Morals an

Morals and Markets

The Dangerous Balance

Second Edition

Daniel Friedman and Daniel McNeill

palgrave
macmillan

First published in 2013 by
PALGRAVE MACMILLAN®
in the United States—a division of St. Martin's Press LLC,
175 Fifth Avenue, New York, NY 10010.

Where this book is distributed in the UK, Europe and the rest of the world,
this is by Palgrave Macmillan, a division of Macmillan Publishers Limited,
registered in England, company number 785998, of Houndmills,
Basingstoke, Hampshire RG21 6XS.

Palgrave Macmillan is the global academic imprint of the above companies
and has companies and representatives throughout the world.

Palgrave® and Macmillan® are registered trademarks in the United States,
the United Kingdom, Europe and other countries.

ISBN: 978–1–137–28258–3

Library of Congress Cataloging-in-Publication Data

Friedman, Daniel, 1947–
    Morals and markets : the dangerous balance / Daniel Friedman and
Daniel McNeill.
       pages cm
       ISBN 978–1–137–28258–3 (alk. paper)
       1. Economics—Moral and ethical aspects. 2. Economics—Sociological
aspects. 3. Capitalism—Moral and ethical aspects. 4. Economic history.
I. McNeill, Daniel. II. Title.

HB72.F75 2013
174'.4—dc23   2012046886

A catalogue record of the book is available from the British Library.

Design by Newgen Imaging Systems (P) Ltd., Chennai, India.

Second edition: June 2013

10 9 8 7 6 5 4 3 2 1

Printed in the United States of America.

To the memory of my mom, Marion Thelma Siegel Friedman (1918–1997). Biology teacher and humanist, skeptic and spiritual seeker, she first got me thinking about many of questions asked in this book.

—D. F.

To Rosalind Gold, with love.

—D. M.

Contents

Prologue: A Tale of Two Tilts

Mikhail Gorbachev was relaxing in his lavish villa in the Crimea at 4:50 pm on August 18, 1991, when he learned he had visitors. One was a secret police official. He picked up his phone to see who the others were, but the line was dead. He tried others. They were all dead. He had heard murmurings of a coup before taking this vacation, but had waved them away. Now he gazed around at his palace, with its marble stairways and escalator down to the Black Sea, and felt dread.

"I paced the room and thought," he said later. "Not about myself, but about my family, my granddaughters."

His wife Raisa entered and they talked. She recalled the family of Czar Nicholas II, slaughtered in a cellar in 1918. Then he called the whole family in to tell them they were in real danger.

They waited.

The men arrived. It turned out they were administrators well known to him. His chief of staff, whom he had long trusted absolutely, informed him his reign was over. Gorbachev countered that he had to return to Moscow to sign an important treaty, but they said the treaty now lay in a Kremlin trash bin. They placed him under house arrest and added that Russian President Boris Yeltsin was also in custody.

The plotters then flew back to Moscow and joined the coup leaders: Gorbachev's own defense and security ministers. Many opened bottles and started drinking. The next day they told the world that Gorbachev was ill and a State Committee on the State of Emergency had taken charge. In case anyone missed the point, they sent tanks rumbling down Moscow streets.

But Yeltsin was hardly in custody. He climbed atop one tank to denounce the putsch on global TV. As the plotters got drunker and drunker, they waffled. Defiant radio stations kept broadcasting, and hundreds of thousands of protesters thronged the streets. Troops defected, and buoyant crowds pulled down statues of communist supermen. On August 21, the coup collapsed.

Gorbachev had his presidency back. Yet everything had changed. The coup triggered a cascade of events that would spread further and further.

For Gorbachev didn't have his power back. His appointees on the right had tried to oust him, and his appointees on the left had already drifted toward Yeltsin, so he stood starkly alone in the center. Indeed, he had looked impotent in the revolt, while Yeltsin seemed the bold hero.

Within a few months, Yeltsin and his counterparts in other Soviet republics shoved Gorbachev aside and broke the USSR like a walnut under a hammer. New nations like Belarus and Kazakhstan hoisted flags. After 74 years, the Soviet Union and its grueling experiment in communism had ended.

Most observers celebrated. Economists predicted a splendid future for the core of the old empire, Russia. With a bonanza of natural resources, advanced technology, and a well-educated workforce, Russia no longer had to prop up the more backward parts of the Soviet realm or contort itself to satisfy orthodoxy. True markets could pump out wealth.

Yet things got worse. Responding to critics one year later in 1992, Harvard professor Jeffrey Sachs, a top advisor to Yeltsin's government, wrote that reform would yield "very great" benefits. Data about Russia's progress after a year was "incomplete and misleading," he said, "and easily misinterpreted to give an overly bleak account... [resulting in] undue pessimism about the reform policies."

But the pessimists were way too optimistic. The economy collapsed, and during the 1990s Russia was the sort of place that gives anarchy a bad name. The new tycoons, called "oligarchs," and their partners in government and in the Mafiya, the Russian mob, destroyed almost as much Russian wealth as Hitler's invasion 50 years earlier.

The economic team had rightly viewed private ownership as essential to national growth, and began privatization in late 1993. This was a massive enterprise. The state had owned almost everything but minor personal household goods, so a vast treasure was being uprooted and floated to new destinations. The insiders of the Communist Party and KGB found the lure irresistible. In alliance with black market figures, they seized the pelf and stashed it in safe places like Switzerland.

Pillage is essentially a medieval operation, but in Russia the looters used 20th-century tactics.

The first was bank fraud, a kind of telecom Bonnie and Clyde. In this ploy, one company sent a wire transfer of funds to another, and it went through the Central Bank, as all transactions did in Russia. The Central Bank checked the first company's account, okayed the deal, and placed the funds in the second company's account. The second company then withdrew them. So far, so good. Except that the second company quickly disappeared. Then the Central Bank discovered that the first company never really had that money after all, but it too had vanished.

How could such a scheme possibly work? It required a carrot and a nasty stick: 1) modest payoffs to Central Bank employees who provided the codes to approve the bogus transfers, and 2) the murder of resisters. Over 25 bank officials met violent ends between 1992 and 1995. In a particularly exotic killing, banker Ivan Kivelidi died in 1996 after swallowing a nerve toxin placed on the lip of his cup. Bank fraud worked especially well in 1990–92 and involved tens of billions of dollars.

Capital flight was even more lucrative. The Soviet Union had kept prices artificially low, so citizens could afford basics like bread and gas. To prevent operators from selling these goods abroad and making a fast ruble, the government enforced strict export controls. In this ploy, the looter evaded them. He first bought oil, natural gas, or even wheat at the low Soviet price. He then got permission (sometimes with a bribe) to export and sold the goods at a low price to a foreign partner or shell company. The foreign partner in turn sold on world markets at a much higher price and earned a huge profit in hard currency. The booty went into a Swiss bank account or the equivalent. This scam became easier after 1991 "reforms" eased most export controls. Crooks siphoned off some $100 billion this way during the 1990s, wiping out the Soviet Union's entire gold and foreign currency reserves, as well as large loans from the IMF.

Basic organized crime flourished, involving protection rackets, smuggling, drugs, and prostitution. Protection schemes were tapeworms in the economy. They sucked away business profits, boosted costs, and slowed trade. And once the Mafiya got rolling in the early 1990s, it began to move upscale. For example, it opened new casinos and took over many legitimate hotels. In 1993, Yeltsin estimated that two-thirds of all commerce was connected to organized crime—an astounding figure but in line with subsequent estimates by experts.

The biggest scam of all was auction rigging. It yielded several trillion dollars in plunder. The basic idea is simple: Hold an auction and gag everyone else. Looters often bid less than one percent of fundamental value for an asset like an oil field or factory, while their partners in the government and the mob suppressed rival offers. For example, Gazprom, with natural gas reserves worth about $500 billion, sold to insiders for one twentieth of one cent on the dollar. Almost all state assets went on the block, in the largest and most corrupt auctions the world has ever seen.

Some top "conservatives" in the KGB and Communist Party commenced this looting around 1990 as the Soviet system was ending. But even more ruthless operators soon displaced them. In Russia, men at the edge of power often saw the opportunities sooner and more clearly than the old rulers. Of course, everyone still needed a "roof"—protection against intervention from government and other thieves—so the old-timers and their minions still got some of the loot. But Russia's crown jewels went to men like Boris Berezovsky, the crooks who became the "oligarchs."

As these new men soared in the 1990s, Russia's economy starved. You could see the impact everywhere. As black-windowed Rolls-Royces purred through the streets and the new elite drank $150 Scotch in nightclubs, the justice system and government agencies crumbled. Taxes were huge and often bizarre—there was a tax on business *losses*, for instance—but went unpaid by companies with good connections like Gazprom. Among the police and military, morale and discipline vanished, and officers survived mainly by selling weapons and protection services to the highest bidder. The 1993 Russian murder rate set new records quadrupling that of the United States in one of our worst years ever. Thugs assassinated eminent individuals, yet seemed beyond the reach of the police and courts. At the same time, Russia's world-class medical and educational systems collapsed. Teachers could no longer earn a living wage, and doctors gave their own blood for transfusions. Live birth rates dropped while alcoholism and disease reached new highs. Life expectancy plummeted, especially for men, resulting in about 6 million excess deaths.

The final blow was a huge default on international debt in July 1998. The nation's economy fell to less than half its former size and ranked behind those of Brazil and Mexico. It was no longer a superpower.

In sum, Russia's transition from communism was among the 20th century's worst disasters. What had the US economists missed? Why did the invisible hand that bred wealth in the West steer it to criminals in Russia and cripple the state?

*   *   *

"It felt like war," said doorman Dimitris Arvanitis. "I could not believe I was in Athens. I have never seen this in my almost 60 years of life, and I have been working here all my life."

It was morning, February 13, 2012. The previous day 80,000 Greeks had demonstrated, and violence began that night. Angry rioters flung gasoline bombs into shops and torched 48 buildings, including banks, cafes, and two movie theaters. They vandalized some 150 other buildings and injured scores of police. After sunrise, as smoke wafted up from gutted structures, pedestrians coughed from the tear gas as they stepped around shards of glass and broken marble on the sidewalk.

The cause of it all? The Greek Parliament had just approved austerity measures in order to get $170 billion in rescue financing. The nation had to make payments on a bond the following month and needed these funds to prevent a default. In exchange, it promised the Eurozone to cut the national budget, reduce salaries, and alter an array of government practices.

The latter was ironic, because Athens was the site of the first formal democracy we know of. There, 40 times a year, adult male citizens assembled on a slope overlooking the Agora, the public square, and decided public issues by a majority vote. Athens had the most responsible system on earth, and it became the inspiration for the fledgling United States and eventually much of the world.

In 1981 Greece joined the European Community, the forerunner to the EU, and Europe felt honored to embrace it. From 1996 to 2008 the nation enjoyed the highest growth rate in the Eurozone. Salaries rose, fancy shops appeared, and gleaming new cars purred down the streets. In 2004 a proud Athens hosted the Olympic Games, and for two weeks it held the world's attention. The European Central Bank had based the euro symbol on the Greek letter epsilon, in honor of the "cradle of European civilization," and now Europe seemed the cradle of a new Greece.

Yet it all peaked in 2009, and by 2012 economic wreckage lay everywhere. Tax revenue was plunging. Workers were getting termination notices right and left. Indeed, unemployment reached Great Depression levels: 25 percent overall and almost 30 percent for Greeks between 25 and 34. Filling a 16-gallon tank of gas cost $136, so cars spent more and more time as garage ornaments. Trash collection waned in Athens, and rats multiplied. Once quiet neighborhoods throbbed with crime, and thieves even stole ancient treasures from the museum at Olympia. The national insurance system got so unreliable that pharmacists began demanding full payment for drugs, and some patients went without medicine entirely. Malaria and HIV rates increased.

In September 2012, a general strike closed the Acropolis as well as gas stations, ferries, and schools, and hospitals resorted to emergency workers. One hospital staffer who left his post was Alkis Betses. His salary had shrunk from €1,300 to €800 ($1,690 to $1,040) a month, he said, and he expected it to drop to €600 ($780). "How can you survive on €600 a month, with ever-rising taxes, and continue to pay bills and buy necessary supplies?" he asked. "If the washing machine breaks down, where do you get the money for repairs?"

Meanwhile, taxes were rising, so more and more citizens shifted transactions into the shadow economy. On one business trip to the tourist isle of Santorini, three tax collectors spotted a gas station owner demanding payment in cash to avoid declaring it as income. When they asked what he was doing, he raged at the government and snapped a bullwhip at them.

A deathly mood settled in. "There is a depression in the Greek people, in all my friends," one college student told the *New York Times* in 2012. "They keep saying: 'I can't take it. There's depression about our jobs, depression on the news, depression about the economic situation, depression in our family, depression and fighting among friends.'"

With the riots and gloom, anyone might think Greece was the biggest victim of the European crash. Yet other Europeans claimed Greece had ripped them off, that the most responsible government of antiquity was the least responsible on the continent today.

Greece had become the gangrenous leg of the Eurozone. It didn't respond to treatment, yet no one wanted the trauma from cutting it off. The country itself was aching and every remedy worsened the pain. And at times the whole European crisis seemed to pivot around Greece.

What had happened to this fabled nation? Why did others hate it so much? And how could its prosperity just evaporate?

* * *

Each of us is a wonder of balance. We may be over six feet tall and weigh 200 pounds, yet we stand effortlessly on two small feet. Even cats, with their marvelous grace, use four legs and a tail. Balance comes naturally to us since we've had millions of years to evolve it. We have vestibular systems in our inner ears that automatically send signals to the muscles that keep us upright. The whole thing works so well that we take it for granted, as we realize with amazement when we suffer labyrinthitis and can't stand despite our hardest efforts.

Morals and markets lack this well-tuned balance. Though they need equilibrium, they have no vestibular system for it and no automatic signals to keep them in tune. If anything, our instincts deceive us about morality and markets, so trouble occurs more often. Yet the result is similar: Economies like Russia's and Greece's can lose their footing and wind up on the floor.

"Morals" has a fusty ring, through its association with nags and killjoys, but morals lie at the heart of our most gripping concerns. They are full of life and juice. They animate issues such as abortion and the death penalty. We ignore their power at our peril, as cheaters like Enron's CEO Jeff Skilling and slugger

Mark McGwire discovered. It's unclear how many countries have learned the same lesson.

Markets need morals. A farmers' market, say, must have trust to function well. Buyers won't come if too many vegetables are rotten inside. And a market economy like the United Kingdom needs morals too, for it is a vast interlocking web of promises and understandings. We can think of a market economy as a broad vine with richly colored blossoms that rises to the sky. But morals are the trellis it hangs on, and without them, it is just a low shrub.

Though few realize it, markets have also made us more moral. They not only encourage cooperation, but since they've increased wealth, they've enabled boons like police and public health systems. As we brought morals and markets into alignment a few hundred years ago, warfare dropped off and so did crime. Markets bred the world of peace we live in today.

But if the benefits run both ways, so do the hazards.

Morals can sabotage markets. The ethical compass is a poor guide to the market landscape, and the world has seen plenty of examples of good intentions leading off the cliff. Markets can also corrupt morals, and many believe Wall Street has suffered this blight. And since we lack an inner guidance system, we not only cause such tilts, but sometimes celebrate them until it is too late.

The dangerous balance led to the crash of 2008 and the aftermath, but it also affects economies more broadly. It has deeply influenced corporate life, terrorism, the War on Drugs, and global warming, among other issues related to our happiness. It is a core dynamic of our world. It touches the lives of people everywhere.

And unfortunately it's not a simple seesaw. We can't just aim for equal weight on both sides. The balance is subtle and multidimensional, and the influences flow several ways at once. Yet we must understand it, or we're in for debacles again and again.

To grasp it, we have to look deep into history. Ultimately, Russia wound up helpless against gangsters because of ideals that go back to prehuman tribes, and Greece got into trouble partly because of moral barriers that arose from morals themselves. The great events in our economies stem from the forces that created us in the first place.

So let's go back to the origin of morals. What are they? Why do we have them?

I

Two Halves of the Balance

The great division of our affections is into the selfish and the benevolent.

—Adam Smith

I

The Savanna Code: What Good Are Morals?

We must, indeed, all hang together, or assuredly we shall all hang separately.

—Attributed to Benjamin Franklin

Dawn can be cool and quiet in Olduvai Gorge in Tanzania. The hyenas cease wailing and thorn bushes on the canyon's brink tremble in the breeze. Soon, the sun will light the gray strata of the ravine, and eventually it will rise higher in the blue sky and oppress the land with heat. Tourists will arrive from all over the globe, snapping photos and uploading them to their Facebook pages.

For Olduvai is the most famous site of our prehuman ancestors, where the maverick Louis Leakey and his wife Mary labored unknown for over 30 years, seeking our origins on a continent others scorned. In 1961 they discovered *Homo habilis*, the first member of our genus, and triggered a rush of scientists to Africa.

The 300-foot gorge is no Eden. It is dry and dotted with spindly plants. Tourists can't see the priceless fossils unless they go to museums, and more important sites now exist elsewhere in East Africa—especially in the north along the Rift Valley, beside green Lake Turkana, and in the Afar region of Ethiopia near the Red Sea.

Yet Olduvai is symbolic. And here, at the origin of humanity, the first half of the dangerous balance began to take shape.

The Great Leap Forward

Our evolution from other creatures was swift and stunning. Today, the four great apes struggle against extinction, but our own species has eight times more biomass than all wild land vertebrates combined. From the Kanto Plain of Japan to the Antarctic ice shelf, we've altered the physical world more drastically than any other animal in history. Physically, we're much taller than chimps. We have seemingly hairless bodies, flat faces, and ultra-nimble hands, all novelties. We're smarter, with the highest brain-to-body mass ratio of any creature. We have music, art, and language with syntax. We've built tools, from the hoe to the Large Hadron Collider, and we've left some on Mars.

And those are just the obvious differences.

Chimps will never build an Eiffel Tower, and it's not just because they lack the intelligence, dexterity, technology, and communication skills. They don't cooperate well enough. But we work together on a scale and with a finesse unseen in the planet's history. We convey complex ways of life—cultures—across generations, so we benefit from the experience and ingenuity of the long dead. And supporting it all we have morals: standards for our own behavior and the conduct we expect of others.

We developed these traits in a flicker of evolutionary time—just 2.5 million years. By one estimate, our ancestors' brains gained an average of 100,000 neurons and support cells with each generation. How did it happen? What created you and me?

These are among the most fundamental questions we can ask. They are basic to our understanding of who we are and why we act as we do. They have tantalized humanity as far back as we can see, and every culture has spun out fantasies to quell the itch. We still don't know the answers in detail, but we finally have solid evidence and many persuasive ideas.

In *An Essay on the Principle of Population* (1798), economist Thomas Malthus (1766–1834) made a famous argument that social hardship was inevitable. We breed more than we can feed, he said. Creatures always have more offspring than the environment can support, so some percentage must die in every generation. Charles Darwin read this work in 1838, and in his 1876 autobiography he said, "It at once struck me that under these circumstances favorable variations would tend to be preserved, and unfavorable ones to be destroyed. The results of this would be the formation of a new species." The environment filters for good traits. It's like a game where round after round—generation after generation—the better players advance, and the poorer ones drop out. In *The Origin of Species*, he wrote, "I have called this principle, by which each slight variation, if useful, is preserved, by the term Natural Selection."

In East Africa around 4 or 5 million years ago, a few apes moved out of the forest to dwell in a new environment: the proto-savanna, or forest interspersed with grasslands. There, Darwin's process sieved generations and changed them into new beings: australopithecines, like the famous Lucy. These creatures were no taller than a yardstick, and their brains were about the size of a chimp's. But the proto-savanna had more open space, and they often walked upright to save energy. Chimps, in contrast, can't straighten their legs and find walking arduous. The australopiths were not wholly bipedal, however, and they used their curved feet to climb trees, perhaps to sleep in safety from predators like *Dino felis*, a saber-toothed cat.

Then about 2.7 million years ago, the Northern Hemisphere began getting a little less sunlight in the summer, because of factors like the tilt of the earth's axis. The small loss of warmth triggered big effects. Glaciers formed in the Arctic, two-mile thick ice sheets spread, and sea level dropped as much as 400 feet. The boundary here is so striking that geologist Charles Lyell (1797–1875) gave the chilly epoch that followed its own name: the Pleistocene (from the Greek for "most new").

This era incubated us. We were born of ice.

In Africa the landscape altered. It grew drier and true savanna appeared: grassland dotted with trees, like the parks we create for our pleasure. The ancestors of gazelles, giraffes, and zebras multiplied, and herds spread. Proto-tourist Africa had arrived.

But the biggest climate change 2.7 million years ago was constant change itself. The ice sheets didn't just expand. They spread and ebbed like tides, since the amount of summer sunlight hitting the north varied. Radical shifts occurred as often as every 10,000 years, and climate graphs of the Pleistocene, based on Greenland ice cores and Atlantic sediment cores, resemble seismographs in an earthquake.

So Africa became a yo-yo world. As glaciers advanced, drought sucked moisture out of the continent. A column of desert often stretched from the Sahara all the way down the Rift Valley to the Kalahari in the south, breaking the savanna into fragments and scrambling ecosystems. Then, as ice sheets withdrew and the planet warmed, monsoons and trade winds brought heavier rainfall. Lake Chad swelled into Mega-Lake Chad, the middle Congo River became a huge inland sea, and the savanna fused again.

In this environment, generalists thrived. We were born of change as well.

The first member of our genus, *Homo habilis*, appeared soon after the Ice Ages created a drier Africa, some 2.5 million years ago. It always walked upright, though it stood just a bit taller than the australopiths. And its brain grew 50 percent larger, to around 0.75 liters, an astonishing development, since brains are greedy for nourishment and therefore costly. (At 1.35 liters, adult human brains consume about 16 percent of our resting metabolism; for most mammals, the figure is 2 to 5 percent.) So next to the australopiths, these primates had almost godlike minds.

Why exactly did *Homo habilis* appear? A species is just a strategy for success, and the big herds were an economic opportunity. They rewarded good new strategies, just as social media and smartphone technology have recently. And carnivores made it easy. They left plenty of meat behind after a kill, so *Habilis* saw little buffets everywhere. It began taking the leftovers. And with its free hands and progressively smarter brain, *Habilis* was made for stone tools. It could carry them easily, and they let it strip a carcass better than any big cat. With sharp flakes it could slice tough hides, and with the blunter tools it could crack open thighbones to get the nutrient-rich marrow. So *Habilis* used tools routinely, and in fact its name means "handyman."

But this advantage may not be the full story. The alternative may have been dire. Overall, the genetic chain from *Habilis* to us was tenuous and we are lucky to exist at all. Our lineage rarely had more than 20,000 to 30,000 individuals—about the population of Key West, Florida. (In comparison, there are today about 50,000 Indian elephants, an endangered species.) Presumably this was the Malthusian limit, the extent to which prehumans could feed themselves.

That limit swung up and down. When the grass withered, lakebeds cracked, herds dwindled, and the food supply shrank. As the death rate rose, prehumans competed more fiercely for necessities. At least twice our ancestors approached extinction, and these crises savagely culled out individuals with poorer survival skills, much as a recession wipes out companies. Indeed, a near-extinction event may preserve only individuals with distinctive qualities and thus change species swiftly.

Did a population bottleneck occur at the start of the Pleistocene? It's possible that in one island of savanna, prehumans with stone tools and progressively better minds outlasted a long famine while the rest failed to pass on DNA. Big brains are costly, but here they paid for themselves. Individuals needed them. We can't be sure what happened, but evolution clearly selected for them and they didn't arise by chance at this time. The australopiths had survived for millions of years without them.

Hanging Together

In 1887 a young Dutch anatomist named Eugéne Dubois sailed with his family to the East Indies in search of "the missing link." He was an utter amateur, but he had a cause. Apes dwelt in the tropics, he reasoned, and prehumans must have left bones there too. Once in the jungle, he faced agonies. He got malaria. Torrential rain drenched his sites. Workers sneaked away and sold bones to Chinese traders. Mosquitoes and heat tortured his family. Yet in 1891, on the edge of the Solo River, he came across an ancient molar and two months later he found a skullcap that was smaller than a human's but clearly larger than an ape's. In 1893 he announced his discovery: Java Man.

But what did it mean? Dubois endured the customary ridicule following a paradigm-shaking revelation and eventually grew so paranoid he installed a mirror over his door, turning away visitors, even eminent scientists. Yet the mystery was endlessly tantalizing, and it only grew after discovery of a second, similar specimen called Peking Man. Who were these individuals? How were they related to us, if indeed they were related at all?

Around 1.7 million years ago, a second big climate break occurred. Africa grew even drier and trees became rarer still, so evolutionary pressure intensified and a bold new species appeared: *Homo erectus*. *Habilis* resembled a short apish semihuman, but this species was clearly a cousin of ours. At around five feet, it was taller than *Habilis*. Its brain ballooned to over twice the size of the australopiths', almost a liter on average. It made far more and better tools, so it likely tapped a broader food supply, and by at least 1 million years ago it was using fire. It was adaptable, and it quickly spread from Africa into ecosystems as far away as East Asia, leaving the bones Dubois found.

Homo erectus tribes were almost certainly nomadic and opportunistic, moving as seasons changed, herds migrated, and water ran low. At sites like Lake Turkana, they dined on hippo, crocodile, and fish. Each band likely had several dozen members, perhaps 30 to 80. The size varied with conditions, since large groups can quickly deplete the local food supply and then split apart. They didn't specialize much—no one made a living as a toolmaker—and such specialization as existed mainly followed the crude lines of sex and age, rather than talent. Men hunted and women gathered berries and tubers, for instance. Overall, they took what they needed from the land and had little surplus.

And there was one more thing.

Australopith males seem to have been significantly larger than females (though evidence is sketchy), and in primates this pattern typically means a dominant male and a strict hierarchy. But *Homo erectus* males like Java Man were just 15 percent bigger than females, about the same proportion as today. This fact implies pair bonds, less violent competition for mates, and flatter hierarchy. That is, better cooperation.

Cooperation is power. In coordinated groups, for instance, our ancestors could have gone beyond snatching leftovers to stealing kills. Think of African dogs: One can't bring down an antelope, but a pack succeeds 80 percent of the time. If a big cat brought down an impala, prehumans working together could make a racket, throw rocks, scare it away, and seize the prize.

Cooperation was especially crucial in hard times. When people worked smoothly together, they could get more food and keep more children alive. They could fight other tribes when necessary and in general keep everyone safer. They could care for each other in disease and injury. They could spread key information. They could use one another's assets (such as strength, intelligence, keen vision, stamina) for the good of all. We are still far more effective in groups—in companies, gangs, and nations—than as individuals. And in crises, prehumans with more genes for cooperation would have done better and passed on more DNA.

People say "genes for" very casually. What do we mean by "genes for cooperation"? It's easy to understand a gene for hair color, say, but a gene for behavior? Where is the anatomy of cooperation?

We now know that too. Fossil skulls only show the increasing brain size of our ancestors like *Homo erectus*. But the soft structure inside the skull was changing as well. Key human organs were developing within—such as our huge insulas and posterior ventromedial nucleus (the size of a poppy seed in monkeys and a macadamia nut in people)—and our mirror neurons and spindle cells were becoming far more numerous. Research has tied these items to our complex social emotions, to self-awareness, and to our unrivaled capacity for putting ourselves in another's shoes ("theory of mind"). Indeed, overall the centers for emotion in our brains are now twice as large as in our ape ancestors. These organs all helped us work together and survive, and prehumans with bigger insulas, say, outcompeted others. We are literally built for cooperation. We probably had to be.

Suppose we could go back in time and communicate with *Homo erectus*. What kind of culture shock—or species shock—would we experience? How did they act among each other?

We don't really know, since our ignorance of this period remains colossal. However, from their remains and our knowledge of modern hunter-gatherers we can cautiously fill in the picture. These beings fell in love and raised children. (In contrast, male chimps neglect fatherhood and often can't even recognize their offspring.) They were bright enough to use an iPad, to some extent, though since their tools didn't improve for eons, they may have lacked a what-if imagination. They likely possessed a sense of justice and felt many of the same moral emotions we do. They could have had facial and vocal expressions similar to ours, and if they had partial language, they might have understood the use of a telephone. They were getting close to us. We might not take them to parties, but we could hardly put them in zoos.

These are, again, surmises. But we can be sure of one thing: Group living raised problems.

The I-Versus-We Dilemma

Suppose a cod fishery is shrinking seriously. What should a fisherman do? They'll all be better off if they limit their take and let the fishery recover. However, each person will make more money if he still catches as many cod as possible. Yet if everyone tries to catch the maximum, the fishery will crash, and all will suffer badly. So should a fisherman keep hauling in cod or not?

Cooperation is tricky, despite the bonanza, and we are among the few animals that have come close to mastering it. We both compete and cooperate, so we face the classic I-versus-we social dilemma: If everyone cooperates, everyone benefits, but if I'm selfish and cheat, I gain a bigger payoff. Yet if everyone is selfish, the rewards vanish. All of us feel this tug-of-war inside, and the dilemma has animated fiction from *The Iliad* to *The Hunger Games*.

Some forms of cooperation are win-win, with no dilemma. Anchovies swim together in tight schools that confuse predators, for instance, and pelicans fly in V formation, saving energy by riding their neighbors' bow waves. Here, individuals act in their own interest and the group's at once. No sacrifice occurs. Biologists call this behavior "mutualism."

Yet in a tribe prehumans had to sacrifice repeatedly, and temptations to shirk abounded. Indeed, all teams face the threat that devious members will free ride on the effort of others. For example, a warrior would be better off lurking in the rear in battle, letting others fend off the spears and clubs. Yet if everyone shunned combat, the tribe would suffer repeated defeats and get marginalized. Overall, cooperation is fraught with the risk of betrayal, and we see dramatic examples of it all the time in the headlines and courtrooms.

So what kept tribes together?

Part of it was kinship. Kinship is the secret of cooperation among bees and ants, which can share up to 75 percent of their genes. Modern hunter-gatherer bands are largely composed of kin, and people have always favored relatives over others, ultimately because when kin pass on their genes, they pass on some of ours as well. Kin groups arrange marriages in most bands, usually with an eye to political alliances, and tribes stick to clear rules about which kin can and can't marry. Kin relations also aid on the road to power. In well-known, historic societies, nepotism has led to dynasties and even put imbeciles on the throne. Today, too, most religions impose special duties on relatives and encourage a bias toward them; for example, family obligation is at the heart of Confucianism. Family-run businesses can be more effective than nonfamily ones, and extended families like Marco Polo's handled much early long-distance trade.

But among us cooperation gets more interesting.

Favors: The Origin of Credit

In a 1971 paper, the brash young Harvard biologist Robert Trivers showed a way cooperation with non-kin can succeed. The essence is trading favors. A streamlined version of his argument runs as follows: One creature does a favor for another, expecting that the other will return the favor eventually. The recipient in fact does so, and a regular exchange of favors follows. And if each recipient benefits more than each giver loses every time, and if the delays and risks of the return favor are not too large, then the favor system pays off. This dynamic is called "reciprocal altruism."

For instance, suppose you got sick. It would cost another person time and trouble to care for you, but your benefit would far exceed that cost. In return, the caregiver would get credit. A debt would arise. If he himself later got sick, you could return the favor and erase the debt. You both would have done better overall, and perhaps even have saved your lives.

In other words, the I-versus-we social dilemma turns into mutualism.

But that was just theory. Then biologist Gerald Wilkinson spent 26 months between 1978 and 1983 studying vampire bats (*Desmodus rotundus*) on a Costa Rican ranch. The creatures dwelt in hollow trees, and at night he and his assistants ventured out and shone flashlights into them. Slowly they increased the illumination and saw more and more.

Life is tough if you are a vampire bat. Every night you have to search for an unwary cow or other large animal whose blood you can drink without interruption. If you fail to tap a vein two nights in a row, you are in danger of starving to death. Without a social safety net, an accident of fate could end your life.

Wilkinson discovered how they cope. Adult female vampire bats live in colonies of eight to twelve individuals, most of them distant cousins. An unlucky adult will beg by licking the wings of a well-fed potential donor, who will often regurgitate some blood into her mouth. Wilkinson reported that refusals are rare if, on previous nights of success, the current beggar had never refused the current donor. He estimated that the survival benefit to the hungry bat of a gram of blood is at least twice its cost to the well-fed donor. Since the colonies are stable over years of nightly excursions, the chance for a return favor is fairly high.

About ten years after Trivers' paper appeared, Wilkinson published his findings. It was a perfect example of reciprocity theory in the wild.

Since his study, very few new examples have cropped up. However, we see the pattern clearly among primates. Monkeys and apes commonly trade grooming favors: one will hunt through another's fur, picking out lice and other parasites, and later the other will return the favor. It is literally "you scratch my back and I'll scratch yours." And since these exchanges improve health, the groomee gains more than the groomer loses in each round; "Wealth" increases.

This activity forges social bonds as well, tying the band together. It can fill several hours each day, and monkeys of similar age and status typically spend about equal time grooming each other. In many primate species, individuals spend more time grooming those who have higher status. The powerful get better favors.

Such relationships lead to politics. Be helpful and you can get help as you need it. For example, when the Roman orator Cicero was running for consul in 64 BC, his brother gave him the age-old advice: "Now is the time to call in all favors." And if two or three chimps regularly exchange favors over time and trust each other, they may form a coalition, and then they can overthrow an alpha male: a palace coup in the jungle.

We can think of favor systems as precursors to loans. Loans go back much further than we can trace, and the first writing arose in Mesopotamia to record debts. Of course, favors are much less formal and much more personal and social than loans. But they anticipate repayment, one way or another. For instance, tribal members aid ailing strangers less often because the chance of repayment is lower.

Hence a favor system has this necessary condition: Freeloaders can't prosper. The mutual benefits evaporate if one person trims the return favor or neglects it completely. People must be able to avoid these cheaters or they grow more common, distrust rises, and cooperation crumbles. As we'll see, that's generally what happened system-wide after the crash of 2008.

Favor systems are also precursors to trade. Its participants must have a sense of value, an inner scales, since others must repay favors with equivalent ones. Adam Smith said, "Man is an animal that makes bargains: no other animal does this.... Nobody ever saw a dog make a fair and deliberate exchange of one bone for another with another dog." And though favor systems aren't trade in this sense, in grooming we do see a kind of "fair and deliberate exchange." It's the foundation for trade.

It's the foundation for something else as well. The Northern Ache of Paraguay are a hunter-gatherer tribe who did not make peaceful contact with the outside world until the 1970s and whom anthropologists have since scrutinized. In the 1980s and 1990s tribal members gained 78 percent of their daily calories from wild game. However, on any one day, a hunter had just a 40 percent chance of making a kill. So his family faced the same plight as one of Wilkinson's luckless vampire bats. And other Ache families responded similarly, by sharing meat. But there was a big difference. Scientists found no evidence that recipients had been good donors in the past. Everyone simply got food. Yet as one anthropologist noted, "It is my impression that those who refuse to share game would probably be expelled from the band." So this proto-unemployment insurance is fundamentally different from reciprocal altruism. It is moral.

Morals and the Tribal Interest

Everyone has seen the driver struggling to enter a clogged street from a parking lot. If no one lets him in, he'll wait for a long time. Yet usually a driver on the road will wave him in. The street driver gains no perceptible benefit, so why does she do it? Reciprocity can't explain it. The other driver can't possibly repay the favor; the two will never see each other again and likely wouldn't recognize each other if they did. Nearby motorists, who might give her credit for her thoughtfulness, will also never see her again, and thus she gains no reputation benefit. Her action seems like pure altruism.

Children show such behavior very early. By around the age of two, they will help an adult who has dropped a pen and spontaneously give their own possessions to others who lack them. Overall, they display a desire to help others and work together toward goals. And from this time on, children actively seek to associate and cooperate with others. Again, reciprocity can't explain this behavior. Yet its early appearance suggests it is hardwired.

And one reason is that we all descend not just from successful ancestors, but ancestors in successful tribes.

Tribes competed with each other, as companies do today. Think of two equally able executives, one working for a profitable company and one for a struggling one. Though both are just as skilled, the person at the effective firm will likely prosper more. Likewise, on the savanna, the better a tribe did overall, the more likely each member would prosper and pass on genes.

For instance, in the Upper Nile region of Sudan a tribe known as the Dinka had followed a pastoral lifestyle over centuries. But sometime in the early 1700s, one local group, which called itself the Nuer, tweaked its marriage customs in a way that created stronger bonds between the in-laws' families. Although the Nuer were otherwise culturally and genetically identical to the Dinka, the stronger intergroup bonds let the Nuer form larger raiding parties than their neighbors. With that military edge, the Nuer took territory from their Dinka neighbors decade after decade. Dinka men either joined the Nuer voluntarily or were driven away or killed. Women willingly or unwillingly took new Nuer husbands and raised their children as Nuer. The Nuer were poised to take over the remaining Dinka territory when the British intervened around 1880.

As Darwin observed in *The Descent of Man*, "From the remotest times successful tribes have supplanted other tribes." The Nuer advantage lay entirely in heightened cooperation and overall, for any tribe, the smoother the cooperation, the greater its strength and the more likely its members will pass on DNA to posterity. In this case, culture made the difference, but genes creating better equipment for cooperation, such as more mirror cells, could have had the same effect. But note that genes give us only the capacities we need for cooperation; they don't transmit cooperation itself.

Cultural and genetic improvements also spread peacefully. Suppose one band is more welcoming to outsiders. Then, if productive newcomers begin arriving, that tribe will grow more quickly than others in the area, and will spin off new tribelets more often. The nearby bands may or may not emulate the first tribe or marry into it. But unless unfavorable conditions appear—say, the latest newcomers are freeloaders—the hospitable behavior will prevail in the region.

So tribal members faced serious pressure to cooperate with each other. That pressure helped breed morals.

Morals are our basic behavior code. They are a shared understanding within a group on how to live and work together. They involve notions we call "right" and "wrong," and "good" and "evil," as well as emotions such as guilt, shame, and gratitude. We can summarize the code in a set of rules. It's an elaborate one, to be sure, and some rules are explicit and others implicit, some clear and others fuzzy. We sometimes call the specifics "social norms," and they vary across cultures. In a large society, norms can clash, as we see in arguments over abortion and the death penalty. That's one way norms change: through conflict.

In hunter-gatherer societies, the moral code imposes regulations that the group enforces. The proper way to behave seamlessly applies to all activities—raising kids, sharing food, finding a spouse, working with neighboring tribes and with the spirits of nature, and dealing with death. What happens when two people want to fight? Norms tell you. How should people of different sex and age behave? Norms tell you. They also govern access to desirable items, such as food, political power, and mates. Tribes everywhere use symbolic means like rituals to drive their norms home. And when people internalize them and use them as a way of life, they can react harshly not just to violations, but to novelties that threaten change.

All known hunter-gatherer groups manage their I-versus-we dilemmas with moral systems. By heightening cooperation, they could better feed tribe members during famines and repel rival tribes seeking their food sources and women. Since the good of all was the good of each, a public interest arose. Everyone benefited by rewarding those who furthered that interest.

And by punishing those who harmed it. The incentive to cheat is ever-present, and hence the code absolutely must deter slackers and swindlers. If they thrive, others will copy them, and all will suffer. Thus every moral code prescribes penalties, and effective groups enforce them. In contrast, chimps don't punish third-party offenders. If they see one chimp harm another, they ignore it. When humans act like chimps, as they have recently in regulatory bodies, crises can result.

In tribes, penalties can seem surprisingly subtle. Members may deliberately misunderstand the wrongdoer or gossip about him and mar his reputation. They may shun a petty thief until he returns the goods with interest. They may even pretend a violator isn't actually standing there in front of them. Yet these punishments cut deep, because members are so interdependent. They show the offender he has lost important moral ties to those around him, and if he doesn't make amends, they are quite effective at getting him to leave the tribe.

When the moral folks prosper more than the free-riders, social dilemmas turn into win-wins. For instance, we are much more likely to trust people with ethical reputations and help them automatically. And where a generalized, group-wide trust runs high, people aid each other reflexively, frequently, and more fully, and everyone profits. Public goods multiply. In the cod example, if a fisherman trusts that all others will obey the limit, he'll be more likely to obey it himself. If they all act morally, the fishery will have a greater chance of bouncing back.

So the existence of public goods depends partly on trust—and at bottom the capacity to trust is partly chemical. We humans have evolved more receptors for

oxytocin, the "cuddle hormone," than any other animal, especially in the pleasure centers of our brains. Oxytocin improves social attachments and parental
care. Spray a little into a person's nose, and she trusts strangers more and acts
more generously toward them. One lab study found that treated people donate
more to charity. Differing alleles (or varieties) of the oxytocin gene make people
more or less willing to trust, so our readiness to trust is heritable. The chemical
is basic to moral behavior and helps explain why genuine trust makes us feel
good.

   On the other hand, suspicion does not feel good. It not only distances people,
but slows the benefit flow, decreases public goods, and weakens the group. If the
oxytocin isn't there, if fishermen think free-riders are cheating, they may feel like
chumps and try to cheat too. And the stock of cod is in trouble. That's part of the
story in Greece, as we'll see.

The Nectar and the Rack: Moral Emotions

Emotions are closely tied to the meaning of life; ultimately, they *are* the meaning of life. Why do people with bipolar disorder see the world as pointless during lows but as rich with meaning during highs? The reason is that the brain
region most affected by bipolar disorder, the ventromedial prefrontal cortex, is
the brain's emotion control center. They are swinging between a world with few
rewards and one with plenty of them. Emotions are the prizes and punishments
in every aspect of life. They create urges and send us cues like "thank that person." If we had to deduce these conclusions—that person has helped me, so I
better thank her—we'd fall short again and again, just as if we had to make eating decisions without the prod of hunger. We aren't smart enough to reach the
right conclusions reliably and quickly, and we aren't disciplined enough to follow
through. So emotions both give meaning to life and guide us through it.

   They shape our ethical responses. And they well up swiftly, subtly, and unbid-
den as we go about our days. We know it from experience, but also from experiments. In one of them, for instance, scientists asked participants to keep either a
short number like 3 or a long one like 6824398 in memory, and then make moral
judgments. The long number is a greater cognitive load, so deliberate thinking
gets harder. But researchers found no difference in people's performance. It didn't
matter whether they carried a high cognitive load or not. Moral responses arise
automatically from within.

   The moral system is so much a part of our everyday sensibility that we often
don't see it well. For instance, as we read a newspaper, we constantly feel subtle
flickers of response to words before we can even think about them. So largely
unbeknownst to us, moral emotions dye our perceptions, and we view the world
in ethical terms. The effect is like an optical illusion we aren't aware of and may
vigorously deny, and at times it has led us to economic disasters.

   Here is a bird's-eye view of how the moral emotions work:

   Suppose someone does us a favor. *Gratitude* tells us that she has put us in her
debt, gives us an idea of how much to repay, and urges us to do it. It creates a sense

of obligation. Without this feeling, it is hard to return favors, and prehumans lacking gratitude were less likely to gain the cooperation of others.

Suppose you do a favor for someone and that person doesn't return it. *Anger* and *resentment* warn us against aiding that person in the future. Or consider the resentment when another worker slacks off on the job. Shirking breaches the duty to do one's share for the group and forces others to work harder. It's theft of time and effort. We also feel anger and resentment toward third parties who violate the code, even total strangers, such as famous criminals we know only through TV. *Revenge* is usually more intense. It drives us to punish an individual for rip-offs and personal affronts, though it can also arise from betrayal of the group and breach of the code in general. *Envy* stems from the other person's superior opportunities. The worry that others might be envious can encourage sharing. All these negative emotions lead us to enforce the code, maintain trust, and keep public goods thriving.

What happens if you yourself follow or breach the code? *Pride*, *guilt*, and *shame* spring from our own behavior. We can feel pride when we exceed group expectations. We can feel shame and guilt when we fail to repay favors or to live up to moral duties in general. Guilt stems from our inner awareness of the breach—you can feel its lash even if no one else knows about your act—while shame arises from others' knowledge of it.

We can also feel moral emotions for the acts of our group, regardless of whether we contributed. Fans swell with pride at great victories of local sports teams, for instance. Some German citizens experienced guilt and shame after World War II even though they had no responsibility for the horror, and Germany has given Israel billions of marks in an attempt at reparation. Our group affects our reputation and our feelings.

The moral emotions fuse rewards and penalties into our core. Indeed, social network scientists have found that others' happiness is contagious. When a friend who lives nearby becomes happy, the chance that you'll become happy too rises by 25 percent. And when it pleases you to help others, you'll obviously do it more often. Hence a driver on a busy street will often let another car in. She can put herself in the other driver's position. She has done "the right thing." It feels good.

Morals are unique to us, but we're not the first animals with moral emotions. Not far from Olduvai, in Gombe Stream National Park in the Tanzanian forests, live the chimpanzees that Jane Goodall studied. They not only have elaborate favor systems but possess a sense of justice. Cheaters upset them. They also console others in distress and fear arousing envy in others. And it's not just chimps. In 1996 media worldwide reported the story of a three-year-old boy who fell into the enclosure of Binti Jua, a female gorilla in the Brookfield Zoo near Chicago. The primate scooped him up, cradled him gently before gaping spectators, and carried him to a door where a zookeeper took him. Similarly, in a 1964 study, monkeys could get food, but only by giving an electric shock to another monkey. Of the 15 animals, 10 prolonged their own hunger rather than inflict the pain. Primatologists report many similar examples. Such qualities are the forerunners of a moral system.

We even share some moral emotions with nonprimates. Dogs and elephants seem to feel gratitude and anger in response to specific actions. Dogs also appear to experience pride and shame, but apparently only humans feel guilt. Self-righteousness, generalized disgust, and righteous wrath also seem uniquely human.

Yet classical economists long downplayed moral emotions in constructing their models. They assumed that people were wholly rational, that they always acted solely to maximize monetary gain. Thousands of scholarly articles and a massive tower of theory arose from this premise, and it yielded important insights. But how correct was it?

In 1977 the economist Werner Güth had just returned from an academic conference with "1000 marks in my bag for running experiments." The bubbly, irrepressible Güth was starting his first semester teaching at Cologne, and he, Rolf Schmittberger, and Bernd Schwarze decided to test the rationalist assumption. They ran the first Ultimatum Game, an experiment now viewed as a turning point in the history of economics.

Here's how the Game works: You begin with a pot of $10, say, and two people: a proposer and a responder. The game has just two plays, one by each person. First, the proposer offers to divide the $10 between himself and the responder, whose identity he will never know. He can split it any way he wants. For instance, he might give himself $8 and the responder $2, or he might divide it $5 and $5. Second, the responder either accepts or vetoes the offer. If she accepts, both go home with the cash as proposed. If she vetoes it, both get nothing.

What would happen? Economists expected that responders would accept any amount. After all, some money is better than none. So the proposer's best move was to offer a minimal sum, say $1 or even $0.01, and keep the rest.

But that didn't occur. Instead, responders often rejected the smaller amounts. And most proposers, anticipating the veto (or acting out of a sense of fairness), offered close to an even split, say $4.50, which responders usually accepted.

For years scientist debated why responders refused the small offers. But recent studies using brain scans and measuring physiological reactions have concluded that the main reason is anger, or moral outrage. Many responders find the satisfaction of punishing a greedy proposer (so he loses the $9 and takes home nothing) worth more than the demeaning $1.

Scientists have reported roughly similar results with players on every continent. However, anthropologists have also tried it in dozens of isolated societies and found a wide range of behavior. Machiguenga tribesmen in the Amazon rainforest played it much more as economists originally expected, accepting small amounts like 10 percent from the proposer. At the other extreme, Au and Gnau bands in New Guinea often vetoed very generous offers, even those above 50 percent. Why? The Machiguenga rarely share outside the family, so they expect less generosity from non-kin and presumably feel less outrage at a $1 offer. On the other hand, a Gnau accepting a very high offer would feel obliged to track down his benefactor and return the favor with interest. The "generous offer" was in fact a burden. In other words, culture affects our moral responses.

Moral Zoology: The Panoply of Right and Wrong

Rain was pelting Damascus one morning in January 2007 as Fawaz al-Azzo got up and prepared for work. He gazed down at Zahra, his bride of five weeks, as she slept on their foam mattress on the floor. The room was chilly, so he bent down to tuck the blanket more tightly around the 16-year-old. Then he left for his construction job on the outskirts of town, being careful to lock the door behind him.

Soon after, Zahra's brother Fayyez slipped a stolen key into that lock and entered the apartment. He knelt beside his sister and stabbed her five times in the head and back, almost cutting her spinal cord in half. Then he called his family in their rural village, said he'd killed her, and walked to the nearest police station to surrender.

"It is my right to correct this error," he told police, according to his lawyer. "It's true that my sister is married now, but we never washed away the shame."

The shame was Zahra's kidnapping and rape in the previous year.

Back at the village that night, her family held a party to celebrate the murder and invited all the townsfolk to join them.

Why would anyone—especially a brother—want to kill an innocent young woman? Why would her family rejoice in her death? How can a moral code even condone such an act, much less compel it?

Morals are part nature and part nurture. We're born with moral preparation for the world. All societies take the same emotional engine and build their own moral codes atop it. Since we learn these elements of the code, they vary. For instance, most cultures catalogued by anthropologists allow polygamy. Many, like our own, demand monogamy, and a few encourage polyandry, two or three husbands sharing one wife. The Bari women of northwestern Venezuela go a step further and seek multiple "fathers" for each child.

The nature-nurture scheme has yielded many advantages in the past. Indeed, cultural evolution is a substitute for biological evolution, and it works much faster and more fluidly. It's not mere individual intelligence that allows generalists like ravens and us to thrive in kaleidoscopic environments, but also our flexible social dynamics.

A tribe's conditions change. For instance, it might move from one environment to another, and with learned morality its members could adjust better. The Nyinba of Tibet show how it works. They live in a harsh climate at 16,000 feet above sea level, and they do very labor-intensive subsistence farming on fields that can't be subdivided efficiently. So a family needs the combined efforts of several brothers to support a woman and young children. The local custom of polyandry among brothers—several husbands to one wife—goes back several centuries, and over time it became increasingly compatible with other parts of the moral code. Until the 1950s, when China annexed Tibet, the custom spread among Nyinba farming families because those who followed it did better than their monogamous neighbors.

We take our own culture's morality for granted, but it can shock those outside our culture, and sometimes even our own young people. For instance, how can we condone breaking up a family over mere personal differences? How can we tolerate a vast and widening gulf between rich and poor? How can we give mild-mannered drug addicts harsher sentences than street thugs?

Yet an evolving moral code favored tribes over the millennia. So it makes sense that we all have the same moral foundation, the apparatus of guilt and gratitude and the rest, but attach differing values to it. And the power of morality can fix these values deeply in the mind.

Mirror neurons play a key role in maintaining cultures over time. They enable our unrivaled capacity for imitation, and we copy others even when we aren't aware of it. So people can transmit morals by example. In fact, imitation is more powerful than instruction, and that's why "Do as I say, not as I do" is a classic piece of advice. Children will copy the unrewarded actions of an adult model, while chimps—with far fewer mirror neurons—quickly cease imitating any acts that don't reward them. In this sense, ironically, chimps are more like *Homo economicus* than any human.

It may seem puzzling that children tend to copy all actions. After all, some adults are hardly role models. But there are powerful benefits. Kids learn faster. They cooperate better, since in a tribe they grow up internalizing similar norms, so mirror neurons help a tribe compete overall. Kids easily imbibe the culture, which presumably has been somewhat successful. And copying fosters morality, for children also tend to think that the actions they are imitating are "right."

Let's look at three ways moral codes can vary: by stain, sphere, and values themselves.

What kind of person are you if you violate the moral code? It depends on interpretations of what you did. Basically, we can view moral rules as either intrinsic or conventional. Anglo-Saxon criminal law captures the distinction in the concepts of *malum in se* (wrong in itself) and *malum prohibitum* (prohibited wrong). Despite the Latin, they're pretty simple. *Malum in se* involves nasty acts like robbery and assault. People feel the vileness in their gut, and these acts stain a person's character. *Malum prohibitum*, on the other hand, is just rule-breaking. If you drive 75 miles per hour in a 65-mile zone and get a ticket, that's *malum prohibitum*. It's not intrinsically wrong, since if the legislature raised the speed limit to 80, you wouldn't have gotten the ticket. Society bans the act, yet you aren't evil. However, cultures and individuals differ in the extent to which they view offenses as basic wrongs. In less developed societies, people consider more acts wicked.

What kind of person are you if a relative violates the code? We can also view morals as either individual- or group-centered. In the West, individualism reigns. We feel we should be responsible solely for our own acts, since they're the only ones we control. But in other cultures, especially outside Europe and the United States, misdeeds can contaminate the group. You have roles in the larger matrix, typically the family, and it matters more than you do in many ways. Hence arranged marriages can seem natural in some countries, though baffling to the West. The group can also be larger. For instance, on the Pakistan frontier a controversial set of laws imposes liability on a whole tribe. If one member commits a crime, all are responsible, and the authorities can fine the tribe, arrest everyone in it, and tear down their homes.

Finally, what kind of person are you if you violate your neighbor's code? Values make up morals, and they come in great variety. In fact, they may have arisen as a cluster of modules, each solving a specific problem on the savanna. Moral psychologist Jonathan Haidt examined cultures worldwide and identified six values: caring, liberty, proportional fairness, loyalty, authority, and sanctity. They may not exhaust the range, and they don't necessarily reflect the values Haidt or we the authors have, but rather those found in the field.

Caring is concern for the suffering of others. It has kept tribes internally strong, for obviously if you allow harm within the group, everyone is at risk. So every society has strictures against acts like murder and battery. Helping others also keeps the tribe strong, and we also see this value in people who urge aid for the poor, the uninsured ill, the bullied, and mistreated animals.

Liberty is doing as you please. It arose organically from the rough equality in tribes, where no one had the power to boss anyone else around. In Western societies we see desire for liberty in rights, such as freedom of speech, religion, and assembly, as well as in the general loathing of oppression.

Proportional fairness is more complex. It can involve trust, reciprocity, and equality of exchange. Most people also deem it distribution of rewards by merit. If you think a shirker in a business partnership should get less of the profits or none at all, you are honoring the value of proportional fairness. Similarly, most people deem it fair to pay highly trained professionals like doctors more than laborers like janitors.

Loyalty is commitment to the group (or, in a marriage, to one's mate). Suppose a pitcher gives a friend on the opposing team easy changeups to hit. If you feel he's acting improperly, you are responding to the loyalty value. On the savanna, tribes with loyal members enjoyed more mutual aid and did better against other tribes. Indeed, the opposite of loyalty is betrayal, and we stigmatize it. Benedict Arnold remains a byword in American culture, his name a poisonous slur, though few know what he actually did.

Authority arose as a moral value for children. Kids who obeyed their parents were more likely to reach adulthood on the savanna, and we inculcate this value in them. If you feel some revulsion on seeing a seven-year-old publicly tell her mother to "shut the fuck up," you are responding to this value.

Sanctity is a quasi-religious value that endows certain objects and ideas with inviolability. We tend to react with disgust or fury when we see them abused. For instance, suppose a hungry homeless person slips into a morgue and started eating corpses. If you feel revulsion at this idea, you're responding on this dimension. No matter how much sympathy we have for his plight, the act offends most of us. It feels immoral, but only a value like sanctity can explain why. Likewise, if you wonder why ayatollahs might sentence cartoonists to death for mocking Muhammad, sanctity explains it.

Now, there are clearly other values, such as citizenship and moral courage. But the weights you give these six basic values determine much about your approach to life. For instance, extensive tests have shown that liberals focus mainly on the first three and pay less attention to the rest, while conservatives value all six almost equally. (Libertarians concentrate almost wholly on liberty and proportional fairness.) Non-Westerners value the latter three much more than liberals and this fact has helped shape their cultures.

So let's go back to that January morning in Damascus. How could morals drive Fayyez to kill his sister Zahra because she was raped?

First, Fayyez was upholding an ancient code of honor. Honor is all about pride, shame, and often sanctity. This particular code holds that any suggestion of extramarital sex, even victimization in rape, dirties a woman and touches the third rail of sanctity. It also defiles her whole family. In Islam morals are much more group-centered than in the West, and a woman's indelicacy—even just meeting with a single man—can dishonor her family. So, as hard as it is for Westerners to grasp, a group can feel shame even if a raped woman has followed all the rules.

This shame plunges everyone into bad territory. Others define an Arab male's status and masculinity in terms of his ability to protect his female relatives. If she is chaste or faithful, the males gain prestige. If she isn't, as if she is raped, the men have failed, and others view them as weaker.

What can they do? For some, the moral code has evolved an aberrant solution.

The woman's death can erase the blot. Indeed, the stigma of helplessness vanishes if the men take dramatic masculine action, such as murdering their own kin. They at once eliminate the ongoing source of embarrassment, showcase their violence to other potential seducers, and through punishment partly shift the blame to her. And, of course, where a whole group has responsibility for a homicide, each individual has less. It gets easier.

These "honor killings" are surprisingly common. For instance, in March 1999, after a man raped a 16-year-old mentally defective girl in rural Pakistan, the tribe's judicial council ruled that she had shamed her tribe and had her executed in front of the group. Some 5,000 honor killings occur each year, mostly in the countryside of Pakistan, Egypt, Jordan, and Iran but also in such nations as Brazil and Italy. A 1980 PBS docudrama on the honor killing of a Saudi princess, ordered by her grandfather, provoked a serious diplomatic crisis.

Various authorities support these killings. Younger males tend to commit them, but older, influential folks urge them to. The in-group offers rewards like celebrations, and custom provides the guidelines. And the strict legal code of *sharia* reinforces it all, so the murderers are punished only lightly and at times not at all. Fayyez went straight to the police after killing his sister and no doubt expected a short sentence. The average honor killer in Syria spent just a few months in jail.

But Zahra's husband filed a civil suit, and the case became locally famous, for honor killings are controversial even among Muslims. This tradition flouts values of caring, liberty, and fairness, and many loathe it. The logic is also flawed, for if the men really are responsible for protecting the women, why should a raped female suffer the death penalty? Overall, these slayings are a mandate to some and a disgrace to others.

Moral emotions can thrill us and sear us. Yet the codes themselves are malleable, so much that they can induce sibling murder. As we'll see, moral codes can turn against their original purpose and undermine fruitful cooperation. They can deem catching endangered cod moral and restraint immoral.

I-Versus-We Revisited: The Ultimate Flat Organization

Most people think democracy began in a brilliant city-state by the Aegean Sea. In fact, it is the oldest form of governance on earth. In virtually all hunter-gatherer tribes studied—from the Ache to the !Kung, from Australian aborigines to Greenland Inuit—people are basically equal. They hold most property in common. All help raise children. They decide by consensus, and leadership stems from judgment and persuasive power rather than edict. "We" prevails.

It's hard to play pharaoh in a tribe. Class structure was unnecessary in a band of 70 or so nomads and, indeed, counterproductive. Hunting parties (mostly male) needed only casual, temporary leadership, and informal peer organization (mostly female) was fine for gathering berries and tubers. An overlord would get in the way.

In fact, most moral codes promote caring and sharing, two leveling virtues. In traditional societies, the healthy help the sick or injured, grandmothers watch the kids when the mother is out gathering food, and hunters give chunks of fresh meat to other families, while gatherers share mainly within the nuclear family. Sharing across families in a band varies somewhat, but it is common. Here we see humanity's original social safety net, bred of eons, beneficial to all, and regulated by morals.

Such acts strengthen the group and bring esteem, or at least avoidance of shame, to those performing them. We see similar phenomena today in philanthropy, where Bill Gates, Warren Buffett, and other magnates donate huge sums to worthy causes with no expectation of return beyond the moral.

What if a tribal member tried to monopolize access to women or control the best food? Since everyone knows everyone else, attempts to abuse power get checked immediately. A bossy guy would face escalating penalties—even if he had a little gang around him. Others would gossip and playfully shun him, and if he persisted, they'd mock him and, in extreme cases, threaten, exile, wound, or kill him. Indeed, some believe technology moved our genus toward equality. If other means failed to curb the budding ruler, a wooden spear to the heart would end his ambitions, as it occasionally does among the hunter-gatherer Hadza of Tanzania today. In contrast, chimps wake up and retaliate when attacked in their sleep.

The lack of formal hierarchy had a huge effect on evolution. For instance, female chimps are reluctant to share food, even with their own offspring. Male chimps hunt together and share the meat, but not equally. The chimps that have done the most to kill a monkey get the most meat, and the others often beg and whine for shares. So chimps have incentive to make the kill, but much less to cooperate in making it. Prehumans did better. Individuals had reason to join even if just to sharpen their skills, and far more benefited from success. Tribes cooperated better when no "big man" was hogging the catch.

Morals in fact substituted for the big man. Tribal members used them to make decisions that were good for the group. As codes of behavior, morals established standards all could understand. As intuitions, they created a sense for social strategy. For instance, they enabled the trick of expelling offenders without breeding a yen to retaliate. Morals helped tribes determine who got how much meat from a kill, who deserved what in general, and how to resolve disputes. Hence morals gave tribes self-direction. They coevolved with equality.

Of course, we were never entirely equal. No group is. Fairness is proportional. And some inequality is productive, since it gives people goals to strive for. Yet for 99 percent of our prehuman evolution, the hierarchy was slight, fluid, and generally meritocratic.

I-Versus-We Revisited II: The Cooperation Contest

The American redstart (*Setophaga ruticilla*) is a New World warbler that gets its name from the orange patches on its wings, breast, and tail ("start" is an obsolete term for "tail"). After its second year, the brighter the male's plumage, the more females he attracts. They respond because vivid color signals genetic fitness. Redstarts can't manufacture the carotenoids they need for orange and must get them from their food. Only effective birds, those that dine often and well, have bright patches. Darwin called this phenomenon "sexual selection." It is evolution based on preferences within the group.

Evolution worked at the preference level with us too. Like redstarts, prehumans competed to gain the best mates and offspring. Instead of strong color, they displayed traits such as prestige and alliances. That is, they competed for others' cooperation. "I" prevailed—via "we."

The more friends we have, and the greater their loyalty and status, the better off we are. With more friends, we can tap a richer flow of information. With more loyal friends, we can mobilize greater support. And with more prestigious friends, we show that the high-status respect us and thus, indirectly, that we are high-status ourselves. Hence others want our friendship more. And our social plumage brightens.

That's why guides to good social behavior have flourished throughout the ages, from Aristotle's *Nicomachean Ethics* to Baldassare Castiglione's *Book of the Courtier* (1528) to Dale Carnegie's *How to Win Friends and Influence People* (1936), which has sold over 15 million copies. Adept cooperators usually know the network better, spot its shifts faster, and can use them more successfully. They can better manage the gossip that affects people's choices about whom to work with and whom to avoid. They also have more allies and power, and others may rely on them. We find these qualities attractive. We prefer mates with charm, insight, and political savvy, so they tend to win better partners and pass on more genes. Once our ancestors reached a certain level of cooperation, this social selection likely took off and developed its own momentum.

So competition and cooperation intertwine. They can reinforce each other and undermine each other. In a company, for instance, people strive toward a common goal and earn rewards for success, but office feuds can turn team members against each other and sabotage projects. In buddy cop films, competitive bickering constantly threatens the effort, though warm cooperation usually prevails. But in a corruption-rife nation like India, competition dominates. There, officials commonly demand bribes to do their jobs. That is, private individuals levy taxes, and these costs slow the economy. Self-interest erodes the public interest. Indeed, because members of the Indian parliament are immune from criminal prosecution, 29 percent of the lower house had been charged with a crime as of 2012, and 14 percent with a serious offense such as extortion, theft, rape, or murder. India is getting richer, yet as its citizens look out for number one, they slow the nation's growth.

The Moral Drop-off: Us and Them

Few societies on earth are as untouched by civilization as those in the highlands of Papua New Guinea. Around 2004 scientists traveled there to conduct a field experiment among the Ngenika and the Wolimbka tribes. The two live a day's journey apart and enjoy friendly relations. But they dwell in a preinstitutional world where laws in our sense are absent. These tribes still rely on social feedback to enforce the moral code.

The researchers ran a more elaborate version of the Ultimatum Game with them. It featured three players: a dictator, a recipient, and a judge. The dictator received 10 *kina*, about the daily wage for a laborer in the surrounding territory, and the judge got 5. There were two moves. First, the dictator had to divide the 10 *kina* between himself and the recipient. He was free to split it any way he wanted, and the recipient was powerless to respond. Second, the judge could, if he wished, use his own money to punish the dictator. Each 1 *kina* he spent reduced the dictator's booty by 3 *kina*.

As it turned out, judges willingly paid to slap down greedy dictators. When all three players came from the same tribe, judges typically punished dictators who gave themselves significantly more than 5 *kina*. Moreover, they increased the penalties to match the selfishness. Presumably the reason is moral outrage, as in the original Ultimatum Game. The experiment cleanly shows that within the tribe, even in an unusual and rather artificial situation, people will sacrifice to prevent one person from taking advantage of another.

But the results changed when the greedy dictator and the recipient came from different tribes. Judges were harsher when dictators from the other tribe victimized members of their own tribe. And they were softer on dictators from their own tribe who victimized members of the other tribe. The other tribe simply seemed to deserve less. At the same time, dictators overall offered better deals to recipients from their own tribe than from the other one. Again, these tribes weren't enemies.

In other words, in-group membership affects people's sense of justice.

Morals are shared understandings among members of a group. They arose to control selfishness and ensure smooth cooperation within the tribe itself, and, only to a lesser extent outside it. Hence the ubiquitous in-group effect. Virtually all traditional moral codes distinguish between in-group and out-group, us and them.

The phenomenon runs deep. Whites punish white criminal defendants less harshly than blacks. In experiments, when whites and Asians see members of another race pricked by a needle, their brain circuits for empathizing with pain show less activity than when they see members of their own race pricked. Out-group members seem to matter less in other ways too. We tend to view out-group members as less individual, more homogeneous. We remember in-group faces better than out-group faces, unless the latter are angry. Embarrassment is worse before an in-group than a low-status out-group. Even among chimpanzees, yawning is more contagious within in-groups than with members of an out-group, because chimps feel more empathy with members of their own group.

If these findings seem disturbing, the ancient moral logic behind them is clear: On the savanna, you knew the individuals in your own group personally, and you shared their code. You understood how to behave with them and how they were supposed to behave with you. Their opinion of you mattered much more, and you had effective penalties. But it was different with outsiders. You might know little about their status, personality, and history. You might have just a blurry idea of their moral code, which could seem quixotic and degraded. Their assessments of you mattered less, and you had much less leverage if they misbehaved. So you had some reason to be wary of full reciprocity.

In-groups arise everywhere: in classrooms, in online chat rooms, in prisons, and of course between different races, political parties, and nations. They even appeared swiftly when researchers divided subjects based only on eye color.

In-group rivalries have divided paleoanthropologists. Hominid fossils in Africa are rare prizes, and scientists have formed coalitions and competed to keep their sites free from out-group intrusion. Accusations of theft and double-dealing have flown back and forth. Kenya arrested at least one anthropologist, and in another case, a member of one coalition implicitly threatened a scientist with a gun.

And we often see worse. In the 1992–93 Hindu-Muslim riots in Bombay, for instance, Hindu thugs beat their way into the apartment of a Muslim family and attacked the dad with an iron rod. Later, the 15-year-old son said, "I saw the boy who was beating my father. He was my friend. He used to come to my home to eat at Eid. He used to play cricket with me." The son pleaded with him to stop, but the friend just told him to leave. The group interest of the savanna had overwhelmed the personal tie.

In 1914, a Serb nationalist assassinated Archduke Franz Ferdinand in Sarajevo, and the deed triggered retaliatory provisions in mutual aid pacts. The result was World War I. Soldiers like French surrealist poet Guillaume Apollinaire marched to the front with glorious notions of battle, only to find themselves in filthy trenches where friends suffered ghastly deaths. Ten million ultimately perished, and shrapnel gravely wounded Apollinaire himself. Behind this slaughter lay the savanna dichotomy of in-group and out-group, and it intensified as each side sought to portray the other as subhuman, undeserving, beyond moral restraint.

This is the ultimate gulf between in-group and out-group: war. Serbs and Croats, Hutu and Tutsi, Greek and Turkish Cypriots, Catholic and Protestant Irish, Sunnis and Shiites—all shed blood partly for reasons that trace back to ancient Africa.

But not all out-groups suffer the moral drop-off. Weak ones like the sick, the homeless, and the elderly tend to evoke charity. For instance, after a 7.0 earthquake killed a quarter million people in Haiti in January 2010, US relief agencies received $611 million in one week. In these cases, there is no reason for wariness, and our moral feelings surge to the fore.

Intriguingly, moral bonds in an in-group seem to strengthen as the gap with others grows. In particular, groups that sense an immediate enemy—like commando units, terrorist cells, and cults—show tighter moral ties. Members realize they need each other, and they do more for each other. The code of "one for all and all for one" may emerge. For example, if an ancient tribe felt threatened, its moral bonds would have strengthened, and if the danger eased, they would have loosened again. Levels of morality can fluctuate.

Social in-groups are flexible and ever-changing, a key challenge in the cooperation contest. For instance, hunter-gatherer tribes are hardly walled units. They fuse and fission all the time. People almost always marry outside the group, to prevent incest and build political ties. There is strength in good relations, as between the Ngenika and the Wolimbka. Your band is healthier, happier, and more productive if you don't have to worry about raids from neighboring bands and if you can get their help in emergencies. Serbs and Croats, for instance, had lived together in peace for centuries before the bloodshed. There is also strength in alliances. For instance, as whites spread over North America, tribal confederations like the Iroquois and Sioux resisted them better. On the savanna, it made no sense for every band to wave the spear at every other band. Like individuals, tribes both cooperated and competed.

African Exodus

Our own species, *Homo sapiens*, appeared in northeast Africa about 200,000 to 175,000 years ago. At that time they developed the need to cut hair, presumably because hairstyle variety was alluring. By 100,000 years ago, if not long before, our ancestors had modern human bodies. Like ourselves, they looked weak and vulnerable. A species that walks upright seems like an easy target—just lunge at its midsection. And these people were slender, lightly muscled, without claws, fangs, or a projecting, weapon-filled snout. This appearance is highly deceptive. They had so few built-in weapons because they didn't need them. They crafted far more potent ones, and they had the smart cooperation of others and thus lived in a halo of safety. In comparison, the great musculature of the Neanderthals suggests not strength but a lack of full *Homo sapiens* powers.

Homo sapiens also had language. These individuals could communicate through symbolic speech just as we do. They could form plans, hypothesize, analyze in detail. And since language let them externalize thought, they could think in groups, use more available information and ideas, cooperate better, and deploy the moral system better. Moreover, language gave morals an aspirational side. That is, almost everyone urged greater altruism, even the selfish, because everyone benefited from it.

Slowly, over many millennia, the hunter-gatherer lifestyle became increasingly sophisticated. Members of our species started to make fitted clothing about 75,000 years ago, according to evidence from the genes of body lice. They developed better techniques for constructing shelter and tending fire. Weapons improved, especially slings and atlatls, spear-throwing devices that allowed our ancestors to kill top predators and big game.

Around 40,000 years ago, cave art first appeared, as well as an array of other novelties: bird-bone flutes, personal ornaments of shell and ivory beads, and complex tools of ivory, antler, and bone. We see far more results of what-if imagination as innovation blossomed and spread. A fundamental transition appears to have occurred around then, and we still don't know its immediate cause.

But the detonator was cultural evolution, made possible by the moral system. Cultural evolution let us adapt much faster and more successfully than the biological parallel, as with the Dinka and Nuer mentioned above. To an extent, just as new operating systems upgrade computers' behavior, evolving moral codes improved our own. Our ancestors transmitted more of the best ideas and practices from one generation to the next, and they shifted their behavior quickly when new conditions arose. Groups that adapted well succeeded, and other groups imitated them, moved away, or shrank. Our ancestors became "behaviorally modern."

A few of these people—perhaps just a few thousand—then left Africa from around Ethiopia at the Strait of Bab el-Mandeb, when the sea level was over 200 feet lower than today. All non-African people descend from this small group. That band and its descendants spread out slowly along the coastline. When things got crowded, a few groups moved into new territory and adjusted to it. Our ancestors eventually reached India, Australia, and the East Asian coast. Then they moved inland into central Asia and Europe, where they encountered descendants of *Homo erectus*. These forebears eventually disappeared, outcompeted, though pygmy *Homo erectus* may have survived deep in the Indonesian island of Flores as late as 11,000 BC. In contrast, the Neanderthals of Eurasia vanished 30,000 years ago

Descendents of the African emigrants eventually moved over the grassy Bering land bridge, with its herds of woolly horses and mammoths, and into the New World. Most recently, using canoes and sophisticated navigation, they spread through most of Polynesia.

So with strong tribal bonds and a face-to-face moral system adapted for small bands, our ancestors inherited the earth.

Then the other half of the balance appeared.

2

The Rise of Wealth: How We Became Civilized and Started Shopping

Why is there something rather than nothing?

—Gottfried Wilhelm Leibniz

In 25,000 BC a few people at Dolni Vestonice, now in the Czech Republic, lived in shelters made of rocks, wood, and mastodon bones. Most tribes back then dwelt in caves or temporary huts, and some on the European steppe made torches by burning animal fat in the bulbs of mammoth femurs. From the era of *Homo habilis* through 10,000 BC, total global wealth was near zero.

Today, we live in high-rise towers, ski chalets, beachfront condos, suburban duplexes, and homes and apartments of every kind, all over the globe. We drive to shops, spas, and office spires. The midnight glow of Tokyo is visible on the way to the moon, and every day we move almost two million tons through the port of Shanghai. In June 2011 total global wealth was $231 trillion. And most of us live so immersed in wealth that "nature" is a special experience.

Where did our brilliant, comfortable, stimulating universe come from? How did we achieve it?

Our genome hasn't altered that much since 10,000 BC—we're basically the same people—so we can't look to biology for the answer. Instead, it lies in a faster pace of cultural evolution. Innovations tumbled out in an array of realms, built on each other, and created our world.

Yet this road was hardly straight. We languished long in dead ends, and only a combination of two unusual circumstances enabled us to get here at all. Even as people have pined for wealth throughout history, they have failed to see its sources. We stumbled into treasure.

The Birth of Economies

The cave painters at Lascaux lived almost without an economy. An economy is a system of producing, distributing, and consuming goods and services.

Value flows through it. Around 40,000 to 20,000 years ago, hunter-gatherers began accumulating property, such as grinding stones, bows and arrows, and animal-skin boats. But they still had little to swap, so their world is a moonscape to the average economist. Classic economies arose when they had enough goods for regular trade.

And that happened when they began coaxing food out of the void.

Climate change provoked this step, as it had so many in the past. The key incidents began about 12,000 years ago in what is now a Kurdish-speaking region near the border of Turkey and Syria. There, after several millennia of warmth and plentiful rain, an era of cooler, dryer weather began. We call it the Lesser Dryas. It lasted only several centuries, and few scientists would study it today if it hadn't revolutionized human life.

By then villages already existed, but as with drying episodes throughout the Pleistocene, tribes faced a dwindling food supply. With more people competing for the local game and plants, almost anything that quelled hunger pangs became important. As we've seen, morals and many other aspects of our nature developed from such challenges. But this time people took a new tack.

They developed agriculture.

Even the earliest tribes doubtless realized that they could increase grass yields by planting and watering seeds. But why bother if your band will move on in a few days? And it may just seem like too much trouble. An anthropologist once asked a !Kung tribesman why he didn't sow fields like neighboring villagers. "Why should we," he replied, "when there are so many mongongo nuts in the world?" But in the Lesser Dryas, for reasons we don't fully understand, folks began raising crops. Very likely women took the lead with the wild grasses now called emmer and einkorn, using digging sticks to give seeds a better chance and resowing the best varieties.

Yet here we have a puzzle. For the immediate result isn't progress, as measured by happier lives. Anthropologists estimate that !Kung adults work only 25–40 hours per week, even though others have now pushed them out of the choicest parts of their range. The Costanoan Indians of California probably toiled even less. By contrast, subsistence farmers labor dawn to dusk every day for most of the year. Comparing skeletons, archeologists conclude that foragers generally enjoyed better nutrition and health than most early farmers. They probably also had a more pleasant social life. In this sense, hunting and gathering was the original Garden of Eden.

Why then did agriculture prevail? Why did people keep at it after the Lesser Dryas ended?

The answer lies not in its appeal, but in simple arithmetic. Nomads depend on the existing food supply. But farmers turn the soil into a factory churning out berries, apples, and corn. So the Malthusian limit balloons, and far more people can dwell on each square mile. With hunter-gatherers, a group of a few dozen is usually the most efficient size. But with farmers, larger groups—say, thousands of people—all in the same place do better at raising crops (especially irrigated ones) and livestock, and at fending off raids.

That greater population density made the difference in conflicts. Suppose there are two small, neighboring valleys, each with a different lifestyle. If a thousand people can live in the first and only a hundred in the second, the first population will shoulder the second aside. Indeed, agriculture beats back the hunter-gatherer lifestyle wherever climate, water, and soil permit. Slowly, over millennia, farmers spread and nomads withdrew to margins like Britain where crops struggled.

Though we can't precisely track the path from the first rude fields to civilization, we know the outlines of the story. Part of it involved new technology. Tools had expanded the food supply for *Homo habilis* and our other ancestors, and they did so here again. Farmers developed better scythes for cutting the grass stems, better storage devices like pots, better grinding tools, better means of separating edible grains from the stems and husks, and better recipes for cooking and baking. Yields kept growing, century after century. Each increase in yield per acre increased the food supply and population density.

With more and more active minds in the community, a greater collective intelligence arose. People shared problems and knowledge until good solutions emerged. Hence innovation accelerated. Some key improvements were better grains, especially a hybrid called wheat, and new sorts of cultivated plants, especially legumes like lentils and garbanzos, whose complementary amino acids give a huge boost to nutrition. Crop production climbed still higher when farmers developed specialized skills and built novel items: dams, irrigation ditches, grain storage bins, plows, hoes, and scythes. Economists call the process "capital accumulation." We all live partly on the capital other generations created.

These advances led to still newer ones. For instance, domesticated herd animals were a special kind of capital. Humans tamed goats around 8000 BC, then sheep, pigs, and cattle in that order. Each increased the meat supply. And though people first raised sheep for food, they soon found the animals were a living factory for wool. You just had to shear it. Humans first raised cattle for meat too, but later used them to give milk, plow fields, and pull carts. The plow boosted crop yield and let farmers cultivate land that previously seemed marginal, so it too, increased the food supply. And with carts, people could haul bulk goods like wool much farther. Markets expanded.

By 7000 BC, people were farming pretty much all the land along the Tigris and Euphrates that they could irrigate. Soon the same was true by the Nile, and then the other great rivers of temperate and subtropical Eurasia. The population exploded, from tens of thousands of people to tens of millions, the majority living in agricultural villages, and then in cities like Eridu, Uruk, and Ur.

Today the world has seven billion people. Agriculture feeds them all, and it can feed many more. Most people don't work in food creation at all, and contribute in other ways instead. The Malthusian limit is still with us, but we don't know where it is. At least for now, we have freed ourselves from it.

Secrets of the Bazaar

Agriculture and technology weren't the only ways to spin wealth out of nothing. Another was trade, and agriculture bred it on a large scale. The new world required storable harvests and livestock; without them most people would starve.

Hence, people gained more and more surplus. They could swap it, and exchange became the road to further wealth. Let's take a look at how trade led to the first cities.

As humans evolved, language enabled face-to-face bargains or "spot exchange": I'll give you this if you give me that. Spot exchange increases wealth in a variety of ways, but at its most basic level it is just a simultaneous favor swap. It's like two primates grooming each other at once. For instance, suppose Jack has a figurine he values at $100. Jill likes it, and for her the value is $200. At the same time, Jill has an old raft she values at $100, but Jack values at $200. They trade, and now each person is richer by $100. This kind of swap is ubiquitous in our history, and children do it naturally, without instruction.

Is it really a mutual favor on the spot? "Favor" implies donation and trust, and since the deal is simultaneous, there can't be any donation or trust in a return favor. But some need for trust remains. For instance, Jack warrants that the figurine will last a reasonable time. If it falls apart at once, Jill will want her raft back. Likewise, Jill warrants that her raft will float. That is, a moral obligation supports the deal. Indeed, without such guarantees, people get wary of trade, and it slows down.

Let's take the Jack and Jill swap several steps further. Suppose Jack actually sculpted this figurine. He totals up his labor and raw materials, and sees that it is worth $100 to him. But Jill values it at $200 and so will gladly pay $150 to get it. If enough people will pay $150, Jack can stop farming and sculpt full time. He can specialize. And everyone's wealth increases.

This kind of trade didn't emerge all at once, but agriculture created just the right conditions. First, it increased the population. More people meant more people with varied tastes, and hence more who would want the figurines. Agriculture also increased the sheer amount of property. There was more stuff to swap in return. So spot exchange proliferated.

Then a few interesting things happened to transform it.

First, people found a customary time and place to trade, perhaps the site of a harvest festival, the intersection of two roads, or a ford in a stream. That place developed a tug. For instance, if Jack wanted to find buyers for his figurines, he'd go where the buyers already were. And if Jill wanted to find figurine sellers, she'd go where the sellers were. So they'd both wind up in the same place. More sellers attract more buyers, and vice versa, so the site expands. The upshot is a central marketplace: a bazaar.

Bazaars almost certainly existed in ancient Mesopotamia and Egypt, but the first we know about in detail is the Agora in Athens. There, merchants sold wine and ointments, cobblers fixed shoes, and barbers cut hair, all in booths marked off by wicker screens. Socrates roamed this plaza for victims because it attracted so many people. The Forum in Rome was also a bazaar, and the central marketplace in Tenochtitlan amazed Cortez, who estimated it drew 60,000 shoppers every day. Bazaars also existed in almost every small town in the Roman and Aztec empires. And they survive today in cities on every continent, as souks in the Arab world, as night markets in large East Asian cities, as weekly street markets in many European cities, and as farmers' markets and crafts fairs in the

United States. Shopping malls are a modern mutation that has spread around the world.

Bazaars increased wealth beyond spot exchange. They cut the "transaction cost," the cost to do the deal itself. Transaction costs include transportation and time spent haggling and comparing prices. They cause friction in an economy. Reduce them, prices fall, and you have more money in your pocket.

For instance, bazaars made trade impersonal. For Jack and Jill to swap goods, they have to know each other. So their sphere of trade is social: their friends, and friends of friends. But a bazaar is relatively impersonal. You can trade with anyone. You don't have to know a vintner to get wine. Bazaars bring more sellers together with more buyers who want their goods, and everyone's opportunities expand. Transaction costs fall.

Eventually, buyers and sellers also came to use money. Suppose Jill desired the figurines but didn't have anything Jack wanted. The deal would die. Barter has always suffered from this problem. But money eliminates it. Everyone wants money—otherwise it isn't money—so everyone will accept it. Jill can simply pay Jack, and the deal takes place. Money not only slashed transaction costs, but made many new trades possible. Overall, it made societies richer.

Money also quantified value. People could measure it in numbers, and prices came to define trades. You pay so much for a bunch of carrots or a haircut. And prices are easy to compare across a wide range of goods. In this way, money created a common language for the market.

Hence another spontaneous improvement occurs: as markets thicken, prices for similar stuff converge. Sellers tend to charge the same price for equivalent goods and services. For example, consider a farmers' market, where the going price today for a standard bunch of carrots is $1.00. You'll wander around and find that the price is $1.00 almost everywhere.

What determines that price? This is a favorite topic of economics textbooks, which show how it stems from the intersection of curves representing supply and demand. In the farmers' market, sellers use their experience and the costs of acquiring produce to decide how much to bring that day and what prices to post. If those prices differ too greatly from other sellers' or if their carrots are selling too briskly or slowly, they change the price. So using price they almost automatically align the amount they've produced (supply) with the amount others buy (demand). Prices move toward a kind of equilibrium.

The centerpiece of economic theory is this: Trade at these competitive equilibrium (CE) prices is efficient. The reasoning is simple: People usually make sensible bargains. If they like carrots, they'll buy them and benefit; otherwise, they'll buy celery or squash or nothing at all. More specifically: Carrot consumers who value a bunch at more than the CE price of $1.00—at, say, $1.25—will pay $1.00 and gain the extra $0.25 value. Likewise, carrot growers who can raise them, bring them to market, and sell them at less than $1.00 a bunch—say, $0.80—will sell them at $1.00 and gain $0.20 in profit. It's the logic of the Jack and Jill figurine deal, but now it plays out among many people. This is how prices find a balance between supply and demand. As a result, buyers and sellers both realize all potential gains from carrots.

And they realize similar gains with everything sold in organized markets. The CE satisfies those customers who want an item more and turns away those who want it less (assuming it is equally affordable to all). But it also rewards low-cost producers and punishes high-cost producers, so it increases efficiency. As farmers seek less expensive ways to grow better carrots, prices fall over time, and quality improves.

The kicker is that the CE filter adapts to changing conditions. For instance, the supply of carrots isn't constant. If a bumper crop arrives, there are more carrots per person. At a farmers' market, sellers are more likely to have leftovers, so they cut their price. On the other hand, if blight or drought strikes, there are fewer carrots per person. Now sellers are likely to run out early and increase their price. On the consumer side, if a craze for carrot juice sweeps the nation, demand and prices rise, and if people hear warnings against too much carotene, they buy less and prices fall. Overall, buyers and sellers quickly adapt to realize all potential gains.

If this all sounds rather mundane, the result is magic. Wealth appears from the void. And thick markets solve a social dilemma. Post prices and haggling falls off, so transaction costs drop. Trade quickens. At the same time, these markets command the cooperation of all participants, even when they are total strangers. Fail to cooperate at the basic level and you lose money.

It all seems too good to be true. What's the catch? Do prices actually converge in the real world? As conditions change, do they really adjust? Textbooks traditionally couldn't answer these questions, because buyers' true willingness to pay and sellers' true costs are usually private information, unknown even by other buyers and other sellers. So until fairly recently the magic of markets always seemed a bit hypothetical. But Vernon Smith won the 2002 Nobel Prize in economics largely for his laboratory dissection of market performance, and his experiments showed that CE in fact emerges quickly and tracks changing conditions. The theory is right.

Marketplaces recast the I-versus-we dilemma. First, they increase cooperation because sellers have reason to nurture relationships with complete strangers to turn them into repeat buyers. They also have incentive to understand their customers' desires and satisfy them. And marketplaces simply bring people together who otherwise wouldn't meet. The ancient Greeks sailed as far away as Sicily and the Crimea to buy grain, for instance. Long before the EU, Greece was enmeshed in a large, cooperative system.

Yet bazaars also bred novel forms of cheating. The farmers' market is unusual in that purchasers know all they need to about goods and prices. Economists say these buyers have "perfect information." But perfect information is rare. For example, no one will travel all around town to compare the price and quality of a bunch of carrots. The transaction cost—all that lost time and fuel—would dwarf the value of the item. So prices can vary. Moreover, merchants who exaggerate or lie about the quality of their goods can profit more as long as others don't find out. However, fraud threatens not just the cheaters, but the market itself. If people think merchants are dishonest, they'll trade less and everyone will suffer. We saw this effect after the accounting scandals in the dot-com bust; investors pulled funds from the stock market because they couldn't tell who was lying. Congress passed the Sarbanes-Oxley Act to address the problem, and it seems to have worked; accounting fraud was rare after the deeper crash of 2008. So shady dealers shrink the reward pool. Moral codes underlie marketplaces and need effective penalties to work.

At the same time, markets absolutely require competition. When it breaks down, markets suffocate. Prices no longer approach that mutually rewarding CE. A legend about the famed Greek thinker Thales of Miletus (624–546 BC) tells how he decided to demonstrate the practical value of philosophy (then understood broadly as "reason"). Working on the sly, he purchased all the olive presses on his island. The presses are the bridge between olives and olive oil. No presses, no oil. So when the olive crop matured, he could charge growers exorbitant prices. This trick—now called cornering and squeezing the market—no doubt earned him a juicy profit, but it must have hurt many olive growers and raised the price that local people paid for olive oil. Overall, the harm to the local economy surely exceeded the boon to Thales.

Markets create wealth as sellers vie to please customers. Greed is good when we channel competition toward creating better, less expensive products. But markets destroy wealth—and the social fabric—when participants compete to harm rivals and rip off the public.

"The Mother of Cities"

The world's first true city, Uruk, arose around 3500 BC, and it must have been a startling sight back then. It lay in Sumeria, in the fertile delta of the Tigris-Euphrates, above modern-day Basra, where fields yielded two to three times more crops than elsewhere in Mesopotamia. A dense network of waterways surrounded it, and canals wound through the city itself. Here the first writings appeared, and from them we know of Uruk's later prosperity and occasional calamities.

What was life like there? Let's suppose you are a young man waking up in Uruk five thousand years ago. You find the water jug and splash your face, then wolf down some wheat-barley mush cooked yesterday with a couple of figs. You grab your bronze-bladed hoe and, along with thousands of others, head off to work. As you pass the city gates, the crowd splits up. You head north to the garbanzo bean fields, where the overseer has you start clearing an irrigation ditch from the great river, the Euphrates. Later you help dry the harvest and prepare the next planting.

That afternoon, work stops an hour earlier than usual. Your crew fills big baskets with dried garbanzos and marches to the goddess Inanna's temple at the city center. The priests take the beans and hand out treats in honor of tomorrow's big holiday. In the evening, you feast on roast duck with lentils and leeks and coriander, and wash them down with a jar of dark beer. You fall asleep and dream of a lissome temple attendant cavorting with you at tomorrow's celebration.

A cave painter from Lascaux, magically transported into this future at Uruk, would have gazed about in wonder. Nomads had little wealth, but here he'd see the great White Temple, streets, homes, canals, orchards, flocks of sheep and goats, workshops, artful mosaics. He'd also see crowds as he'd never imagined. The mudbrick walls of Uruk enclosed two square miles, but within them lived over fifty thousand people—twice the number of our ancestors alive at any one time through 99.5 percent of our history.

The cave painter would see curious behavior as well. People had settled in one place, chockablock with neighbors, and most spent all day in just one task, such as cultivating fields, weaving cloth, making pottery, hauling goods, or keeping records. He'd encounter individuals serving in government and large organizations—cooperation on an unprecedented scale. Instead of several dozen people well-known to him, he'd see a dense hive of strangers living under a single, complex moral code. He might wonder how they could do it.

But he might also find Uruk fascinating. Modern cities certainly are. They are splendid, intricate worlds, full of surprises and unknowns. In just a block or so of Los Angeles, a movie theater, a hookah lounge, two used book shops, a hotel, an "authentic" Mexican restaurant, a courthouse, a motorcycle dealer, and much more jostle together. A place like Paris or Rio or Tokyo beggars description. Millions of varied people have built such cities, millions live there, and millions of intriguing events happen every day. To any lone human, they are infinities. And the overlays in a city like Rome can create an atmosphere thoroughly distinctive and beguiling.

What is a city? We can think of it as a huge market where people happen to live. In fact, Hong Kong, Chicago, Venice, New York, and many other great cities began as trading posts. When people started to dwell nearby, the providers of life's necessities followed, and the bazaar became a habitat. Of course, most cities don't strike us as giant marketplaces. We see the throngs of pedestrians, the faceted glass towers, the rumbling cars, the homes, and the beckoning shop fronts. But like markets and fields, cities are wealth factories.

Cities are all about proximity. And proximity is valuable. It cuts transaction costs. For instance, it shortens transport. It speeds and broadens information flow. It expands market size. It lets people compare prices more easily. In all these ways proximity magnifies the benefits of the bazaar.

Large markets spin out variety. For instance, a small town might have a Chinese restaurant or two, but a metropolis will have cuisine from Sichuan, Hunan, Shandong, Fujian, and other regions. A small town might have a bookstore, but a metropolis may have stores devoted to travel or technical books. A small town might have several primary care physicians, but a metropolis will have specialists in oncology, nephrology, and every other field, and may even have leading researchers in these areas.

The bigger the city, the greater the market for specialists. Indeed, the Lascaux painter in Uruk would see a world where he might make a living as an artist. Specialists are more efficient, because they can focus on areas where they have ability. If I'm good at customer relations and my friend is good at managing inventory, it makes no sense to have us both deal with customers and inventory. We get more done by splitting up the tasks. Specialists also improve their skills and equipment over time.

Thus, we've gone from a world where no one was a specialist to one where almost everyone is. You the reader are almost certainly a specialist. You probably don't collect your own food and make your own tools. Instead, your job fills a niche in your organization and thus the economy itself. And this ubiquitous specialization has boosted total wealth.

Proximity increases teamwork possibilities. It enables larger, more complex organizations. For most of history, organizations have needed people to live nearby, and before cities there were no large organizations. At the same time, proximity increases the brainpower of society, enabling people to learn from others with different skills, knowledge, and background. So a city of 50,000 people can solve problems that would baffle the same 50,000 scattered in farms over the countryside. Innovations have always come from the city.

Let's look Uruk in particular. Why did it arise?

Several factors were basic. Its site yielded more crops per acre, so the wealth from the ground drew settlers. Its waterways let its rulers dominate a wider realm and control more workers. It seems warfare was a constant threat outside, so people abandoned the space between cities and filled the streets of Uruk.

But two other, less obvious factors were likely also crucial: information processing and commerce.

Writing was almost certainly both a reaction and a spur to Uruk's growth. As early as 8000 BC, the Sumerians were using tokens of stone and baked clay for bookkeeping records, typically of agricultural goods. By 4000 BC they were keeping track of manufactured goods as well, with more complicated tokens. As Uruk grew, its need for better records intensified, and these pictures became a written language: cuneiform on clay tablets.

In most parts of the world, the first cities emerged around the same time as the earliest writing, and we can see why. In Uruk, writing vastly increased the size and accuracy of people's memories. By keeping information intact over time, writing enabled verifiable contracts and impersonal laws. It strengthened property rights by enabling permanent records of who held what. Writing made bureaucracy and large institutions possible. Who can run a government on memory alone? Likewise, some kinds of deals were too large, detailed, and complex for people to remember, so they hadn't occurred. But after cuneiform they did. So it spurred commerce and greatly increased the level of cooperation.

Writing also enabled new ways of understanding. For instance, lists and classifications are important both for trade and comprehending the world in general, yet the mind handles them poorly. In text they are pellucid. Writing captured our inmost thoughts as well and made them available to a wide range of readers over time. We began composing poems, novels, schoolbooks, histories, and we define the border of history and prehistory by the appearance of writing. It swelled our knowledge as agriculture had the food supply.

Information is a slippery construct, hard to pin down and study. It's not like an ancient urn. But the big advance in information processing made cities work. Without written records, complexity would have limited them.

Second, Uruk enjoyed a remarkable location. With its maze of waterways all around, its residents could move goods into surrounding areas more cheaply than other towns and increase commerce. For most of history, water travel has been far less expensive than land travel. In the United States in 1816, for instance, a merchant had to spend the same sum to send goods 30 miles over land as he did to send them 3,000 miles across the Atlantic Ocean. When developers completed the Erie Canal in 1825, nearby villages turned into town, towns became cities, and New York grew into the biggest city in the country.

Uruk had the qualities for similar growth. Its elites traded for such goods as flour, beer, preserved fish, vegetables, fruit, leather sacks, bitumen, pottery, silver, and copper tools. Moreover, the more diverse the trading partners—in terms of resources and preferences—the greater the potential gains. Hence, people who live great distances apart have tended to want each other's goods more. For instance, when Columbus first met Caribbean Indians, he was able to swap bits of glass for bits of gold, and both sides benefited. The reason is clear. Suppose I come to the farmers' market from The Land of No Carrots. If I buy carrots at the farmer's market for $1.00 but value them at $10.00—as I might—then I've gotten far more wealth than if I valued them at $1.25. Uruk gained similarly from long-distance trade. It was The Land of No Timber. It needed wood for roofs, and lumber was thus precious, while forests of cedar, cypress, and pine carpeted Lebanon, and logs there were cheap. So the timber trade would have benefited both places greatly.

We have to be careful in reaching conclusions about Uruk. Archeologists still haven't excavated the whole site and much about it remains unclear, including the extent and role of its commerce. But the city was well suited for trade, and it likely played a major role in Uruk's prosperity.

Cutting Up the Antelope of State Wealth

Archeologists believe Uruk used another form of exchange in addition to trade. In a famous Bible story, Joseph foresaw seven good years in Egypt followed by seven years of failed harvest, and the pharaoh asked him to deal with it. Nowadays, Joseph probably would have bought grain in the open market during the seven fat years, but markets on that scale did not yet exist in Egypt, or anywhere else. Instead, Joseph collected grain as a 20 percent in-kind royal tax on the farmers, and then rationed it out to the pharaoh's subjects during the seven lean years. We call this approach redistribution.

Redistribution was a way of life on the savanna and by many accounts in Uruk too. It seems the central temple directed the efforts of tens of thousands of city-dwellers beginning around 4500 BC. The temple staff collected mandatory contributions (in-kind taxes) from everyone in the city, and then gave everyone rations throughout the year. Around 2500 BC, after Ur had replaced Uruk as Sumeria's cultural capital, the city's ruler took over the temple's role in coordinating redistribution. The whole system began to break down after 2000 BC, in part due to climate change and accumulated salt in the fields.

All governments redistribute wealth in a sense, since every tax is a redistribution. But direct redistribution to citizens has its limits. It works best when the authorities proceed according to a well-understood plan, yet such plans can't accommodate special circumstances. For example, one family might not need its entire oil ration that month but might instead need fish for a sick child, and a fisherman might have a large catch that day. It's almost impossible for redistribution to deal with such one-off situations, and yet they occur all the time. So markets emerge spontaneously even in economies dominated by redistribution.

And as societies grew more complicated, more and more special circumstances arose, and it became harder to make redistribution work. So it fell by the wayside—until recently.

Moral Codes in Cities and Empires

Civilization reshaped our ancestors' moral codes. In a place like Uruk, new lifestyles appeared and face-to-face tribal codes faltered. City dwellers had to deal with strangers, and strangers were a problem. They might not be trustworthy. They might have a different understanding of proper way to behave, and their peers might not punish them for misconduct, especially against members of out-groups. The larger and more diverse the kingdom by ethnicity and class, the less effective implicit codes become.

Every civilization has responded with externalized morals—law. The ruler announces explicit rules and appoints professional enforcers. The most complete early system of laws we have is the Code of Hammurabi (c. 1770 BC), which the Babylonian conqueror posted on pillars in temples near the end of his reign. That code had at least 282 laws, and they show where Babylon needed them. About half of them deal with contracts, and a third with household matters such as divorce and inheritance. The equivalent of this code today is the ocean of statutes and judicial decisions available in law libraries and on the Internet.

But law is not the same as morals. Laws are far more complex, and most are unknown to all but specialists. They are usually prohibitions or prescriptions, and legal codes say little about such positive ethical qualities as kindness. New and vexing moral questions arise constantly in disputes and keep judges awake at night. Moreover, you can't get legal remedies for some wrongs, such as a casual insult. The offense is too small and common, the slope to censorship is too slippery, and angry plaintiffs would clog the courts. And of course, some laws—especially in less developed nations—are flat-out immoral. They may permit torture for offenses such as criticizing a tyrant's haircut, and the Nazis took pains to "legalize" genocide.

As laws proliferate, it becomes clear that a violation does not always signal bad character. You may not even realize you have broken the law. In ancient societies one likely upshot was a rising sense of *malum prohibitum*, of morals as conventions. Early cities held far more people than tribes did, and they all had to get along. So if others followed different customs from you—if, say, they compelled the painting of a dot on women's foreheads—you could view it as merely a rule and not a sin. You could disagree without imputing immorality to them, and thus live in harmony.

Laws provide moral infrastructure for markets. They are essential. Hence as Europe awoke from its feudal doze, mercantile law grew to help commerce along. According to economist Avner Greif, traders first relied on community responsibility. Suppose a merchant from Bremen cheated you. Then, the next time you saw anyone else from Bremen, you and your fellow townsmen would seize his goods. The Bremenite you robbed and his friends would then pressure the cheater to compensate you. This system hooks into our ancient moral instincts about tribal identity. It also gives everyone a direct incentive to monitor and discipline fellow townsmen: if anyone misbehaves, everyone from the town is in danger. It is the group morality we see in the killing of Zahra in Damascus.

And it's pretty ham-fisted. Innocent people have to suffer. Honest differences of opinion arise, and false accusations can be hard to detect. Thus a quarrel can escalate into a feud, disrupting trade and conceivably sparking open warfare— not exactly what you want in a dispute resolution system. Moreover, reliance on group morality didn't scale up well as trade increased during the 1200s. When your town has too many merchants to know personally, and when satellite towns spring up, group pressure gets hard to deploy.

A better system developed out of the fairs at Champagne and elsewhere: *lex mercatoria*, or the "law merchant." A respected, experienced merchant listened to both sides in a trade dispute and decided who owed what to whom. His decisions stuck, because defiant merchants suffered stigma and lost their livelihood. Several generations of merchants prospered as the law merchant enforced credit agreements and quality assurances. Even today, in dozens of industries—such as diamonds, independent films, printing, rice, and tea—merchants resolve disputes in such tribunals, and the threat of expulsion from the trade association enforces these decisions. Over time, the law merchant became part of the legal codes enforced by courts of general jurisdiction today.

However, in 1273 Philip III of France invaded Champagne and brought it into the royal demesne. Over the next several decades, taxes rose, merchant privileges were curtailed, and facilities deteriorated. The Champagne fairs withered. This act reflected a larger problem.

The Origin of Power

From 1949 to 1976 Mao Zedong presided over more than half a billion people in China. He had the power of life and death over them, and he regularly ordered the destruction of treasured heritage. He also engineered vast, ignorant economic experiments like the Great Leap Forward, which drove about 30 million into the grave from starvation and exhaustion. Overall, some claim he was responsible for 70 million deaths, a toll greater than that of Hitler or Stalin. He may have been the most powerful creature of any species who ever lived.

Yet power is new—even the power of a CEO in a small business. It scarcely existed before women began raising crops in Kurdistan. The clever wielded influence, yet command structures were alien and rulers unknown. Some prehumans sought power and its perks, but the social world kept this desire in check.

However, farming begat property and villages became fat targets for hunter bands and unfriendly neighboring villagers. Indeed, raiders and rustlers owe their existence to hoards of grain and herds of livestock; they can't make a living off the meager stored wealth of hunter-gatherers. Thus, as wealth and population increased, people needed strong defenses.

Tribal moral codes couldn't cope. In small groups, quick communication— even eye contact—may be enough to organize a counterattack against surprise raiders. But it all breaks down when the group gets too large.

A key requirement for effective defense is coordination. For example, one of us (Friedman) once worked in downtown San Francisco and often met friends near the black sculpture called the Banker's Heart to choose a lunch spot. There were hundreds of options. Would it be something quick at North Beach? Maybe a restaurant in Chinatown? When there were four of us, we usually made a decision in less than a minute, but when there were eight or more, it often took more than five minutes. So the time to reach consensus on a plan of action grows rapidly as the group size increases. When a large village has to react at once to invaders, it can't rely on consensus. Someone has to be in charge and coordinate the others.

Hierarchy is the result. Once the permanent population exceeds a few hundred, the group is more efficient when a single individual or small group has authority. Hierarchy displaced equality because it worked better.

In fact, much better.

As villages expanded in Mesopotamia and along the Nile, and a bit later on the Indus, Yellow, and Yangtze, semi-egalitarian "big man" governments naturally appeared. They gave way to more complex structures in the larger towns, which eventually grew into hierarchies like that at Uruk. These organizations had a new intricacy and efficacy, and they could achieve things that were impossible without a rank order.

At the top of the pyramid sat a military and religious elite. They fought their counterparts upstream and downstream, and the winners were those with the best armies, often because they controlled the most efficient agriculture. Over the centuries, the top guy ruled larger and larger collections of towns, and started to call himself king. Eventually one of these guys would conquer the whole region, as the Scorpion King seems to have done for the Upper and Lower Kingdoms of the Nile about 3450 BC. Empires arose. And when well run, the hierarchy in an empire was more efficient than in a city-state.

But hierarchies conflicted with long-term savanna values, such as liberty and proportional fairness. Even monkeys get upset when experimenters divide rewards unequally between them, and people everywhere seem to loathe oppression. So to gain cooperation, the ruler typically made his moral stature clear. In his code, Hammurabi observes, "I became the beneficent shepherd whose scepter is righteous; / My benign shadow is spread over my city." Likewise, Urukagina of Lagash (c. 2350 BC) proclaimed that he ended injustice, purged corrupt officials, and protected widows and orphans. The perception of the king's benevolence helped justify his rule.

In *Leviathan*, the cool-headed Thomas Hobbes (1588–1679) argued that people were so self-interested that only absolute rule could overcome the I-versus-we dilemma. He was wrong, of course, but shrewd rulers heighten the "we" among their subjects. For instance, they cultivate peace, crack down on extortion, and enforce honesty in the market. They just rarely overcome the I-versus-we dilemma when it comes to themselves.

Abuse of hierarchy has caused some of the greatest moral catastrophes in our history. Moral codes flounder without effective penalties, like the tribal ridicule in daytime and perhaps the knife at night. Yet as power became fixed in a hierarchical structure, those penalties stopped working. Rulers live at the top of institutions, obeyed and even worshipped, and well-protected by walls and guards. Socially apart from the mass of people, the top officials receive feedback mainly from each other. The bottom levels don't matter. So human history has seen a bestiary of tyrants from Caligula to Kim Jong-Il.

Even with decent rulers, moral codes grew layered. Hunter-gatherers have unified codes, with one rule for everyone, but hierarchy bred varied moral codes based on power and status. For instance, in tribes people enforced authority mainly with their children, but civilized societies encouraged adults to take a subservient, childlike role toward the religious and political elite. Divinities helped monitor good behavior, and some, like the Mesopotamian sun god Utu, specialized in overseeing the moral order. Meanwhile, the privileged had special in-group codes justifying their positions, sometimes including paternalistic obligations toward their inferiors. On the savanna, in-group thinking helped keep tribes strong, and though internal power plays often occurred, they were fluid, ever-changing. Civilization cemented in-groups atop in-groups.

So the new moral codes often brought misery to those at the bottom, the 90 percent who tilled the soil. They had little recourse. They couldn't just leave (unless they knew of unclaimed and defensible fertile land elsewhere, which usually didn't last long), and it was hard to oppose professional soldiers. The ruler had to allow out-groups at the bottom enough to survive, reproduce, and work, but not much else.

Toward Market Economies: Cracks and Moral Infrastructure

In AD 1000, Western Europe was an unpromising backwater, a patchwork of pagan territories and petty Christian fiefdoms (including a pitiful collection that called itself the Holy Roman Empire). By 1400, an outsider trying to predict future world powers would have had to take Western Europe seriously, but he probably would have bet on more established players, such as the Ottomans in Turkey and Greece or the Mings in Beijing or possibly the emerging Sayyid dynasty in Delhi.

By 1800 that contest was over. Western Europe had become the muscle of planet earth, and old pyramid societies everywhere else had begun to crumble. A single Western company was dominating India, for instance. European countries were changing in their very essence, becoming market economies. Karl Polanyi (1886–1964) summed up the difference: Before, economies were embedded in social relations; today, social relations are embedded in economies. Yet it seems a bit mysterious. Why Western Europe 1400–1800, and not some other time or place?

Every historian has a favorite way to explain the Great Transformation, as Polanyi called it. For a long time the most popular theory focused on the Renaissance and early Industrial Revolution, and told a heroic tale of brave explorers and brilliant scientists and inventors who created a host of new technologies, such as better sailing ships, guns, and looms. In this explanation the innovations naturally opened new markets and transformed the economy.

But why did all these heroes happen to turn up in Western Europe (or, toward the end of that period, also in North America). Why not elsewhere?

A short answer is that for centuries Europe enjoyed two conditions that rarely coexist: access to long-distance trade and fragmented political control.

Long-distance trade turns cheap goods into valuable ones by moving them from where they're common to where they're scarce, as in the Uruk timber trade. Yet throughout most history only residents of a capital city enjoyed its benefits, and not just in profit, but in information. For example, if you lived in Kaifeng a thousand years ago, you could meet barge operators from South China, and they might have talked with traders or scholars from India and other exotic lands. But the Song rulers would never let you try anything that might undermine their rule. On the other hand, if you lived in a remote province where their control was weak, you could try new things, but you'd lack access to funding, markets, and the latest ideas. It's hard to innovate if you don't even know what's new. Hence, in China as in all traditional empires, growth languished.

In Western Europe, the situation was different. The ragged coastline fostered long-distance, maritime trade, as did extensions of Roman roads. And with the discovery of the Americas and the reach of ships to Africa and Asia, trade flourished across much of the earth. Spices from Indonesia, for instance, became a prize in European courts. And though Spain monopolized the gold and other wealth from Mexico southward, that wealth spread into neighbor nations. The Spanish failed to develop their economy and had to buy things with it.

Western Europe's political weakness was also a crucial asset. The coastline, the mountain barriers (especially the Alps, Carpathians, and Pyrenees), and the lack of rich resources (not much gold or spice) discouraged the rise of stable empires. No dynasty ever ruled the entire continent. Instead, the feudal system created fragmented loyalties to kin, overlord, and church, and they exercised weak and erratic control of Europe's 2,000 free towns and cities.

Moreover, in traditional empires, towns and cities flourished best near the imperial capital, the center of money and royal favors. But in medieval Europe, free towns sprang up in cracks between fiefdoms. Usually dominated by merchant and craft guilds, these towns fed vital tax revenue to the feudal lords. The lord therefore found it in his interest to protect the guilds' local monopolies, to defend the town against bandits and invaders, and to grant townsmen privileges, such as exemption from corvée. Hence the medieval German proverb *Stadtluft macht frei*, which translates roughly as: "Freedom is in the city air."

How did this work? Suppose you were an ambitious young apprentice dyer in Bruges in 1400, and you discovered a cheaper, better way to dye cloth. The spread of your innovation would threaten the livelihoods of established dyers and their suppliers, so in a traditional empire the dyers would work through their patrons in the ruling elite to quash it. But in Bruges, you'd have choices. Your master could profit by using your method, and if the local dyers' guild cracked down, then you (or perhaps another apprentice who picked up your idea) could go to Amsterdam or some other city where the dyers' guild wasn't so strong, or where the guilds wanted to grow. Weavers and tailors in your new town would then have an advantage due to their access to a cheaper, higher quality dyeing process. Eventually, others would have to adapt.

You or your friend might not even have to move. Paper had reached northern Europe by the 12th century, and paper documents were much less expensive than parchment. Economies rely on information—contracts, records, basic knowledge—and paper increased it. By 1400, Europeans had access to the best ideas in the world, and had the chance to try them out. If an idea failed in one town, the others didn't suffer. If it succeeded, like the dye process, competition among the piecemeal fiefdoms virtually guaranteed that others would use it too. If they didn't, they dropped behind.

The printing press appeared around 1452 and made publishing—copies—cheap and accessible. Information exploded. Just 30,000 books existed in all of Europe before Gutenberg, but by 1500 there were between 10 and 20 million, and in the next century as many as 150 to 200 million. The printing press alone was not enough, and it failed to spark a market revolution in large autocracies like the Ottoman Empire, which clamped down on it. But in Europe, fragmentation unlocked the doors. The faster information moves, the harder it is to kill. People and ideas could go elsewhere.

At the same time, since the 1400s changes in military technology had increased the towns' economic leverage. In particular, cannon and gunpowder favored offense over defense, and professional soldiers for hire were increasingly effective against local knights and conscripted serfs. Military success required a rising spiral of cash, and nobles more and more needed the wealth machines of towns.

Impatient (or foolish) lords tried to squeeze nearby towns harder, but the tactic was self-defeating. Profitable businesses simply decamped, like the young dyemaker in our example, and soon the lord's take declined. Shrewder and more patient lords kept taxes moderate and offered better privileges, so their towns prospered. Greater wealth, and greater battlefield success, increasingly went to regions with laws and politics favorable to townsmen. As on the savanna, the more effective groups pulled ahead and the rest grew relatively weaker unless they copied the high achievers.

Britain and the Low Countries led the way. From the 1500s onward, a growing moral infrastructure fostered trade there. Political power flowed toward elected representatives of the people (at least, the wealthy people). Elections eased the hierarchy problem somewhat. By making government more responsive to the needs of the economy, they made it more efficient. At the same time, these countries developed new and effective commercial law and courts, and private property enjoyed unprecedented protection. Overall, rulers and merchants moved toward better balance. Commerce quickened and wealth increased, and to avoid oblivion, other places had to follow. This ratchet pulled Europe's political and legal systems toward modernity, expanding markets, further improving these systems, and so on.

What happened to those who didn't adjust? Look at Spain. In the 16th century it was the superpower of Europe. Christian rulers had united the Peninsula (except for Portugal) in 1492, and by funding Columbus they gained the inside track to the New World. Spain soon enjoyed the richest stream of plunder the world has ever seen. In an average year in the 1500s, Spain's galleons brought home two to four tons of gold, mostly from her New World colonies, and the annual silver haul averaged over 200 tons by the end of the century.

Spain's rulers then could pretty much do whatever they wanted. So what did they want? As you might expect, they built up their capital, Madrid, and adorned it with huge, luxurious palaces. They also funneled vast sums to religious fanatics. The Inquisition smothered dissent and new ideas, and well-funded missionaries spread a particularly intolerant version of their faith. Spanish rulers spent even more on military adventures, building a huge armada and hiring enormous armies. Though they had some successes, they were never able to conquer England or Holland.

With its geography and wealth, Spain (with Portugal in tow) could isolate itself from the market-driven changes sweeping the rest of Western Europe in the 1600s and 1700s. But like a billionaire who does nothing but spend, Spain eventually started to decline. In the early 1800s Napoleon overran it and its richest colonies then threw off the yoke, and in 1898 the United States snapped up the few remaining. The glittering empire had sunk into irrelevance.

Throughout the Great Transformation, personal moral codes also changed. Historians have noted that the countries leading the Industrial Revolution were mainly Protestant, and Catholic countries like Spain and Italy tended to lag. Sociologist Max Weber suggested that the reason might be the "Protestant work ethic." His point was that Calvinist doctrine encouraged wealth accumulation, savings, and investment, and that investment (in new factories, for example) is essential to economic development. By contrast, traditional Catholic teachings—such as: "It is easier for camel to pass through the eye of a needle than for a rich man to enter heaven"—discourage savings and investment. In Catholic southern Europe, wealthy people focused more on brightening their social plumage, through conspicuous acts such as building larger castles and making hefty donations to the Church and charities. David Landes and other economic historians point up Spain's hidalgo mentality: scorn for people who had to work for a living, the Protestant ethic in reverse.

Yet the Protestant predilection for savings and investment was part of a whole suite of personal traits—rationality, skepticism of authority, orderliness, diligence, productivity—that helped people succeed in an ever-changing market economy. So too were the emerging middle-class habits of passing moral judgments on neighbors and exerting tribe-like peer pressure. These traits were more common in Protestant Western Europe than in traditional cultures, and they surely helped accelerate the economic transformation.

So Weber's thesis is valid as far as it goes, but it misses half the loop. The "Protestant" virtues spread like effective moral codes in tribes. They invited imitation because they worked. They gave people a real advantage when new opportunities opened in commerce. That is, these virtues were not the lucky *cause* of the Industrial Revolution, as some of Weber's followers claim, but rather both *cause and effect*, a part of the runaway dynamic, a virtuous circle like the one that bred writing in Uruk.

Moral traits conducive to the new market system were bound to appear somewhere. If the Protestant Reformation had not been handy, similar values would have evolved directly from Catholicism or some other religious or philosophical tradition. Once present, the new morals would spread, boosting and boosted by the new market system.

So, sparked partly by refugees from Iberia, an age of prosperity bloomed in the Low Countries and artists like Hals and Rembrandt memorialized comfortable burghers. Britain blossomed and took the lead in industrial technology. And both these nations had one other advantage.

The Maxwell's Demon of Economics

The Italian Renaissance is famous as a hubbub of artistic vitality and worldly curiosity, with storied names like da Vinci and Galileo, Michelangelo and Vesalius. But its spark arguably came earlier, from new forms of finance. Beginning in Florence around 1250, banks developed interpersonal networks of *fiducia* (trust) that crossed family lines and soon embraced most of the city's elite and later their contacts across the continent. These supple credit networks eventually could draw on resources throughout Europe. For example, in May 1399, banker Giovanni da Pessano in Milan reported to senior partner Francesco Datini in Florence about a new loan he had given to a merchant traveling to Venice, funded by a repayment from Avignon. Loans, centered in Italy, were flowing across Europe.

Complex networks in previous eras soon collapsed in mutual recrimination, or never really got off the ground. The problem was typically cheating or suspicion of it. But Florentine banks reinforced their exacting moral code of *onore* (honor) with new aids, such as double-entry bookkeeping (for precision, to prevent squabbling and embezzling), letters of credit (to reduce theft while transporting money), and a republican government led by bankers or merchants who had earned high *onore* and respect (to limit corruption and nepotism). Best of all, the Florence-centered system multiplied wealth itself, since one florin in the bank could typically support five florins of bank loans. For over 200 years this financial magic energized the economy in Florence, northern Italy, and much of Europe.

Finance is yet another great wealth factory. One way it works is, of course, by shifting resources from those who don't need them to those who do. The idea is clearly older than written history. It is a formalized favor swap, and prehistoric villagers must have promised shares of the autumn harvest to those who gave them seeds or tools or labor in advance.

Finance provides another baseline boon, almost without trying.

In 1867, the physicist James Clerk Maxwell proposed a thought experiment about the Second Law of Thermodynamics. That's the idea that "entropy," or disorganization, is inevitable. It increases over time. For example, mixing a hot gas and a cold one always yields a lukewarm, less organized one. Maxwell described a little creature later called Maxwell's Demon. Textbooks show the grinning, red-skinned devil sitting between two boxes linked by a small hole. With blindingly swift hands, he sorts the air molecules, moving fast ones into one box and slow ones into another. As a result, one box warms and the other cools. So organization has increased. Entropy is not inevitable.

Unfortunately, Maxwell's Demon doesn't actually work in physics. The Demon himself requires too much energy.

But it does work in finance. Lenders overall act as Maxwell's Demon, sitting above the wealth flow and shunting funds into good ideas and away from bad ones. They assess credit risks and decide which plans have a future and which don't. And they get "energy" from interest. When they work properly, they act overall as an invisible hand steering a society in the right direction. Instead of a single mind, an informed, collective intelligence guides the economy.

Loans gain further value when they are tradable. So do ownership shares in businesses. Recall how the Jack and Jill sale changed when many people became involved. A market developed, with competing buyers and sellers and its own wealth-creating dynamics. Likewise, we can trade stock and loans (usually bonds), and we do so in financial markets.

Financial markets have become the dynamos of modern economies, but they emerged only after the moral infrastructure had stymied greedy rulers. Arguably, legal protection first appeared in the Roman Republic, and scholars have discovered there a prequel to financial markets. A type of organization called the *societas publicanorum* contracted with the government to provision temples, collect taxes, and construct and repair public works. Surviving texts suggest that these firms lived on beyond the death of specific members and were owned by shareholders who could trade shares in the Forum. This inchoate stock market apparently vanished after emperors took power in the first century BC.

However, in response to favorable laws in fragmented Europe, the first true financial markets appeared in Lyons and Antwerp in the early 1500s. The Lyons market dwindled away after a few decades, and when Spanish soldiers seized Antwerp in 1585, non-Catholic traders moved to Holland. There they bred the Dutch "economic miracle" of the 1590s.

Financial markets took permanent root in Amsterdam and London. Investors traded shares in the Dutch East India Company after its launch in 1602, meeting in the open air (and in churches in bad weather). By 1610 they had a *beurs* or bourse in an attractive building on Dam Square, and in 1688 Penso de la Vega described tradable items there beyond shares and bonds, including forward contracts and options. In the 1680s another stock market arose in London's Exchange Alley, a pungent lane bustling with butchers, fruitmongers, and coffeehouse patrons. "Broker," which once meant "tapster" and even "pimp," now went upscale and new terms like "underwriting," "puts," and "stockjobber" entered the language. Financial markets spread further as people saw that they attracted more efficient investment and made cities prosper. Ambitious societies adapted morals and laws to nurture the new markets.

They thus strengthened the funneling power of finance. For instance, canal owners in the mid-1800s competed for backing with the new railroads. Using the emerging financial markets in the United States, investors provided funds to build the railroads, and those with a stake in canals (such as barge builders and toll collectors) could do little to stop them. So finance steered support to railroads and they got built. Markets expanded, organizations grew, and the nation got wealthier.

From Steam to Forex

The world had about a billion people in 1800; now it has seven times that many. In 1800, no city held more than 5 percent of its own society's population; today, more people live in urban areas than outside them. With market economies, wealth has skyrocketed.

Scholars have long cited Industrial Revolution technology as the key reason, and of course it played a major role. For most of history, people had to travel to mechanical energy. It came mainly from mills—windmills, water mills, and so on—all planted in the earth. But as Europe grew richer, inventions freed, simplified, and amplified energy creation. The steam engine let us not just make our own power but move it around. We could put a steam engine in a factory and make new goods, such as steel. We could put it on a boat or a railroad car, and propel it almost anywhere. Then oil made steam almost obsolete. We could burn gas in much smaller vehicles, and the car and jet plane arrived. We could drive to the top of Pike's Peak and fly around the globe.

These tools arrived in a competitive economy hungry for them. The railroad, for instance, slashed the cost of transportation, bringing the hinterland nearer the coast. It let city dwellers buy fresh produce from a much wider radius, so their populations could swell. They could thus gain more from proximity, and their markets and organizations could grow. The car cut transaction costs further and turned cities into "metropolitan areas," with suburbs spreading out to obliterate fields and orchards.

Electricity today is the great power source. Most of the power we get from Hoover Dam, for instance, goes straight to the electric grid, and the movement of electrons came to power engines everywhere. And it did much more. It lit homes and streets. It enabled instant communication, first with the telegraph, then the telephone, radio, and TV. The telegraph led to nationwide companies, for a manager could now directly control operations far away. Organizations grew much bigger and, often, much more efficient. Markets widened and commerce quickened, since people could make long-distance trades at once. The information flow expanded so dramatically that it made the printing revolution seem a blip in comparison. Ultimately, electricity led to computers, which automated information flow and commands, so today Internet-phones are commonplace and we see vast global markets like the forex. The planet is our Uruk.

And the moral infrastructure has matured. Democracies have spread widely since 1800 and made leaders more responsive to needs people perceive. At the same time, regulations have evolved to cope with the new complexities. For instance, we have antitrust laws to maintain market competition. We have laws compelling disclosure, as in the grocery aisle and stock market, to move markets closer to perfect information and increase trust and buying. We enforce laws against bribery and extortion, and we keep most streets safe.

Without such an infrastructure, the Industrial Revolution would have died young. The brilliant ironmonger Thomas Newcomen (1664–1729) invented the first steam engine, but if the right economy hadn't already existed—the mine owners to buy the engine and laws to protect his rights to it—he wouldn't have invested the decades of effort necessary. Morals bred economies that bred world-changing technology.

The need for moral infrastructure stands out clearly in the nations that lack it. Countries in sub-Saharan Africa can get modern technology too, yet most have spurned the moral scaffolding and have struggled. Perhaps the worst dictator in a nightmare half-century was Francisco Macías Nguema of Equatorial Africa, a bloodthirsty near-psychotic who annihilated his own economy. His 11-year reign saw the population fall from 300,000 to 125,000 and the capital Malabo empty out as stores closed and barter replaced trade. On the other hand, there is Botswana. After independence it rejected the African template and built a moral infrastructure. It became an honest, multiparty democracy focused on the public interest, and as a result the economy averaged 9 percent annual growth from 1967 through 2006. Morals made it the greatest success on the continent, by far.

Like Botswana, prosperous societies both liberate and regulate trade, so more takes place and people get richer. Citizens trust the system to enforce contracts, shield property from confiscation, keep banks sound, minimize violence and corruption, and foster real competition.

* * *

To sum up (and simplify), we have risen from bare encampments to a world of spectacular wealth through:

- *Agriculture*, which took us beyond subsistence and created a surplus for trade.
- *Technology*, which lets us produce more, saves time, and confers new powers, some of them breathtaking.
- *Trade*, which lets us buy cheap and sell dear (in our terms), and whose profits spur efficient production and invention.
- *Proximity*, which thickens markets, improves information, saves time, enhances specialization, and spurs competition.
- *Finance*, which multiplies wealth and navigates the future.
- And the *moral infrastructure*, which holds it all together.

We've come a long way from the first seeds in Kurdistan, yet for all we know, future generations will look back on us as we look back on Uruk. For we keep advancing further. Cities are growing faster than ever in history. By one estimate, the world's 600 biggest will see their GDP rise by $30 trillion from 2010 to 2025, and they'll need new floor space the size of Austria. And as smartphones enter rural Africa and India, they bring commercial opportunities to places now virtually devoid of them. People in dusty crossroads towns can become literate, gaze out at the world, get loans, buy and sell, video-chat with others anywhere. Markets will expand and middlemen drop out. Rulers of the Nguema stripe will die away, or learn the lesson of yielding power to gain it.

But it all relies on the moral infrastructure, bred in us over millions of years and modified by institutions. And it's a balance between I and we, competition and cooperation. Go too far in either direction and you'll harm the wealth generators and shrink the economy.

It can happen easily.

II

Worlds Out of Kilter

Losing one's balance is like a little death.

—Scott McCredie

3

From Melqart to Zombieworld:
Adventures in Imbalance

Loops feed back. We began with two stories: the heist of Russia's economy itself and the torment in Greece. But we told you chronicles, almost fairy tales. Great events occurred, but they just seemed to happen. In fact, neither makes sense without the moral background. In both cases, markets and morals were disastrously misaligned. And these are just two examples. Let's look deeper into these and several others.

When Moral Codes Are Too Weak

In 1827, the great Mughal poet Ghalib visited Calcutta and saw an exhibit of Western technology. Much impressed, he urged the absolute rulers in Delhi, "Cities are being lighted without oil lamps. This new law makes all other laws obsolete. Why must you pick up straws out of old time-swept barns when a treasure trove lies at your feet?" It was understandable advice, but like the African nations, Mughal society couldn't take advantage of it. It lacked the economic framework, of course, but also the moral infrastructure. And when the moral infrastructure is weak, two phenomena tend to occur: Rulers siphon profits from merchants, and people siphon money from everyone else.

The Prince and the Paupers: How Monarchs Kill Markets

Around AD 1000 Basil II ruled the Byzantine Empire, the terminus of the Silk Road to China. When bolts of fine silk cloth arrived at the eastern end of his domain, traders had to sell them. But Basil didn't let just any Byzantine buy them. Silk was a royal monopoly, a crucial source of revenue and power. So he let only favored dealers purchase bolts and sell them on to customers like Maghribi traders in the west. In return, these merchants gave Basil a chunk of the revenue as well as political support. If they balked, he could exile or execute them and find more pliable traders.

Potentates have trumped market forces for most of history. For instance, everywhere they seized monopolies. Suppose salt is rare in the realm's inland capital but common in a coastal province. By controlling the salt trade, the king (or a loyal retainer) can buy it cheaply, sell it expensively in the capital, and tuck away the profit. If anyone could deal in salt, merchants would compete, and its price would drop to the competitive equilibrium (CE). The low price would save money for the residents of the capital. The economy would grow. At the same time, dealers would get more efficient at collecting and transporting the salt, so the CE would keep falling.

But the king faced constant threats, both inside the castle and out. An ambitious nephew or duke or neighboring ruler was always ready to grab the pyramid's top spot whenever he thought his soldiers could beat the incumbent's. Therefore the king's first priority was a strong, loyal military. So he chose I over we. He was a vampire on the economy, draining its blood and keeping it lethargic.

And of course the problem arises not just with salt, but silk, slaves, and pretty much anything that could move funds into the ruler's never-filled coffers. The ruling elite typically made sure nobody but its own inner circle could deal in those goods and thereby earn what economists call "monopoly rents." ("Rent" here has the sense of profits in excess of normal competitive levels.) These rents killed drive, stifled innovation, and stunted markets. They are a key reason why, from 5000 BC to AD 1600, annual worldwide GDP per capita remained almost unchanged, at between $400 and $550 (in 1990 dollars).

Rent-seeking sapped even empires based on trade. At their peak, from 1200 to 800 BC, the Phoenicians dominated commerce from Turkey to Spain, and monopolized commodities such as royal purple dye, clear glass, and cedar. The Bible mentions King Solomon's Phoenician ally, King Hiram of Tyre, and his gifts of cedar and skilled artisans in building the Temple in Jerusalem. From their base on the coast of Lebanon, the Phoenicians founded colonies in North Africa, Cyprus, Sicily, and Spain, and reportedly roamed far into the North Atlantic and down the West African coast. Phoenicia had one of the first alphabets, ancestor of the Greek and our own.

Trade expeditions were the lifeblood of the Phoenician empire, and at their head were princes and priests—especially those serving the god Melqart, the "protector of trade" who, according to hostile accounts, required child sacrifices. To maintain rents for the priestly cartels, the Phoenicians launched wars against foreign rivals and often triumphed. As usual, the cartels bled the economy as they steered profits to the temple and palace. Eventually, Phoenicia faced competition from its own colonies. Carthage in North Africa was the most prominent as the Phoenician homeland faded around 600 BC.

Kings furled the sails in other ways. For instance, they often borrowed large sums and defaulted, leaving banks little recourse and at times killing valuable institutions. An early example occurred in 1788 BC. Perhaps to clear his own debts or to curry favor with borrowers, King Rim-Sin of Ur declared all loans null and void. Surviving cuneiform texts show that the edict ruined a money-lender named Dumuzi-gamil and all his competitors. The texts also hint that such events occurred occasionally in previous and subsequent reigns.

Kings abused the mint. When they needed quick cash, they could debase the coinage by lowering its gold or silver content. A florin or ducat was suddenly worth half its previous value, so inflation erupted. Such events were a debtor's holiday. Now borrowers could repay loans of, say, 5,000 drachmas in coins worth 2,500 drachmas. But this cheating disrupts markets and financial affairs throughout the realm. Intriguingly, some Eurozone economists today have pined for the old trick, since indebted states based on the euro can no longer devalue.

And then there is in-depth meddling. Hundreds of books discuss the fall of the Western Roman Empire and offer a welter of competing interpretations. Let us highlight just one episode. In AD 301, Emperor Diocletian was facing economic decline and sought to stop it. So he issued more coins. People would have more cash in their pockets. At the same time, he imposed price and wage controls, so merchants couldn't nullify the added money by hiking prices to match. And violators, he said, would suffer the death penalty. It seemed like a clever scheme: More money + same prices = more stuff to buy. Why hadn't anyone ever thought of it before?

The results were disastrous. Money isn't wealth or value. It's a marker of value. So with more money in circulation, each unit of money was worth less. Buyers would now have paid higher prices for goods—since higher prices reflected the same value as before—but those prices were illegal. It was just as if carrot growers at the farmers' market suddenly had to sell all bunches for $0.80. The CE couldn't adjust. Meanwhile, sellers' real costs also rose, since Diocletian froze some prices and not others. When dealers couldn't recoup their expenses and started losing money, they stopped selling. Markets ceased functioning.

Many Roman citizens by then were accustomed to producing for the market and buying what they needed, and they were devastated. Entire towns went bankrupt, especially those producing cloth or wine for trade. Imperial tax revenues plummeted. Diocletian and his successors tried ever more desperate measures: in-kind taxes, permanent tax exemptions for political and financial supporters, and minting more and more coins with less and less gold or silver or copper. Nothing worked. Over time, and for numerous reasons, trade dried up across the Mediterranean and Europe entered an economic abyss.

So here is one way insufficient morals hurt markets: through lopsided power structures and ever-whispering greed. If "L'etat, c'est moi," then moi can stunt the economy.

Are kings doomed? Can an absolute ruler ever build moral infrastructure and create a functioning market economy? It had never happened, but then came the last half of the 20th century. For instance, when Singapore gained independence in 1965, it was a drowsy, malarial, almost helpless city-state. It had to import its food, water, and energy—everything—and its per-capita income was a fifth that in the United States. The dictator Lee Kuan Yew took charge, and today, because of his policies, Singapore is a cluster of shining skyscrapers with the highest GDP per capita on earth, according to one 2012 report. Brutal despots in Taiwan and South Korea also built powerhouses. So the problem all along lay not in the nastiness of tyrants per se, but their greed and short-sightedness.

Yet Taiwan and South Korea are now also democracies. Moral infrastructure bred strong markets, which in turn improved moral practices. The parallel rise of democracies and market economies suggests that they work better in tandem. It makes sense, since distributed power reduces the Great Self at the center and the effects of its self-interest. One huge test, as we'll see, will be China.

Russia's Transition to Kleptocracy

The coup against Mikhail Gorbachev in August 1991 was just another example of Soviet bungling, but it was one of the last.

The Soviet Union was bloated, corrupt, and rudderless in 1991 as it began its crossover to the market system. A huge experiment in redistribution and central planning, its economy had expanded, especially after World War II, and by the early 1960s it was the world's second largest. It grew by drawing on its cornucopia of natural resources: free-flowing oil, natural gas, metals (including almost all the world's nickel), diamonds, and vast stands of timber. A rising population and good schools helped as well. State policies more or less forced citizens to put much of their earnings into the bank. The government then funneled these deposits into factories and other production facilities. Central planners—bureaucrats headquartered in Moscow—orchestrated everything and announced healthy overall growth year after year.

The economy looked good from a distance, but up close you could see it was a sham. A common joke was: "They pretend to pay us and we pretend to work." The system generated colossal waste as managers tried to meet their production targets on the cheap. A typical tale: A nail factory has only a few weeks to meet the annual quota, measured in tons. It succeeds by producing 20 tons of 30-centimeter nails—a foot long and useless, but much easier to make than real nails.

Central planning needs shadow markets, because a large national economy is ultimately unknowable. Even the best planners see only the broad outline and miss the world of detail and ripple effects. A shortage of bolts in Kiev, for instance, could cause a Leningrad factory to fail to meet its quota, surprising planners and disrupting downstream operations. So unofficial traders filled in the gaps and lubricated the whole process. Soviet managers swapped favors in the gray market ("Ship me a boxcar of seat fabric so I can meet my car production quota, and I'll send you eight new cars"), and they occasionally ventured into the black market, as by selling extra tampons and buying French wine. And of course even if planners had been omniscient, they didn't have the final word. The Communist Party did, backed by the KGB. Party kingpins had often butted in, as when Nikita Khrushchev ordered corn planted on 85 million dry, empty acres and 69 million failed.

But by the 1970s the state was caring less and less. Officials were selling permits and jobs and growing fat on the cream of the economy. The resemblance of Leonid Brezhnev to a dissolute banana-republic supremo was no coincidence. He was the greediest and most venal of the Soviet dictators. According to one story, his mother comes to visit him from her drab life in the provinces, and he proudly shows her his diamonds, luxury cars, and opulent homes. "Well, it's good, Leonid," she says, amazed. "But what if the Reds come back?"

Meanwhile, citizens dwelt in a world of ineptitude. Store shelves were vacant, workers cheapened goods to meet impossible quotas, and government spun lies about production. Thefts from the government rose; in 1975 the official newspaper *Izvestia* guessed that a third of drivers were using gas filched from the state.

In fact, the ethical problems were systemic. In-group comradeship was the state myth, endlessly promulgated over the media; in reality, mutual support was hard to find, and mutual suspicion was everywhere. People trusted only close friends and relatives, if anyone. They had come to expect short-run selfishness from everyone else, especially from those in authority, and they tended to respond in kind.

It was a moral vicious cycle that choked the economy.

Then came the Crimean coup. Within months, the USSR dissolved into nations. The richer areas like Russia and the Baltic republics especially sought the breakup, for they were weary of subsidizing backward areas like Tajikistan. Yet the fracture stunned the economy, for overnight it raised huge bars to trade. Imagine Florida, New England, and California seceding and hindering normal shipments across their borders. In fact, the consequences were even worse in the ex-Soviet Union: because of a highly centralized industrial structure, many factories had neither alternative suppliers nor customers within their republics.

At the same time, Boris Yeltsin's economic team and its Western advisors had such faith in the magical powers of the market system that they chose this moment to remove price controls. The "shock therapy" turned out to be all shock and no therapy. People cashed in their long-saved ruble bank deposits and started buying. Money flooded into the system, inflation skyrocketed, and to the surprise and dismay of the economic team, it roared on for several years. Inflation destroyed the life savings of most families and retirees as their rubles lost 99.99 percent of their value in less than a decade.

The problems had just begun. Next came the huge enterprise of privatization. As a first step, all Russian citizens got vouchers they could use to buy state property for themselves. But with their income, savings, and faith in government all exhausted, most people sold these vouchers immediately—often to glib operatives—for less than one percent of the potential value.

Then the Great Steal began. Bank fraud, capital flight, new monopolies, organized crime, and rigged auctions combined to rip away the wealth men like Stalin and Khrushchev had collected for decades from the toil of sweating comrades. In the end, communism gave its centralized riches to criminals.

Why did it happen? The pot was so big it might have tempted anyone. But the Soviet Union had lacked markets, and hence the moral infrastructure for an honest transition. Laws had long been a joke, so officials didn't enforce them. Citizens heard endless lies from the state, didn't trust it, and stole regularly from it. In 1994, the Russian import-export executive Vladimir Aleksanyan put it this way: "You rob your workplace. You cut in line. You skip out on contracts if it's convenient. Dishonesty is deep-rooted. When a person in business is honest, it is because he has made a conscious, and usually temporary, decision to be honest.

There is not a deep-rooted sense of ethics." Moreover, money had bought little, so contacts mattered more. And the oligarchs used their contacts and raw force to pry away the life savings of the Soviet Union itself. In a sense, the Great Steal was just business as usual.

To work their magic, markets and economies need the right kind of competition. When firms vie to offer customers better quality and lower prices, we get a value overflow that markets split among customers, suppliers, and owners. The magic vanishes when competition instead is for currying government favors, stealing property, and murdering rivals. That sort of competition killed economic growth in ancient empires and in medieval times and did so again in Russia under the oligarchs and Mafiya.

Markets live on voluntary exchange, which requires trust. You have to feel that strangers won't be cheating you before you'll deal with them. You have to believe your property is secure before you'll work to improve it. You have to think the banks are honest before you'll put your money in them. You need confidence that your profits won't drain away in protection payments before you'll start a business in the first place.

In Russia this trust didn't take root. Markets were new and vulnerable, and yet there was, if anything, an immoral infrastructure. Morals and markets were nowhere near equilibrium. Honest economic reformers did their best but never gained traction. Part of the problem was the old socialist dream—happy workers laboring for the common good. Three generations of Soviet citizens had learned at school that property is theft and that capitalists are parasites and crooks. Their experience in Soviet black markets reinforced that lesson. So when criminals flourished in newly capitalist Russia, public outrage was muffled.

The upshot was that politicians and officials found it more expedient to join the thieving than oppose it. The courts and police were toothless, and legitimate businesspeople feared for their possessions and lives. The incentive from the top down was not to invest and improve, but to strip and loot. The Russian pie shrank as the oligarchs feasted.

When Morals Are Too Strong

It's not just moral weakness that hurts economies. Moral strength can too. The road to hell is paved with you know what. Morals can make us shun wealth-creating policies, and since they pervade our sense of the world, they have deep persuasive power. If we follow their lead in economics, we can wind up in startling locales.

Utopia of Cooperation

Where did the strange creed of communism come from? Why did it seem so successful for so much of the 20th century? The appeal of communism, and its fatal flaw, was moral outrage at the market system. In attempting a divorce from it and a more ethical world, it bred moral catastrophes and the world's most perverse markets. It's a spectacular story, and it began in innocence with the 19th century Romantic reaction against the emerging markets for land and labor.

Not everybody loved market economies as they started to take hold around 1800. Take William Blake (1757–1827). His poems glorified a natural and spontaneous lifestyle ("Bathe in the waters of life") and depicted industrialization with its "dark Satanic mills" as a threat to the environment and the human soul. Of urban labor markets he wrote:

> There souls of men are bought and sold
> And milk-fed infancy for gold
> And youth to slaughter houses led
> And beauty for a bit of bread.

The antimarket spirit of Romanticism pervades Blake's work and that of many of his contemporaries.

Why did so many eloquent writers of the day hate the market system? Indeed, why do so many people today?

Two aspects were particularly noxious. First, markets turned embedded social relations into commodities. Land and labor, once defining fixtures of life, became saleable like shoes. As Christopher Lasch (1932–1994) later put it, "Money, even more than other good things like beauty, eloquence and charm, has a tendency to 'seep across the boundaries' and to buy things that should not be for sale: exemption from military service; love and friendship; political office." The shift was especially pronounced in the early 19th century, when markets for the key resources—land, labor, and capital—were just detaching from the moral sphere.

Second, the market system brings quick, unsettling transitions, often accompanied by great pain and dislocation. When faced with a major new opportunity—such as railroads, electricity, microprocessors, a new colony, or a new form of organization—the system grants huge rewards to the first few lucky and skillful enough to seize the new turf. The winners are people like Cornelius Vanderbilt, Andrew Carnegie, John D. Rockefeller, and Bill Gates—not necessarily the innovators, but rather those who got there early, grew fast, and didn't let go.

As competitors flock to the new opportunity, the rewards eventually return to normal, but that may take decades. Meanwhile, the new opportunity starves the older ways, and many people lose their livelihoods. Railroads impoverish the canal owners and workers, new agriculture and industry leaves behind the landed aristocrats and their retainers, and technology displaces skilled craftsmen such as blacksmiths and weavers. Joseph Schumpeter called the process "creative destruction," and venture capitalists now search day and night for true "disruptive technologies." A hallmark of the market system in times of rapid change is to bestow enormous wealth on a few lucky or greedy individuals, and to dispossess many good people. It seems extraordinarily unfair.

Moral outrage is natural, yet the market system has greatly improved material conditions for workers as well as capitalists. In virtually every country that truly joined the market system in the last two centuries, the population boomed as nutrition and public health improved, and death rates plunged. With free entry into new activities and appropriate transfers (such as social safety nets), any innovation that increases productivity will benefit everyone. Even without appropriate transfers, the great majority of people can expect to come out ahead once things settle down. The problem with the market system is not that it takes from the poor—it gives to them—but that it disrupts lives and clashes with established moral codes.

Around 1800, new factories were sprouting up everywhere, boosting demand for unskilled workers. Their supply increased even more rapidly, thanks to the population boom and in Britain to the enclosure movement as well. So labor markets thickened while real wages remained low. Easy access to cheap labor and new technology encouraged factories to refine the assembly line and other new methods of organization. An unprecedented variety of goods poured out of the factories at unheard-of low prices, displacing traditional craftsmen and guilds. In the Portsmouth dockyard in 1801, for instance, machinery tended by 10 unskilled workers replaced 110 skilled block makers.

The human toll was incalculable. In 1824 young Charles Dickens, age 12, got up early every morning to work at Warren's bootblacking factory, near Charing Cross in London. Each day he did the same dreary job—pasting labels on jars of shoe polish, as fast as possible—for ten hours straight. He loathed it. Still, it could have been worse. His job was far less dangerous and unhealthful than many, and he received his wage, six shillings a week, on time. It allowed him to live in a simple boarding house and buy a few treats for his family, locked up in Marshalsea debtors' prison. It also let him daydream occasionally about his happier early days in the Kent countryside and about finding a better life in the big city. Of course, Dickens was lucky. In the next few years he was able to get an office job, add to the two years of schooling he already had, and hone his writing skills. But he never forgot his workhouse experience, as novels like *Hard Times* show.

The human moral system is tuned to help us work spontaneously with our peers and family. It grates on us to have our time regulated by the factory whistle and to take orders all day from bosses we hardly know. Factories bred other problems. They typically demanded 15 hours a day six days a week, and often were hazardous to life, limb, and health. Most industrial jobs were deadly dull. As Adam Smith observed in *The Wealth of Nations* (1776), on the assembly line the typical worker spends his whole life "performing a few simple operations...and generally becomes as stupid and ignorant as it is possible for a human creature to become."

The dumbing down of work did more. It made child labor viable. It thwarted ambition, blocking personal advance as from apprentice to journeyman to master. The dead-end jobs required more external discipline—overseers—and their intrinsic unpleasantness increased. The need for close coordination squelched spontaneity and initiative, and alienated worker from product. On the assembly line, responsibility was so diffuse that nobody could take personal pride in the quality of the final product.

The emerging market system of the 19th century created sprawling political problems. Among the poor, lower food prices mainly meant more surviving children and thus more poor people. They became more urban and visible, and remained near the Malthusian edge; think of *Oliver Twist*. The rich grew richer than ever, and hundreds of English families accumulated wealth beyond the imaginings of, say, Basil II. So as workers toiled in the factories, the wealthy seemed to float above it all, living off their employees' very substance. The gulf between rich and poor widened extravagantly, and the public clearly saw it. The hatred of oppression, which seems universal, had plenty of room to grow.

Meanwhile, even before this time, market economies had spread wealth more widely and the middle class, the bourgeoisie, expanded as never before. Leisure was now a real possibility for a substantial fraction of the population. At the same time, the king seemed more and more of an impediment. Nations that limited royal powers did better.

Leisure and dispersed wealth combined with moral outrage to create an unprecedented demand for dissident thought. Romantic philosophers, perhaps taking Jean-Jacques Rousseau too literally, extolled the life of the "noble savage," and some individuals (including young Sam Houston, future leader of Texas) found that they preferred tribal life to modern civilization. Thomas Jefferson idealized the yeoman farmer, as did several other fathers of the American and French Revolutions. But reality in 19th-century Europe (and the eastern United States) was ever greater urbanization and industrialization.

Young people from working-class and bourgeois families began to look for practical ways to change this world, and a rich stew of competing dissident groups simmered in Europe during the 1800s.

What does it take for a dissident group to survive and grow? Then as now, helpful tactics include:

- *Building tight in-groups.* Slogans, songs, and a sense of community all help forge close social bonds.
- *Appealing to a high moral sense.* An egalitarian style and a compelling picture of a better world engage people's moral sympathies.
- *Reaching out to idealistic young people,* especially those with an education and some leisure time.
- *Finding interest groups with resources.* Dispossessed artisans and unemployed intellectuals had resentments, time, and talent; working people had numbers and muscle; aristocrats had money.
- *Maintaining a flexible ideology,* able to respond to new opportunities and rapidly changing political and economic conditions.
- *Creating an efficient internal organization* to spread the word to new groups and in new provinces or countries, and to mobilize for political (or perhaps military) pressure at the right time and place. Groups won style points by seeming egalitarian, but in practice it helped to be hierarchical.
- *Having opportunistic leaders,* not too constrained by ideals to seize all available means to achieve their goals.

Marxism, and its later mutant Leninism, turned out to be especially well adapted to the harsher environment after 1848. To see why, let's first take a quick look at the founder and his ideas.

Karl Marx (1818–1883) was a brilliant, wide-ranging thinker with a PhD in philosophy, a thundering prose style, and a dismissive attitude toward opponents. The Prussian government shut down his academic career and then his newspaper, so he moved his family to London, where they lived in clutter and poverty as he scribbled away in the British Museum and fended off creditors.

Marx agreed with Adam Smith and William Blake about the urban labor market: "Labor produces wonderful works for the rich, but it produces poverty for the worker. It produces palaces, but hovels for the laborer. It produces beauty, but deformity for the laborer. It replaces labor with machines, but at the same time it throws the laborer into the most barbarous labor and at the same time makes the laborer into a machine. It produces intelligence and culture, but it produces senselessness and cretinism for the laborer."

Marx turned Ricardo's classic economic doctrine, the labor theory of value, into a scathing critique: Capitalists were getting rich by stealing the surplus value that the workers created. This idea dovetailed nicely with those of the first anarchist, Pierre-Joseph Proudhon (1809–1865), who, referring to landlords and factory owners, famously wrote, "Property is theft." Marx described class structure based on economic interests, emphasizing the proletariat (factory workers) versus the bourgeoisie (managers and owners). Above all, Marx told a compelling story about the course of history: an inevitable rise from primitive communism to feudalism to capitalism to scientific socialism. He predicted that workers in industrial nations like England would soon rise up and take charge of the means of production.

How do Marx's ideas stand up early in the 21st century? His (and Ricardo's) labor theory of value is now discredited; it looks like moral outrage in economic dress. The idea that evolution means upward progress toward an inevitable goal is a Victorian fallacy that Darwin never endorsed, and, of course, Marx turned out to be no better than anyone else at predicting the future. However, sociologists still benefit from Marx's economic analysis of class structure and dynamics.

Together with his friend and patron, Friedrich Engels (1820–1895), Marx published *The Communist Manifesto* in 1848. Compared to his other writings, it was short and crisp, and it had a stirring conclusion: "Proletarians have nothing to lose but their chains. They have a world to win. Workers of the world, unite!"

The new creed attracted idealistic young people, who saw themselves riding the wave of history and science. As with other socialist and anarchist movements, Marxist politics fostered close emotional ties among comrades, brothers and sisters in the struggle. People worked together intensely in small groups, laughed and sang songs, and met in larger groups for occasional mass demonstrations. These movements harnessed moral emotions going back to hunter-gatherer bands and filled a psychological void left by the market system.

Marxists didn't sweep the field, however. In the late 19th century, they often trailed the anarchists, and the trade unions grew far larger than any of the more radical groups. As the factory system matured, demand for labor rose faster than supply, and real wages rose. Workers achieved higher standards of living, and reformers achieved major goals, like child labor laws, the 10-hour working day, and universal male suffrage. The market system was working better than ever, and Marx's predictions seemed increasingly dubious.

Vladimir Lenin (1870–1924) argued for radical changes in ideology and organization. Standing Marx on his head, Lenin in 1902 dropped the idea that the working class would spontaneously revolt and install communism. He acknowledged that, left to themselves, workers would simply join unions. So instead he called for a "vanguard" of professional revolutionaries to disrupt elected governments and infiltrate union leadership. Lenin also abandoned the notion that only advanced industrial countries were ready for communism, and instead pushed for revolution first in czarist Russia, which still was trying to shake off feudalism.

World War I gave Lenin's vanguard its chance. The Russian czar was overthrown in early 1917, and moderate democrats took over. Lenin had been living in squalor, next to a foul sausage factory in Zurich, but now everything changed. To destabilize the enemy to the east, the German kaiser gave him free passage into Russia. There, Lenin's Bolsheviks sprang into action. In October 1918, allied with cooperatives, anarchists, and peasant groups, they swept away the moderate democrats and seized power. Then, one by one, the Bolsheviks picked off their erstwhile allies and consolidated power, and finally, in 1919–1920, they beat back a counterattack by the remaining czarists and their foreign supporters. By the time of Lenin's death in 1924, the Bolsheviks controlled all of Russia.

An inside view of the takeover comes from the American writer Emma Goldman (1869–1940). A 4-foot-10 dynamo with thick glasses, Goldman had emigrated from Russia to the United States as an idealistic 16-year-old. After working in a Rochester factory and studying political tracts at night, she joined the anarchist movement; by 1900 she had become its leading American spokesperson and journalist. US authorities jailed her in 1917 for antiwar agitation (and for helping women get access to birth control), and deported her to the USSR in late 1919.

The Bolsheviks saw Goldman as a propaganda tool and gave her interviews with Lenin and other top officials. But she was shocked by their cold, manipulative ways, and by the brutal house arrest of her anarchist hero, the saintly Peter Kropotkin. She saw sullen workers, resentful of their clumsy and hypocritical new bosses. Her new friends confided to her how the secret police, the Cheka, ran kidnap and extortion rings. Supposedly as an emergency measure, the Cheka forbade free speech and blocked news from the outside world.

The final straw for Goldman came in March 1921, in the Kronstadt naval base. The sailors had been an advance guard in ousting the czar and the moderate democrats, and now they wanted to elect their own leaders. The Bolsheviks knew the anarchists would win a free election, so they brought in their best troops to crush the Kronstadt sailors. They shot any of their own soldiers who held back, while their propagandists denounced the sailors as counterrevolutionaries. Goldman wrote, "The Bolsheviki now proved themselves the most pernicious enemies of the Revolution. I could have nothing further to do with them."

Later that year Goldman was able to sneak out of the country. After stewing for six months, she began writing a book about her experiences. It concludes, "The tyranny of the dictatorship has cowed people into slavish submission and all but extinguished the fires of liberty; organized terrorism has depraved and brutalized the masses and stifled every idealistic aspiration; ... coercion at every step has made effort bitter, labor a punishment, has turned the whole of existence into a scheme of mutual deceit."

Lenin's heir in 1924 was the Bolshevik hatchet man, Joseph Stalin (1879–1953). Stalin was not burdened by the socialist fantasy that, with the greedy capitalist owners driven off, the workers would happily work alongside their comrades and spontaneously increase production. Instead, he made Lenin's emergency measures permanent. The Communist Party and the Cheka (later renamed the KGB) controlled everything—where you lived, what your children learned in school, all agriculture and industry, radio and newspapers, even grocery prices—and Stalin personally ran the party and the KGB. To maintain power, he murdered millions, many of them by firing squads, more in the Siberian Gulag. Another 10 million or so perished in famines engineered to bring peasants to heel. The survivors lived in fear.

Many Western idealists, seeing the ethical deficits of capitalism up close, still responded to the noble moral call of communism. They had no idea and little curiosity about what life was really like in Russia, now called the Soviet Union. Soviet propaganda hijacked the high ground, but the Soviet reality was exploitation of workers and everyone else to serve their masters' imperial ambitions.

The utopia of cooperation had become a nightmare.

Finance: The Hard-Eyed Genie

To look at Greece, you'd hardly guess a great civilization might arise there. It has a jagged coastline with deep inlets, valleys isolated by craggy ridges, and hardscrabble soil too poor to feed a large populace. But these drawbacks forced the ancient Greeks out onto the sea to trade with each other. Like Uruk, Greece had useful waterways all around. So trade enriched them willy-nilly, and those city-states that lowered class barriers and opened themselves more fully to trade outdistanced their rivals. Athens is a prime example. It became the first among equals, and Athenian silver coins helped monetize trade throughout the Greek world and beyond.

Yet unlike the Phoenicians, Greek upper classes scorned commerce and finance especially. To them, plunder and even humble farming and crafts production seemed morally superior. Our moral sense can not only lure us into bad strategies like communism, but deter us from fruitful ones, and it did with the ancient Greeks.

Biologically, favor systems were always highly personal. Monkeys know whom they are grooming, and the act tightens their bonds. Lending among people also began with personal ties. In ancient Greece, some took the form of an *eranos* loan. An Athenian merchant with a customer in Alexandria for 100 amphorae of olive oil, say, would not want to buy all the goods himself. After all, a storm might sink the ship, and then he'd be penniless. He could share the risk and reward by borrowing from extended family, neighbors, and wealthy friends. These *eranos* loans bore zero interest, but the borrower had to reciprocate later by lending to others in his circle. So *eranos* was a tit-for-tat system, very much like the blood swapping of vampire bats. And the social element was vital. Lenders knew when the borrower was trying his best to repay and would forbear when bad luck hindered him. If the borrower was not trying his best, lenders knew that too, and pressured him through the social network.

This is just the sort of thing the moral system is designed for, with its emotions of gratitude and resentment. And it works pretty much the same way in farming and fishing villages throughout the world today, perhaps because it's especially suited to group-centered morality. Members of a close-knit group provide financing (and insurance) to each other, and the group's moral code enforces the obligations. Recently, *eranos* financing has emerged spontaneously in towns in Africa, Asia, and Latin America. Roscas (rotating savings and credit associations) typically involve about half a dozen families who pool their savings and take turns purchasing things like bicycles or roofing materials. With this strategy, they can purchase sooner on average, cut risk, and encourage each other to save more.

Polonius, the garrulous court advisor in *Hamlet*, pointed out one problem with *eranos*: "Loan oft loses both itself and friend." You might have relatives whom you love but would never lend to because their lifestyles make repayment problematic. And unpaid loans can be very awkward. Personal lending can cause personal trouble.

More importantly, it is also inefficient. It draws only on the funds of your own social circle. If you are like most people in recorded history, those funds are limited, so you can't jump on great opportunity or get enough help in a crisis. Even if you belonged to the wealthy ruling elite, you probably would find most money tied up in trying to maintain power and not much available for really new opportunities.

In sum, *eranos* finance is a throwback. It is not dynamic. It doesn't scale up as societies grow larger and more diverse. It gains less of a Maxwell's Demon effect. Other forms of finance become increasingly important.

Professional moneylenders took up the slack as the commercial empire of Athens expanded. They used interest-bearing loans backed by collateral, an approach called *daneizein*. This sort of finance goes back at least to Uruk, and by 2,500 years ago it was an accepted part of city life from the Mediterranean to China.

Most Greek moneylenders belonged to the lower class and were not citizens. The lender Pasion, for example, was born a slave but gained his freedom and started his business around 400 BC. Twenty very successful years later, and after conspicuous public philanthropy, he was made an Athenian citizen. By the time of his death ten years later, his net worth of 70 talents made him the city's richest man.

Yet Pasion's rise to citizenship was an exception. Plato's *Republic* disparages moneylenders as parasitic wasps, and in general Greek citizens regarded them as a necessary evil. Most ancient civilizations (and those since) seem to share the Greeks' ambivalence. But why? Why have people been blind to free wealth?

The answer lies in our moral emotions. Giving an *eranos* loan feels virtuous—you help a friend in need, you share in good outcomes and bad, and you expect reciprocation. You're part of a warm social group linked morally. In contrast, the *daneizein* loan feels unfriendly. The moneylender collects interest without actually working for it, and if you are down on your luck and can't repay, he worsens your problems. At your time of greatest vulnerability, he seizes the family heirlooms or land you put up for collateral. If you had no collateral, he might put you in prison or sell you as a slave. Not nice.

The ancient rules on collateral and default, though seemingly distasteful, rest on compelling moral logic. Once the borrower has received the money, his direct incentive is to free-ride: to delay or avoid repayment. So he will be tempted to abscond or pretend he can't repay. Economists call the problem "moral hazard," and it must be solved for lending to succeed.

Of course, the borrower may feel morally bound, and she's more likely to with *eranos* loans from in-group friends. Her reputation is at stake, and everyone has an interest in seeing the loan repaid. But moral bonds are much looser for *daneizein* loans from an outsider, and as in the New Guinea Dictator Game, the borrower's friends are far less likely to side with the lender when trouble arises. *Daneizein* lenders who rely on the borrower's good faith tend to go broke.

Hence the standard solution is collateral plus enforcement. Borrowers will do their best to repay if they know that otherwise they will be worse off materially. Thus the collateral must be precious to the borrower, more valued than the repayment.

Unfortunately, the collateral solution is not perfect. Fate can doom even scrupulous borrowers. Crops might fail, or robbers or invaders might strike, and then the borrower forfeits the collateral. A decent hardworking family could lose everything to a low-class moneylender, a stranger who doesn't even "work for a living." It seems terribly unjust.

This tension between moral sensibilities and economic logic has predictable consequences. First, moneylenders seldom belong to the social mainstream. They often have a different ethnicity and tend to have relatively weak moral ties to borrowers. For example, overseas Chinese dominate the moneylending business in Southeast Asia, as do Lebanese in the Mediterranean and beyond, and Jews did in medieval Christian Europe. As outsiders, their threat to seize collateral is more believable, and they can also tap resources beyond those in the borrowers' circles. Another consequence is political risk. Moneylenders have traditionally been an inviting target for rulers.

Christian and Muslim teachings forbid *daneizein*-style lending, but of course it often crops up anyway in a black or gray market. The Old Testament calls for cancelling some debt contracts every seventh year and others every half century, at Jubilee. This custom would cause credit to dry up as cancellation approached, and it was apparently soon abandoned. Whether or not *daneizein* is officially tolerated, widespread moral feelings make lenders vulnerable to expropriation.

Plato was hostile toward moneylenders but even more scathing about demagogues who buy off the people by confiscating moneylenders' property. He praised Sparta, the archrival city, for never repudiating debts, and rightly so because that policy surely strengthened Sparta's economy. The danger of politically motivated debt forgiveness and expropriation always has the same sad effects: higher interest rates to cover the extra risk, stunted finance, and a weaker economy.

Financial markets have had, if anything, a worse reputation. We can see the problems as early as 1688, in Penso de la Vega's description of shenanigans in the Amsterdam stock market. The value of stocks depends on both present and future value. So anything a speculator can do to affect perceptions of future value—such as circulating false rumors or selling large amounts of a stock to cause a frightened run and then buying it back—will be done. These markets are worlds of intrigue. But their value outweighs the immediate lies and cons. Our morals correctly tell us these charades are wrong, but in the larger sense, in terms of benefit to all, our morals should also tell us to tolerate the lesser evils, to be pragmatic.

Zombieworld

World War II left Japan a rubble. Atomic bombs had leveled two cities, firestorms had charred huge tracts of Tokyo, Osaka, and other urban areas, and the economy was on its knees. Yet when the US occupation ended in 1952, Japan began one of the most amazing spurts of wealth creation the world had ever seen. By the late 1980s, its economy was the world's second largest and one of the fastest growing. Pundits, including Lester Thurow, dean of MIT's prestigious Sloan School of Management, argued that Japan would leave us far behind unless we copied its policies.

Even more remarkably, Japan seemed to have overcome the conflict between morals and markets, by stressing social harmony (*wa*) and tradition. Firms enjoyed friendly ties with regulators, as management did with labor, while bosses made decisions by consensus with their underlings. Japan's economy appeared different, and better, than everyone else's. It really did seem a utopia of cooperation.

But Japan's growth collapsed in 1990, and its financial system stopped functioning. Stocks lost more than two-thirds of their peak value. And the economy stagnated and endured deflation reminiscent of the Great Depression for 15 years.

The problem was too much *wa*. The moral ties that had helped the nation for so long now strangled it.

An island nation at the edge of China, the great Middle Kingdom, Japan kept its independence for over 2,000 years by a remarkable mix of adaptability and cultural unity. With the threat ever close, in-group ties strengthened among the Japanese. They again and again copied from China, taking not just ideograms and the Confucian social structure, but techniques of metallurgy, military technology, city planning, architecture, and much more. At the same time, Japan's internal networks spanned the islands, maintaining a single culture and a single ethnicity. Its cultural unity and up-to-date military capacities protected it from invasion century after century.

Japan's in-group feeling has led to a vast back-scratching system, with bureaucrats, business managers, and politicians all swapping favors and helping each other. Mutual support is the linchpin everywhere. Workers are expected to actively aid others on their team (and generally do), and the team is expected to take initiative in improving performance. The moral code also calls for management to consult extensively with workers, and for everyone to build consensus before changing anything important. In-group morality had a similar effect as it did among ancient savanna tribes. It softened market competition within and across firms in the giant conglomerates called *keiretsu* (and to some extent, within the country) and it made them tougher competitors in foreign markets.

When something went wrong, it was taken care of quietly, usually within the *keiretsu* family. Nobody wanted to lose face. For example, Maruzen, an oil refinery company, expanded too fast in the 1960s and became unable to meet its debts. The lead bank in its *keiretsu*, Sanwa, in cooperation with the Ministry of Trade and Industry and a host of supporting banks, gently encouraged the family owner-managers to retire. It then brought in a professional leadership team, reduced the workforce (mostly through attrition, not layoffs), infused capital, and restored profitability. Maruzen never formally declared bankruptcy. Similarly, when the car manufacturer Mazda got into financial trouble in the 1980s, its lead bank stepped in. Working with Ministry of Finance officials, the troubleshooters from Sumitomo eased out the founder's grandson Kohei Matsuda, and the bank's own top manager, Tsutomu Murai, took over. He cut costs, partnered with Ford, and nursed Mazda back to profitability.

By 1970 manufacturers like Matsushita and Toyota were setting the world standard for quality and efficiency. Japan's new manufacturing system had unprecedented agility. Supported by their partners in the *keiretsu*, by government ministries, and by cheap long-term loans, Japanese manufacturers could plan deeper into the future. They could build market share without worrying about next-quarter profitability, and could give each other price breaks until they had driven out foreign rivals in export markets. Meanwhile, a snarl of very adhesive red tape discouraged foreign firms from entering Japan. Its economy delivered breathtaking growth, and in the 1980s it appeared destined to rule the world.

Except all was not as it seemed.

In retrospect everyone can see that Japan entered a bubble in the late 1980s. Land and stock prices, which had risen steadily since the 1950s, shot upward. The Nikkei stock index first hit 8000 about 1980 and 10,000 about 1986, but then rocketed to just under 39,000 by the end of 1989. Even with very rosy views of profitability, stock prices were exorbitant. The textile sector sold for 103 times earnings, for instance, and fishery and forestry firms for 319 times earnings. The stock prices implied that Japanese companies were worth more than all those in the United States and most of Europe combined. Land prices in Japan also ballooned, and by 1990 they reached about 100 times the US level.

Japan's policy makers had grown incautious. They deregulated banks in the 1980s, letting them invest in stock and real estate schemes directly and via loans to customers investing aggressively in similar schemes. Funds were going out to people who had less chance of paying them back. Deregulation also loosened *keiretsu* ties, so banks no longer reliably vetoed risky ventures by other firms in their family. Yet government agencies were slow to pull in the regulatory slack. Forty years of prosperity and government protection gave Japanese investors a false sense of security.

Moreover, as in the US savings and loan industry a few years earlier, deposit guarantees created a moral hazard. Remove the penalty from risky or unethical behavior, and it increases. Why not sit down at the blackjack table if someone else will cover your losses? Furthermore, the Bank of Japan (BOJ), the monetary authority, kept interest rates artificially low too long in the mid- to late 1980s.

Loans were easy as well as cheap. A borrower could use inflated stock or land as collateral for a new loan, and use those funds to buy more stock or land. Hence the number and size of loans increased. But habitable land is scarce in Japan and so is domestic stock. As demand grew for this collateral, the supply of it remained limited. So just as when more people want carrots at the farmers' market, the price for Japan's land and stock spiraled upward.

Yet there were plenty of cheaper buys elsewhere. Why not purchase foreign assets instead? Japanese international investors for decades had shown a remarkable knack for buying blue-chip properties—like Pebble Beach golf course, the Lincoln Center, and Dutch Master paintings—at all-time high prices and selling years later near historic lows. With such experiences, foreign investment didn't seem so attractive. As a result, the two Japanese bubbles—land and stocks—continued swelling for several years.

The air supply eventually runs out in all bubbles, and in Japan it happened in 1990. The public had fully invested and began to worry about the oil price spike due to Iraq's invasion of Kuwait. Then the Bank of Japan let interest rates rise to more realistic levels. Money cost more, and borrowing got harder. Demand for collateral slowed.

Stock prices paused.

Then the self-feeding dynamics halted and went into fast reverse. After peaking at 38,912.87 in late December 1989, the Nikkei lost about half its value in a year. Later it lost half of the remaining value and in mid-2012 it was around 8700. Land prices dropped more gradually, but except for a brief rise in 2007, they have continued to fall for 20 years. Transaction volume plummeted—buyers had fled—and people found it very difficult to sell their property. As stock and land prices dropped, bank assets shrank, so the banks stopped lending to finance new purchases. Many of the more aggressive speculators couldn't pay back their loans. And in Japan that is a particular problem.

Three company presidents faced it in 1998. One, Masaaki Kobayashi, had been highly successful, and his two friends grew wealthy as his suppliers. Kobayashi loved spending money, buying racehorses and flashy cars, and when the economy went into first gear he kept spending, even though his two friends begged him to halt. The Internet brought further woe as customers abandoned him for online retailers. Finally, he realized he was badly in debt and turned to his two pals. Both felt they owed him, and not just as a friend but as a patron. So they embezzled from their own firms and passed him cash on the sly, $650,000 from one and $225,000 from the other. It didn't help, and Kobayashi's quicksand soon became theirs. Unable to face disgrace, on February 25 they all committed suicide.

But why didn't they just declare bankruptcy a year earlier?

Bankruptcy law is crucial to modern society. When borrowers can't repay their debts, the law spells out which lenders get what. Bankruptcy laws should induce debtors to swiftly abandon unprofitable businesses, to sell the assets and distribute the proceeds to lenders. Good bankruptcy laws cleanse the system, quickly redirecting resources so as to minimize the overall loss. Confidence in bankruptcy procedures encourages lenders and thus benefits borrowers. It is essential to financial markets in good times and bad.

Classically, here's what is supposed to happen when bubbles burst: The overspent firms go bankrupt and their assets are sold off. The government makes sure that healthy companies have the chance to recover from their links to bankrupt firms. Asset prices once again reflect fundamental value and restore their tie to reality. The financial system is back in business and the economy recovers.

That didn't happen in Japan. Encouraged and even pressured by government regulators, Japan's banks did the opposite. They gave first priority to loans to firms facing bankruptcy and kept them afloat. The Maxwell's Demon of finance that normally guides funds toward success was moving them toward failures, reducing wealth instead of increasing it. The new walking dead or "zombie" firms were money sinks, absorbing loans that could have energized more promising enterprises. They also cut the profitability of their sounder competitors, who had to match their subsidized prices. The zombie effect depressed investment, new job opportunities, and economic vigor throughout Japan, especially in construction, retail, and real estate.

We know a lot about one zombie: Sogo. Founded as a kimono store in 1830, by 1962 it was a second-tier department store chain with three branches. In that year Hiroh Mizushima took over. He had been an ambitious executive at the Industrial Bank of Japan (IJB), a semiofficial spigot of bureaucratic largesse about to be privatized, but he bailed out at age 50 when he realized he probably wouldn't reach the top spot.

Known within the firm as the "Emperor" or "God," Mizushima ran Sogo like a real estate speculator. He'd buy up property near busy train stations, install a department store or mall, and rent out the extra space. When the land rose in price, he'd sell it off or borrow against its now greater value, and buy more land near the next train station. His method worked well from the beginning and looked brilliant during the land bubble. But then the bubble burst.

Mizushima had never run Sogo's department stores efficiently, and they made little profit. During the 1990s they racked up increasingly large losses. Mizushima, by then an autocrat in his eighties, was unwilling to switch tactics. With his goal of being Japan's largest retailer almost in sight, he continued to open new stores even as the value of his holdings sank alarmingly. So he needed huge bank loans.

In a proper market economy, Sogo would have declared bankruptcy by 1991 or 1992, and Mizushima, along with thousands of employees, would have lost his job. The government might have retrained some employees and helped basically sound suppliers make the transition. Instead, it kept the zombie upright and walking.

Mizushima called on his old friends from IBJ. Soon IBJ became the lead bank, and its prestige and close ties to government ministries encouraged other banks to pitch in. It seemed reasonable: Join in and help make powerful men happy, gain reflected prestige, and contribute to *wa*. Everyone was doing it. The fact that Sogo's property was unsalable and that cash flows were negative seemed beneath the notice of the lenders. (Echoing Louis XIV, Mizushima liked to say, "Collateral? It is me.") Eventually, Sogo ran up more than $17 billion in debt to 73 banks.

In 2000 the government introduced new accounting rules, which showed that Sogo had a negative net worth that began at $5 billion. (The total was surely worse, but Sogo didn't have to disclose it.) Mizushima and his pals worked out a typically quiet, backroom deal. The banks would cancel about $6 billion of debt, and the government ministers and elected officials would earn the gratitude of Sogo's employees, suppliers, lenders, and customers. Would all 73 lenders go along? Normally, they probably would have. When the herd began moving, no one wanted to get caught walking against it—especially when the well-being of everyone in the Sogo empire seemed at stake.

But this time it was different. A few months earlier, the government had sold off a failed lender called Shinsei Bank to an American group, which had insisted on guarantees for bad loans. Thus the bank was able to pass its hit, about $1 billion, back to the government, which had to disclose the backroom deal with Sogo. Insiders were embarrassed—one of IBJ's key officials committed suicide—and the public was outraged. The deal unraveled and Sogo declared bankruptcy in July 2000.

Mizushima publicly stepped down, but kept power behind the scenes. Despite his age and government connections, his legal problems mounted. In March 2005 he was convicted of hiding personal assets he'd skimmed from Sogo, and he received a suspended sentence. He celebrated his hundredth birthday on April 15, 2012.

We know so much about Sogo because it was a fluke. Mizushima ran into bad luck with the timing of the crisis and especially the presence of the American-controlled lender, outside the system of *wa*. Thousands of other zombies remained in operation, subtracting wealth from Japan, their losses still unknown.

Where did the banks get the money to give to firms like Sogo? Most banks fear dud loans, since they can be fatal. Indeed, Japan's banking industry had a net operating loss every year from 1993 through 2003. The banks' international credit ratings, once the envy of the world, crashed to Third World levels.

The natural result should be that some banks themselves declare bankruptcy, their assets are sold, and the banking sector recovers. Society cuts out the dead tissue. Instead, in the 1990s Japanese bureaucrats and politicians propped up banks by dipping into the public treasury. Ordinary citizens were keeping the zombies alive. Taxpayer money went to bank subsidiaries called *jusen*, which specialized in real estate lending. Voter outrage at the huge giveaways to these firms (or to their parent banks) in the late 1990s only persuaded the politicians to use more covert handouts, such as subsidizing megamergers among Japanese banks.

By 2001 the total debt of Japanese banks was over one trillion dollars. Due to the disproportionate role banks play in the Japanese financial sector, the impact was huge. Subsidies, direct or hidden, also shored up the two other major financial market subsectors: insurance and government-run financial institutions, such as the Postal Savings bank. The result was a zombie financial sector, no longer able to do its job, and an economy on Ambien.

Why did government regulators and the public tolerate this mess? Why didn't they demand that banks and other financial firms restructure and start lending for activities with a real future?

Bankruptcy in Japan is not a simple risk of doing business, but a moral transgression, "regarded as close to a crime," according to Seiichi Yoshikawa, a Tokyo attorney. The bankruptcies Japan needed would have shamed important people in government and industry, and increased unemployment for awhile. Some of the disgraced might take their own lives, as the three company presidents did. Friends don't do that to friends. They lock arms with them, even if they wind up in free fall too. So in-group solidarity spreads success in good times and trouble in bad. *Wa* has two sides.

The personal traits that help you succeed in markets are quite different from those that help you socially. For instance, good stock investors make money by quickly spotting chances to buy at a low price or to sell at a high one. They don't buy shares as favors to the CEO. Economies too must know how to impersonally jettison losing enterprises like Sogo, as through bankruptcy, and how to reward promising ones. Where moral feelings—like gratitude, loyalty, and *wa*—get snared in the process, it can all go awry.

How Markets Improve Morals: The *Pax Economica*

The Greek philosophers gave much thought to improving morality. For instance, how do we teach virtue? Plato says we should learn from those who are virtuous, just as we'd learn navigation from skilled navigators. But improving morality goes beyond human instruction. The environment cultivates morals, too, and does so more effectively. When it rewards cooperation, people become more obliging and virtuous. And markets have long bred cooperation.

To be fair, Plato lacked perspective on morals and markets. Yet without trade, Athens wouldn't have existed at all. Indeed, without it our species would have no cities, and hence no large organizations and probably no writing to record Plato's thoughts. Cities, organizations, and writing all bring us out of the kin group and village, introduce us to people different from ourselves, and give us reasons to act well toward them. They enable guides to moral behavior, like the New Testament. And they're just the start. For instance, over the past five centuries, as markets have grown in the Western world, crime has dropped sharply. Directly and through follow-on effects, markets have made us better people.

Look at war.

War is not just a breakdown of morals. It's an assault on them. Murder, forbidden within societies, becomes mandatory. Looting, also forbidden, becomes a bonus for good performance. Unless restrained by their superiors, soldiers commit crimes with impunity, as in the Rape of Nanking. At the same time, huge numbers of men can die, and Mathew Brady's photographers showed the world real, corpse-strewn battlefields for the first time.

The Prussian philosopher Immanuel Kant (1724–1804) called perpetual peace "the entire final end of the doctrine of right," but felt it was unachievable. In the 1960s, some Vietnam War protesters urged an end to all war, and many observers deemed this goal unachievable too. We had always had war.

Or had we? Scholars debate the amount of warfare among prehumans and we won't try to settle the issue here. But among known hunter-gatherers today, violence caused 55 percent of all deaths among the precontact Ache of Paraguay and 30 percent among the Hiwi of southern Venezuela. Yet the rate is just 3–7 percent among the !Kung and Hadza of Africa and the Agta of the Philippines. Figures like 55 percent and 30 percent smack of the front lines rather than a functioning society, but even 3 percent is high. It's about one in 30. You know people who will die violently.

As stored wealth rose, theft beckoned the daring, and organized warfare almost certainly increased. We can see one way it worked in the Turkana nomads who live in the dry savannas of east Kenya, near the great lake named after them. In 1919, the English army officer Henry Rayne described a typical Turkana: "You are struck by the grace of his carriage and the independence of his demeanor, as with a light, sure tread that would scarcely crackle a dry twig, he advances out of the bush to meet you." The Turkana aren't hunter-gatherers. They are pastoralists, cultivators of meat. They own flocks of cattle, goats, donkeys, and sheep, and survive off their flesh, blood, and milk. When drought strikes, the precious herds thin, and the Turkana face starvation. So they raid others. Sometimes a group of men grabs stray cattle from a nearby tribe. Other times, a much larger party circles a camp at night and swoops in at dawn. Neighbors naturally reciprocate, and Turkana have to battle for their own animals and waterholes. The upshot: An average Turkana male has a 20 percent chance of dying in warfare.

As states arose, rulers drew wealth from the populace. They created armies for self-defense and often enough, in cases like Alexander the Great, to broaden the tax base as well. War was relatively common. In ancient Greece, flare-ups occurred regularly between city-states. With larger nations came larger massacres. In 88 BC, for instance, Mithridates of Pontus (134 BC–63 BC) slaughtered 80,000 Romans and Italians in Asia Minor. It is scarcely a footnote in Roman history. When Timur the Lame (Tamerlane, c. 1336–1405) conquered Isfahan in Persia, he built a pyramid of some 70,000 skulls, and if we remember this deed better, it's more for the showmanship than death toll.

As market economies grew in Europe, conquest took on a different hue. The colonial empires seemed to be all about trade, though it was trade where one side determined the price and goods supplied. The prize of these empires lay in market control, and in some instances, like the Belgian Congo and the silver mines of Bolivia, simple rapine and slavery.

Thinkers at least since Montesquieu (1689–1755) had suggested that true international trade reduces the chance of war. "The natural effect of commerce is to lead to peace," he wrote. "Two nations that trade together become mutually dependent." Victorians like Richard Cobden (1804–1865) and John Stuart Mill (1806–1873) further drove home this idea. As the World Trade Organization puts it: "Sales people are usually reluctant to fight their customers."

Europe is a prime example. From pre-Roman tribal battles to World War II, one bloody war followed another in a continent divided by political boundaries and trade barriers. Yet today Europe is a single market, and war between France and Germany, say, is unimaginable. Markets have made Europe more moral than morals alone ever had.

And it's not just Europe.

No two nations on earth are at war today, as we write. In fact, over the past several decades, few nations have waged war against each other. When they do, a colossus often stomps an ant, as in the Iraq War. Armed conflicts now tend to be internal, like the citizen revolts in Arab states and separatist actions in Darfur and Chechnya. States rarely battle each other; they fight nonstates like the Taliban, if they are fighting at all.

Even in these conflicts, the fatalities are declining. In the 21st century, total deaths from war-related violence have averaged 55,000 a year. That's about 0.0008 percent of the global population. In the 1990s the figure was around 100,000, and from 1950 through 1989 around 180,000. And since the world's population has almost tripled since 1950, rising from 2.5 to 7 billion, the percentage declines are even greater. Better medicine partly accounts for these figures, but even so, war seems in retreat.

What about World War II? It occurred between highly developed market economies. Does it weaken the case?

Actually, it's pretty much in line with the Montesquieu argument. The world de-globalized through World War I, the Depression, and World War II. Nations turned isolationist, and the percentage of world output entering world trade did not recover its 1913 levels until the mid-1970s. To some extent, this reduction was deliberate. For instance, Mussolini strove to eliminate international trade and make Italy a sealed, self-contained economy—an autarky.

And then there was Hitler. In 1936, he heard his economists debate whether or not Germany should boost its prosperity by increasing trade with nearby nations. He retired to contemplate the matter and then wrote in a confidential memo, "I consider it necessary that now, with iron determination, 100 percent self-sufficiency should be attained in all those spheres where it is feasible." If he had picked wider trade, Europe might have remained at peace. But self-sufficiency required conquest, so the bloodthirsty enterprise ensued, ending with Germany vanquished and carved up by nations whose citizens it had butchered. Instead of self-sufficiency, Hitler achieved prostration.

The moral dynamic has actually enflamed war, given our old tribal sense that out-groups deserve less. To prepare for battle, leaders still stoke their warriors' sense of honor, and their sense of us-versus-them. Typically, "they" are semihuman: gooks or krauts or ragheads. "They" are evil or corrupt or bullies that need to be taught a lesson, vengeance is our due, and we must defend ourselves, pre-emptively if necessary.

And World War II is Exhibit One of this moral drop-off, a spectacle of us-versus-them so extreme it remains hard to talk about. Hitler had plenty of in-group feeling to work with in Germany after World War I: widespread chauvinism, resentment, and poverty. In the 1936 memo he states that the "Bolsheviks" would inevitably invade the Fatherland and their victory would lead to the "final destruction" and "annihilation of the German people." In other words, Russia was preparing the kind of genocide he himself would launch. So Germany had to act first. Posterity would never ask how "we achieved the salvation of the nations, but only *whether* we achieved it." Any method was okay. The future wouldn't judge Adolf Hitler by a moral standard.

By 1945 the number of dead from all war-related causes in Europe was about 36.5 million. Germans had killed six million Jews and a further six million others at industrialized murder sites. At the same time, two out of three German males born in 1918 did not survive this war. Germany had visited grisly slaughter on the Soviet Union and the Red Army took revenge as it marched to Berlin, killing male civilians and raping hundreds of thousands of women. It dropped 40,000 shells on Berlin in the last two weeks of the war, damaging 75 percent of its structures. American and British planes also carpetbombed such German cities as Hamburg, Dresden, and Cologne. By the summer of 1945, the ruins had ceased smoking but people were starving and ailing all over Europe; the mortality rate of children in Vienna in 1945 had quadrupled since 1938. Railroad tracks lay twisted, and factories were empty or collapsed. With economies eviscerated, there was little to buy, and most currencies were worthless in any case. And the point of it all? In fact, the Bolsheviks had triumphed and occupied East Germany. They wouldn't have if left alone.

World War I is a harder and more illuminating case. As market economies rose in 19th-century Europe, the continent swept away obstacles and international trade burgeoned. Near the end of the 18th century Goethe had pined for the day when "my luggage may pass unopened through all thirty-six German states," but by 1871 the country had united. So had Italy. The railroad replaced the horse-drawn cart, and the telegraph and telephone moved information almost instantly. Markets widened and tightened, and prices for similar goods edged closer to a CE. And throughout this period, from the 1815 Congress of Vienna on, war fell off dramatically in Europe. Some felt trade had brought peace to stay.

Then in 1914 Archduke Franz Ferdinand took a bullet in the jugular, and Europe burst into flames. Yet even as the war began, many thought it temporary, partly because trade ties were too important.

If international trade is so good at keeping peace, why did World War I break out? Why didn't companies and merchants pressure rulers to stop it? Why didn't governments consider the damage to their economies? The topic has received extensive analysis, and we'll just make a few points here.

The structure of international commerce was quite different in 1914 than it is now. European countries didn't just make things and trade them. Like the Turkana, many owned stealable property: colonies. As nationalism swelled into imperialism from 1870 to 1914, the scramble for Africa commenced, and even Germany grabbed a bit of the swag. If a nation could seize, say, Kenya, war with Britain might be worth it. So us-them tensions grew and took on a life of their own, the Triple Entente and Triple Alliance glowered like two angry men over a fence, and a distant Balkan gunshot could set off violence.

This whole system changed after World War II. The European powerhouse lay weak and battered, and only recovered slowly. In fact, Britain didn't end food rationing till 1954. So the colonies took action. India, Pakistan, and Burma terminated Britain in 1947, Sri Lanka (then Ceylon) in 1948, and Egypt with the Suez crisis in 1956. The Dutch tried and failed to reconquer Indonesia after a four-year war, leaving for good in 1949. France lost French Indochina at Dien Bien Phu in 1954 after several years of combat, and then its colonies everywhere. Portugal hung on longest, forcing Mozambique to grow cotton instead of food and thus causing local famines. But eventually the empires vanished.

And as the North-South trade declined, a new form took its place. European nations had swapped finished goods for raw materials. For instance, Britain early on imported cotton and exported bolts of cloth. Since every bolt was pretty much the same, few developed countries traded bolts back and forth. Why bother? Today, however, we make complex products like cars. Cars come in myriad varieties, and a German may prefer a Honda, a Japanese a Mercedes-Benz. So advanced economies now have much more to trade with each other.

More importantly, production fragmented. A bolt of cloth takes just a few steps to make, so manufacture could take place wholly in Britain. But a car needs far more steps, and highly specialized ones too. As transport costs fell, companies began making parts and using labor in many countries. The factory straddled the globe. Interdepartment transfer became international trade. We moved past entwined economies to entwined production.

So the global fabric has tightened. Connections interpenetrate more. When a factory lies in ten or more countries, war can injure us more easily. Destroy a link in the supply chain, and widespread processes slow or stop. Even third parties have an interest in preventing war because of ripple effects. If you trade with nations that trade with nations that go to war, you can suffer. This interrelatedness was far less common in 1914 and 1939. So the chance of a disaster like either World War drops. The lesson is: It's not just the amount of international trade, but the kind of it.

Moreover, though war declined among nations in 19th-century Europe, these nations used armies to maintain their colonies. Resistance overseas led to conflicts like the Sepoy Mutiny, the Boer War, and the two Opium Wars. The empires of the 19th century rested on military force, and if you could use it elsewhere, you could use it nearby. But now that structure has disappeared.

Our attitude toward war has also changed. The Turkana treat warriors as heroes, since they save lives, and works like *Beowulf* throb with praise for hearty fighters. But it is hard to find anyone who glorifies war today. We know too much about it, first of all. News accounts and movies like *The Deer Hunter* and *The Hurt Locker* have made its nature all too clear. But markets have also reduced the defensiveness that led to World War I. No one reasonably expects Brazil, for instance, to attack any country. It's harder to sustain an us-them attitude when we are partly them.

Instead of wars, we now have flash points, throttled wars that become theaters for brinksmanship. Hostilities between China and Taiwan were among the Cold War's greatest dangers, but over the past 20 years the two have become so commercially bound together that, despite posturing, invasion seems unlikely. For instance, in late 2011 the two signed a treaty easing import tariffs into China on over 500 categories of Taiwanese goods, and in the first six months of 2012, cross-strait commerce was worth $75 billion or 4.1 percent of China's huge foreign trade. Markets are making these nations act more morally.

This happy story hasn't played out at certain other flash points. The global economy helped defuse the India-Pakistan crisis in 2002, but trade just trickles across the border, with about 1 percent of each nation's foreign trade flowing to the other. Religious differences have heightened in-group defensiveness, and the roving killer mobs of the 1947 Partition linger in many minds, much as Sherman's March did in the South. But since both sides have nuclear weapons, we're seeing mutually assured destruction and a Cold War-ish standoff. Efforts are afoot to reduce trade barriers, but attitudes remain prickly.

There is as yet hardly any trade between Israel and her Arab neighbors, despite tremendous potential gains. The world's future surely would brighten if this trade took off. Indeed, since the Israelis aren't going anywhere, mutual trade and perhaps the passage of generations seem the only solution here.

Not only has war diminished, but the world now applies a working moral code to it. The fourth Geneva Convention of 1949 has become international law ratified by every UN member. War crime tribunals appeared swiftly after World War II. Nuremberg is the best known, but Nazis stood in the dock throughout Germany as well as Norway, the Netherlands, Belgium, Denmark, France, Czechoslovakia, Greece, and other countries. Today, the International Criminal Court in The Hague prosecutes bloodstained leaders from everywhere, and mass murderers like Slobodan Milosevic and Charles Taylor have faced its judges. Its deterrent effect is unclear so far, but the satisfaction of subjecting such men to moral authority and punishing them is deep. Like tribesmen playing the Dictator Game, we now intervene to penalize unfairness between third parties at war. The moral forces that helped keep savanna tribes together are now at work across planet earth.

The causes of war are complex and other factors are at play here too. For instance, the rise of democracies may have curbed war, since autocrats could send armies across borders more freely. The global US military presence helps damp down conflicts. Moreover, modern sources of wealth are simply harder to grab. In the past, you might try to capture silver mines or oil fields, but today's software designers and film studios are not tempting targets even when they generate greater wealth. In addition, the most powerful nations have nuclear bombs and are less likely to fight each other. And global TV triggers mirror-neuron effects and has led to interventions to stop conflicts like that in Bosnia. Much of the world is networked together and has an interest in muting war.

Yet Kant was right. We won't end war. The dynamics of in-groups and out-groups remain a threat. Ideologues like the Iranian ayatollahs are a threat, and Hitler probably would have found an excuse for war no matter what. Cyberwar is a threat, especially since it's hard to trace attacks back and locate blame. Water shortages may become a threat, as with the Turkana. Nations that trade less, like those in Africa, are a threat. And internal conflicts will persist. We could even see another terrible surprise like World War I. Markets are not perfect peacekeepers.

But that's not the point. They have largely smothered the mayhem, a remarkable fact. And markets have improved morals in many other ways. We are better people for them.

In general.

How Markets Can Undermine Morals:
The Anemia Drugs

The Greek philosophers were not entirely wrong about markets. When they reward cooperation, people become more obliging and virtuous—but markets don't always reward it. Though on balance they have greatly improved our moral behavior, they can also degrade it. Cases of cheating go back beyond Uruk, and in our time we have witnessed extraordinary frauds such as Enron.

Let's look at a small-scale example to show how it can work.

For years Amgen and Johnson & Johnson have sold a trio of anemia drugs: Epogen, Procrit, and Aranesp. Together, they've been the pharma equivalent of Ghawar, the vast Saudi oil field. They brought in $8 billion annually for these companies, and the star, Epogen, was the most lucrative drug under Medicare, yielding $3 billion.

But in 2011 Medicare issued a study which found no solid evidence that most kidney patients—the main users of these medicines—lived longer, felt better, or indeed got any "clinical benefit" from the drugs, other than an increased red blood cell count. At the same time, the pharma firms had understated the risk for maladies like cancer and stroke. In other words, the drugs benefited few people but could harm many who were taking them needlessly. In most cases, they were no different from the 19th-century patent medicines.

Yet market incentives had led doctors everywhere to prescribe them. A 2012 story in the *Washington Post* outlined the steps.

First, the drug companies held trials of the drugs that inflated the benefits while missing the true harm. Amgen, for instance, assured the FDA, "The risks associated with therapy are minimal." Yet conflict of interest is an obvious hazard when firms test their own potential blockbusters. It's like asking a job applicant if she's qualified for a high-paying position.

Then the companies won approval from the FDA and, according to the *Post*, lobbied Congress assiduously to allow higher dosages. Of course, the more patients take of a drug, the more companies earn. Moreover, though investigators eventually learned that the medicines only seem to help 16 percent of dialysis patients, those who need blood transfusions, the companies won approval for milder cases and a variety of other ills. So by 1994 one drug's label stated that it could improve "health, sex life, well-being, psychological affect, life satisfaction, and happiness."

Next, the companies tilted decision making among doctors. For instance, they gave discounts to physicians who ordered a large volume of the drugs. They also overfilled vials, sometimes adding as much as 25 percent extra, presumably so doctors could resell the surplus. And the companies lobbied Congress to allow a markup to physicians of up to 30 percent each time they prescribed these medicines to Medicare patients. Markups were even higher for patients with private insurance. It's called the "spread." For instance, one clinic paid $600 for each dose of Aranesp, but the insurance company paid the clinic $900 for it, so with each dose the clinic pocketed some $300. "An oncologist could make anywhere from $100,000 to $300,000 a year from this alone," said Charles Bennett, professor at the University of South Carolina. "And all the while they were told that it was good for the patient."

Finally, in November 2006 an independent study in the *New England Journal of Medicine* revealed that kidney patients who got higher dosages also had higher rates of stroke, hospitalization, and death. The following month scientists in Denmark stopped a trial of Aranesp in cancer patients because tumor growths and deaths had increased. Amgen sat on this news for three months, until a newsletter revealed it. Asked why his company had not reacted faster, CEO Kevin Sharer replied, "Perfection says we should have done that."

Use peaked in 2007. At that time, over 80 percent of the 175,000 dialysis patients on Medicare were getting higher levels of these medicines than the FDA now deems safe. In 2007 despite intense lobbying, the FDA limited use of the drugs, lowered dosages, and warned doctors to prescribe the smallest possible quantities in many cases.

Amgen initially denied any deception. It issued a statement claiming that it updated the product labeling 15 times and "quickly and responsibly communicated" new findings as they appeared. "Any assertion that Amgen misled the public about the risks and benefits...is a gross misstatement of the facts. On the contrary, Amgen's primary concern is for patients."

Amgen's primary concern in fact seemed to be for the bottom line. But were company executives evil? Did they choose to commit statistical homicide, to kill a percentage of customers they would never meet, in exchange for big profits?

We can hardly know. But we think it far more likely that they simply didn't scout too hard for negative test results. Indeed, they may have thought of themselves as highly moral, bearers of vital therapy to suffering patients. All of us concoct rationalizations of self-interest. Desire comes first, and then reason jumps in to help it out. And if we badly want to believe a fact—say, my drug is widely helpful and harmless—the bar of proof drops significantly. We'll seize on evidence suggesting it does and downplay the counterevidence. Indeed, if a job applicant falsely says she is qualified for a position, she may not even be lying. Self-interest may convince her that she is.

And once we form and express an opinion, we will pay more attention in the future to supporting evidence and slight the rest, a well-known mental quirk called the confirmation bias. We're all vulnerable; no one likes to learn news that undermines one's beliefs. And where billions of dollars and entire careers are at stake, the bias grows much stronger. So markets can degrade morals by offering gleaming rewards and playing on our need to see ourselves as moral. Corruption finds its own excuses.

Note that this was hardly a farmers' market. The balance between buyers and sellers leading to a CE was just not there. The government defined many terms of its operation. Yet officials had to deal with relatively sketchy data, as it turned out, and heavy lobbying. Market pressure swayed votes in Washington, DC, and allowed the selling of these drugs far beyond the need for them, despite the dangers.

Moreover, the decision maker was not the buyer, but the doctor. So to an extent this market resembled that for college textbooks. There, professors assign the books but don't have to pay for them, so students see eye-popping prices. Here, doctors prescribe the drugs, but patients, insurance companies, and the government all pay.

Overall, the checks and balances of the model market receded, and the opportunities for moral corrosion grew. For whatever reasons, these companies clearly failed to investigate the safety of their drugs well enough while advocating intensely on Capitol Hill for high dosages of them. In the end, it is hard to believe Amgen's claim that its "primary concern is for patients."

The larger question here is: Have markets changed the zeitgeist? Have they marginalized the moral dimension in public policy and made market efficiency its key arbiter?

Many think so. In 2009 then-President Nicholas Sarkozy of France wrote, "Purely financial capitalism has perverted the logic of capitalism. Financial capitalism is a system of irresponsibility and is...amoral. It is a system where the logic of the market excuses everything."

The charge has grown common. For instance, in 2012 economist Lawrence King and coauthors decried the "low levels of official opposition to—or even questioning of—the primacy of markets," and added, "This pattern is reflected in the evolution of political and economic responses to the current financial crisis, which began in 2008, but has so far proven stubbornly resistant to all efforts to resolve it."

We'll address the issue of marketolatry in the final chapter, but first let's take a look at the immediate claim. Let's look at the panic.

4

Madness, Lies, and Crashes: When Prices Run Free

A lot of people behaved like idiots.

—Fu Wei, trader, on China's 2007 tea bubble

Financial Armageddon hit Wall Street early Monday morning September 15, 2008. Following a damp weekend filled with ominous rumors, anyone tuning into the morning news heard that venerable Lehman Brothers had filed for bankruptcy, and that Merrill Lynch, stock broker to millions of ordinary investors, had collapsed into the arms of an obscure North Carolina bank that had, a few years earlier, hijacked the Bank of America name.

As 25,000 stunned Lehman employees cleaned out their offices that morning, everyone in the world's financial system had to reconsider his or her own situation. That's when real panic struck. Lehman had huge trades with all the biggest players, who in turn had trades with everyone else. If it couldn't pay its bills, many other big players would see their assets drop and might also be pulled under. Citicorp, the world's largest bank, had been tottering for months, and AIG, recently the world's largest insurance company, was sinking fast. Timothy Geithner, then chair of the Federal Reserve Bank of New York, could not believe that an insurance company failure might cripple the global economy, but others soon edified him. AIG, like Lehman, had made massive deals in exotic financial instruments called CDSs and CDOs, and if it went under, it could drag down Goldman Sachs and Deutsche Bank, and probably everyone else.

The consequences boded worse than those of the Great Depression of the 1930s, because at least then lots of people could go back to the farm. The 21st-century economy was different. If its financial heart stopped, the economy might collapse completely, and hundreds of millions of people could starve.

No one knew how far the debt network extended. It was far too complex. But government officials realized they had to act at once. On Tuesday the Federal Reserve in effect nationalized AIG. On Thursday, after intense conversations with President Bush's team earlier in the week, Fed Chairman Ben Bernanke (a former Princeton professor of economics) and Treasury Secretary Henry Paulson (former CEO of Goldman Sachs) met with Congressional leaders to propose a $700 billion fund to bail out the financial industry. Their words reassured investors, and on Friday the S&P stock market index, which had dropped almost 10 percent earlier in the week, returned nearly to the 1250 of the previous week.

But things didn't go so well in Washington the following week. The Senate Banking Committee rejected the original three-page proposal, which would have given Paulson unprecedented powers with no oversight. A revised version, called Troubled Asset Relief Program or TARP, went forward and on September 23 President Bush explained on prime-time national television why swift approval was essential. But even with revisions, TARP provoked outrage from both ends of the political spectrum. Democrats hated the way it protected Wall Street fat cats but did almost nothing for homeowners. Republicans said it amounted to socializing risk and was un-American.

On Monday, September 29, the House of Representatives rejected TARP 228 to 205 on a bipartisan vote. A sizeable minority of Democrats voted against it, as did a 2–1 majority of the Republicans.

The financial system went into freefall. The S&P index slid 4 percent in five minutes on news of the House vote, and almost 9 percent that day, the worst drop in decades and one of the worst days of all time. Short-term credit, which had become shaky over the past year, suddenly vanished, and Paulson called this moment his worst of the whole crisis. It disrupted international shipments and even ordinary business. Firms began to lay off employees at a rate not seen in decades. Giants toppled and died, notably Washington Mutual (the largest S&L ever) and Wachovia, both serving vast numbers of depositors. Congress finally passed TARP on October 3, but by then it was too late. Financial markets now seemed to have no floor at all, and the selloff apparently had no limit. In March 2009 the S&P index finally bottomed out around 680, about half its value a few months earlier. The Great Recession had begun, and the world economy has still not fully recovered.

How did it come to this? The global economy was supposed to be shock-resistant ("the Great Moderation," economists called it) as well as enriching, due in no small part to sophisticated finance. What went wrong?

The crash of 2008 started innocently, in quiet neighborhoods all over the country. Most families wanted homes, and home ownership is surely a good thing, right up there with motherhood and maybe even better than apple pie. Why not encourage it? US politicians had already done so several times since the 1930s, and their efforts worked. Fannie Mae (more formally: FNMA, the Federal National Mortgage Association), Freddie Mac (FHLMC, the Federal Home Loan Mortgage Corporation), and the whole savings and loan industry helped keep mortgages affordable, and US homeownership stayed ahead of that in most other countries. New initiatives in the 1990s and early 2000s went further. By encouraging the securitization of mortgages, they let new borrowers in and boosted homeownership further.

And lending to young homeowners is indeed a good thing. Without financing, most families couldn't save enough to buy a house until their children were almost grown. By taking out a mortgage, they could buy early and fix up the home so that it worked for their kids, without worrying about a landlord's desires.

Mortgages also expanded the market for homes, so more were built. This is just the sort of thing financial markets are supposed to do, and it helps spread and increase national wealth.

Here's how the US financial system made it happen during much of the 20th century. After saving about a year's income, a family would look for a home that cost no more than five times that amount. Then they would talk to a loan officer at a local bank or S&L who would gather confidential information on their savings, income, expenses, and resources. Often a bond of personal trust would develop between the family and the official, much as that between people and their insurance agent. The family would borrow up to 80 percent of the purchase price of the home and agree to repay it over the next 30 years in fixed monthly payments, each no more than a third of the family's current monthly income. The S&L or bank would accept early payment if the family came into extra money. On the other hand, if they had a temporary problem (say, a seasonal layoff at the factory), the loan officer would renegotiate the mortgage terms. Fannie and Freddie's loan guarantees reduced the lender's risk and helped keep interest rates low.

This arrangement changed dramatically early in the 21st century, due largely to securitization. Instead of holding a mortgage for 30 years, the bank would sell it right away to a mortgage broker. Working with an investment bank, like Lehman Brothers or Goldman-Sachs, the brokers would securitize the mortgage. That is, they would pool the monthly payments from several thousand mortgages and sell shares in the pool, called a mortgage-backed security. Buy one and you were were essentially buying a fraction of monthly payments from all over the place.

Some securitized pools structured payments into several tiers. The top tier of shares (the "senior tranche") would pay off first every month, then the second tier, and the bottom tier (the "junior tranche") would absorb any shortfall. So if a homeowner missed her payment that month, each of the junior tranche investors would get a little bit less. The middle tranche investors would get paid in full unless a very unusually large segment of homeowners missed their payments. Rating agencies (like Moody's and Standard and Poor's) almost always gave the senior tranche their highest grade for safety: AAA.

Such products proliferated under various names, such as CDOs ("collateralized debt obligations"). Why were they so popular? Because mortgage interest rates paid by homeowners are normally 2–3 percentage points higher than traditional bond yields. Financial engineering transformed illiquid and somewhat risky assets into much safer and more liquid assets, greatly increasing their value to investors. It might seem like magic, but the underlying principles were (and are) quite sound.

The problem with securitization in the early 21st century is not that it didn't work, but that it worked too well. Lured by high yields and top safety ratings, investors around the world clamored for products like CDOs. As a result, mortgage brokers and investment banks shouted for more raw material for securitization, more home loans. But how could supply meet demand? How could you increase the number of home loans?

It turned out that there were several innovative ways. One was lending to "subprime" borrowers who would not have qualified before. Another was reducing down payments from 20 percent to 10 percent and eventually essentially to zero. Yet another was not bothering to verify borrowers' stated income. These became the famous "liar loans," and they enabled almost anyone with a decent overall credit rating to get a large sum of money and buy a house. Aggressive innovators, companies like Countrywide Financial, shot to the top. They paid their loan officers on commission and hired almost anyone.

The federal lawsuit filed against Countrywide in 2012 makes for an interesting study. According to prosecutors, the company launched a program called Hustle (a sort-of acronym for "High-Speed Swim Lane"), in which it: a) junked the forms its employees had used to determine whether granting a loan made sense, b) encouraged employees to bolster the applicant's numbers when the computer flagged weakness, c) granted bonuses based solely on the quantity of loans issued, regardless of caliber, and d) sold over $1 billion of these poisonous loans to Fannie and Freddie while claiming that Countrywide standards were getting stricter. This list includes only charges relating to the fraud case regarding Fannie and Freddie, and is not a full roster of Countrywide's schemes.

The traditional lenders either followed Countrywide's lead or dwindled toward insignificance. Half a trillion dollars worth of securitized loans were issued in 2001, and the number climbed steadily to over $2 trillion in 2006—compared to a US GDP of about $13 trillion that year. Countrywide was then the nation's leading mortgage writer, with a 20 percent market share.

As more buyers entered the market, they bid up home prices to unprecedented levels. Demand outraced supply, and the great real estate boom began. Homebuilders worked overtime, and speculators made fortunes flipping houses—buying, quickly reselling, and buying again elsewhere. People saw the value of their homes skyrocket, and sometimes took out home equity mortgages to buy new things. The economy grew.

The same lure of outsized profits (and the same threat of losing out) transformed the incentives higher up the financial pyramid. Rating agencies had always earned their revenue from the companies they rated, but the need to safeguard their reputations helped them resist that conflict of interest—at least until Moody's and S&P became stand-alone companies around the turn of the 21st century. At the same time a third company, Fitch, entered the market and fueled more intense competition. So the rating agencies too innovated and vied with each other in building impressive-sounding new risk models that justified grade inflation. It became quite easy to get that AAA rating, even on pools built from liar loans. The near-blind stamp of approval encouraged further innovations with securitized mortgages.

Consider, for example, the CDO squared. An investment bank scooped up just the lowest tranches from lots of ordinary CDOs, and made a new CDO out of them. It then tiered that cash flow. Remarkably, the rating agencies gave the top tier the AAA rating, even though it was built from distilled junk. Next, the bottom tiers could be collected and tiered to form a CDO cubed and so on. Thus, even the most dubious liar loans eventually became part of a complicated asset sold to investors as AAA, safe as Fort Knox. More than half a trillion dollars of such multitiered securities were sold between 2004 and 2007. The buyers knew very little about their composition, and analysts later discovered that the rating agencies and financial engineers also knew only average FICO scores, not borrowers' actual credit histories or loan terms.

You've probably noticed that these investment innovations cross the line. In fact, they range deep into the realm of delusion and outright fraud. The problem was even worse than it seemed because, for historical reasons (and lack of motivation and talent), the rating agencies all used models that conflate two very different sorts of risk. Idiosyncratic risk arises from an individual homeowner's fortunes, while systemic risk arises from adverse events that affect the whole economy. Tiered claims on mortgage pools do indeed help wash out idiosyncratic risk, as the raters' models recognize. But at the same time, tierings, especially multiple tierings, concentrate systemic risk. A top tier CDO squared, for example, is highly vulnerable to an overall slowdown or decline in US home prices. Such declines hit the least creditworthy the hardest, and as they stop paying their mortgages, a palace of liar loans will fall quickly. Many prominent economists predicted such a decline by 2002 or 2003, but the bubble didn't run out of air until 2006.

One reason was credit default swaps (CDSs). These were insurance for items like CDOs squared. They offered backup for conservative entities such as money market funds that were boosting depositors' yields by holding CDOs. But they could also go beyond insurance. They could be bets. With a CDS, a seller could agree to pay a buyer if a *third party's* bond defaulted. So more adventurous CDS buyers could make huge wagers against mortgage pools. The result was a casino dwarfing anything in Las Vegas, and for the savvy it was hardly a casino at all. This is the main story line in Michael Lewis's delightful *The Big Short*. CDS sellers made nice profits for awhile. Then, as default loomed, they faced claims from both the holders of mortgage-backed securities and from those who had bet against them. This was AIG's downfall.

Moreover, CDSs created a huge systemic problem. Everyone knew that vast numbers of such agreements existed out there (eventually, due to multiple offsetting agreements, grossing hundreds of trillions of dollars), but nobody knew exactly who the other CDS sellers and buyers were. This dark market created an epidemic of counterparty risk that paralyzed finance post-Lehman, and it was completely unnecessary.

The emerging financial structure, with CDOs and CDSs and their cousins, was called shadow banking. It is banking in the sense that it channels funds from depositors to borrowers. In this case, the depositors were often foreigners looking for another 1 or 2 percent extra interest on AAA-safe deposits, and most of the borrowers were homeowners. But it was shadowy in that there was very little public information or oversight. Traditional banking takes place in the light. Authorities gather statistics, and everyone knows in a timely way how many bank loans are out there, and to which industries. But CDSs and CDOs dwelt in a barely visible realm, and with the CDOs squared, not even the rating agencies knew which tranches held mainly liar loans and which tranches were good even if home prices declined.

So by August 2008, everyone knew there was a lot of toxin in the system. They just didn't know who was holding it.

This lack of public information is perilous, as suggested by the Groucho Marx Theorem. Based on Groucho's quip, "I don't want to belong to any club that would have me as a member," the theorem states that you shouldn't buy an asset from someone with clearly superior knowledge about it, at any price they might name. You'd join the club of suckers. So if someone offered to sell you securitized assets after the crash, you'd hold back. They might actually be high quality, but as far as you could tell, bad mortgages might taint them. You wouldn't even want to make a loan to a long-time trading partner who might be about to go bankrupt because he wrote too many CDSs or merely because he lent too much to some other CDS writer. After Lehman, such opacity magnified risk and paralyzed finance.

To pull back: The problem lay in money loaned—or thrown—to entities that could never return it. Favor systems, all the way back to the grooming of monkeys, thrive on reciprocity. Yet in the years before 2008, the balance tilted toward freeloaders. The home buyers received money through mortgages they could never repay, the real estate brokers earned money and avoided responsibility for toxic loans by selling them to Wall Street financiers, the financiers earned money and tried to avoid responsibility by reselling them in packages like CDOs, the rating agencies earned money by falsely assuring the world of their safety, and the shadow insurers like AIG earned money by letting others bet against toxic CDOs without the reserves to pay when doomsday arrived. All these freeloaders thrived at first, as anyone accepting a favor does, and the economy grew. But when it became clear that many loans were hopeless, everyone counting on repayment suffered. As the CDOs plunged toward their true but unknown value, organizations realized they had less wealth and some couldn't pay their bills. Investment banks collapsed, suspicion soared, a credit squeeze began, and normal economic cooperation broke down. The recession was a stinging consequence, and controversies are still boiling over how to reshape the system to stop freeloading.

Shifty Business: Ponzi Schemes

The great real estate and financial bubble leading to 2008 was unique, of course, but so was Japan's bubble of the late 1980s. To better understand bubbles, it may help to consider a stripped-down variant: the Ponzi scheme. In both, the returns are alluring at first, but they rest on illusion, and with time they vanish. Recent history has graced us with two special examples.

New York City, 2008

Bernard Madoff seemed the insider's insider, savvy and well-connected. As one broker put it, there was "something about this person, pedigree, and reputation that inspired trust." In 1960, still a senior in college, he borrowed money from his father-in-law and launched Bernard L. Madoff Investment Securities with $5,000. He first traded in over-the-counter (OTC) stocks, a pool so dark it is hard to imagine today. Newspapers didn't print daily prices, the public couldn't check them, and they varied so much from one broker to another that a smart man could get rich just by learning how to make others believe in him. Madoff later made a name in high-volume trade in stocks, buying order flow (legal, but closely related to illegal front-running) in the 1980s, and then became a founding member of NASDAQ. In 2008, Madoff Securities had $700 million of equity capital and handled 10 percent of all trades on the New York Stock Exchange.

But he also had a different operation two floors below. It was a bit of a sideline at first. It was very exclusive and its clients were mainly charities and wealthy coreligionists. Madoff earned relatively small annual returns of 10 to 12 percent, but he earned them year in and year out. It was like a huge annuity, and he attracted clients like Stephen Spielberg, Mort Zuckerman, and Elie Wiesel. But partly because he wouldn't take just anyone, investors craved to join this in-group. A few individuals bragged, "I know Bernie. I can get you in," and his nod gave supplicants a status rush.

Madoff said he made money by buying a portfolio of large-cap stocks like General Electric and also buying call and put options on them. The strategy is called split-strike conversion, and Wall Street knows it well. Done right, it can yield small, reasonably safe, yet volatile returns. So the head-scratching arose over Madoff's consistency. His profits were pretty much the same in good times and bad, as if the sea that lifts and lowers all boats didn't touch his. That didn't make sense.

Around 1999, financial analyst Harry Markopolos began arguing publicly and persistently that Madoff's steady returns were statistically impossible for any legal strategy. Madoff not only earned too much too steadily, but the options market wasn't big enough for all the orders he claimed to be placing in it. Markopolos demanded that the SEC investigate Madoff for front-running and Ponzi finance. But the SEC viewed the complainant as an odd, scarcely comprehensible quant and took no action.

In 2001 Barron's got curious about Madoff's wizardry and asked how he did it. "It's a proprietary strategy," he replied. "I can't go into it in great detail." And he never did, beyond generally describing split-strike conversion. The publication also put this question to a partner in a firm that marketed Madoff's securities, who replied, "Why Barron's would have any interest in this firm I don't know."

However, an unnamed money manager understood the interest. He had taken over assets that included a Madoff investment and talked to its guiding mind. "What Madoff told us was, 'If you invest with me, you must never tell anyone that you're invested with me. It's no one's business what goes on here,'" the manager recalled. "When he couldn't explain how they were up or down in a particular month, I pulled the money out."

The widely-read Barron's piece also spurred no action.

The SEC did investigate three times. The first inquiry occurred in 1992 and ended with the SEC deciding that Madoff had been right in a dispute. The second took place in 2005, in response to the relentless Markopolos. The sole SEC attorney conducting the probe cited Madoff for three small infractions, and later married Madoff's niece. The third investigation occurred in November 2007, and again the SEC found no evidence of fraud. Some SEC staff members won promotions for their work on this case. These failures were a tribute to Madoff's stature, secrecy, and political skills, as well as to SEC's lack of expertise and funding.

Then came the crash.

On the evening of December 9, 2008, Madoff admitted to his brother that the fund had been a Ponzi scheme since at least the early 1990s. Now, as the market tanked, investors were clamoring to withdraw their money, and Madoff had to cover $7 billion. If he had actually invested their funds, he could have done it easily. But since he simply shifted new money to older clients, he didn't have it, and in the panicked atmosphere he couldn't get it. The next day Madoff informed his astonished sons, who contacted police.

On the morning of December 11, two FBI agents visited him at his apartment. Wearing pajamas and a bathrobe, Madoff admitted them into his foyer, with its carriage lamp and grandfather clock.

"I know why you're here," he said.

"We're here to find out if there's an innocent explanation," an agent said.

"There is no innocent explanation," he replied.

They arrested him, and the revelations staggered the public. Bernie Madoff had run the biggest con of all time, a swindle next to which the enterprise of Carlo Ponzi looked like a shell game in the back of a bus. He had over $50 billion in liabilities—four times the 2010 GDP of Iceland. In comparison, stockholders in Enron lost about $11 billion and creditors perhaps $23 billion.

But the size of the scam was just the start. His customer base was also the broadest ever seen. Despite the pretense of elitism, Madoff had engineered the first globalized Ponzi scheme. He had begun in the United States, but since he needed steadily growing revenue, he expanded to Europe. A Swiss hedge fund manager recalled his encounter with a Madoff agent: "He told me the fund was closed, that it was something I couldn't buy. But he told me he might have a way to get me in. It was weird." Then Madoff's salespeople moved to the Persian Gulf, Southeast Asia, and China. By now, there were hints of desperation. A potential mark in Beijing said Madoff's people were urging the fund on "anyone who would listen."

The fraud was also unusual in that it lasted at least 17 years, a methuselah in the Ponzi world. Its modest yields, also atypical, may have helped. Most Ponzi schemes promise eye-popping returns and flame out in a few months or years. But Madoff was careful. He operated in a more sophisticated realm and claims of, say, 4 percent per month would have drawn a hornet's nest of skeptics.

In March 2010 he pleaded guilty to all charges. Then the question of proper sentence arose.

Bernie Madoff was also special in his rapacity. He cheated the most vulnerable and beneficent: charities, foundations, and even his closest pals and relatives. He emptied the bank accounts of his best friend Carl Shapiro and those of the heirs of his mentor Norman Levy, and he conned a widow right near the end. One effect of oxytocin is that it makes us more likely to trust others similar to us, and Madoff preyed especially on fellow Jews. Hence many victims felt wronged both financially and personally, because they had trusted Madoff not just as an advisor, but as fellow Jew and friend. One victim wrote Judge Denny Chin, "If he were tortured for the rest of his life, it wouldn't be enough punishment." At sentencing, Madoff spoke tonelessly, admitting "a terrible error in judgment," and his attorneys argued that he had committed a bloodless crime. But Judge Chin accurately described it as "extraordinary evil" and sentenced Madoff to 150 years. He will die in jail.

The court-appointed trustee, Irving Picard, is still trying to claw back as much as possible of investors' original investment, about $18 billion, mostly from gains of those who cashed out earlier.

Yet as breathtaking as the Madoff scheme was, an earlier one was perhaps even more remarkable.

Tirana, 1997

Albania was Europe's poorest and most isolated nation when it flung off communism in 1991. Then the new Democratic Party took over, radically reformed the economy, and touched off an economic boom. The official banking system, burdened with bad loans to communist-era enterprises, couldn't keep pace with growth. Regulation was stunted and ineffective, and financing came mainly from unofficial institutions.

Vefa was a prime example. Founded in 1992 by Vehbi Alimucaj, a former army officer with $700 in the bank, Vefa started to build shopping centers, finance trade with Italy across the Adriatic, and begin a host of other new activities. Vefa promised investors a return of at least 6 percent per month (or about 100 percent per year) and delivered on that promise month after month for several years. This record had mouths watering. Families poured in their life savings (especially remittances from sons and daughters working in the West), and Vefa's assets soared to hundreds of thousands of dollars in 1993 and to hundreds of millions in 1996. The business activities produced some revenue, but mostly Vefa paid early investors with funds raised from dazzled new investors.

By then, rivals offered even higher interest rates, up to 50 percent per month. Vefa had 85,000 investors, but two new entrants, Xhafferi and Populli, together lured in almost 2 million people or 57 percent of Albania's population. Scammers had now become a major market segment, and the newer ones were pure Ponzi schemes. They invested no money, but relied entirely on funds from a growing pool of new investors. Legitimate investments couldn't compete, nor could wages. People quit their jobs and looked for ever-quicker ways to get rich. Investors sold their homes, and so many farmers butchered livestock to buy in that one observer griped that Tirana smelled like a slaughterhouse. Outsiders warned that collapse was inevitable, but government officials gave their blessings to Vefa and several competitors.

Ponzi schemes fail when they run out of naïve investors. In Albania's capital city, Tirana, things started to unravel with a prominent default in November 1996, a month in which the prime minister and the speaker of parliament accepted medals from one of the Ponzi firms. By January 1997, Vefa and the other major players had shut down.

Spring 1997 was bitter. The majority of Albanians had lost their life savings, totaling about half of GDP—an all-time record. Citizens were outraged to learn that officials who blessed Vefa and its cousins had been on the payroll, and many rose in revolt. In the town of Lushnje, for instance, an angry crowd descended on the deputy prime minister and one man clubbed him with an iron bar. The official fled to the local sports stadium and a squad of policemen arrived to shield him. But the mob seized their weapons, and though the frightened police claimed the government had forced them to come, citizens beat them anyway. By March a semi-civil war had erupted and the government lost control of southern Albania. Rebels stole one million weapons from the government and burned and looted its buildings. Police and soldiers began deserting. The government fell, and over 2,000 people were killed before order was restored.

Decisive action in late 1997 helped heal the wounds. National and international authorities imposed martial law and seized and sold off assets of the bankrupt companies. The nation elected a new government, and, remarkably, the economy began to grow again in 1998.

Many of the scammers had escaped with their loot. But authorities caught Alimucaj transferring funds to Switzerland. He was arrested, charged with fraud, and in 2002 found guilty of 57,923 counts of deception, one for each of Vefa's creditors. He received a 20-year jail sentence, but was released in May 2010.

The Albanian trauma had many hallmarks of a bubble. First, the events occurred in ignorance. Albania was just emerging from decades of communist isolation and it had little financial regulation, so citizens lacked reliable data about these companies, which government officials vouched for. Second, the scam tapped into people's urge to top others in prestige. As citizens saw their neighbors getting rich, they flung money into the same ventures. If you ignored the wealth fountain, others might treat you like a fool. Third, the profits might be here today, but they'd be gone tomorrow. That is, people were giving loans to others who at the end would never pay them back. Fourth, and basically, these schemes arose from a contrast between fundamental value and market value. For example, think of the fundamental value as the worth of the assets Madoff claimed to buy. Since he bought nothing, the fundamental value was zero. But the market value was high and kept rising.

Ponzi scams can cause scathing damage, but in the end what's wrong with them? It's the business model. They require more and more new investors, and when the stream of them ends, they face a debt crisis. The fraud-meister can no longer pay what he owes and collapses.

That's what happens in bubbles too.

Planet Finance

Can Ponzi effects self-generate? Can similar events happen on their own, just because of market dynamics? Sure, and every seasoned investor has seen it. You can too if you check a chart of the stock price of certain companies. You'll see spikes, occasions where the stock rose quickly on optimism, perhaps based on news or rumor. At the peak, the news turned bad or the rumor proved false, and the stock price plummeted. If you'd bought near the top, you could easily have lost money. The same thing can happen in market sectors like base metals. Rumors about demand from China, for instance, can cause them to rise and fall.

Bubbles are almost as old as stock markets. In the 1550s an early bubble occurred in Lyons around a loan, called *le Grand Parti*, to King Henry II. As one observer noted, "Everyone ran to invest his money in *le Grand Parti*, the very servants brought their savings. Women sold their ornaments and widows their annuities.... In short, people ran for it as if to see a fire." The craze ended abruptly when the king stopped repaying the loan.

And then there are the grand spectacles. The Great Crash of 1929. The zombie depression in Japan. The dot-com bubble of 1999. The Panic of 2008. The entire financial market runs amok, and everyone gapes.

How do they happen? We can understand the process better with a visit to Planet Finance. It's much like the earth.

Our earth has three main layers: crust, mantle, and core. The crust is the varied world we see, with all its mountains, rivers, and gentle plains. Indeed, we tend to think the crust is the planet itself. But it's just the skin. Beneath it lies the mantle, mostly semimolten rock, whose movements create earthquakes, tsunamis, and volcanoes. The mantle drives most of the variation we see, as its drift tugs continents, forces up mountain ranges, and opens and closes oceans. Below the mantle lies the earth's molten core, a rather simple mix of nickel and iron.

Planet Finance is similar, and we'll look at the crust and core before describing the mantle.

The Crust: Investment Vehicles

On Planet Finance, we mostly see a world of varied instruments, include commodity futures, CDOs, options, bonds, and stocks. This landscape is complicated and innovations constantly disrupt it. At times, a sudden, damaging change can occur, like an earthquake. For most of history, we had no sure sense of what caused them.

The Core: Promises

At its center, finance is nothing but promises. Even a sophisticated modern financial instrument is just a complex vow. For example, the writer of a CDS for a CDO-squared promises that in exchange for specified payments by the holder she will pay her specific amounts in specified situations.

Most promises are too personal to trade. If I promise to pay you $5,000 for painting my house, you can't simply trade that contract to a friend. Financial markets need special kinds of promises, ones that are standardized and depersonalized.

How do you standardize them? You adopt conventional phrasing, such as, for bonds, "periodic interest payments plus a repayment of principal on the maturity day." You disclose information and include easily verified guarantees, as by very visible collateral. And you involve publicly known third parties, such as underwriters.

How do you depersonalize them? One key is mass. Add enough promises together, as with CDOs, and the personal submerges into the general. Another is a secondary market. Two people trading a share don't need to know much about each other; they just have to understand the company.

So an upshot of financial trading is the need for knowledge. And these promises aren't like cars, for example. They're invisible, and complex interactions constantly change their value. And since the borrower company knows much more about them than you do, you need to counter the Groucho Marx Theorem and reduce the information imbalance. In a viable promise market, the borrower publicly reveals a great deal about his circumstances, and often another person or organization vouches for the information or for the promise itself. In the United States, for example, the SEC requires extensive disclosures from companies issuing new stock or bonds, and the companies often pledge not to incur additional debt and to keep liquid assets. In addition, other companies called underwriters offer additional guarantees; and rating agencies, like Moody's, monitor and report on the companies and their guarantors.

Something is lost in making promises tradable. No longer do we have a rich human relationship between the person making the promise and the person who accepts it. We put aside feelings of trust, gratitude, worry of betrayal, and guilt and vengeance if the promise isn't honored. Tradability pushes these social emotions to the background and creates more space for opportunistic behavior.

Yet much is gained. The secondary market gives an investor valuable flexibility, so she can trade more often and faster. She will pay more for a promise that she can sell whenever she wants than for a promise that she must hold until it matures. Since she'll also pay more in the primary market, the borrower gets a better deal too.

Financial markets also tap invaluable mental resources. They pull together everyone's ideas on how to best to provide for the future, and this power is the deep source of their influence in the modern world.

The Mantle: The Instability Cycle

In the mantle we see the dynamics that drive bubbles and crashes. Note that economists still argue these matters and have not yet reached full consensus. Our story relies largely on the work of three men: the maverick economist Hyman Minsky (1919–1996), preceded by the shrewd John Maynard Keynes (1883–1946) and followed by Charles Kindleberger (1910–2003), a key architect of the Marshall Plan. Hence we call it the KMK perspective. As hot, soft rock in the mantle circulates up toward the crust and back down toward the core, so too this description proceeds in a sequence of phases.

Phase 1: Normalcy. Investors share a broad consensus on the earnings prospects for tradable assets and take normal returns. In the United States, we spent most of the second half of the 20th century in this phase.

Phase 2: Novel Intrusion. Every so often, a remarkable new economic opportunity appears. In the 1840s it was the railroad, and in the late 1990s it was the Internet. How much were they worth? No one could tell. There was nothing to compare them to.

Now, that was a problem, since virtually all of fundamental value is value in the future. (More technically, the fundamental value is the expected present value of the promised repayments, taking into account everything that anyone currently knows about the borrower's prospects.) You want to buy low and sell high, so you need some gauge of prospects. But now all is dreamy. Hence phase 2 innovations defy consensus. Optimists believe these novelties are transformative and envision once-in-a-lifetime profits. Pessimists think otherwise. Yet given the paucity of knowledge, optimists have the easier argument: "It's changing the world." For instance, dot-coms really were changing the world, and everyone sensed it. Pessimists have to contend that the change has limits, that profits might come in somewhere below cloud nine, a more nuanced and less welcome task.

The novelty need not be a new invention. Anything creating widespread misappraisal will do. In the US real estate bubble, for instance, it was the rating agencies deeming CDOs squared as safe as treasury notes. Pessimists such as Robert Schiller noted that home prices were getting out of line relative to historic rents and incomes, a critical point. But the bubble kept growing anyway.

Phase 3: Takeoff. Then the optimists start getting rich. Think of the Albanians whose Vefa investments doubled in value each year from 1992 to 1996. Or the dot-com buyers whose net worth skyrocketed in 1999. The steadily increasing returns are a strong reinforcement, both positive and negative: I'm getting richer month after month, and you poor skeptics aren't. So the pessimists now play along or get ignored. When pessimist Warren Buffett refused to touch dot-coms, some said he was out of touch.

Even investors who clearly see the bubble can join in. Buy now on a rising curve and you may sell later at a higher price. It's easy money, if you can handle the brinksmanship. So speculators like house flippers arrive and drive prices up further.

At the same time, wealth spreads out into the larger economy. As values soar in a real estate bubble, for instance, people take out home equity mortgages and buy more jewelry, vacations, and stock shares. Financial markets rise. Everyone feels more prosperous and the economy seems to glow. It's good times.

Yet, meanwhile garbage enters financial markets, partly because pessimists lack the stature to stop it. So liar loans and CDOs cubed appear. Buoyed by profits and perhaps a heightened regard for their own skill, some investors eagerly enter agreements that only make sense in sound markets. Hence AIG wrote CDSs that could immolate the firm if overall home prices fell. Such overvalued assets riddle the economy with air pockets and worsen the wreckage after collapse.

Mass judgment grows confused. By now the market has stopped distilling the wide range of private information into prices and instead amplifies overoptimism. The tie to reality has frayed and asset prices float skyward. As a young financial analyst in the late 1970s, one of us (Friedman) personally watched top managers at a large US bank decide whether to expand energy lending, despite warnings that the sector was overextended. The clinching argument was that the bank had to make the loans to remain a major player—not that the loans were safe. Even Isaac Newton succumbed to the pressure during the South Sea Bubble in 1720; he bought near the peak, lost £20,000, and was traumatized. "I can calculate the motions of the heavenly bodies," he wrote, "but not the madness of people."

Unlike Newton, true optimists pour everything into the new opportunity. The Albanian farmers slaughtered their flocks, but American investors got heavily leveraged, as much as 99 to 1. Basically, they were borrowing $99 to buy every $100 of stock. So if the stock went up to $101, they doubled their $1 per share investment. But if it dropped to $97, they suddenly owed twice as much as they'd ventured. Such extreme risk forced them to sell quickly at the slightest downturn.

Phase 4: Peak and Swoon. Eventually the supply of eager new investors and financial innovation runs out, as it sadly must in our finite world. A minor event can then touch off a cascade. In January 1990 it was the rise in interest rates in Japan, which cut the easy flow of cash to investors. The trigger can also be less direct. Lehman's demise would not normally have shaken a vast economy, but in late 2008 it occurred in an atmosphere of panic, sabotaged other balance sheets, and shifted the financial tectonic plates. As prices started to fall, the most leveraged investors had to sell, so the market dropped. At the same time, even calm investors saw that if they sold now and bought later, they might reap huge bargains. Congressional rejection of TARP quickened the plunge. And since lower asset prices erode collateral, and borrower defaults can cause lender defaults, so a financial crash can be contagious. Hence, phase 4 generally runs faster than phase 3.

A national or global recession may result. That's because the whole economy is web of promises and understandings. Agreements tie employee to employer, supplier to customer, and borrower to lender. Normally the web is resilient, and you can repair broken links at moderate cost. In a thick market, you can find transaction partners almost as good as the current ones; in thin markets it might take longer, but the new partners are always out there somewhere. Yet when the promises and understandings are jointly inconsistent, local disruptions spread. Firms that lose customers can't immediately find new ones and (especially if leveraged) have to cut back and lay off employees. Then they purchase less, try to wind down borrowing, and may default, and more firms lose customers. A vicious circle begins.

Phase 5: Bottom and Reconstitution. Eventually, prices drop so low that savvy investors purchase again. With effective bankruptcy laws, society quickly parcels out the losses from phase 4, companies redeploy useful assets, and recovery begins promptly, as it did in Albania in 1998. Consensus beliefs return, and financial asset prices are again grounded in reality. Then phase 1, normalcy, begins anew and usually lasts for decades.

But the crash causes lasting damage when it is unclear who gets stuck with the losses, as in Latin America in the 1970s and 1980s, and in Japan in the 1990s. A political struggle determines the outcome, and it can make phase 5 long and painful.

In a nutshell, bubbles inflate as early optimists succeed, pundits exaggerate the potential, and skeptics play along. Abraham Lincoln was right that you can't fool all the people all the time, but you can fool lots of them occasionally—and they can surely fool themselves. The crash restores realism and inoculates investors. Hence bubbles tend not to repeat themselves: it takes a rather different novelty, in a distant market segment, location, era, or arena, to touch off the next enthusiasm.

Engines of Trust

If financial markets can burn so many citizens, why do we allow them? Why have all modern countries done so, at least since the fall of the Soviet Union? Do they compensate for the occasional havoc? Both casinos and financial markets attract gamblers, so do these markets accomplish anything at all, on balance?

In fact, they lie at the heart of the economy. That's why news media pay such close attention to them. Financial markets pull money into companies, helping them grow and enabling more to exist. And as with loans, they are an invisible steersman. Using the collective knowledge of investors, they guide funds to the best and away from the worst. Countries that let them flourish tend to grow faster than economies that don't. Indeed, for the last 400 years, the world's most advanced economies have relied mainly on them to make crucial choices: How much should we consume now and how much invest for the future? And which new ideas should we ignore, which try, and which develop further?

Financial markets summarize vast information. Ideally, they embody the knowledge, feelings, and best thinking of all investors, and crystallize everything into price. Investors can then use price to decide the best courses of action.

But financial markets only work this magic when asset price equals fundamental value. Then they inform us and funnel resources into the best opportunities. Bubbles occur when prices balloon up from true value. They make the financial market inefficient. It then funnels resources into bad bets like pets.com and CDOs cubed, and away from sound investments.

Financial markets are what allow modern economies to soar, but they only got started in the early 1600s. Why did it take so long?

One likely obstacle was moral repugnance. Financial markets tend to corrode the traditional social order. When people can freely buy and sell financial assets, some will cease being farmers or craftsmen and become full-time traders. Occasionally, through skill or fraud or perhaps blind luck, a trader will gain wealth beyond the dreams of ordinary folk. At the peak of Tulip Mania in 1637, for instance, the heirs of deceased tavern keeper Wouter Winkel sold his flower collection for 90,000 guilders—in an age when midlevel merchants earned 1,500 guilders a year and carpenters 250. But the Winkel kids were lucky. Traders could also go bankrupt, bringing ruin to their families.

Traditional morals find both extremes—jackpot and disaster—deeply offensive. There is a Protestant-ethic sense that the winners don't deserve their fortune, that they haven't earned it, and hence that it is disproportionate and unfair. Meanwhile, all around other people are working harder and getting less. In Aesop's terms, the grasshopper becomes a millionaire while the thrifty ant seeks food stamps. Critics also resented the siphoning of talent from "honest" activities, and ordinary members of the public saw the complex financial markets as black boxes, hiding a welter of potential sins. And successful dealers sometimes have offensive natures. Think of Ebenezer Scrooge's crabby talk and shrunken heart in Dickens' 1843 tale *A Christmas Carol*.

Therefore, like moneylenders, financial markets are a tempting target for politicians. Twentieth-century despots Lenin and Hitler (and Zimbabwe's Robert Mugabe in the early 21st century) found it politically advantageous to expropriate the "leeches and parasites" who make their living in financial markets. Unbeknownst to them, they were sending the navigator down to the bilges. Yet even representative governments may find it expedient to outlaw these markets when citizens see them as no better than keno parlors.

The real problem with financial markets is not that they don't work, but that they usually work so well that participants (and regulators) let down their guard after a few decades. They trust too much and treat illusions of payback as real wealth. More and more people deceive themselves, and the bubble swells. It always seems to happen sooner or later, at least since the dawn of financial markets in the 16th century.

However, reforms can lengthen the time between bubbles by creating more vigilant watchdogs and better information, and can minimize the harm when they do occur through a robust bankruptcy infrastructure backed by strong political institutions.

As evidence grows from labs and financial markets around the world, our understanding will keep increasing, but we may never solve all the mysteries. Meanwhile, policy makers must do the best they can. The history of bubbles suggests that they should try to keep access to financial markets open to everyone and perhaps encourage pessimists if they see a bubble inflating. They should also create incentives for transparent and honest behavior by all participants. The smaller the bubble, the less the damage from its collapse.

And of course that raises the question of what to do afterwards.

5

Blundering Back to Balance: TARP and Tear Gas

He entered the territory of lies without a passport for return.

—Graham Greene

Western economies crawled for years after 2008. Riots lit up Europe even as a gray miasma settled on household confidence. Citizens began speaking of finance as a predator, and scandals like the rigging of the Libor interest rate kept coming. Once-remote moral issues were now on everyone's lips.

And the questions began on the American side of the Atlantic.

Suppose part of a shopping mall collapses. What do you do? Well, some goals are obvious. You need to clear away the debris. You need to decide who pays for what damage. You want to repair the mall as fast as reasonably possible. And you want to be sure it doesn't happen again.

Suppose part of a financial system collapses. Economists broadly agree that we take the same steps as for the mall. The process just looks different, since promises have caved in rather than walls and ceilings. Bankruptcy is the key (along with mergers and acquisitions). The legal system should swiftly sort out the bad promises from the good, determine who bears the losses, and put the working resources in the hands of people who can best use them. The process should be smooth and fast, and government should reform policies that helped cause the disaster. It seems like pure common sense: Discard the junk, assign losses, get things humming again, and prevent future calamities.

However, most economists (not all, as we shall see) prescribe a further role for government: limiting the contagion. They say the shopping mall analogy isn't quite complete, because damage from broken promises radiates out in a complex of forking paths, many unseen.

The global economy is a network. Nodes are individual people, and links between them are relationships of customer-supplier, or borrower-lender, or employer-employee, or service provider-client. Other kinds of links arise within an organization, and for many purposes an organization can be a single node. Strong, numerous links indicate a vigorous economy, as does the ability to change links in response to new opportunities.

Hunter-gatherer societies consist of simple versions of such webs. The nodes there don't vary much, nor does their nature. The connected components tend to be small but fluid, with fusion perhaps annually and fission in most seasons. Agricultural economies build much wider webs, with a simple hierarchical structure. They are less fluid.

A market is neither a node nor a link, but a pond from which the web draws nourishment, selling outputs and buying inputs, increasing throughput and value. Links grow in number and strength. So we can view the Great Transformation as a shift from a set of isolated shallow ponds—markets—nourishing the network to a sea in which the whole intricate web of connections floats as rafts and islands.

But an economy grows fragile when people cannot honor the promises and understandings behind many links in some realistic circumstances. Systemic risk arises when broken promises spread, as with excessive leverage, where node A defaulting on node B can cause B to default on nodes C and D, in turn causing defaults further along the links. Thus, a financial bankruptcy may bring innocent people down, even if they don't seem nearby, and they in turn can undermine more people. That's what happened in September and October 2008. The damage ripples outward, and it can take years to restore the network to health.

Hence government should cordon off the best-connected, most threatening nodes, and it should also make sure wounded firms can form new links as the economic web begins to repair itself. Economists first articulated the latter role in the Great Depression of the 1930s, and it became the centerpiece of macroeconomic textbooks half a century ago.

How did this prescription and the others fare in the United States after 2008?

The government's performance was (to put it kindly) a bit muddled. Of course, the coincidence of a presidential changeover with the financial crash complicated matters immensely.

TARP and the Stimulus

The outgoing Bush administration prided itself on its hands-off, market-friendly ideology, but TV viewers could see fear in the president's face and even his advisors thought we needed the $700 billion TARP bailout to prevent catastrophe. In the administration's last few weeks, it redirected some of these funds to keep the auto industry afloat a few more months.

The incoming Obama administration had fewer ideological constraints than its predecessor, but still faced moral and political problems seldom mentioned in economics textbooks. Before taking office in January 2009, the economic team prepared a $300 billion stimulus package, but doubled down as net job losses in the United States accelerated that winter to almost a million per month. Congress passed the final $787 billion American Recovery and Reinvestment Act (ARRA) in February 2009, and that spring the government loaned $80 billion to GM and Chrysler.

Republicans fiercely opposed these measures. The hostility stemmed in part from partisan politics. Had they cooperated in passing a bigger and more effective stimulus, they probably would have received little credit and done badly over the next election cycle.

Yet arguably the larger part of opposition was moral. ARRA incoherently bundled tax cuts and highway projects intended (with little success) to attract Republican votes together with extension of unemployment benefits and miscellaneous initiatives favored by Democrats, such as school reform, alternative energy investment, health care reform, and infrastructure. At the same time, it failed to fire the public imagination. Unlike the best Depression-era programs, it wasn't clearly putting Americans back to work. Many felt that it was a huge and unfair use of taxpayer funds.

ARRA indeed was huge. At 4 percent of GDP spread mostly over two years, it exceeded the WPA and its Depression cousins. But was it effective? Most impartial economists believe that the Great Recession otherwise would have been far worse, but that ARRA was not large or well-targeted enough to speed the economy back to normalcy.

On the other hand, the GM and Chrysler bailouts worked pretty much as advertised. Both automakers emerged from bankruptcy with lower labor costs, lower executive pay, and fewer old plants and pension obligations. They introduced more attractive new models and (aided in part by the Cash-for-Clunkers program) soon reached profitability and began to repay the loans. It now seems that US taxpayers will largely (or perhaps entirely) be repaid and that these bailouts saved millions of jobs.

Should We Bail Out the Bad Guys?

Effective or not, bailouts somehow seem unjust. Why use taxpayer money to save the firms that actually caused the meltdown, the banks that made the reckless loans, and insurance companies that wrote too many CDSs? More broadly, why save the state and local governments that offered overly generous pensions? Or auto companies too fat and lazy to match foreign competitors? They deserve to suffer the consequences of their behavior.

Let's start with the word "bailout." To most laypeople, it suggests a gift to a giant, inefficient, highly connected octopus. But bailouts are typically investments: loans or purchases. In 1980 the US government bailed out Chrysler with a $1.5 billion loan and earned acid criticism, mostly from liberals. But by 1983 Chrysler had paid it back and, with interest and stock warrants, the government made a $660 million profit. Taxpayers spent less overall, and the nation saved jobs. So these companies often pay for the lifesaver we throw them.

More basically, the trouble is that we don't live in Adam Smith's village. We live in a much larger world.

Take AIG. The mammoth insurer had links everywhere. On February 28, 2008, it had branches in 130 countries and received half of its revenue from overseas. Its assets exceeded $1 trillion and its stock sold for $50.15. Yet for an insurance company it showed breathtaking disregard for risk. In August 2007 Joseph Cassano, head of the unit that made the fateful CDS deals, said, "It is hard for us, without being flippant, to even see a scenario within any kind of realm of reason that would see us losing one dollar in any of those transactions."

In late 2008 AIG faced death from "those transactions" and begged for help. The government could have punished it and let it succumb, but the harm would have been global. AIG owed money everywhere, and its bankruptcy could have brought surprising creditors, like the supposedly safe money-market funds, to their knees and spurred further panic. We condemn secondhand smoke, but here too others nearby would have suffered from self-destructive acts—and far more quickly, widely, and violently.

Yet most AIG divisions earned a profit. So to keep this crumbling tower upright, the US government pumped $182.5 billion into it and took 77.9 percent of its stock. The gamble seemed hazardous, since at one point its stock fell to around $1 a share. And it was the most hated bailout, partly because AIG went on to shower millions in bonuses on executives who had caused the fiasco.

But the strategy had key advantages. For instance, the government was buying inexpensively, when most investors thought the company mortally ill. And it could be patient. It didn't need repayment at once. According to one analysis, by 2012 the US government had earned all its money back and made a profit of $15 billion, and it still owned 16 percent of a company whose stock was selling for around $34. (Note that in these cases, funding and paybacks are complex and different analyses yield different figures.)

Similarly, with the banking system, the most direct strategy would have been to take control of the most overleveraged big banks, fire the top executives, strip out the toxic assets and liquidate them slowly, and spin off new banks with cleansed balance sheets. This approach worked well in the US S&L crisis of the 1980s and more recently for banks in Scandinavia. Taxpayers ended up paying relatively little, and the economy suffered minimal damage.

However, like all investments, bailouts don't always turn a profit. The Treasury gave the big banks around $230 billion in TARP and has received around $255 billion, for a gain of $25 billion. However, the smaller banks still owe some $15 billion, and overall the public may never get the full $700 billion back from TARP. But its cost will be far less than pundits originally warned. Beyond TARP itself, the biggest losses have come from Fannie Mae and Freddie Mac, which remain deeply in the red. However, the government can reap all future profits from these two, and we won't know the final score here for a long time.

So we have to counter the moral impulse to pull down irresponsible goliaths with the economic—and ultimately moral—benefits of saving them. After a financial crash, well-targeted bailouts and stimulus spending can hasten repair of the torn network. They can keep the economy stronger, spare the hardship of lost jobs, and earn money for taxpayers. The moral reaction, often manipulated to political advantage, hinders such repair work and prolongs the suffering.

The government can respond by educating the public about the nature of bailouts and thus help overcome the sense that they are ripping money from citizens' paychecks to cushion fat cats from their blunders. This task may be difficult, but even so the Obama administration proved deficient in it. Indeed, in the 2010 midterm elections, the moral backlash fueled the Tea Party and made further stimulus impossible. Repair of the financial system then had to proceed slowly, using awkward indirect subsidies.

Should We Help Loan Liars?

The problems in the financial sector begin with bad promises at the base of the mortgage pyramid. A mortgage is a promise of monthly payments or an early repayment in full. That promise is good as long as the owner can sell the house for more than the remaining principal balance of the mortgage. But when she no longer can—when she owes more than the house is worth—the promise is in jeopardy. She may do better by defaulting. And after 2007, falling home prices in much of Florida, California, and elsewhere pulled millions of homeowners underwater. Monthly payments stopped from those who lost their jobs or were never able to pay to begin with.

But here is the interesting and important question: What about the underwater homeowners who can make the monthly payments? The value of a good credit rating and the possibility of a rebound in house prices might make it financially advantageous for them to keep paying on homes that are only slightly underwater. At some point, however, it may make bottom-line sense to walk away from the loan.

The specter of massive foreclosures worried both politicians and economists. As a result, the Obama administration offered many programs to renegotiate distressed mortgages, some carved out of TARP funds and others created separately.

And that raised questions. Is it moral to use taxpayer money to ease the mortgages of people who should have understood and avoided them in the first place? Why funnel cash to them rather than to prudent buyers who didn't get into trouble? Doesn't every homeowner take a risk that the property's value will decrease?

There is a moral tension here. On the one hand, most of us feel a desire to aid others in distress. On the other, we have homeowners with varied levels of culpability and merit:

1. People who received typical mortgages, fully understood them, and wound up underwater anyway. The "good people."
2. People who trusted lying agents and signed mortgages with nasty provisions they didn't know about. In some cases, they may have had limited English. Here, we may sympathize with them as victims and want to help them even more, but we can't ignore the fact that they had an obligation to check the document thoroughly themselves, even if it meant going to a lawyer.
3. People who simply didn't understand harmful provisions buried in the stultifying fine print.
4. People who lied to get mortgages they couldn't pay back. These individuals had to realize they would likely default, and obviously they bear responsibility.

The weights you place on helping out versus punishing in these cases will determine your moral attitude toward them.

But here too we have to be careful not to let our moral instincts outweigh good policy. So what are the economic dimensions of this situation?

Businesses routinely walk away from contracts when it is more profitable to, and we hear no uproar about it. Moreover, the law imposes no punitive damages on them or on anyone breaking a contract (in most cases). If you default, you pay only for the harm you cause, and the courts pass no moral judgment on you. The rationale is that our economy ultimately benefits, since business moves faster and more nimbly. Homeowners whose mortgages are sufficiently underwater are in a similar situation. By defaulting, they can enjoy living in a home at lower cost, even taking into account the impact on their personal credit rating and the loss of the tax advantages from home ownership. And, they may argue, what's the harm from a default, ultimately? The big, impersonal corporation just subtracts a sum from the balance sheet, yet a family with kids can benefit directly.

But this dynamic changes when a tide of defaults looms. The more defaults, the more foreclosures, and the damage radiates from them too. They bring down the price of all homes nearby. If foreclosures are nationwide, people's wealth drops significantly. They can't get home equity mortgages, for instance. At the same time, as housing prices fall, owners get deeper underwater and default looks more and more appealing. So while an individual default here and there does not affect society much, a rash of them does. Yet if you lighten too many mortgage burdens, as the Obama administration proposed to do, you lower income for the banks and make them less likely to lend. And that damage radiates too.

So what actually happened?

Intriguingly, despite the dire predictions, most underwater homeowners chose not to default. Recent research suggests that the reasons were mainly moral. Many homeowners apparently didn't want the guilt and shame from skipping out on the deal. Perhaps too they didn't want to hurt their neighbors by abandoning their current home and contributing to neighborhood blight. So our savanna heritage prevented the havoc that a world of amoral *Homo economici* would have caused.

At the same time, the federal aid programs had few takers. For instance, the Homeowner Affordability and Stability Plan (HASP), announced in February 2009, sought to help up to nine million homeowners avoid foreclosure. However, far less than 10 percent have received any substantial relief, while about four million people lost their homes to foreclosure between 2007 and early 2012. And many of those losses have been processed improperly, in some cases fraudulently, to the banks' advantage.

These foreclosure problems are doubtless due in part to the complexities higher up the food chain. But we share the opinion of many commentators that the larger problem is political. The financial industry spends more money on lobbying and campaign contributions than any other industry except healthcare, led by the pharmaceutical industry, and it seems to get an excellent return on its investment. The industry opposed the mortgage renegotiation programs, and Treasury Secretary Timothy Geithner did little to get them off the ground.

So when we think about fixing the future, one question naturally arises.

Is the System Rigged?

Two well-placed officials took a moral stance different from Geithner's in the aftermath of the collapse. Elizabeth Warren, a former Harvard law professor and now a senator, was appointed to the TARP oversight panel in 2008. "Some of the largest financial institutions can build a profit model on tricking people," she told a reporter, explaining the need for a Consumer Financial Protection Bureau and citing, among other things, home mortgages with poorly explained teaser rates that disproportionately led to foreclosure. Warren's larger point is that wealthy interest groups pressure government to grant them special favors, contrary to the public interest. "The system is rigged. Look around," she told the 2012 Democratic convention. "Oil companies guzzle down billions in profits [from special tax breaks]. Billionaires pay lower taxes than their secretaries. And Wall Street CEOs—the same ones who wrecked our economy and destroyed millions of jobs—strut around Congress, no shame, demanding favors and acting like we should thank them."

Neil Barofsky, inspector general for TARP from the outset through 2011, told his story in his 2012 book *Bailout*. "The suspicions that the system is rigged in favor of the largest banks and their elites, so they play by their own set of rules to the disfavor of the taxpayers who funded their bailout, are true," Barofsky said in a July 2012 interview. "It really happened. These suspicions are valid." He added that another crisis is likely because of the failed response to this one. "Incentives are baked into the system to take advantage of it for short-term profit," he said.

Regulators must achieve a delicate balance. Clumsy intervention surely can reduce profits of the regulated industry and may also hurt the public as markets themselves operate less effectively. Often regulators need to deftly tweak the rules of the game, so competitors offer better value to consumers. In financial markets, the goals should be to improve transparency—that is, to gather dispersed private information and make it easily available—and to foster competition by breaking up inefficient cartels.

Getting this right is almost impossible in Washington's highly polarized environment. The pressures distort action. Most legislators fear offending wealthy interest groups, who can easily fund a barrage of negative advertising the next time they stand for reelection. Regulators know that poor relations with the industry will dim their future job prospects. Of course, industry insiders see lobbying as a means of protecting their well-deserved and customary livelihood. Outsiders (including us) see it as rent seeking, and even attempts to buy licenses to gamble with other people's money, pocket most of the gains, and pass most of the losses to others, ultimately taxpayers.

Ordinary citizens usually can't counterbalance the wealthy pressure groups, but in his book Barofsky suggests that maybe enough people will get angry. "Only with this appropriate and justified rage," he writes, "can we sow the seeds for the types of reform that will one day break our system free from the corrupting grasp of the megabanks." But rage is not enough. The Occupy movement had it, yet didn't know the pressure points. As lobbyists understand, a single meeting in a Washington office can sometimes do more than all the Occupy demonstrations combined.

So though the need for financial reform was undeniable after 2008, industry pressure and partisan gridlock slowed the process. Finally, in 2010 the president signed the Dodd-Frank Wall Street Reform and Consumer Protection Act. This legislation realigns existing regulatory agencies and creates some new ones, notably the Consumer Financial Protection Bureau that Elizabeth Warren championed and the Financial Stability Oversight Council along with a new research unit.

The effect of this reform measure will depend entirely on implementation details. Some observers, such as Barofsky, think that the financial industry will mute its impact and that the next financial crisis is not far off. The possibility is there, however, for the new agencies to change the rules of the game and greatly reduce the likelihood of a financial crisis for several decades.

The question of enforcement remains. As Barofsky said, "The incentives are to cheat, and cheating is profitable because there are no consequences." By October 2012 the federal government had filed not one criminal indictment against a top executive of a major Wall Street financial firm. "It's perplexing at best," said Phil Angelides, chair of the Financial Crisis Inquiry Commission. "It's deeply troubling at worst." Indeed. Is it moral to *not* prosecute and jail guilty Wall Street traders, even after a firm like Citigroup publicly admits to years of fraud?

To repeat a key theme, a moral or legal system without effective enforcement doesn't work. And fining large financial institutions is ineffective. The company just passes the cost on to investors and customers. Even if you destroy a firm like Lehman Brothers, its wealthy traders can move to another firm or just retire and travel the world. What do they care if the old shell is gone?

Many observers, such as former FDIC head Sheila Bair, the top banking regulator during the crisis, recommend the cellblock for individuals involved in frauds around items like CDOs squared. This punishment seems essential, considering the enormous damage these scams can cause. Even individuals with high risk appetite, like Joseph Cassano, might think twice about the prospect of swapping a penthouse for a room with a lidless toilet.

After the dot-com bust, we saw a wave of accounting scandals. These disgraces had typically surfaced after a crash. A company has been rigging its books to make its performance look good, but suddenly it can't hide the losses any longer, and everyone sees the lies, as with WorldCom and Global Crossing. However, the Sarbanes-Oxley Act of 2002 made CEOs personally liable for accounting fraud. Now they had to attest that they had examined the auditors' report and found that it "does not contain any material untrue statements or material omission" or anything that could be "considered misleading." Jail awaited CEOs for deceit. The result? After the far bigger crash of 2008, almost no major accounting scandals occurred in the United States. If they had, we would have seen an even worse calamity, as people pulled funds from the stock market out of uncertainty about what they had bought. The threat of prison worked.

The Quandary for Economists

Why didn't the politicians just follow the advice of economists after the meltdown? In fact, conflicting advice from economists added to the muddle.

Macroeconomics, one of the three main branches of the discipline, began with John Maynard Keynes's attempts to come to grips with the Great Depression of the 1930s. Keynes was a witty, mercurial figure whose intellect Bertrand Russell described as "the sharpest and clearest that I have ever known." Early in his career he was part of the bohemian Bloomsbury set, and after he saw firsthand the shenanigans that bred the Treaty of Versailles, he wrote a sardonic, prescient best seller about it. Keynes and his followers put together a body of ideas by the early 1960s that justified stimulus in recessions and depressions, and that seemed to fit the facts.

Despite many heroic efforts since then, it proved extraordinarily difficult to fit these ideas into a coherent theory compatible with competitive equilibrium, as understood in the other two branches of the discipline, econometrics and micro-economics. Controversies raged in the 1970s between Keynesian macroecono-mists and monetarists led by Milton Friedman (no relation) who thought the only legitimate role for government was to keep the money supply stable. Events in the 1980s discredited both schools, and by 2005 a new generation of macro-economists converged on a more flexible version, awkwardly named "dynamic stochastic general equilibrium" (DSGE).

DSGE models were able to accommodate inflation and GDP data from 1960 to 2005. They helped macroeconomists believe that depressions were a thing of the past, that advanced economies had entered a time in which we could expect nothing worse than a mild pullback. The Great Recession beginning in 2008 thus took them by surprise.

Here's the underlying theoretical question: When is a stable competitive equi-librium easy to reach after an event like the Lehman bankruptcy, and when is it hard? Unfortunately, DSGE models have nothing to say here. They assume that the economy is always at equilibrium, though one that might take random jumps.

With no clear guidance from theory, macroeconomists had to fall back on opinions, drawn from some reading of historical data and perhaps shaded by per-sonal political beliefs. Almost all economists agree that a credible plan to reduce government deficits is essential to sustained growth. A majority of economists (including most Nobel laureates) also believe that: 1) a well-targeted stimulus will help bring the economy out of recession (and a poorly targeted one may do more harm than good), 2) infrastructure projects now are especially valuable, due to historically low interest rates, and 3) aid to states and low-income individuals is also highly valuable since they will spend the money at once and thus recycle it. But a substantial minority of economists (including some Nobel laureates) dis-agrees. They think that equilibrium will be restored more rapidly if the govern-ment stays in the background.

So the quarrel among economists reinforced the political impasse, which blocked enactment of a stimulus to match the scale of the Great Recession. Despite ARRA, TARP, and lesser programs, combined spending by federal, state, and local governments has declined in the United States. We may never know whether the sort of stimulus Keynes recommended would have worked here. At least, we can hope that by the next financial crisis, there will be better models (perhaps that quantitatively model the economic web in and out of equilibrium) to help guide policy makers.

Europe: The Bubble of Many Shapes

Europe is the site of the most complex economic disaster of recent times. For years Greece dominated headlines about it and compelled the anxious attention of the world's most powerful bankers and politicians. Greece isn't quite typical, but it has a story we're familiar with in the United States.

On October 4, 2009, George Papandreou and his socialist party won parliamentary elections in Greece after five years of opposition rule. Almost exactly one year had passed since the Panic of 2008, and in that time Iceland had virtually bellied up and the Irish government had sucked in the venom of its banks' bad debts. People realized Europe had further booby traps, but were unclear about where they lay. In that context, Greece's new finance minister George Papaconstantinou began drawing up his budget.

The prior administration had publicly projected a budget deficit of 3.7 percent of GDP, a little above the EU limit of 3 percent. But Papaconstantinou called meetings to inquire. Again and again, embarrassed functionaries revealed some new and amazing expense missing from the budget. "At the end of each day, I would say, 'Okay, guys, is this all?'" he told Michael Lewis. "And they would say, 'Yeah.' The next morning there would be this little hand rising in the back of the room: 'Actually, Minister, there's this other one-hundred-to-two-hundred-million-euro gap.'"

On October 18, Papaconstantinou informed European officials that the Greek budget deficit would reach 12.5 percent in 2009 (the eventual figure was 15.4 percent). He listed an array of causes for the surprise, but the eye-catcher was the lying to the EU. Other finance ministers grew furious and spat out terms like "fraud" and "statistical chicanery." The prime minister of Luxembourg intoned, "The game is up."

The Greek scheme came straight out of Enron. If you're paying hundreds of millions a year in pensions and you hide the records in a separate computer in the back room, you seem to have far less debt. Everyone thinks you're a better risk. You can get loans more cheaply. And you can get more of them. So the Greek government was borrowing directly from the EU at low rates and using this money to run its public services.

The idea that a nation would scam fellow EU members was shocking, but it became less so when you looked at the Greek state itself. It was a carnival of corruption. The public sector employed about a quarter of all employees. Get a government job and you had it for life, and each administration handed out further plums to supporters. Wages in this sector rose 50 percent between 1999 and 2007, the fastest rate in the Eurozone, yet in 2009 no state firm reported earning a profit. In 2010 Transparency International rated Greece the most crooked country in the EU and said the average Greek family paid $1,850 per year in bribes.

The greatest risk for the corrupt is jail. But Greek judges treated these cases as if people had the lifespan of sequoias. Prosecutions dawdled endlessly. According to economists Theodore Pelagidis and Michael Mitsoupoulos, corrupt acts rarely received effective advocacy, and politicians who went along with special interests won immunity for "almost any unlawful acts they may engage in." Hence officials developed a pleasing sense of impunity.

Moreover, the courts did not publish all judicial decisions, and publication is essential. It reduces judicial whim and helps keep judges accountable. But as economist Carlo Bastasin aptly observed, "This attitude was extended toward Greece's reporting to the European Union."

Democracy first arose in Athens, but Greece was like a child movie star whose achievements lay far in the past. Other countries had ruled it for millennia, and under the Ottoman Empire tax collectors were rapacious, bribes common, and the nation itself so backward that Orthodox Church authorities were railing against Copernicus as late as the 1790s. After independence in 1828 Greece remained the playground of kings and, later, military figures. Even with democracy in 1974, just two families, the Papandreou and Karamanlis, dominated Greek political life. So while Greeks are very loyal to their families and local areas, they keep the government at arm's length.

Most notably, the median Greek family paid no tax. Tax laws existed, but enforcement was rare. For instance, owners of swimming pools had to pay an extra tax, and in the suburb of Ekali north of Athens 325 people stated on their returns that they had one. When tax inspectors studied Google Earth photos of Ekali, they counted 16,974 pools. That is, 98 percent of households had lied on their tax returns. Similarly, in another suburb, many physicians were declaring an annual income of €3,000, a sum which put them at the level of vagrants, yet investigators almost never inquired. Indeed, tax collectors who aimed at big targets could find themselves relegated to a desk in a quiet back room. The EU taskforce on Greece says the nation's 11 million citizens owe €60 billion in back taxes, most of which has vanished forever.

The EU might have kept Greece out of trouble. Its officials weren't blind. They knew the Greeks were cheating; they just didn't realize how brazenly. Indeed, they knew that Greece had lied to get into the EU. Moreover, though the limit on budget deficits was 3 percent of GDP, both France and Germany exceeded it without punishment in the early 2000s. Eventually, enforcement simply ceased, and EU officials looked the other way. Breach was too common. If you were breaking the 65-mile-per-hour speed limit, you probably wouldn't make a citizen's arrest on the speeder next to you. So the Greek government had been getting massive liar loans. It spun its little tales, Europe gave it cash without checking up, and nationwide its comfort grew and grew.

But after late 2009, Greece was unable to pay its debts, so it did the only thing it could. It turned to its victim for more loans.

Germany had the strongest economy in Europe, and with France it took the lead in European affairs. It could have reasonably bailed Greece out right then. Greece owed $435 billion, less than the $613 billion debt of Lehman Brothers. So the amount was feasible, if daunting. The Maastricht Treaty of 1992 forbade outright bailouts, but there were ways to skirt it. A bailout would have fed money right back to German banks, many of which had issued the earlier loans to Greece. Moreover, a bailout would have prevented contagion and the ills of uncertainty.

But two moral problems stood in the way.

First, 67 percent of German citizens opposed aiding Greece. Most viewed rescue as a redistribution of funds to distant folks, and they didn't like it. They preferred to keep their own money in their own pockets, and the feeling was especially strong among those with a deep in-group sense. Germans had also had an unpleasant experience with redistribution. After reunion, they had paid to help revive East Germany, an economy desiccated by communism. They were not eager to do so again with Greece, a foreign country that had lied its way into trouble.

So aid posed political risks for leaders. And in 2011 a Finnish party called The True Finns ran on a single issue—no help for Greece—and shocked observers by seizing a fifth of the vote. Finns complained that between 1991 and 1994 they had suffered an economic crisis, yet had paid back all their debts. Why shouldn't Greece do the same?

Like a tribe on the savanna, Europe had admitted a cheater into its midst, one whose lying seemed rooted in character. But unlike an ancient tribe, it couldn't easily expel the freeloader. The act would be so disruptive that most were loathe to risk it, and in fact the only course seemed to be *helping* the cheater. Yet we aren't wired that way. We find it hard to even tolerate free-riders, much less reward them—even if we ultimately benefit.

So leaders moved cautiously. In March 2010 the IMF tentatively decided to give Greece €22 billion, and soon it was contemplating €30 billion. Then it reconsidered again. In early May, it gave Greece a three-year loan of €110 billion, but as part of the payback the nation had to reduce its grasping public sector, curb government spending, actually enforce tax laws, trim its pension and healthcare systems, and open up markets for produce and labor.

Austerity seemed a win-win response to a moral problem like Greece. Indeed, if Athens collected its taxes, citizens in Marseilles and Hamburg wouldn't have to pay to support it. The public sector was a black hole that afflicted Greeks and all of Europe. Freer markets would let its economy churn out more wealth. Europe was offering rehab. Everyone would benefit.

But that's when the protests began.

The second moral problem was Greece itself. It's easier to get a nation to change its policies than its habits.

The Greeks dallied with these reforms, and by April 2011, despite global wrath, the circus continued. If you were an official working with Papandreou, you got 16 monthly checks per year instead of 12—and some public employees took home 18. Public functionaries received bonuses for showing up on time or washing their hands. On retirement, each member of Parliament still pocketed €250,000. The loan of May 2010 was paying for it all.

Not surprisingly, the first loan proved insufficient. So on October 26–27, 2011, Eurozone nations approved a write-down of 50 percent on private holdings of Greek debt—if you'd bought $100 of Greek bonds, they were now worth only $50—as well as €130 billion in loans and other contributions to shore up the national balance sheet. The riots that stunned doorman Arvanitis occurred after the Greek Parliament okayed this deal.

Why did the Greeks react with such vehemence?

First, austerity directly damaged many. Again, one quarter of all employees were on government payrolls, and if you learned you were going to lose your bribes, perks, 18-months-per-year salary, and other treats, you might take to the streets too. In 2001 one million people had demonstrated when the government tried to tweak the corrupt pension system. This time, it seemed, one out of five civil servants was going to get fired.

Austerity also wounded almost everyone indirectly. As economists know, it can be a recipe for deflation. The Greek government had to lay off workers into a recession, and while it had plenty to shed, they swelled the unemployment ranks. They began collecting benefits from government, further draining its coffers. Since fewer people had jobs, the population spent less, and the economy shrank further. Tax-paying businesses saw revenues slide and some folded, so more layoffs occurred, and the effects rippled through society. It's the classic vicious circle of recession: a nation spends less and earns less, spends less and earns less, and winds up digging its own hole.

By mid-2012 Greece claimed it had cut government salaries and pensions by up to 50 percent, but it still wasn't balancing its books. Meanwhile, austerity still hadn't reduced the corruption. It had only reduced the price of bribes. Government officials were charging less because citizens couldn't afford more.

Greeks were suffering, yet they seemed unwilling to take the blame for their plight. In a Pew survey of 9,108 European citizens in eight countries, most cited the Germans as the hardest working—but the Greeks named themselves. Greeks were also among the bitterest critics of the EU, which their nation had bilked for so long.

So austerity had backfired. Greece remained a stewpot of self-interest and distrust, and it was less and less able to pay its debts. What went wrong? How could smart EU policy makers have made such a mistake?

The answer is that austerity can work. For instance, it had succeeded in Latvia. After eight years of robust growth, Latvia's economy shrank by 18 percent in 2008, and its GDP dropped 10.5 percent in the last quarter alone when the shock of the panic sent the small nation into a tailspin. In May 2009 inflation reached 17.9 percent. Its government asked the IMF and EU for a bailout of €7.5 billion and got it. Austerity led to the same downward cycle as in Greece. But Latvia popped out of it, and quickly. By early 2010 Latvia was enjoying growth again, and in 2011 it grew at 5.5 percent. In the 1990s austerity had also succeeded, and for similar reasons, in Finland and Sweden. EU officials thought the policy would work in Greece too, and elsewhere.

Why didn't it?

Austerity revived Latvia for a variety of reasons, but one key was the nation's openness to—indeed, dependence on—foreign trade and money. Its banks were largely foreign owned and outsider demand was crucial. In contrast, 85 percent of the profits of Greek industry generally came from within Greece itself. It was much more of a cloistered system. So prices fell, but spending fell too—and buyers from other nations didn't rush in to scoop up value. The fall continued.

And then there was the euro.

The euro had brought genuine advantages to Europe. It had ended the transaction costs of currency exchange and made prices comparable throughout the

Eurozone. Of course, there was a trade-off. It put individual nations like Greece in a straitjacket. Non-euro Latvia could let its currency drop in value, so its goods grew inexpensive to international purchasers, and they returned to buy. At the same time, imported goods got costlier for Latvians, encouraging them to spend more domestically. But the single currency deprived Greece and other euro nations of this strategy. It locked them into the exchange rate of the whole.

The tale in Greece was simply the most bizarre and spectacular of those in Europe and its implications the most worrisome. There the government was cheating. In other nations, the problems arose from the banks. But in all cases the problem boiled down to one source: easy money.

A bubble.

The easy money began the 1990s, and perhaps before, as global wealth grew and the 1992 Maastricht Treaty boded well for Europe's future. When the euro debuted, lenders assumed that loans across the Eurozone were all equally safe or at least that nations on the margin would soon have a standard of living like that in Britain and France. So banks throughout Europe could get loans at almost the same rate as those in solid Germany, and everyone dipped a cup into the sweet-scented vat.

It was as if someone handed out low-interest loans freely to a group of friends and watched to see what they would do with it. One person—Greece—spent it and lied about it. The rest invested it, but followed different paths. Let's take a look at three nations that fell from heyday into an abyss deeper and more frightening than they could ever have imagined.

Iceland

In 1970 Jan Morris wrote of Reykjavik: "The stink of the fish factory at the end of the quay hovers perpetually over that end of town—'Mm,' say the Icelanders appreciatively. 'The money-smell.'" By the mid-2000s the money-smell was money itself. It was everywhere. Porsches filled the streets, and people who a century ago often lived in sod houses now built summer retreats. The stock market was one long upward joyride. If you had bought an average Icelandic share in 2002, it would have been worth 10 times more in 2008. Banking assets ballooned to over seven times GDP, and one bank flush with cash even considered building a city from scratch, right next to an existing one.

Iceland looked like a wonderland of economic savvy, but its wizards were really just launderers of tainted Wall Street products. Iceland's banks offered depositors in the United Kingdom, the Netherlands, and beyond an irresistible deal: interest rates 1–2 percent higher than they could get at home, with a sense of complete safety. The deposits were backed by AAA-rated securities and seemed to have EU government insurance. The money poured in and funds became so easy to get that brewers and shippers opened banks. As they borrowed more and more from overseas lenders, cash flooded the tiny isle. Foreign loans paid for Armani suits in boardrooms and Louis Roederer Cristal Brut at nightclubs. The bank that contemplated building a city was intoxicated on outside loans.

Then came the crash of 2008. The AAA securities turned out to be creations like CDOs squared, worth very little, and EU insurance had been vaporous all along. The three major banks collapsed, and the nation seemed at the edge of bankruptcy.

Now Iceland had to find an escape from the trap. The government lacked the money to bail out its gargantuan banks, and they weren't too crucial to fail. Hence despite international protests, Iceland let them die and hung the losses around the necks of lenders and depositors.

The bankruptcies cleared away the debris and reallocated all the resources, so the economy could move ahead. The value of the króna, the national currency, plunged by half, but just as in Latvia that drop made its exports more appealing internationally and boosted trade. The IMF and other nations also loaned Iceland $5 billion, or 40 percent of its GDP. Hence Iceland began recovering fairly quickly. By 2012 its unemployment had fallen to 6.3 percent, and immigrants were seeking its jobs. But the money-smell came from the fish once more.

Ireland

The Emerald Isle was a land of misery for centuries. In 1845, before the Great Famine, a British royal commission found the condition of the average Irish home almost beyond description. "A bed or blanket is a rare luxury," it said, "and nearly in all their pig and a manure heap constitute their sole property." Yet after 2000 the average Dublin home sold for as much as one in Beverly Hills. The Irish were riding dizzy prosperity. In terms of GDP per capita, Ireland was richer than Britain, Germany, and even the United States. Reversing the trend of centuries, Irish immigrants began flocking home for jobs. In *Ulysses*, James Joyce's Stephen Daedalus famously complained, "History is a nightmare from which I am trying to awake," and now Ireland had fully woken up and it was grinning. It was the Celtic Tiger.

But as in Iceland, the nation was like a roller coaster on the crest before the plunge. Irish banks had heavily financed a real estate bubble that was, in percentage increase, bigger than that in the United States. For example, in 2006 Irish companies built over 90,000 new homes, twice as many as the nation needed, and this kind of construction amounted to over 12 percent of the Irish economy. Indeed, Ireland gave tax breaks to the free-spending property developers, and they occupied the same slot as the subprime borrowers in the United States.

By the summer of 2008, the real estate bubble was collapsing, and Irish banks began suffering. After Lehman Brothers folded, the withdrawals commenced. On September 29, 2008, the price of bank shares took a sickening dive, with the scandal-tainted Anglo Irish Bank falling by 45 percent. Panic spread, and late that night, bankers held an emergency meeting with top government officials. The next day the Irish state announced it was shouldering the debts of the six major banks. That is, citizens would pay for all the unneeded, half-built homes littering Eire, and the government in an astonishing attempt at consolation referred to "specific terms and conditions so that the taxpayers' interest can be protected."

At once, the annual Irish budget deficit swelled to 32 percent of GDP, more than twice the Greek figure that had shocked the EU. Many have questioned whether Irish officials acted too quickly or fully understood the extent of the obligation. Others have been blunter. Early in October 2010, the entire front page of the Irish *Daily Star* read: "Ireland RIP," and below it: "Our Future Killed by Wanker Bankers and Stupid Politicians."

Ireland's strategy was patently unsustainable, and in November 2010 the EU gave it an €67.5 billion rescue package, on which the Irish people would have to pay about 5.7 percent annual interest. Austerity measures included spending cuts, the firing of 25,000 public employees, and tax hikes, and in 2011 there was an uptick in the economy. However, by 2012 unemployment had risen to 14.9 percent, and young Irish workers were once more leaving the country. Ghost estates pocked the landscape. Some 1,850 housing developments lay unfinished, and 240,000 homes were vacant in a nation of 4.5 million people. Economists estimated that Ireland would owe a total of €68 billion, or €19,000 for every man, woman, and child. Joyce was long gone, but Peggy Nolan, mayor of Longford village, summed up the situation: "The people that bought into a dream inherited a nightmare."

Spain

Spain once bestrode the world, but kingly misrule and the Franco dictatorship had dropped it far behind northern Europe. Yet by the 2000s bulldozers were leveling ground for construction everywhere, especially by the sunny Mediterranean, where hotels and retirement apartment towers were lining the beaches. Cranes also loomed over Madrid and architectural spectacles sprang up, such as Frank Gehry's Guggenheim Museum in Bilbao. In 2006 Spain consumed half the cement in the EU, and its housing starts exceeded those in Germany, Italy, France, and the United Kingdom put together. Indeed, the "Iberian Tiger" was the biggest job creator in the Eurozone. Some began referring to a new "Armada Invencible," or Spanish Armada: Its economic savants.

But here too the boom rose on easy money. In fact, the ECB would in essence pay people to take its cash. In 2006, inflation was 4.0 percent, but interest from the ECB was 2.75 percent. So you could take out a loan, buy random stuff, resell it a year later at a 4.0 percent higher price, repay the loan, and end up with 1.25 percent more than you started with. It's hard to resist such easy money, and most of it went into buying real estate, amplifying the boom. With repayment almost an afterthought, loans poured in. One giant receptacle was a dark pool of subprime loans. They lay in the regional S&Ls called *cajas*, which accounted for about half of Spain's banking system. The *cajas* often lent to small borrowers whom the regular bank system avoided as bad risks. Moreover, since these S&Ls were largely free of oversight, they could conceal enormous questionable loans. No one knew what they were doing.

The frenzy peaked in 2007 when construction accounted for 13 percent of all employment. Then the regulated banks sensed trouble and slowed funding to the sector, but the *cajas* filled the void. By 2009 they owned 56 percent of the country's mortgages. And their financial status and the depth of their involvement in real estate were only then becoming clear to the government.

In that same year the housing market crashed, and the construction industry suddenly owed billions. Spain bailed out its first *caja* in March 2009. This act spooked investors and bank stocks plunged. As in Ireland, a run soon ensued. Depositors withdrew €21.6 billon in the first four months of 2010, putting even more stress on the banks and inducing the government to bail out more of them.

Like Greece, Spain was locked into the euro and couldn't depreciate its currency. So its government began imposing austerity in 2010, and in mid-year the Bank of Spain estimated that the total exposure of banks in real estate alone was around €180.8 billion. As government spending and the demand for homes ebbed, unemployment rose to 10 percent. Citizens now paid less in taxes while tapping government benefits more, and the economy spiraled downward. From a budget surplus of 2 percent of GDP, Spain soon had a deficit of close to 4 percent.

By 2012 unemployment had risen to 24 percent, a rate close to that in the United States during the Great Depression. In early June 2012, Spain asked the EU to lend it money. Prime Minister Mariano Rajoy, elected on a pledge to cut taxes, depicted the plan as a relatively painless "victory" for Spain. About a month later, he revealed the details of the austerity program: A €65 billion package of tax hikes and spending cuts, reduction of unemployment and housing benefits, shrinkage of regional governments, closures of state-owned companies, a 3 percent jump in the value-added tax to 21 percent, and the privatization of ports, airports, and railroads. Rajoy's negatives instantly soared 20 percent in the polls.

After centuries, of empire, Spain became a shell because it confused gold with wealth. It never developed the diversified export economy that appeared in Britain and the Netherlands, so it had to trade its limited gold for their limitless goods. Modern Spain had a sclerotic labor market and, like Iceland and Ireland, it built its castle with the fool's gold of easy money. But it also focused too little on its export economy. Housing, after all, serves mainly domestic demand, and as Spain's citizens grew poorer there was no one to revive its world.

*   *   *

Bubbles always seem well-camouflaged, but Europe's was particularly hard to spot because it wore a different disguise in each country. The result was a potpourri of disasters that economists now call Europe's sovereign debt crisis. Even so, the bubble has many parallels to the events in the United States. In both the United States and Europe there was basic misappraisal, in the United States (and little Iceland) of CDOs and in Europe generally of the credit risk in certain nations. In both, ratings or enforcement agencies could have stopped the bubbles but didn't. And in both, the euphoria was widespread. From the wine bars of Reykjavik to the cabanas of the Costa del Sol, people reveled in the rise of wealth all around, unaware of the swelling vacancy inside that caused it.

The Greek fraud seemed to jolt lenders awake. If *that* could happen, what else was going on? By early 2010, markets finally realized that all Eurozone nations were not equally good risks. Moreover, though Greece resembled Enron and the liar loan recipients, it also resembled AIG. It was interconnected, and its failure could harm other nations. So interest rates began climbing in Greece, Spain, and Italy. As fear spread, the rates brought Spain and Italy to dangerous levels. For instance, the interest on Italian government bonds rose from under 4 percent in April 2010 to over 7 percent in November 2011. Nations already weakened by austerity had to pay much more every year for money. And most analysts deem 7 percent too much in the long haul.

One problem here is competing notions of fairness. German taxpayers think it unfair to foot the bill not just for Greeks but Irish and Spaniards as well. This attitude parallels the reluctance in the United States to bail out underwater mortgage holders. It's their fault, Germans say. The Spanish had a duty to watch over the *cajas*, for instance. The Germans view fairness as proportional: The better performers should get better rewards.

On the other hand, citizens of nations with the derogatory nickname PIIGS— Portugal, Ireland, Italy, Greece, and Spain—think it unfair for them to endure crippling unemployment and shredded safety nets to repay rich neighbors who have profited from the status quo. They view the proportion here as too extreme, and they may also feel that inequality is inequity. Moreover, most are not at fault as individuals. If a decent, law-abiding Spaniard has to root through dumpsters for the food her family needs, she is suffering a punishment meted out too broadly. She belongs to the wrong tribe, but it's poor consolation if her kids are crying.

Overall, this is a tale of moral hazard. That's often a threat when group union is incomplete: Some semi-integrated members will be tempted to take advantage of the rest. The EU rather resembled the 13 colonies under the Articles of Confederation, when each consulted its own interests first. The Continental Congress could not collect taxes and had no control over foreign or interstate trade, and threats from abroad grew as each state negotiated with nations on its own. The problems were clear from the start, especially after Shays' Rebellion in 1786. The new nation largely solved them with the Constitution of 1787, which imposed much stronger federal authority on the group.

Europe needs either a tighter or looser union. It needs effective enforcement bodies or a partial breakup so nations can respond to trouble with measures like currency devaluation.

How can the EU grow more united? Economist Joshua Aizenman suggests several steps. To overcome the political problem in Germany, leaders must mete out direct punishment, the kind of thing that shows taxpayers that new reforms are serious and that the EU won't tolerate freeloaders.

Step One, he suggests: Punish Greece. Europe can suspend Greece's membership in the euro (though not the EU) and force it back to the drachma. Once Greece enters this penalty box, its sovereign debt will lose most of its face value, as the bond markets already anticipate, and thus it will get easier to repay. Moreover, Greeks must stop blaming outsiders, and they're more likely to do so on their own, outside the euro. In addition, the lure of potential return to the Eurozone will give them a carrot, and encourage them to tax the wealthy, balance the budget, and reform rigid labor markets. At the same time, the EU and ECB can provide aid over a five-year transition to economic health, such as food stamps for people who fall out of the middle class. The EU also needs fiscal reforms. A Euro-FDIC would stabilize banking, if it had regulatory bite. It would need tax money behind it to be credible, perhaps 2–3 percent of Europe's GDP.

This approach could also work for other troubled countries, like Portugal. Most importantly, it would put in place the essential missing piece: an enforcement device that doesn't backfire on the EU itself and that ultimately helps nations grow more prosperous. Perhaps, he also suggests, Europe should find its way with evolutionary mechanisms. No one can predict the future here, so instead of imposing policies without knowing if they'll work, it should test options and cultivate the successes.

That's an approach worked in China.

6

China: Morals and the Rush to Wealth

In 1976, China seemed in ruins. The ten years of strife called the Cultural Revolution had torn society apart, turning kids against parents, emptying schools and universities, and paralyzing the national government. The economy was a wasteland, and both the United States and the Soviet Union seemed poised to take advantage. Yet somehow the Chinese Communist Party (CCP) managed to renew itself and put China on a path of astonishing economic growth.

Since 1978, China has tipped the economic axis of the earth. It now has the world's second largest economy, and it is a dominant force in international trade. China's poverty rate—the fraction of her people living on less than $1 a day—fell from 50 percent in 1978 to less than 7 percent now, lifting half a billion people from the depths. The world has never seen development at this scale and speed.

How did China do it? Not by following textbook prescriptions on economic development. The CCP meddles in the economy constantly, corruption is rife, and the rule of law is weak. With these handicaps, how could China possibly have created so much wealth?

Rapid economic change often brings difficulties in its wake, and China's growth has raised a great cloud of moral problems. They start with dispossession and include a two-tier caste system and poisoned environments. How are its people coping? And what are their prospects for a better future?

For perspective, we begin further back.

In AD 1000, China had the world's most advanced civilization, and more than a quarter of its population. Peasants irrigated fields in the great floodplains of the Yangtze, Hwang He (Yellow), and other east-west rivers. The thousand-mile Grand Canal ran from Beijing and Kaifeng in the north to Hangzhou in the south, linking the nation's five largest rivers. This network of watery highways cut the cost of trade, as in Uruk and Greece, and unified China's economy and often its government as well. China's infrastructure also included the world's first civil service, which drew talent from the entire kingdom.

But by 1900 China still hadn't modernized. Qing emperors had ruled since 1644, and they sucked life from the economy. By the 1800s Western traders dominated China's coastal cities, and by the 1920s the emperor was gone, replaced by a patchwork of feuding warlords. Meanwhile, Japan had gone through its own Great Transformation, and its economy and military were burgeoning. It attacked China before World War II, and the Chinese Communist Party (CCP) helped battle the invaders. Its rebel army played a key role in beating back the Japanese as World War II wound down, and afterward it swept aside the warlords and then the Nationalist government, which fled to Taiwan.

By 1950, the CCP controlled the entire Chinese mainland, and had to figure out how to rule. Although the military remained large and important, the CCP itself became China's only political institution and also its sole moral authority. Ancient theocracies had fused these two roles, but modern states seldom did.

As a political institution, the CCP ruled top down. Mao Zedong issued edicts to his trusted lieutenants, who passed orders down to provincial party leaders. They in turn commanded the city, county, town, and village party cadres, who exerted tight control over all ordinary citizens.

The CCP's other role, ideological and moral, was equally important. Most of China's citizens at that time had known nothing but hardship and sacrifice for their families. The CCP told them—and they accepted with little apparent resistance—what was good, what was bad, and who needed forcible "reeducation."

Surviving ex-warlords, of course, had already fled to Taiwan, but lots of minor landlords remained. The party seized their property in the name of the Chinese people. Private property was deemed inherently bad, so the party confiscated private enterprises and turned them into state-owned enterprises (SOEs). The party also seized the farmland where most of China's half a billion people then lived and divided it into communes, each typically comprising several hundred families. Commune members, under the direction of the local CCP cell, were to share the farm labor and turn over the entire harvest to local authorities for redistribution. It echoed our ancestors' sharing on the savanna, but on vast scale and under compulsion from a dictator.

In 1945 Mao had written, "Our point of departure is to serve the people wholeheartedly and never for a moment divorce ourselves from the masses, to proceed in all cases from the interests of the people and not from one's self-interest or from the interests of a small group." He was articulating a level of selflessness never before seen in rulers, and by 1957 he was publicly complaining: "A dangerous tendency has shown itself of late among many of our personnel—an unwillingness to share the joys and hardships of the masses, a concern for personal fame and gain. This is very bad." It was the old problem: lack of negative reinforcement from below. He proposed to solve it with negative reinforcement from above, by demoting selfish officials, but he himself remained immune from this kind of corrective.

In 1958 Mao launched the Great Leap Forward, intended as a fast track to industrialization and true socialist living. But the Leap went backward. Massive investment in inefficient technology and strict enforcement of commune rules led to sharp drops in output, and famine spread through much of China. At a closed-door meeting in Shanghai on March 25, 1959, the minutes indicate Mao said, "When there is not enough to eat, people starve to death. It is better to let half of the people die so that the other half can eat their fill." From 30 to 45 million people did die before Mao ended the Leap in 1961. After that, pragmatists like Deng Xiaoping took an increasing role in daily decisions, and Mao felt power slipping from his hands.

In 1966 Mao struck back with the Cultural Revolution. This time he recruited fanatical young people to join the Red Guards, and encouraged them to turn on their parents and to arrest even high-ranking CCP officials who seemed insufficiently hard-line. One of those imprisoned was Bo Yibo. Yibo had joined the CCP a few years after its inception, and by the end of World War II he was a top commander in Mao's army. He later became China's finance minister, the chairman of the State Planning Commission, and Mao's swimming partner. Now he survived years of torture by virtue of his determination and charisma, and some luck. His wife died in captivity, but their four children—including Bo Xilai—all survived.

Another revolutionary stalwart, General Gu Jingsheng, also suffered during the Cultural Revolution. He had foreseen imprisonment and wrote his daughters, "Don't be threatened by the door-knocking and confiscations during the night, and don't be misled by the neighborhood children [if they accuse us]." Both he and his wife were indeed accused of being rightist deviants and spent years in jail, while the state pulled the daughters out of school and set them to work to "learn from the people." One of them, Gu Kailai, swept the floor of a textile factory and served as a butcher's assistant.

The Cultural Revolution shut many of China's ministries, and virtual civil war broke out in many provinces. The basic tasks of managing the economy devolved to provincial or even county governments.

This national self-mutilation finally ended a few weeks after Mao died in 1976. A coup d'état took place, and the new leaders arrested Mao's heirs, the famous Gang of Four. By 1978 Deng Xiaoping had claimed the CCP's top position. He brought back Bo Yibo and other old comrades, who became known as the Eight Immortals after a band of Taoist deities.

The Tournament of Riches

The devastation of the Cultural Revolution had undermined the legitimacy of the CCP—only communist illuminati could see how chaos served "the people"—so Deng and the Immortals had to forge a new social compact right away. Their first priority was to maintain the CCP monopoly on political power while changing its style. There would be no more personality cults but rather collective decision making by the party elite. The second priority, crucial to support the monopoly of power but also crucial in its own right, was rapid economic development. Now presented as the quintessence of socialism, modernization would restore the party's legitimacy and prevent the developed world from reasserting dominance over China.

But how can a communist regime spur economic growth?

The textbook prescription calls for the creation of secure property rights, removal of government from the business sector, fighting government corruption, and opening up the financial system.

China did none of these things. To the contrary, government officials are at least as corrupt as they have ever been, and the central authorities have kept tight reins on the financial system and a firm grip on all economic levers. China's courts were late in acknowledging property rights and are still quite lax in their enforcement. Nor has China privatized most of the largest state-owned enterprises.

What is going on? Since 1950, the real competition in China has always been for advancement in the party. The difference since 1978 is that the competition has focused on economic performance. That is, the CCP decided to run a contest.

Regional authorities at all levels—province, city, town, and village—had already been making economic decisions during the upheaval of the Cultural Revolution, but now the CCP encouraged them to experiment with new ideas. The officials who spurred the most growth won promotions, and the least successful lost their jobs. This novel form of competition and experimentation, some scholars believe, has been the true engine of China's growth.

Consider the Household Responsibility System (HRS), a Chinese version of land reform. It took the commune's land and food production quota and contracted it out to individual households. That is, small farmers could make decisions on their own and sell into the market. The bland name barely disguised its bold violation of Maoist principles, so it was introduced very quietly in the late 1970s in villages like Xioagang in Anhui province. Due to relatively weak cross-jurisdiction ties and decentralized authority, the local officials collaborating with provincial-level reformers were able to prevent sabotage from the many enemies of reform.

Results were so good that the village CCP bosses and their patrons at higher levels all got promotions. They moved to top positions in different counties and provinces and, with suitable adaptations to deal with local political and economic conditions, they spread the HRS to new locations. Once again, crop yields skyrocketed. Hard-line Maoists gazed at the cartloads of fresh produce and softened their criticism. More local officials adopted HRS, early adopters got second promotions, and by 1984 it was common throughout China, greatly boosting the national food supply.

The contrast with the Soviet Union is instructive. The USSR was far more centralized than China. The Kremlin presumed godlike knowledge of the economy, and even where it admitted ignorance, it rarely encouraged or rewarded good ideas. So insights seldom moved up the chain—especially when they flouted dogma. The top didn't learn and ultimately didn't seem to care. The Kremlin also presumed that its command structure could effectively regulate the myriad parts. Issue an edict, and people will obey. But the system got in the way. It was interlocked, hard to move, and hence hard to change by fiat. Beginning in 1985, Gorbachev attempted land reforms, among other things, but reform required close coordination among national ministries. One ministry in Moscow had to reallocate fertilizer quotas, another ministry had to approve the construction of more silos to collect and store the crops, yet another ministry dealt with farm equipment, and so on. The reforms brought disappointing results, due in part to the top-down information flow and the unwieldy structure, but perhaps in greater part due to lack of motivation by some key players.

In China, land reform was just the start. Hundreds of other experiments took place, and most failed in the pilot phase. But Special Economic Zones (SEZ) turned out to be a second big hit. In 1980, the sleepy coastal town of Shenzhen was declared an SEZ, along with three others in Guangdong and Fujian provinces. The local authorities offered unusual enticements—such as convincing guarantees of property rights—for foreign direct investment in export-oriented industry. The experiment expanded in 1984 to another 14 cities and went national in the early 1990s, launching China as a (or the) world power in exports of manufactured goods. Again, the tournament approach blunted strong national opposition. The experiment stayed small until its initiators worked out the bugs, and then governmental entrepreneurs clamored to try it in their own regions. Entrepreneurship was needed because each locale had to solve problems such as which specific goods they could profitably manufacture with which foreign partners, whether to market their goods mainly domestically or to specific foreign markets, and how find enough of the right kind of workers.

The early career of Bo Yibo's son Xilai illustrates the process. Bo Xilai survived his imprisonment during the Cultural Revolution, and when the elite universities in Beijing reopened, he enrolled. He graduated with a master's in international journalism in 1982, and for the next two years he worked in research departments at CCP headquarters in Beijing. With guidance from his father, Bo lobbied for a job in the provinces, and in 1984 he became deputy party secretary of Jin County in northern Liaoning Province. He associated himself with successful economic development at every stage and hence rose quickly through the ranks.

However, friction developed between Bo Xilai and his wife, the daughter of a high party official, and she returned to Beijing with their son. But Bo didn't stay lonely for long. General Gu Jingsheng's daughter Kailai, the butcher's assistant during the Cultural Revolution, visited Liaoning Province on a field trip from Beijing University and found a way to meet the rising CCP princeling. Bo Xilai and Gu Kailai married in 1986, and their lone child, Guagua, was born a year later.

Meanwhile, Bo's career moved ahead nicely. He was promoted to the governing council of the Economic and Technological Development Zone of the province's second largest city, Dalian. He then rose to the governing council of the city itself, became its mayor in 1992, and a few years later its party boss as well. At that point he could do pretty much anything he wanted in Dalian, but he knew that further advancement depended entirely on his success in boosting economic growth.

How did Bo use his power? According to an article in *Bloomberg Business Week*, this "suave, charming" man "transformed the drab, unassuming port into a cosmopolitan showcase for foreign investment and tourism. He also gave a boost to small business," attracting investors from South Korea, Japan, and the West. To make room for modern office and apartment buildings, Bo bulldozed the old neighborhoods and moved their residents, willing or not, to the edge of town.

In 1997, with his father's backing and his wife's support, Bo campaigned publicly for appointment to the Central Committee, but he met resistance and lost.

Some resented his funneling of provincial resources into Dalian, others opposed his faction, and still others just disliked the appearance of nepotism. But this setback was hardly permanent. In 2001, a corruption scandal involving the governor of Liaoning Province conveniently erupted, and Bo stepped into the job. There, he put into place a three-province regional plan for industrial development, again featuring export-oriented foreign direct investment. A year later, in 2002, he gained a high-profile cabinet post as China's secretary of commerce. He continued to seek investment from abroad, but at the same time he found ways to shield China's domestic firms from direct foreign competition.

Behind the rise of men like Bo Xilai stood several other successful experiments. For example, in the early 1980s, bloated, money-losing state-owned enterprises (SOEs) weighed on the economies of many provinces. In the early 1990s, experiments with bankruptcy reform showed how to wind down doomed SOEs and straighten out those that could succeed. By 2004 the problem had faded.

Another late-1980s experiment led to creation of Township-Village Enterprises (TVEs)—sort of like halfway houses between private companies and SOEs. They let startup firms have access to labor and capital, and gave local governments an entrepreneurial stake that shielded the firms from expropriation. Officials experimented with incentive contracts in TVEs, and they spread those that worked well, such as higher marginal profit retention and medium-term contracts. Disciplined by regional competition, many TVEs prospered and their CCP patrons got promoted.

More recently, since the mid-1990s, access to private labor and capital markets improved, and most of the successful TVEs went private. Under the tutelage of party patrons like Bo Xilai, the pattern now in some ways resembles Germany's Mittelstand or Italy's Prado: networks of specialist firms clustering around a local industry such as toys or textiles. A legacy of the TVEs is that local government is part of the mix and acts as a facilitator, helping the cluster compete with clusters in other locales.

Yet corruption abounds. As in Russia, CCP officials can rig privatization to favor cronies and get huge kickbacks. Start-ups need patrons in government to get a foothold and stay ahead of rivals, and clusters offer untold opportunities to funnel favors. The CCP has not placed a high priority on resisting these lures, and by the usual measures China is far more corrupt than most developed countries. In 2011, China ranked 75th of 178 countries in Transparency International's Corruption Perceptions Index. Brazil, whose official extortion is legendary, was 73rd.

What is surprising is that China's massive corruption has had such a small impact on its growth rate. Moral questions aside, economists think of corruption as analogous to a very inefficient tax, a hungry parasite that keeps the economy bedridden. But the secret was simple: CCP officials had a strong self-interest in both corruption *and* economic success. In post-1978 China, if extortion slowed local economic growth, officials didn't get promoted and could expect less future pelf. So they sought the salient qualities of Lee Kuan Yew as well as Boss Tweed.

Bo Xilai again is a case in point. He made cities and provinces thrive, but he had another side. Journalist Jiang Weiping had broken the corruption story that unseated Liaoning's provincial governor and gave Bo this position. A few years later, Jiang accused Bo himself of shielding corrupt cronies. Police soon arrested Jiang on trumped-up charges, and a judge sentenced him to eight years in jail. International pressure got him sprung after five, but by then Bo had moved on to Beijing. There, his wife Gu Kailai opened a law firm that quickly became very lucrative due to her connections and aggressive marketing. They raised their son Guagua in great luxury, which increased in 2007 when Bo became party chief of Chongqing. They sent Guagua to some of England's most exclusive schools where, by all accounts, the youth indulged a fondness for sports cars and partying. The family clearly had cash flows far beyond the modest official salary of a party chief.

China's grand growth tournament was novel, but few things under the sun are utterly new. If Europe rose through a kind of natural selection, China rose through what Darwin called "artificial selection": People choose the propagators instead of nature, as in tulip breeding. China's tournament in some ways also resembled competition in large multinational corporations, like Exxon or Citicorp, where top corporate managers set the ground rules, and the middle managers vie for promotion by trying to increase profits faster than their rivals. Of course, there are differences. For instance, the corporate climbers usually face greater constraints from market competition and the rule of law.

Nor is China's growth path completely different from Japan's since 1868 and South Korea's since 1965. Like these now-rich countries, China began with land reform, and its growth was mainly self-financed. China's investment rates for the last 35 years reached even higher levels than theirs, roughly half of GDP, sustained by savings rates of roughly the same size. Productivity has also soared, spurred by purchase of modern (or even ultramodern) manufacturing equipment combined with China's vast supply of diligent semiskilled workers. We'll see later that the labor force is now changing rapidly in China, much of it becoming highly educated and skilled.

Japan and Korea also developed unique forms of industrial competition managed by their governments. Government ministries identified the bottlenecks and key technologies and offered subsidies to firms that most successfully adapted Western technology and ideas to local conditions. In these countries, though, the competition was more by industry than by region, and the winners formed families of firms called *keiretsu* in Japan, like Mitsubishi and Toyota, and *jaebol* in Korea, like Samsung and Hyundai. As in China, the government sheltered chosen industries from foreign competition until they could compete in world markets.

In China, as in these other countries, the government built financial walls that kept interest rates artificially low on domestic deposits and (for many years) prevented ordinary savers from earning higher returns abroad. Despite the low interest, households in China (as earlier in Japan and Korea) saved a huge fraction of their earnings. Two powerful reasons for China's high savings rate were rapidly rising incomes and the lack (until quite recently) of a social safety net outside the old SOEs.

Does the Chinese model have any weaknesses? Certainly it required conditions seldom seen elsewhere, including vast numbers of semiautonomous towns and villages (about 42,000), counties (2,900), cities (333), and provincial-level units (31). Hence, the model doesn't work for smaller countries like South Korea, or large centralized countries like Russia. And autonomy is only partial. The tournament naturally led in the 1980s to moves that favored local growth at harm to national growth—such as hoarding key local resources like silk and coal—and forced Beijing to intervene. These autarkic tendencies seem to have faded as local markets have become more integrated with world markets.

The Moral Whipsaw

The path to modernity always changes morals, but we have never seen a back-and-forth as dizzying as that in China. Older citizens today remember the weak and corrupt Nationalist government headed by Jiang Jiesh (also written "Chiang Kai-Shek"), and the often hypocritical neo-Confucian ethics it preached, urging deference to authorities and noblesse oblige for the rich and powerful.

Then, after 1950, the CCP sought to flip this structure upside down. Morality now came from below, ostensibly from peasants and workers, but via the mouthpiece of Chairman Mao and his party. Especially during the Cultural Revolution, stigma poured down on rich peasants and businessmen. The state reeducated them, redistributed their property to itself in the name of "the people," and encouraged children to betray their own parents if they didn't fully adhere to the socialist ideology.

Then in 1978, Deng decreed, "Poverty is not socialism. To be rich is glorious." The fountainhead of ethics shifted from peasants to the once-reviled wealth producers, and China suffered another jolt, though this time in a better direction. For it turns out that loosening the hold on internal markets (and joining the world economy) is very good at promoting growth and well-being.

At the same time, the CCP continued to suppress every alternative moral authority. It still insists on appointing its own religious leaders, such as Tibetan lamas and Catholic bishops. It threatens evangelical Christians and members of Falun Gong with jail and beatings. China spends a huge share of its resources on internal security, and it blocks YouTube and social media like Facebook which might spread embarrassing information.

Yet other major moral problems have arisen simply from China's all-out dash for growth. When people or nations compete intensely in one dimension, they often neglect others, and may even launch a race to the bottom. In China, the dangerous imbalance has led to forced uprooting of peasants, a rigid new class structure with widening inequality, environmental havoc, neglect of long-term health and safety, and authorities' indifference to citizens.

The Developers and the Dispossessed

Let us start with forced eviction. The government (or CCP, really) owns all the land in China. Farmers just use it. So local developers can cut deals with local officials to buy real estate. They are supposed to compensate the farmers, but only for the value of lost crops. (In a competitive market system with secure property rights, of course, they'd have to pay farmers' asking price.) So peasants get dispossessed and often cheated of much of their already-meager compensation, and typically they are relocated in downscale apartment complexes at the fringe of a growing metropolis. It is a modern version of England's old enclosure movement, replayed at lightning speed.

China's land regime enables rapid and relatively cheap urban growth, but it has perverse incentives. It is surely China's largest source of corruption: a developer can quickly gain millions or billions of dollars worth of property simply by convincing a few party or government officials. Kickbacks fuel the system, both secretive illegal cash payments to the officials and legal offers of partnership. The developers and officials, together with the owners of the buildings and largest businesses, have a key to join China's wealthy elite. The dispossessed know that if they protest too publicly, they risk jail and beatings by hired thugs, and they have a minuscule chance of success. Nonetheless, China has seen over 100,000 protests a year, the vast majority by uprooted farmers, villagers, and town and city residents.

For instance, consider Wukan. A sleepy fishing village of 12,000 about 80 miles east of Hong Kong, Wukan was long known for its civility and prosperity. In September 2011, developers started surveying some 1,000 acres just outside of town, startling villagers who had heard nothing about a land sale. Hundreds of townsfolk (2,000 by some accounts) protested noisily in front of the local police station, waving signs that said, "Give us back our farmland." Some were arrested, and when protests continued the next day, the village government called in riot police and the developers called in goons. Roughnecks injured even elderly villagers and reportedly killed a child. Then the provincial party chief, Wang Yang, stepped in to cool tempers. He withdrew the riot police and forced civil authorities to negotiate with representatives of the protesters.

But in December 2011, local officials arrested four of these representatives, and one, Xue Jinbo, died in custody. His relatives, after seeing his body, said he had been tortured to death. The town rioted. On December 14, local police and party officials fled, and regional authorities cordoned off the town. The siege ended December 20 when Wang Yang again intervened and promised quick and free elections. On February 11, 2012, Wukan voters overwhelmingly rejected the local party chair of 42 years, and replaced him and his cronies with protest leaders, including Xue's daughter Jianwan. The developers left town.

Wukan is a rare counterexample; the dispossession almost always goes forward. Local governments rely heavily on fees from developers, and of course officials' careers depend on rapid economic growth.

The example with the highest profile is Beijing's Olympic Park. Before China's bid to host the 2008 Olympic Games, the site, roughly one square mile at the northern edge of the city, was a mix of nondescript recent apartments, office buildings, and older residential neighborhoods. To make way for new construction (including subway lines and ring roads), the government relocated an estimated 1.25 million people, but public protests were few. Workers cleared the ground, and in early 2005 construction began on the major buildings, such as the famous "bird's nest" track stadium and the "swim cube." Developers and their patrons surely made huge profits from the $43 billion officially spent preparing Beijing for the Olympics, but the country got a return on its investment. Beijing now has a world-class public transit system, and the Olympic Village brings real pride to vast numbers of Chinese tourists who visit it every year.

The No-Permit Underclass

The two-caste system is an even more important, and underreported, side effect of rapid growth. Communism promised economic leveling, but China has now created an urban underclass of perhaps a quarter of a billion people. These are the workers with no *hukou*, or residency permit. A holdover from the 1950s when Mao imposed it to keep peasants out of the cities, the *hukou* system denies basic public services—education, health insurance, often desirable housing—to internal immigrants and their children and even grandchildren. Workers with no *hukou* are always subject to deportation to their ancestral home village, and they are therefore exploitable. They hold the most dangerous and onerous jobs, and employers often cheat them by imposing arbitrary fees. Most of them barely earn enough to pay the rent on squalid apartments and to send a little home to help aging parents.

The no-*hukou* underclass thus faces similar but harsher restrictions than undocumented Latinos in the United States. Yet its members have the same ethnicity—Han—as the more privileged. Their parents (or grandparents) were simply born in poorer parts of the country, and they are willing to suffer discrimination for a slightly better chance to get ahead. It is possible to get a *hukou* for a new city, but successful applicants are almost always wealthy or well-connected people in desirable professions.

In August 2012, we interviewed (via an interpreter) two of the more prosperous members of China's underclass. The 27-year-old Zhang Yong (a pseudonym; he asked that we not use his real name) was especially eager to tell his story. A bachelor, he grew up in Taiyuan, in Shanxi province, where his parents still live. That city has changed greatly in the past 100 years, but it still has lots of impoverished people. It made news in September 2012 when riots erupted at dormitories housing some of the 80,000 employees of Foxconn's plant. The workers, many teenaged, complained about their employers' brutal guards, horrible food, and the dorms' filthy shared bathrooms and tiny rooms with four beds for eight people.

Zhang, our interviewee, had been eager to get out of town after graduating from a local college in 2007, and accepted a job offer that brought him to Beijing. With a friendly but intense air and an oddly unfocused gaze, he said he was not happy with his life since then. His company, a large state-owned electronics firm, pays him about $500 per month, and occasionally $700 with bonuses. That's enough to do reasonably well back in Taiyuan, but it doesn't go very far in Beijing. He lives in a company dormitory, sharing about 1,000 square feet with eight coworkers. To have good marriage prospects in Beijing, he says, he would somehow have to triple his income. What really bothers Zhang, though, is the discrimination against no-*hukou* folks like him. He has no state-supported medical insurance, housing, or access to education, and he believes his company favors locals in promotions. Zhang feels that government policies lead to too much pressure on the job and too few opportunities to go back home to visit his parents. In Beijing, despite its excellent public transportation, he feels lonely and isolated. His fondest ambition is to work his way to a well-paying job back in Taiyuan.

Zhang found us while we were interviewing Wang Jianjun (another pseudonym; he was much more forthcoming after being assured of anonymity). A jovial man of 41, Wang has sold fruit from his native Hebei province for the past several years on a busy Beijing street corner. His business brings him a very livable $1,600 per month, enough to support his wife and 16-year-old son, who often helps him but cannot legally attend local public schools. The family lives in the neighborhood, occupying about a sixth of a 1,200-square-foot apartment they share with other no-*hukou* families. He has seen the neighborhood, just outside Beijing's Fifth Ring Road, grow tremendously since he arrived, but thinks he may soon be priced out of the area. Basically, he likes living in Beijing and not having his Hebei relatives constantly asking him for financial support. Of course, the Beijing traffic and air pollution are bad, but his greatest hope is to one day get a Beijing *hukou* and maybe secure a better education for his future grandchildren.

No-*hukou* citizens like Zhang and Wang are one reason for China's huge increase in inequality, which overall mirrors its economic growth. In 1978 China's Gini coefficient was 0.28, comparable to egalitarian countries such as Finland and Denmark. (The standard measure of inequality, the Gini coefficient is zero if everyone has the same income and 1.0 if one household gets all the nation's income and everyone else gets nothing. In the real world, Ginis range from a low of 0.25 in Denmark up to the 0.60s in certain forlorn African nations.) China passed the embarrassing US figure of about 0.40 some years ago and is now probably beyond Brazil's Gini of 0.52. Thus China has gone from one of the world's most equal countries to one of its least. One study notes that rural development in China increases equality, while urban development reduces it—and China's cities have grown fast. According to another study, income differences are shrinking between regions and growing within villages and cities. As Chinese move to the cities, the wealth spectrum widens.

Clearly, the new elite, the top 1 percent, is skimming a large fraction of China's new wealth. This elite consists of entrepreneurs who help open new lines of business, as well as land developers and corrupt officials. Meanwhile, there is a vast underclass of no-*hukou* workers and their relatives in remote villages.

Rise of the Middle

In our view, however, the biggest story of China's transformation since 1978 is its burgeoning middle class. It scarcely existed in 1978, but now (depending on the measure used) it comprises at least a third and perhaps more than half the nation.

We suspect that as long as most middle-class families feel that hard work pays off, increasing inequality will not seriously destabilize China.

The story of Zhu Jun (another pseudonym) illustrates the changes China has seen over the past few decades. A lively and confident 26-year-old woman with a pageboy haircut and stylish black-frame glasses, Zhu is now poised to enter the upper end of China's prosperous professional class. But it was a long journey to get there.

Her parents were born in villages in Hebei province and grew up in huts of mud and straw. Her mother remembers her own parents hiding food in the thatched roof through months of famine during the Cultural Revolution. A matchmaker brought Zhu's parents together in the early 1980s. Zhu's mother worked as a cook in a local factory, and Zhu's father is still a coal miner for a large local SOE. She remembers how excited she was in 1995 when her family first got a refrigerator. It was such a treat to have a popsicle whenever she wanted!

Zhu's mother always pushed for improvements, and wanted to live more like the richer families in town, but her father was content with his job. It supported the family and required him to work underground only six hours a day. Both parents expected Zhu to work hard at school. Her excellent performance in elementary school earned her a full scholarship to an elite boarding school in the nearby city of Tangshan. The city had largely recovered from the earthquake of 1976—with around half a million deaths, it ranks among the world's all-time worst natural catastrophes—and now is a modern city of 7.6 million.

The most difficult part of Zhu's life so far was studying for the Gaokao, the National College Entrance Exam, a modern descendent of the national civil service test. Like millions of her peers, Zhu put in years of hard study, during and after school, to prepare for the three-day test. She took it in June of her senior year, dreading that her whole future was at stake. She scored well enough to become a management major at Hebei United University. There she excelled, particularly in math and statistics, and by her junior year she was invited to join the Communist Party. Zhu was happy to, as membership required just a two-hour meeting twice a year and would probably help her meet her career goals.

Her outstanding undergraduate work and impressive graduate exam scores earned her a spot in the biostatistics PhD program at top-tier Nanjing Medical University, where she is today. Lying along the Yangtze River, Nanjing is one of China's Four Great Ancient Capitals and has become a modern metropolis of eight million. Her boyfriend, also 26, has a plum position with China Mobile, the world's largest telecom provider (and in 2011 the 16th most valuable company in the *Financial Times* Global 500 rankings, just ahead of JP Morgan Chase and Wal-Mart). His job is 300 miles away in the ancient port city of Ningbo. Zhu thinks that his salary, currently about $20,000, will be enough for him to buy an apartment in three years, and then they can marry. After that, she hopes to obtain her degree and move into a university job in Ningbo.

Zhu is unusual in that she has a younger sister. She came from a county that was very lenient about China's one-child policy, and let families with a daughter try again for a son to carry the family name. But since 1978, authorities in most parts of China have strictly enforced the policy. One consequence is that families have female fetuses aborted often enough to skew China's sex ratio. In Zhu's age group there are about 12 percent more men than women, and currently six boys are born for every five girls.

The one-child policy boosted economic growth in its first two decades. That's because the percentage of young people dwindled, so those of working age formed a very high proportion of the population. The policy probably also increased savings rates, since workers anticipated less support in old age from their kids. But the demographics are starting to reverse now, and China's proportion of working-age people is dropping rapidly.

The one-child policy also has moral consequences. The skewed sex ratio gives a lot of bargaining power to young women and their parents, and new norms have emerged. As our interviews with Zhang and Zhu suggest, a man is not considered eligible to marry until he has climbed the "Three Mountains"—owning an apartment, owning a car, and holding a well-paying secure job—and they grow taller each year. The traditional bride price that the groom's family pays has also climbed, and now is on the order of a year's middle-class salary. Fancy weddings are also part of the middle-class lifestyle. Grooms tend to be older and brides younger than before; indeed, unmarried women now are derided as "leftovers" (*shengnu*) after age 27.

Relations between the generations have changed as well. Respect and lifelong deference to one's elders have been the linchpin of Chinese morality for millennia. The Cultural Revolution disrupted the tradition temporarily, but the one-child policy may have permanent impact. Most people of Zhu's generation grew up as only children and often feel tremendous pressure as carriers of the whole family's hopes and fears. Yet they were also the sole recipients of attention, so they developed a sense of entitlement and became less deferential. Teachers (including Friedman) have seen a sea change in the attitudes of Chinese students over the past decade or so.

The rise of the middle class has transformed the moral fabric in other ways. Since the Cultural Revolution, community life has gone from ubiquitous to endangered. When people were crowded together in dormitories and worked in the same factory or commune, they knew their neighbors intimately, perhaps too intimately. Nowadays, members of the new middle class own much more spacious apartments, with their own kitchens and bathrooms. People enjoy a lot more privacy, but often no longer know their neighbors.

What's Next for China?

The party offers membership to those it sees as role models, like Zhu. Regarding the 95 percent who are not members, the party now seems happy if they are shallow materialists and self-promoters with little or no civic spirit. It's the true altruists who pose a danger to the party's moral monopoly.

But the larger danger to China's future is the behavior of the elite 1 percent. All bets are off if corruption seriously undermines growth, or sabotages middle-class confidence that hard work and education will pay off.

The Macau-Vancouver connection illustrates one problem. Late in 1999, China took over the last remnant of Portugal's empire: Macau, a small island not far from Hong Kong. Within five years, in partnership with Sheldon Adelson and other Las Vegas magnates, Macau built the world's largest gambling casinos, whose revenues now dwarf those of Las Vegas. Adelson became an instant billionaire, but has been charged with violating the US Foreign Corrupt Practices Act. Macau is now the world's hub of money laundering, and it is the premier destination for wealthy Chinese who want to evade capital controls and move their money out of the country. Their favored parking place seems to be Vancouver, Canada. On a recent visit there, Friedman was struck by the city's block after high-rise block of new luxury apartment buildings. They are largely empty, like the nearby streets, since most owners live an ocean away and have no need to sublet. They have invested in a form of wealth insurance that does nothing for China's future.

In November 2012, seven of the nine members of the all-powerful Politburo Standing Committee (PSC) stepped down in a once-a-decade transfer of power. Bo Xilai seemed a leading contender to join the PSC, and it is instructive to pick up his story at the point we left it, in 2007.

His father, Bo Yibo, died that year at age 98, revered as the last of the Immortals. In that same year Bo Xilai became party chief of Chongqing, one of China's four provincial-level municipalities. Chongqing now has a population of almost 30 million, about the same as all four Nordic countries plus two Baltic states. There, Bo began a new experiment in governance, dubbed the Chongqing model. Along with his police chief, Wang Lijun, he launched a well-publicized campaign against organized crime. Bo Xilai beefed up security and police forces, and with little regard for legal niceties, arrested anyone with potential ties to organized crime and, it is said, many of his political and personal rivals as well. He expropriated billions of dollars from those he had charged and used the money to subsidize housing for favored groups. The model also promoted a public morality, "red" culture, and revived the old Mao-era songs and public spirit. At the same time, Bo Xilai continued to court foreign investment and industrial development, and encouraged flattering press reports. He liked the comparison with the Kennedys in the United States, but to us the Chongqing model looks more like Russia under Putin or Venezuela under Chavez.

Some of China's top bosses loved the neo-leftist Chongqing model. But several of Bo Xilai's peers saw it as a mortal threat, especially because it violated Deng's rule against personality cults.

These tensions came to a boil in February 2012 when police chief Wang Lijun took refuge from his boss in the US embassy overnight, and was released to Beijing authorities the next day. Bo Xilai's enemies in Beijing pounced, and he and his wife Gu Kailai were both arrested. Based on evidence provided by the police chief, prosecutors charged Gu with murder. She had, they said, enticed a British businessman to her room in Chongqing's Lucky Holiday Hotel, gotten him drunk, and spiked his drink with potassium cyanide. (There are indications that she had emotional breakdowns a few years earlier and that Bo had separated from her.) Despite heroic efforts of her 90-year-old mother, who had marched with Mao, Gu Kailai was convicted that August and received a life sentence. In late September, the CCP expelled Bo Xilai and charged him with—intriguingly— corruption. The accompanying comments on his violation of party discipline and keeping of mistresses suggest that his allies were unable to protect him and that he will spend the rest of his days in disgrace and behind bars.

Xi Jinping has now taken the top spot. His career eerily parallels Bo Xilai's. Like his erstwhile rival, Xi is the son of a top official under Mao. He graduated from Beijing University, worked with top officials for a couple of years, and then went out to the provinces and moved up the ranks, associating himself with successful economic experiments, especially in the Shanghai region. The main difference is that he kept a lower and less confrontational profile.

Today China is at a crossroads. As of early 2013, the economy is weakening. During the prior year export and domestic demand slowed but production roared ahead, creating mountains of unsold inventories. Far more important, it should now be clear to the new rulers that the policies of the last 35 years have run their course. They rushed China from the bottom of the economic ladder to mid-tier; today, per capita income is higher in China than Thailand but still lower than in Turkey, Mexico, and even Russia. China will need new economic policies and true moral renewal if it is to complete its return as a leader of the civilized world.

III

Life Around Us

Without commonly shared and widely entrenched moral values and obligations, neither the law, nor democratic government, nor even the market economy will function properly.

—Václav Havel

7

From Hudson's Bay to eBay: Why Some People Like Going to Work

The more evolved and psychologically healthy people get, the more will enlightened management policy be necessary in order to survive in competition and the more handicapped will be an enterprise with an authoritarian policy.

—Abraham Maslow

In 1805 the venerable Hudson's Bay Company was sinking fast. Since 1670 its Royal Charter had given it a monopoly on the best trade routes to Europe for fine Canadian furs, but the lucrative business had recently attracted a new firm, North West. Its trappers and traders had to haul furs an extra 1,500 miles in birch-bark canoes, often over killing portages. Despite that huge cost disadvantage, North West had somehow managed to snare over 80 percent of market share, and Hudson's Bay's stock was in free fall.

How did North West do it? Not with technology, but organization. North West offered trappers incentive pay and partnership opportunities. It bred a self-reinforcing trust, and aligned the trappers' goals with those of the organization. North West shared more of the benefits, as tribal members on the savanna had. Hudson's Bay Company, on the other hand, was a feudal hierarchy. It passed orders from London down through the ranks, paid employees low fixed salaries, and flogged them for disobedience. In 1809 new owners took over and began to emulate North West. Hudson's Bay profits rose quickly and in 1821 it bought out its pesky competitor. Today it is the world's oldest company still in its original line of business.

The Hudson's Bay revival is a parable for the 21st century, when upstarts like Google have threatened established organizations. Some of the older firms, such as Wal-Mart and IBM, are adapting, but both the upstarts and the familiar names seek the North West advantage: quick reflexes and motivated workers. Nowadays, good organizations of all sorts reward hard work materially, with bonuses and promotions, and socially, with the respect of coworkers and superiors. They follow the Maslow prescription, encouraging autonomy and soliciting good ideas from every level.

But why have corporate hierarchies ruled for so long? Why are moral codes mutating in today's workplace, and how do they intensify market competition?

Dilemmas and Holdups

What is the best way for human society to organize work? Thinkers from Plato to Lenin thought the answer was obvious: let the most talented experts plan everything, and have loyal citizens follow the plan. They believed that a single unified organization, run by philosopher-kings, would eliminate all the chaos, waste, and confusion.

The error was, of course, egregious. Monolithic planned societies have performed terribly, in part because a unitary organization can't properly coordinate and motivate large numbers of people in complex settings.

So why not go to the other extreme? Atomize organizations so that each person operates directly in the market. Imagine a complete set of markets, where at every moment anyone could buy or sell every kind of raw material, labor, equipment, good, or service at a competitive price. You would make your living by renting out your own labor and other resources to the highest bidder, or else by renting other people's labor and resources in order to produce and sell a product. Everyone would do this on an individual basis. Markets would coordinate everything, and firms would vanish.

But things have never worked that way.

Why not? The answer is that markets, especially labor markets, can never be perfect. There are inescapable frictions. Coordinating activities across individuals is costly, sometimes very costly. Even for a task as commonplace as remodeling a house and even with blueprints already in hand, it takes a lot of time and energy to line up the carpenters, roofers, sheetrockers, tilers, plumbers, electricians, and building inspectors, and to get the right materials and right specifications to each of them at the right time. The general contractor usually gets about 25 percent of the entire cost just to coordinate the work.

The problem isn't just coordination and communication. Social dilemmas lie just beneath the surface. The goals and priorities of an organization do not automatically align with those of its members. In the contractor example, each workman would like more money and a more convenient schedule. If an agreement isn't worked out in advance, quarrels might stop the job. A key point of contracting, of course, is to minimize such setbacks by writing down an agreement.

Modern contracts usually cover a vast range of contingencies, as anyone with a credit card knows. But unforeseen events still occur, even if the contract addresses them. The special tile for the remodel job might be defective and have to be back-ordered, and the tiler might not be able to reschedule. Or maybe dry rot has ruined the wall studs and the job turns out to be much harder than expected. And, of course, the contract language itself may be incomplete or ambiguous.

The problem is especially tricky when you have to make specialized investments. For example, about 10 years ago Caligula University (a pseudonym, in case somewhere there actually is a Caligula University; the other names are fictitious too) hired TSC Software to modernize the student record system. Unfortunately, lots of problems surfaced once the CU registrar started using the system. Grade point averages for alums out more than four years were incorrectly reported, for instance, and the system froze when everyone tried to enter new grades at the end of the semester. Meanwhile, TSC had been purchased by software giant Orator. Backed by an impressive legal team, Orator executives argued that CU was at fault for providing bad specifications. They offered to fix and guarantee everything for an extra $5 million. CU had no practical alternative, so after intensive negotiations they signed a new $4 million contract. Happily, no further problems emerged, but CU budget analysts now guess that the fix more than doubled TSC/Orator profits, and (due to the registrar's lost productivity) the unanticipated cost for CU exceeded $6 million.

This kind of problem resembles one that Himalayan mountaineers used to face. After they'd hired local porters and moved high up the slopes, the porters would suddenly demand much higher wages. Pay up, they'd say, or find other porters. Climbers were locked in and had to comply. Economists call this sort of episode a "holdup," and it happens all the time in daily life. Printer ink is the best-known example. You may have paid a ridiculously low price for your printer and then found yourself paying ridiculously high prices for compatible ink cartridges. The device was saying: Pay up or find another printer.

Here's a general description of holdups. You put resources into a specialized system, a system that is valuable as long as you maintain a relationship with a customer (or a supplier) but is not worth much if the relationship breaks. The bargaining power you once had now evaporates because, having sunk the resources, you have little recourse if there is a disagreement. The customer (or supplier) can hold you up, demanding better terms at your expense. Long-term contracting can help, but it can't eliminate the problem because special circumstances might arise (or be invented).

The larger danger is that, fearing eventual holdup, you never create the specialized systems even when they are extremely valuable. The holdup problem cripples market transactions for all sorts of goods and services that require specialized investment.

Motivating with Morals

Organizations made up of many persons are the universal solution to such dilemmas and holdups. Each organization—not just businesses but also colleges, government agencies, and charities—can transact with other organizations and individuals. It can buy supplies, hire labor, own equipment, and create products and services of value. Once it establishes its own identity, an organization can do well even with turnover of its individual members.

Each organization ideally finds the size and activity set that best meet its goals. It often makes its own specialized investments, thus avoiding holdup problems. It undertakes activities that need close coordination, for example, the assembly, testing, and delivery of printers. It avoids activities that others can do better, say, accounting or training engineers or building delivery trucks, but instead buys what it needs under contract or in the spot market.

To keep everyone on task, organizations need internal and external regulation. The tools of internal regulation are material—wages, benefits, bonuses, and promotion opportunities—and also moral—the formal and informal corporate culture.

"Corporate culture" sounds vague, but it refers to the everyday social experience in an organization. Its core is a unique moral code, a shared understanding of how to work together to achieve the organization's goals. For example, when Friedman worked at Bank of America headquarters in the late 1970s, a printed copy of the formal rules, the Standard Practices Manual, occupied an entire bookshelf. Weeks might go by without anyone in his department looking at it, but they were all well aware of the main informal rules. For example, it was quite acceptable to take a long lunch break on a slow day, but carelessness in checking facts for the boss's presentation to top management was unacceptable. The informal corporate culture rewarded some sorts of efficient specialized investment, such as mastering some unique software, but did not reward others, such as measuring the performance of the bank's regular consultants.

Business firms and other organizations divide up into departments or other small groups of people who work together on a daily basis. A good department manager uses all the ancient moral devices to increase productivity: exchange of favors, appeals to friendship and team spirit, reminders of threats posed by rival teams, and promises to improve things later if current goals are met.

Some department managers are better than others at motivating people. Success obviously depends on the manager's skill, but it also depends crucially on external market conditions. As with hunter-gatherers, workers can always quit and go elsewhere. In the modern world, the labor market determines how good that alternative is. So overall that market sets limits on how hard managers can push, and how lucrative and pleasant an experience they must provide.

The market environment and the moral codes for internal regulation are the main forces that determine whether a business firm expands or shrinks, merges or splits up, and enters or exits new activities. Occasionally, the same forces create a major transition in the way firms organize themselves, as happened about a century ago.

The Corporate Takeover

Early capitalist firms were mostly family operations. In the United States around 1800, "apprentices, journeymen, and clerks typically lived in the master's household and were subject to his discipline in the same way as children were," according to one account. These firms dealt mainly with local suppliers and customers. To cope with motivation, coordination, and communication problems, the firm used the old-fashioned moral devices: reputation and hierarchy. Of course, problems still occurred; for instance, sometimes apprentices ran off to the western frontier.

Francis C. Lowell helped change things. He watched firms like Rhode Island's Almy & Brown earn good profits in the new cloth manufacturing business. They would build a mill on a river, and pay local parents to send their children in to work. But as textile and transportation technology advanced and more distant markets opened, Lowell came up with a more profitable business model. Around 1820, he and his partners started to build entire new towns in Massachusetts. The towns centered on huge factories that turned stretches of river into brick-lined canyons, and also included dormitories, stores, and churches. Lowell recruited unmarried young women throughout the region and paid them piece rates to run the specialized equipment. The factories pirated basic technology from England, got cotton bales from the South (cheap thanks to Eli Whitney's recent deseeding device), and used giant waterwheels to power the spinning and weaving equipment. The factory-made cloth sold throughout New England and beyond, and made Lowell and his partners rich.

In later decades, with the development of steam-powered equipment and national markets, the leading textile firms became more specialized and clustered. By 1870, over 600 such firms operated in Philadelphia. The New England factories went out of business, but the brick canyons are still visible along the Merrimack River near Lowell, Massachusetts.

Adam Smith was the first to explain the factories' underlying logic, called economy of scale. A bit ahead of his time in 1776, Smith began his most famous book by explaining how factory assembly lines could manufacture vast numbers of pins at far lower unit cost. Instead of a skilled craftsman doing everything himself, the factories divided the process into tiny tasks—such as drawing wire, cutting it, sharpening the pin point—so unskilled workers could do each task with specialized equipment. The idea spread to the textile industry and, along with the concept of interchangeable parts, to clock and gun manufacture. In the early 20th century, Henry Ford pushed it even further with his assembly line. Such economies of scale could slash labor costs down to one tenth of those of an independent craftsman.

Of course, economies of scale aren't much use without mass markets. The new manufacturers' cost advantage depended on operating near full capacity over long periods of time, and local customers couldn't absorb all that output. Itinerant peddlers helped expand markets in the early 1800s, but some of them overcharged customers or palmed off damaged or inferior goods. Markets work much better when buyers trust the quality of the merchandise, and the seller's reputation can make all the difference. Some manufacturers, like Singer with its sewing machines, built national brands through their own retail networks. Others earned buyers' trust by selling to mass retailers, like Sears and Woolworth, who developed their own reputations for quality.

Transportation was critical. Expanding to (or beyond) national markets works only if shipping costs are low. The supply of transportation networks expanded to meet demand, and costs plummeted, spurring (and spurred by) advances in shipbuilding, canals, railroads, and highways.

Transportation networks themselves demanded new sorts of organization. For example, railroad companies earned much greater profits when shippers and passengers could choose from a wide set of destinations and expect to reach them quickly and reliably. Meeting these expectations required unprecedented coordination and communication. Successful railroad companies like Southern Pacific honed methods used during the Civil War for military operations and logistical support. The internal organization began to look less like a family and more like a specialized army, with general staff, commanders, and geographically dispersed units pledged to execute the orders passed down the ranks.

In the late 1800s the corporate form of organization began to invade a wide variety of industries: manufacturers like Singer, chain stores like Woolworth, mail-order retailing like Sears Roebuck, new industries like petroleum, and old ones like tobacco, coal, and steel. The process was contagious. Some company in a new industry, or an innovator in an established industry, would figure out how to make specialized investments that ensured economies of scale, how to tap low cost inputs, and how to distribute the product to masses of customers. To survive, the other companies in the industry had to follow the leaders, or leapfrog them.

Corporate organization evolved further in the early 20th century at companies like General Motors, Standard Oil, Du Pont, and Bank of America. The competitive advantage went to firms whose organization allowed them to produce a wider range of higher-value products at lower unit cost. This increasingly meant managing a multiunit hierarchy involving workers and several levels of managers as well as professionals, such as engineers, accountants, and lawyers. Aside from the chain of command in the production process itself, the organization needed to coordinate purchases of materials, to hire and train workers, and to manage marketing and distribution. It also had to engage in research and development and to coordinate planning. Making it all work together smoothly is an intricate challenge.

Corporate hierarchies are built to meet just that challenge. The law regards a corporation as an individual person, with a separate identity from its owners, managers, and workers. This legal status lets the corporation make deals that survive changes in management or ownership, and helps stabilize reputations with customers and suppliers. Just as important, the owners are not personally liable if the corporation gets in trouble. Owners don't have to worry so much about everyday activities of the corporation or its other owners. The upshot is that people can freely trade ownership shares in a stock market. Hence, corporations can more easily gain backing by selling shares or issuing debt. In 1814 Lowell financed construction of his first textile mill by selling stock to the general public, and ever since American corporations have raised money the same way.

Throughout the first half of the 20th century, the corporate transformation created new resources to fuel further growth. It became a positive feedback loop. More efficient corporate forms, combined with lower transportation and communication costs, helped expand and stabilize markets. The growth of mass markets created dynamic new industries. As national wealth increased, more children survived but fewer were needed in agriculture, as it too became mechanized. So the pool of blue-collar workers deepened. The white-collar pool—managers and professionals—also grew as families and governments invested more in education.

Profits went to innovators who found new ways to serve the corporate machine at lower cost. The innovations drove transportation and communication costs even lower, expanding the mass market and building new corporate industries like advertising, broadcasting, and consulting. Corporations became conglomerates, adding new product lines and merging with firms in distantly related (or even unrelated) activities. Despite the distractions of two world wars and the Great Depression, the corporate bulldozer chugged forward.

Tribe on the Factory Floor

The overriding goal of a firm is to earn money for its owners, but in so doing it touches the lives of other stakeholders: managers, workers, suppliers, and customers. As the corporate system developed, there was little problem in motivating the managers—the prospect of climbing the corporate ladder did the trick. The corporate system catered to customers, and prosperity served suppliers well.

Blue-collar workers were always more problematic. Neither piece rate pay nor intrinsic satisfaction work well on the assembly line, since each worker's personal contribution is hard to see. Effective worker incentives were mainly negative: punching the time clock, close supervision, intrusive monitoring, and the threat of being fired. When the alternative was subsistence farming or worse, plenty of workers were willing to take these jobs, but they paid a personal price. Critics from Karl Marx to Charlie Chaplin decried the factory as a moral wasteland, alienating and demeaning.

Trade unions helped fill the void. Workers found that joining a union made them part of an in-group that could stand up to corporate management and demand better pay, better working conditions, and more respect. At first the corporations fought the unions fiercely, but that didn't always work. For example, Lowell's successors defeated the Factory Girls' Association strike in 1834, but three years later they went bankrupt in a recession. Strikes and boycotts hurt corporate profits: some unions turned out to be very effective in holding their members' loyalty and in arousing sympathy from consumers and voters. Unions in the United States slowly gained ground as the corporate system matured, especially in the New Deal years before World War II.

Following that war, unions in Japan and Germany worked closely with corporate officials and government to rebuild their countries and enrich everyone. In the United States, many industries found that the most profitable course was to sign industry-wide union contracts. For example, General Motors, Ford, and Chrysler wrote contracts with the United Auto Workers that tended to equalize their labor costs. This reduced the incentive to compete on price or quality, and made it more difficult for new US firms to enter the industry. Thus, the unions helped make the Big Three a stable oligopoly. Of course, soft competition in domestic markets later helped foreign automakers catch up and become tough rivals, but that danger seemed distant at the time.

As a student in the late 1960s, Friedman worked summers in union jobs on San Francisco's docks and warehouses. The International Longshore and Warehouse

Union (ILWU) still had older members who told him stories of their service with the Lincoln Brigade, fighting fascists in Spain on the eve of World War II, and of how they brought racial equality to the union. Their fierce moral code and militancy had made the union strong, but their influence already was fading. All the younger union members Friedman met had only personal material concerns: better wages and benefits and easier work for themselves. As these younger folks took over, the ILWU, like many other unions, slowly lost bargaining power as well as its moral edge.

A Delicate Balance

A research team studied internal regulation a few years ago by having human subjects play games in a Zurich laboratory. Some players (the managers) offered a wage, either high or low, and other players (the workers) chose which offer to accept and how much costly effort to exert. Standard economic theory predicted that the workers would take highest offer and still shirk, but that wasn't what happened. Players who accepted higher offers tended to exert more effort. The experimenters interpreted their results in terms of reciprocity. The workers wanted to repay managers' generosity, and realizing this, the managers were more generous.

Surprisingly, explicit incentive contracts didn't work well in this experiment. Workers tended to make more selfish choices when their take-home pay was tied directly to how much effort they exerted. When workers could see exactly how much their effort helped the manager, they tended again to behave more selfishly, especially when the managers earned more.

The lesson is clear. There is a delicate balance between workers' financial incentives and moral imperatives. Workers' willingness to give a good effort is one of the most valuable assets an organization can possess.

A nasty counterexample surfaced a few years ago. Ford Motor Company's profits in the late 1990s came largely from its bestselling sports utility vehicle, the Explorer. In 2000 sales started to drop on reports of fatal rollover accidents. Tread separation on Firestone tires produced at the Decatur, Illinois plant turned out to be the main cause of more than 270 deaths. Firestone and Ford barely survived the huge tire recall and marketing disaster.

A careful study showed that the problem at Decatur was not technical, but moral. In 1994, despite improved profits, the tire company decided to play tough with the Union of Rubber Workers. It demanded a large wage cut and longer hours rotating between day and night shifts, and immediately hired replacement workers ("scabs") when the union went on strike. The union eventually went bankrupt and capitulated. After that the workforce at Decatur was a mix of scabs, union men who broke the strike, and men returning from the broken union. Morale was poisonous. Workers had no loyalty to the company or pride in their work, and they produced lots of defective tires. Everyone lost: workers, company managers and owners, customers, and the driving public.

The Agility Revolution

On the whole, though, in the second half of the 20th century the balance held. Big business—Coke and Pepsi, the Big Three automakers, US Steel and its brethren, the five major airlines, the six money center banks, the seven sisters of Big Oil, the Big Eight accounting firms, and so forth—dominated the industrialized world. Union wages and benefits climbed steadily, pulling millions of families into the middle class. Nonunionized workers did almost as well because their employers had to offer prevailing wages, set in part by big union contracts. Prosperous workers became a force for stability and economic growth, and corporations thrived.

Now, however, things are different. A transition is underway in the way organizations operate, and once again markets are corroding the old order and opening things up. Big Business and Big Labor are fragmenting, and company loyalty has become passé. Networks are taking root in huge sectors including retail, manufacturing, services, and high technology.

But why now? What changed?

In the 20th century corporations thrived on large, stable, predictable markets. The corporations, with major investments in specialized capital, benefitted from economies of scale. Economic stability and predictability allows such investments to pay off. But in the last quarter of the century things began to shake loose. The 1970s and 1980s saw oil price shocks and two major recessions. A wave of deregulation swept through airlines, banking, and other industries. Markets became more fluid and powerful than ever, and less predictable.

The pace of change accelerated in the late 1980s and the 1990s as the Cold War wound down. The market system invaded Eastern Europe and China and advanced in much of Asia and Latin America. The pool of accessible labor tripled. Vast new investment opportunities opened, along with a flood of new savings. Wealthy consumers grew more numerous, and their tastes became more fickle and fragmented. Containerization drastically lowered shipping costs: sealed cargo from the factory could be trucked to the dock, put on a boat, off-loaded to a train, and then delivered by an 18-wheeler truck, with minimal costs for labor, inspections, and delays. Most famously, advances in semiconductors and fiber optics touched off the information technology revolution, enabling new organizational structures as well as novel products and a new generation of competitors.

These changes rocked the cozy world of big business and big labor. Many of the largest employers, facing global competition, could no longer afford the customary wage increases. To tap the growing labor pool, corporations increasingly built new manufacturing facilities abroad and also started to outsource some service and professional jobs. Most firms that tried to maintain the old ways were unable to compete on price and quality and had to shed jobs. Leading unions also suffered from demographic changes. Worker solidarity and political influence waned as older members moved to suburbs and eventually retired.

In this unstable environment, corporations faced unforeseen threats and new opportunities. All of a sudden, being nimble trumped being big.

But why not be both? Of course, some giants are nimbler than others. Later in the chapter we'll look at the growth of corporate Lebron Jameses like IBM and Wal-Mart. But first let's consider why it is so difficult for large corporations to be agile.

The laws of physics prevent a 300-pounder like Shaquille O'Neal from changing direction as quickly as a Tony Parker. The problem for corporations is not physical, of course. Their economic inertia has three main sources. The best known, but probably least important, is the difficulty of coordinating a larger number of people, which often requires a longer chain of command. A second source is fear of self-cannibalization. Giant corporations have major profit streams from current technology and business models, and they must trade off losses in these streams against gains from innovation. For example, when Apple jumped into the music industry with its iPod and downloadable tunes, the industry behemoth Sony worried about losing CD sales and reacted too slowly. Keeping current profit streams is a concern for giants but not for newcomers.

Third, any giant corporation must cope with influence costs. As it allocates resources among its units, each manager will try to influence decisions to favor her unit. These managers will squander time and talent making dueling PowerPoint presentations, puffing up their own performance, or spreading rumors about the other units. The comic strip Dilbert features endless examples. Small companies, run by entrepreneurs who already know the entire business, face much smaller influence costs. They can devote more resources to dealing with customers and suppliers because they are less tied up with infighting.

In a stable environment, big corporations incur cannibalization and influence costs only occasionally, so they can still prosper. However, when serious threats and new opportunities bombard the firm from all directions, these costs can be killers.

But what's the alternative to big corporations? Old fashioned family firms? Why would they work any better now than a hundred years ago?

Good Old Networks

Interpersonal networks, of course, have been around even longer than family firms. They dominate tribal life, and in medieval times the Florentine banker networks spurred economic progress. The largest networks in medieval Europe, however, were the guilds. Each trade in each town had a guild with connections to its counterparts in other towns and in other trades. The guilds worked together to exclude rivals and to maintain the incomes of their senior members. These cozy networks thrived on the status quo and feared innovation. The Great Transformation swept them away.

Or most of them. A few guild networks adapted to the new market system and prospered. Consider, for example, the Italian wool trade, centered in the city of Prato, near Florence. Recently home to about 9,000 factories with 45,000 workers, Prato is laced with independent small-to-medium operations, each with a specialty in spinning, twisting, warping, weaving, dyeing or finishing. The owners, called *impannatori*, form temporary teams to design new products, and to produce and market the finished products. This fission-fusion network has enabled them to set world-class standards in speed and quality for hundreds of years. More recently, however, they have had trouble meeting price competition from China, where the textile industry is also fission-fusion.

Hollywood always has relied on a similar network. A unique team of writers, directors, cinematographers, actors, producers, and crew creates a film, and they split up once it's done. Commercial success makes reunion of key team members more likely for a new project.

The major production studios, such as MGM, Fox, Paramount, and Warner Brothers, once controlled distribution and financing and signed many participants to exclusive contracts, but now the interpersonal networks are wider and more flexible than ever. Financing comes from hedge funds as well as media conglomerates, revenues derive increasingly from online sales and foreign distribution, and production often takes place outside of California. Next time you watch a movie, linger for all the credits. The span of the participating networks may amaze you.

The higher education industry may have the world's oldest professional network. Even in the first colleges (founded in 11th-century Bologna and Oxford), professors were more loyal to students and to distant colleagues than to their nominal bosses, the deans and provosts, or to their wealthy sponsors. Like members of some prehistoric tribe, and probably like members of the original academies of ancient Greece, the scholars formed bands that sometimes split up and sometimes gathered together. Learned societies took root, like the British Royal Society, founded in London in 1660, and they sponsored regular meetings and circulated journals reporting new findings. Young scholars moved from one campus to the next, building their personal networks and spreading ideas.

Market forces roared through most industries in the 1800s, utterly transforming them. Higher education was an exception: it sailed along nicely, growing briskly while only gradually changing course. In leading nations, wealthy industrialists and governments spread around their increasing wealth, and universities got a share. These sponsors eventually realized that innovation promoted industrial leadership, and that innovators often drew on new scientific knowledge generated in the universities. For example, the new sciences of thermodynamics and chemistry helped craftsmen design better steam engines, and advances in organic chemistry spurred the discovery of new dyes. European governments began to support university science and engineering more generously, and the United States also sponsored land grant colleges aimed at boosting farm productivity.

Germany, Europe's most ambitious rising power in the 1800s, introduced a more corporate university system. The government funds each professor directly, and each of them hires his own team of assistants. The system worked well and spread, but never displaced the decentralized networks in the English-speaking world and beyond. Since World War II, universities in the United States have dominated the industry with an especially competitive fission-fusion network. Ambitious campuses bid against each other to sign up the most promising new researchers, and they often try to hire away other schools' established stars.

A researcher's prospects in academia depend mainly on her reputation among network members sharing her specialties, and on the importance and trend of those specialties within the wider research network. Multicampus teams of researchers assemble themselves to write grant proposals to national agencies. Teams that get grants present their work at conferences and write it up for journal publication, then they dissolve and reform in different configurations. For example, at the time of the first edition of this book, one of us (Friedman) was a member of three research teams funded by the United States National Science Foundation. One team included assistant professors of economics at liberal arts colleges on both coasts. A second team included an emeritus professor of mathematics at UC Santa Cruz. The third included members of a leading industrial lab as well as economists and computer scientists from research universities in the southeast and the southwest. Some members of each team had worked together before, but none of the full teams existed before their current project nor was any expected to continue beyond its completion.

The New Networks

Recently networks have expanded their domain. They have invaded some of the old, corporate industries, and started to take root in industries that never existed before.

The network advantage is always agility. For example, one night in December 2003 an Italian system administrator detected a dangerous virus attack on his Linux server. He contacted Linux network experts in Australia and Atlanta, who identified the vulnerability in the code. They linked up with specialists in California and elsewhere to build a patch, test it, and disseminate it to users. Despite the fact that they had never previously worked together, or even met face-to-face, the team finished the job just 29 hours after first detection. It might have taken a traditional organization days or weeks just to identify the problem, and months to fix it.

This story illustrates the boost that networks get from 21st-century specialized education and mobility, as well as from the new information technologies. The span of networks is no longer a single town; they can reach to the other side of the world to find just the right person or equipment to add to the team.

The story also illustrates decentralization and scalability. Any well-connected person can get the ball rolling. Once she becomes aware of a new opportunity or threat, she can begin to assemble a team from her network contacts. The new teammates can draw on their own contacts to complete the team, and the team can grow (or shrink) as appropriate.

Such teams avoid the overhead costs of large corporations, who must keep paying for their specialized equipment and employees even when there is a lull. Networks, by contrast, have minimal ongoing expenses—phone, email, IM, blogs, occasional travel and meetings—that their own members are happy to cover. When teams form, they can offer key members very intense material rewards, such as stock options or a substantial share of the profit. The profit stream belongs to the particular team, not to the network itself, so the network avoids cannibalization and influence costs.

Fission-fusion networks also bring a new solution to the holdup problem. Many sorts of specialized skills (or human capital, in economics jargon) are valued in the network. You can build these skills and your reputation in your network over time and not lose bargaining power, because you can always look for another team if your present one doesn't reward you properly.

Life in the Netzone

Even more important, however, is the human advantage. Networks are far better than hierarchical organizations at mobilizing our moral sentiments. Being a member of a team handpicked for a special project is like playing on an elite basketball team. Each person's efforts are crucial and are easy for teammates to recognize, and the team can generate incredible bursts of energy and creativity for many months. That's what pays off in unstable times.

Google's famous story illustrates the point. In 1996, two new computer science PhD students at Stanford University found that they enjoyed arguing with each other. Sergey Brin and Larry Page collaborated on class projects, and worked overtime on one they called BackRub. It improved Internet search by tracing links backward and ranking each website by the popularity of the links pointing to it. By the summer of 1998 their search engine was up and running with impressive results. Angel investors raised a million dollars, and Sergey and Larry moved out of their dorm rooms, hired their first employee, and launched their start-up company from Susan Wojcicki's spacious garage. A few months of hard work and five employees later, they moved into a real office and started signing up clients. Two top venture capital firms in 1999 took a piece of the action for $25 million, which allowed Google to move to its own building, hire professional staff, and grow.

Google grabbed a great new market niche. As Internet content mushroomed, search became crucial. Existing search engines got their revenues from advertisers, who could buy higher rankings in user searches and bombard users with unwanted ads. Google offered sharper, faster, and more honest searches, with relevant ads shown separately and discreetly. Its moral code also made Google more attractive to young talent. The egalitarian atmosphere, at once whimsical (starting with the company name) and serious, encouraged everyone to try out wild new ideas and to work around the clock to develop the best ones. Google's 2004 IPO was also unconventional, using an equal-access auction instead of the usual procedure that favors investment banks and their top clients. Hundreds of its employees are multimillionaires and can do whatever they want. What most of them want to do is to keep on working with talented teammates on exciting new projects. In 2012, for the third straight year, *Fortune* ranked Google the best company on earth to work for.

Google is a supernova, but ordinary start-ups draw on their networks too, and not just in good times. For instance, a 1996 Silicon Valley start-up we'll call

Kntek began with a core of Russian engineers. The company went through several cycles of expansion and contraction, constantly increasing the web of personal and professional contacts. Layoffs in bad times hit mainly Kntek's less productive departments and individuals. (Larger companies generally have worse aim.) In good times they heeded the saying, "A players hire A players, but B players hire C's." They found several A players trained at the Indian Institute of Technology, and a few more at American schools.

In summer 2000 Kntek's engineering team faced its toughest test. A key customer pushed the key product harder than usual, found it defective, and gave Kntek a deadline to get it working properly. The problem turned out to be fundamental: an inadequate software engine. Working around the clock from a single room, leaving only to gather specific information and report back, the seven-person brain trust found a way to replace the engine. But the huge job remained of retrofitting and debugging everything the engine drove. After a week, the team was able to parcel out specialized tasks to the rest of the engineering staff, who in turn worked around the clock for the next two weeks. The company met the deadline with a day to spare, and survived. Indeed, it became stronger than ever, because the shared experience—mortal danger averted by outstanding teamwork—brought everyone closer together.

Bonding can take many forms. For example, an American Buddhist temple in California supplemented the usual classes in meditation and philosophy with offerings in martial arts and Java programming. In Northern California, programming seemed as natural a spiritual practice as gravel raking in Japan or thangka painting in Tibet. You bring your mind to one point, see the connections that need to be made, and then type in the code. The class took on increasingly ambitious joint projects. The teacher suggested that they build a software company, and a dozen of the top students signed on.

For the next 18 months the team spent virtually all waking hours together. Most days they carpooled to a large office and programmed for at least 10 hours, the key clatter punctuated by occasional bursts of chatter and laughter. They usually ended the workday with a martial arts class and meditation, and then returned to a decaying mansion that most of them called home. After 18 months, they had a prototype, but money was running low. Even team members with no prior experience had accumulated skills in high demand, so most of them moved to a different city and took outside programming jobs. With coffers replenished but no major customers for their product, the team recently moved once more to a city noted for its angel investors.

What has kept the team together for five years and three long moves? Partly it is the prospect (not yet realized) of getting lots of money and recognition for their unique products. Money is handy even for those uninterested in fancy cars and vacations; it could be used to build a great Zendo, for example. The larger motivation, though, is the teamwork itself. They love being part of a working spiritual community and want to keep it going.

Valve Software is another extreme example. Founded in 1996 by Gabe Newell, it now dominates its niche: downloadable video games. Its user base passed the 50 million mark in 2012, and its annual revenue is on the order of $1 billion. Its many popular games include Half-Life, Team Fortress, Dota, Left 4 Dead, and Portal, but it also offers a suite of game-building tools called Source, and the leading online gaming platform, Steam. Though Valve has only about 300 employees, it is the heart of an ecosystem with dozens of other organizations and thousands of individuals who use the game engine and platform. Since Valve is privately owned and completely self-financing, it is free to choose its own path.

And it does.

Its proudest boast: "We've been boss-free since 1996. Imagine working with supersmart, supertalented colleagues in a freewheeling, innovative environment—no bosses, no middle management, no bureaucracy. Just highly motivated peers coming together to make cool stuff. It's amazing what creative people can come up with when there's nobody there telling them what to do."

One of us (Friedman) visited the company's facility in Belleview, Washington, in September 2012, and can attest to its nonhierarchical organization. All employees (including the founder) work in the same space, four or five open floors of a modern office building. Work groups, called "cabals," self-organize. When any employee thinks that he (or, for maybe 20 percent, she) would be happier and more productive in a new cabal, he simply unplugs his desk with its two huge flat screens and powerful computer, wheels it over, and plugs in alongside the new teammates. Internally, there are no ranks or job titles, but everyone is expected to have deep expertise in at least one subarea and general competence in a range of other subareas of visual design, story writing, coding, or perhaps marketing, finance, HR, PR, or customer relations. To deal with the outside world—such as suppliers, retailers, or journalists—cabal members may draw straws to choose who is to pretend to have the bigwig job title, and that person will go play the role.

Morale seemed to be excellent, and Valve surely is a world leader in productivity as measured by revenue per employee. Bonding experiences include testing shoot-em-up games together and an annual Hawaii vacation for all families on a charter jet. The annual peer review procedures are intended to pay each employee his marginal value product; unlike most other things at the company, much of the information regarding compensation is kept confidential.

Nets at Work

Google is not the only startup to reshape an industry, nor is it the most net-driven. The world's 13th largest retailer by sales volume now is Amazon, and along with the Apple Store and iTunes as number 21, it is the fastest growing. Indeed, in 2012 Amazon was growing at three times the rate of e-commerce itself. Another online giant, eBay, outsources almost everything to its network of 700,000 sellers, who acquire the merchandise, price it, sell it to the highest bidder, and ship it. The network of registered users totals around 100 million, but the organization relies heavily on much smaller networks of teachers, shippers, and web consultants that serve the sellers' needs. For itself, eBay retains the electronic auction platform, the direct online sales, more and more important classified ads, and the trust-building institutions like buyer and seller reputation records. Meanwhile, its subsidiary PayPal, the secure payment system, has passed the rest of eBay in number of users and may be the main revenue source for the future.

Fission-fusion networks don't just succeed at making money. They have also revolutionized military tactics. In April 2003, the US Army captured Baghdad with remarkable speed and very few casualties using fission-fusion combat teams with peer-to-peer communication. On the other side, Iraqi insurgents formed at least three different networks, and more recently these became a model for insurgents in Syria. The insurgent networks all seem very decentralized, and they exploit the Internet and cell phones to share information, recruit new members, coordinate actions, and then disperse. Unfortunately, military network structures help all sides to become more lethal.

Networks are also taking over more peaceful activities. Consider the open source movement. It has produced the leading website server software, Apache, as well as Linux, the impressive operating system. Perhaps its most famous product is the online encyclopedia Wikipedia, now a vast pool of articles and readers, as different from the old Britannica as a library is from a book. Open source contributors aren't paid directly, but the teamwork is emotionally rewarding and builds valuable reputations in the professional network. The open source communities also provide a livelihood for companies that repackage and customize the product for paying customers, as Red Hat does with Linux software.

Networks and Corporations: The Blurring Line

Are fission-fusion networks poised to take over the world? We doubt it. The future will be much more interesting and complicated than that. Networks and corporations are already partners as well as rivals, and are coevolving in new directions.

Take, for example, two of the most important networks in Silicon Valley: venture capitalists and engineers. They require each other—VCs exist to finance new ideas, and engineers with new ideas are always looking for financing. But the two networks have different moral codes and conflicting incentives, and things don't always go as smoothly as they did with Google. For instance, one of us (McNeill) has helped introduce startups to VCs. One fledgling firm had highly promising technology, but to its amazement it couldn't interest a single VC. Its PowerPoint presentation for the initial meeting showed why. It ignored the issues VCs care about, and indeed it was so technical as to be incomprehensible to them. As in many startups, this company's engineers completely misread the people they needed most.

One engineer recently related a life-and-death struggle for control of his company. Its technology seemed very capable in early tests, and the company received a very generous offer letter of second-round finance from a new VC partner. However, the original lead VC (with the new CEO's support) first wanted to get rid of a charter provision that gave veto power to the founding engineers. The engineers refused, the new VC got spooked, and the financing fell through. The original VC then issued an ultimatum: fire the founding engineer and change the charter, or no more money. The engineers held their ground, and the company went bankrupt. The VCs got nothing back on their $20 million investment. However, a new company quickly snapped up the engineering team and gave them even better options than before.

The boundaries between corporations and networks are starting to blur. Most corporations are dissolving some units and functions traditionally under central command and control. They often can reduce costs and increase shareholder value by spinning off some units or splitting up into several smaller companies. For example, in 1999 Hewlett-Packard, one of the original Silicon Valley firms, spun off its huge scientific instrument unit under the hopeful name Agilent. About the same time, HP opened the VC Café. Its mission is to spin off start-up companies led by HP employees. Toyota and Boeing now emulate the Linux community, emphasizing knowledge sharing, peer recognition, and reputation systems.

Outsourcing has become widespread. The idea is to hire out some corporate functions, like information technology or payroll processing (or even manufacturing or purchasing or distribution), to specialized service companies that can do the job at lower cost. Due to globalization and information technology, the specialist companies now can offer real-time service to many different clients in different cities, and reap economies of scale. They also can draw on low-cost skilled labor in Eastern Europe, India, or even Indiana. By now, most corporations have outsourced some functions to reduce overhead and influence costs and to become more flexible. Some have outsourced so many functions that they look almost like a network, or like eBay.

However, outsourcing can lead to holdup problems. For example, if you outsource your specialized computer systems, you can become dependent and then have a hard time switching to a new vendor if the current vendor raises prices. This is a dilemma that can sometimes be resolved with joint ventures and cross-holdings.

Fission-fusion thinking undermines traditional hierarchical organizations. Once a network forms, workers begin to put more value on personal contacts with peers in different parts of the firm and among the firm's suppliers, customers, and even competitors. They become less concerned with pleasing the boss and being loyal to the employer. Young workers now expect several career changes, maybe every two or three years. Flatter hierarchies mean fewer opportunities for promotion. Ultimately, what matters is the size and quality of your professional network and your reputation among peers. Thus, loyalty shifts from firm to network.

Traditional corporations are trying to adapt to the new worker attitudes and to the new unstable environment. In the 1980s, IBM couldn't properly exploit the personal computer because really aggressive shifts would cannibalize mainframe computer services, its core business at the time. In particular, IBM didn't react quickly to the new opportunities for better PC operating systems and microprocessors. This allowed Microsoft and Intel to seize what soon became the most profitable parts of the computer industry. In the early 1990s, squeezed between the two nimbler firms, IBM had a near-death experience.

Lew Gerstner, an outsider who became CEO in 1993, saved IBM by radically transforming it. Internally, IBM dissolved its traditional silos and helped weave personal networks across the research labs, business consultants, and computer systems specialists. The new IBM still sells lots of hardware and software, but most of its revenue now comes from global services. These consist of business solutions, such as showing a client how to reconfigure its business to take advantage of outsourcing opportunities, as well as information technology services such as running the client's computer systems. Now Microsoft and Intel have the more traditional business plans, trying to exploit market power in maturing industries. They all want to be agile giants, but at the moment, Big Blue seems to do it better.

Wal-Mart has deployed a unique blend of techniques to become the world's largest retailer, with annual revenue now totaling almost $350 billion. Its hierarchy is lean and rather flat for a giant corporation. Borrowing Japanese labor practices, Wal-Mart calls its workers "associates" and engages them in company cheers and morale building exercises, but offers rather low pay and benefits. Wal-Mart's supply chain is a marvel. Using advanced information technology and local decision-making authority, Wal-Mart responds almost instantaneously to customers' purchasing trends, and with unmatched efficiency moves the goods from manufacturers to warehouses to stores. It aggressively outsources production to a network of suppliers, especially to new Chinese mass manufacturers. Most of the suppliers would find it difficult to survive without Wal-Mart orders, so the corporation retains bargaining power. Wal-Mart's captive supplier network gives it flexibility without sacrificing economies of scale.

The old union model is collapsing in the private sector as blue-collar jobs are outsourced to worldwide supplier networks and the remaining corporate jobs become more professional and shorter term. Sara Horwitz, the daughter of a union lawyer and granddaughter of a top union official, recently created a new model. The 190,000 members of her Freelancers Union do not pay dues or bargain with employers. Instead, these self-employed workers use their union's networking website to strengthen their professional and social links and, more concretely, they save lots of money by buying health, dental, and life insurance through the union. It also offers a 401(k) pension plan.

As the 21st century advances, we can expect more cooperation, more conflict, and increasingly blurred boundaries between corporations and interpersonal networks. It is not the world Maslow imagined, but his upbeat prediction on work life may yet come true.

8

Markets and Sin: Murder, Megacasinos, and Drug Wars

Victorian philosophers confidently predicted that crime and vice would fade away as the human species evolved. That hasn't quite happened. For example, the State of California used to spend twice as much on universities as jails, but now the two are almost equal—though students enrich the economy and prisoners sap it. The War on Drugs cost US taxpayers about $15 billion in 2010, down from $40 billion in the Bush era, and it has been about as effective as Caligula's war against the sea.

Why does the United States spend so much on fighting crime, and why don't we get better results? The search for answers begins by looking at the nature of crime, and at crime prevention before the rule of law matured. It traces the rise of courts and the fall in crime until the 20th century. Then progress somehow went into reverse. Crime is among the most intensely moral of issues, and yet in some ways our moral instincts are worsening it.

Murder among "The Harmless People"

Why do societies outlaw some deeds and not others? Which sort of acts *should* society outlaw, and which ones tolerate or discourage by other means?

Crime is a flagrant violation of the I-versus-we balance. In the common law it always features *mens rea*, or "guilty mind," a malign intent, in contrast with negligence and insanity. The criminal knows what he is doing, knows it is wrong, and does it anyway. Property crimes like robbery, fraud, and embezzlement wound the target and turn the reward system upside down. If I earn $500,000, I've presumably devoted time and sweat to the effort, and perhaps taken risks, and I've probably benefited others. But if a thief steals that sum, a parasite gets the prize. The most vicious crimes are the personal attacks like battery, rape, and murder, and they benefit the perpetrator far less than they hurt the victim. In all these cases, the community suffers injury as well, for the criminal may strike others. People hear of barbarities, grow fearful, and take costly preventive steps. In sum, criminals shrink the pie when they assault the moral code, and almost every society punishes and stigmatizes them.

The first lines of defense are moral. The moral emotions inside us prevent most potential crime. We feel empathy for the potential victim, and we expect to feel guilt and (if caught) shame. Outer moral restraints—social penalties, informal and formal—stop most of the rest.

Hunter-gatherer societies fight crime the old-fashioned way. Everybody understands the norms and knows which infractions are minor and which serious. When people see a major violation, they quickly spread the word. Until the culprit repents, his outraged peers will apply growing pressure. He can expect ridicule, insult, avoidance, and reduced status, and if he persists, the group will expel him or even kill him. Within a well-functioning group, most crime doesn't pay because the social penalties are effective and costly. Awareness of them reinforces people's internal restraints, and serious crime is uncommon.

Consider how a 20th-century tribe dealt with a murderer. The !Kung, hunter-gatherers in Africa's Kalahari Desert, have been dubbed "the harmless people" because they favor verbal sanctions and generally avoid violence. Still, anthropologists documented about two dozen homicide cases among them over three decades. Four of them concerned a foul-tempered man named /Twi. After /Twi committed his second murder, relatives of the victims and others agreed that he had to go. One winter day in 1948, a distant kinsman named /Xashi ambushed /Twi, and shot a poisoned arrow into his hip. /Twi tried to stab /Xashi, but /Xashi escaped, aided by his mother-in-law. Some people in the encampment offered /Twi sympathy and started to suck out the poison, but /Twi lashed out at them, wounding one woman and killing her husband. Everyone then took cover and shot poisoned arrows into /Twi until he "looked like a porcupine." After burying him, the encampment split up to avoid confronting /Twi's relatives. An anthropologist describes this as an example of "collective action and collective responsibility in a...nonhierarchical society."

The Land of the Vendetta

No one ever called the Corsicans harmless. But with its unique geography and history, 19th-century Corsica became an ideal place to observe traditional group morality at work. Although it is the Mediterranean's fourth largest island, Corsica has never been very important strategically or economically. Invading forces—Phoenicians, Romans, Vandals, Byzantines, Moors, Lombardians, Aragonese, Genoans—viewed it as a minor outpost and controlled only a few coastal towns. Their civilizations hardly touched most Corsicans, who lived in isolated mountain villages connected (after the winter snow melted) only by mule tracks. These hamlets were almost a living Pompeii.

Things started to change in 1769. That year the French took over Corsica, and a boy named Napoleon was born to the Buonapartes, one of the wealthier families in the coastal town of Ajaccio (Ajax). The child grew up in France, and after he rose to power, the French court system reached deep into the Corsican interior. Beginning around 1800, the French compiled a vast archive of official documents (and unofficial memoirs and novels) on life in "the land of the vendetta."

The Corsican people—mainly herdsmen, farmers, and chestnut growers—spoke a variety of dialects related to ancient Tuscan. They were quite egalitarian and had no separate class of nobility. Family and *honore* (honor) were paramount: the larger your family (including first and second cousins and tenants, and sometimes third cousins) and the better their reputation, the stronger your position. *Honore* for a man in some ways defined crime, since it demanded that he avenge insults to himself or kinsmen, and especially threats to female chastity. A Corsican proverb put it this way: "At weddings and in trouble, one knows one's own people."

The French records show relatively little property crime, despite poverty, and most of that was banditry or theft from distant merchants or peddlers. Stealing from neighbors or within the family brought serious *bergogna* (dishonor or shame). On the other hand, the records contain stories like this one:

In June 1835, wonderful news spread in the troubled Corsican village of Arbellara: the rich and handsome Guilio Forcioli, returned from his medical studies in Rome, was to marry Maria Giustiniani, the mayor's beautiful daughter. The marriage would bring together the two leading families of the village and end the bad blood between them. In half a dozen recorded episodes over the last several years, the families had found their oxen, cows and horses poisoned or shot, and now everyone in the village was afraid to go out after dark.

But in July more Forcioli livestock were found dead and, amid finger pointing and threats, the marriage was called off. On July 22, Guilio's brother Antono and his cousin ambushed four members of the Giustiniani clan, killing one and seriously wounding the mayor. The gunmen disappeared, and everyone barricaded their homes. On August 11, a third Forcioli brother, Rocco, was shot in the leg, and in the ensuing melee, one of the Forcioli women stabbed Maria three times. Despite a string of truces and peace pacts, some of them celebrated in church, the vendetta sputtered along for decades, eventually claiming half a dozen more lives.

The honor code required Corsican males to own guns, and young men sometimes humiliated others to impress the girls. For example, if someone took your gun and spit down the barrel, you had to retaliate when you got the chance. If you didn't, you were *rimbeccu* (a wimp), a disgrace and liability to your family. Etiquette required that you give fair warning (once) before launching a vendetta, and if you couldn't get to the culprit, then attacking a close relative was almost as good.

This law enforcement method might sound completely dysfunctional, but most of the time it worked better than one might think. It maintained order within Corsican families, despite increasing overpopulation and crowded homes during the 1800s. It normally imposed good behavior across families and villages as well, since the potential cost of impoliteness could be so high to one's family. Even when a man raped or killed a member of another family, cooler heads in both families usually would discuss the matter and often would agree on punishment, perhaps exile or even being shot by his own kinsmen. For example, in January 1848, Susino Maestrati killed Bastiano Guidicelli in the village of Zonza, and the same afternoon Bastiano's nephew killed Susino's brother. The elders saw a balance of *honore*, and to keep things from getting out of hand, they made everyone tell the authorities that the two victims had killed each other.

Of course, the French records tell us mainly about times where the moral code failed to keep order, as in Arbellara and hundreds of other episodes. The problem is that plaintiffs were also judges and juries. And even very cool heads suffer from self-serving bias. It is easy to disagree on fault and proper punishment, and on whose *honore* had been slighted most. The moral code demanded vengeance to obtain a favorable balance of *honore* and, too often, that in turn demanded countervengeance. The result was a homicide rate about 100 times higher than in most modern societies.

How Markets Cut Crime

Murder and other major crimes are more common in hunter-gatherer cultures. Civilized people took this assertion for granted until about 200 years ago. But then Rousseau and other Romantics argued that "savages" were naturally noble and moral, and many 20th-century anthropologists agreed. By the late 20th century, however, all evidence favored the original assertion. Even !Kung homicide rates are higher than in any modern nation, and rates in some Amazonian and Borneo tribes are about ten times higher, similar to those of 19th-century Corsica. Archeological evidence suggests that murder rates among our ancestors tens of thousands of years ago were also pretty high.

Investigators use the homicide rate as a gauge of crime overall because it is the offense people are most likely to report. And as civilization advances, homicide and other serious crimes decrease. Historians combing the archives of medieval European towns estimate an annual homicide rate of about 50 per 100,000 residents. The rate dropped by about half in the 16th and 17th centuries, and by the time of the great market takeover it was below 10 per 100,000. Even as the total amount of property exploded, the trend continued downward throughout the 1800s with the introduction of modern courts, police, and prisons. By around 1880, the annual homicide rate in London was less than 2 per 100,000 and headed lower. No wonder the Victorian philosophers were so optimistic.

The trend in many advanced industrial countries justifies their optimism. Japan and Iceland now have homicide rates below 0.5, and most of the others lie in the 1 to 3 range. However, developing countries often have rates over 10. In 2010 Honduras had the highest murder rate in the world, at 82 per 100,000, and El Salvador was second at 66 per 100,000.

Did the market system itself cause the drop in crime? The correlation is hard to ignore. The main point of a 2006 book by Benjamin S. Friedman (no relation) is that economic growth (that is, rising income for the average person) historically coincides with a more tolerant, mobile, and democratic society, presumably with lower crime rates.

Why? One reasonable explanation is that a wealthier society can spend more on crime prevention. It can hire efficient, honest police officers and use better detection and prevention technology, such as fingerprinting, burglar alarms, and in-store videos. Digital car keys have slashed auto theft, and smartphones let people easily call police and photograph offenders. Moreover, when wealth is widespread, individuals have more legitimate opportunities and should find crime less tempting. Yet another explanation goes beyond the standard perspective. Markets lead to legal systems, so *honore* codes fade away. Punishment falls to professional, objective institutions like courts, so insults don't justify violence, and amateurish revenge doesn't spark counterattacks. Markets also broaden social webs, strengthen bonds, and foster moral behavior. So the market takeover transforms the moral system. Personal traits like patience and prudence tend to displace traits favored in feudal societies. The new qualities are less conducive to crime.

This logic suggests that the United States, with the world's most advanced market economy, would have the world's lowest crime rates. Unfortunately, we have one of the highest in the developed world. In 2009, for example, the US homicide rate was 5 per 100,000, five times higher than in the United Kingdom. At the same time, crime rates in other industrial countries, although lower than in the United States, stopped falling in the last quarter of the 20th century while their economies continued to grow. Something else must be going on.

And it is. Murder rates swing up in developed countries if they have violent gangs, extensive drug trafficking, organized crime, and easy access to weapons. The market overall tightens the social web and makes us more moral, but where law enforcement falters, we get situations much like that in Corsica, and the killings increase. Honduras and El Salvador score so high because they have the worst of both worlds: low development and extensive drug cultures.

Which brings us to the garden of vice.

Ecstasy and Agony

What's the harm in vice? It's easy to think that vices are victimless crimes, because they affect mainly the perpetrator. She makes the decision, and she should be free to choose what she wants even if she chooses badly. Though most of us avoid activities like gambling and drug abuse out of self-interest, our calculation of costs and benefits is clearly not hers. If we intervene, we are thwarting her liberty.

Why then do most societies try so hard to suppress some vices? Why waste the money and energy?

The answer is, first, that these crimes are not victimless. Self-damage radiates. Vices divert funds from the person's family, sabotage trust, and coarsen conduct. Heroin addicts, for instance, learn to lie to conceal their habit and get more drugs, and their inner restraints to crime weaken. Indeed, at least half of criminals in US prisons have a drug-related history (though the causality is complex). So vices are not really victimless, and often it is in society's interest to suppress them.

Some teenage girls like to cut their flesh. It makes them feel calm, they say. "I was cutting 10-plus times a day," explained a student named Becki, "and still, if I didn't do it, I would feel like I was missing something." How do you respond to her? These acts are "victimless," yet most of us feel an urge to help. We developed morals because aiding others in the tribe aided us, and we have a generalized desire to help. We let trapped drivers onto the road, and we help other trapped and vulnerable people too.

Yet vices remain tempting, even in our age of extraordinary information flow, when their hazards are known. Why do they flourish now more than ever?

Most start out as fun. They hook into pleasure centers in the brain, which generally guide us in the right direction and which have evolved to help pass DNA down the generations. For instance, our taste and scent receptors make meals enjoyable. Without the rich flavors of food, we might not eat enough. But vices are like sugar. We evolved our pleasure centers for the needs of the savanna, when sugar was uncommon and signalled good nutrition, such as ripe fruit. Today, when sugar is common and signals poor nutrition, we still like it very much.

Take prostitution. Nature has endowed us with sex drives, since without them a vertebrate species dies out. Yet, as Bill Clinton showed the world, they can overpower good sense. When a hooker whispers and winks, a john can know he'd be better off walking on, yet still respond. In earlier times, male promiscuity passed on DNA, so this behavior makes sense—genetically, at least. But prostitution is illegal in most of the United States partly because it can break the pair bond, shatter trust, and harm the raising of children. It also spreads disease and, perhaps most basically, it offends a sense of sanctity about the relation between sex and love.

Substance abuse and gambling have similar roots. Alcohol, opiates, cocaine, "bath salts," and other addictive drugs first hijack the pleasure mechanisms. Morphine, for instance, feels good. So a person tries more. And soon it becomes almost part of the brain's operating system, essential to prevent the agonies of withdrawal. Strong inner promptings of pleasure and pain, the normal guides to self-interest, now betray self-interest, so the addict wants what she really doesn't want. Self-interest devours itself.

Gambling is a variation on the theme, since studies show that the prospect of higher wealth and status can also trigger changes in brain chemistry. These changes are healthy and spur us to achievement. But most people also assess risk fairly carefully. Why would nature spur you to bet on winning wealth and status, when on average you lose and fall further behind? Evolutionary psychologists focus on the greatest risk takers: low-status adolescent males. Their argument is that if you are a low-status adolescent male in a premodern society and you play it safe, you'll have few if any mates and surviving children. Your fitness is close to zero. So if you take a big risk, how far can you fall? You might score big and gain far better opportunities to father children, legitimate or not. Although wealth payoff may be negative on average, the fitness payoff—in average number of descendents—is positive. Hence, nature gives us a taste for risk taking, especially when we are low-status, adolescent, or male.

Naïve pundits and most voters assume that outlawing an industry will make it disappear. But all they really do is increase the cost of delivering the product. Merchants must take extra measures to avoid arrest, and they pass the cost on to the buyer. So the price rises, and the amount sold drops. But the dealer's revenues fall only if demand is "elastic," that is, if consumers buy a lot less as price rises (technically, if a 1 percent price increase will decrease the quantity purchased by more than 1 percent). Otherwise, the price hike more than offsets the smaller amount sold, and revenues actually increase. Moreover, production costs fall (since less is sold), partially offsetting the increased delivery costs. The upshot is that outlawing commerce in an item with inelastic demand will increase revenue and might increase profit.

Demand for vice (as for all addictive products) tends to be very inelastic. Anyone who discovers a business model that keeps down the cost of delivering an outlawed vice, then, stands to profit. Such a business model is bound to spread, expanding the industry. In sum, economic logic tells us that outlawing a vice can make it into a larger industry than before.

So much for economic logic. How did modern markets for vice actually evolve? We'll look at three of the largest.

The Turn of the Card

Demand for gambling must have expanded as people developed agricultural and urban societies, in part because low status is much less prevalent among hunter-gatherers, and mobility is higher. The rise of property gave people more to gamble with, and money must have spurred demand further, since it let wealth flow faster and more countably. It's easier to bet with shekels than chickens or pots. As people of all classes grew richer and could afford larger and more frequent bets, innovators developed a wider variety of opportunities, such as wagering on new games of chance and sporting events.

State-sponsored lotteries in the United States go back to the Virginia colony in 1612, and gambling was widely tolerated until the late 1800s. Then a wave of scandals—such as payoffs to state officials and the rigging of winning numbers—helped fuel religious opposition and the rising Progressive movement to "improve the working classes." By 1900 most gambling was unlawful. Only a handful of states allowed any at all, and then usually just at the racetrack.

Of course, demand for gambling turned out to be inelastic. Revenues and profits soared as delighted entrepreneurs found new ways to serve gamblers. The Mafia business model worked especially well: monopolize the local action, pay winners reliably but keep a large "rake" (fraction of the total bets), and bribe local police and officials to maintain lax enforcement.

Political support for the ban began to fade in the 1960s, and in the 1970s an unholy alliance of starved public schools and gambling nabobs brought back state-run lotteries. The amount Americans legally wager—the "handle"—is now over a trillion dollars a year. The net revenue (or rake) expanded from $10 billion in 1982 to over $92 billion by 2006, and is clearly much higher today. Some 80 percent of US adults report having engaged in gambling at some time in their lives, but about 5 percent account for half of all wagers. Experts estimate that 1 or 2 percent of Americans are addicts, whose gambling habit dominates their lives and can lead to bankruptcy. As predicted by evolutionary psychology, the addicts are more often male and come disproportionately from lower income groups.

Three new business models seem to be catching on.

Megacasinos. Las Vegas is the most extravagant city on earth, with its golden towers, fantasyland castles, marble piazzas, fake Statue of Liberty, black pyramid, and dancing waterspouts. And when the lights go on at night, it's a vision beyond the human capacity to dream. Yet an even bigger city of dreams was once a sleepy isle owned by the Portuguese off the coast of China. Mao Zedong had forbidden gambling, but fan-tan and other games lingered on in tiny Macau, across the bay from Hong Kong. This little place is now a spectacle. The Venetian Macao is the largest casino on the planet, and five times more money flows through Macau than Las Vegas. In 2010 Macau gamblers wagered $600 billion, about the total amount Americans withdraw from ATM's in a year.

Yet the gaming industry remains vigorous in the United States. Casinos dominate Las Vegas and Atlantic City, they bounced back on the Gulf of Mexico after Katrina demolished them, and they daily shower cash on obscure Indian tribes. And as the recession withered tax revenues, states embraced gambling. Atlantic City's casino revenue has now dropped by over a third because of competition from Pennsylvania, Maryland, and Delaware. Valley Forge, Pennsylvania, has a casino and so does New York City, near the Aqueduct racetrack in Queens. In Nevada the gambling industry pays 12.5 percent of state expenses. Lotteries tantalize the low-income and unemployed with visions of overnight fortune, but typically only 55 percent of wagers are paid out to winners, while 10 percent goes to promotion, salaries, and so forth, and the state keeps the remaining 35 percent.

A backlash seemed to be gathering strength a few years ago as the social costs grew clearer and the benefits to education proved disappointing. Academic studies suggested that the social costs—increased crime, reduced demand for other goods, and especially other forms of entertainment—exceeded the gains for most communities. But states are hardly turning off the casino lights. Only Hawaii and Utah have no legalized gambling.

Online betting on events. Sites such as betfair.com allow people around the world to wager 24/7 on the outcome of soccer, basketball, and tennis matches as well as other sports events. Online betting companies have expanded their product line to include wagers on financial markets (e.g., will the Dow end the year above 14,000?), weather events (will a category 3 hurricane hit the US coast this season?), political contests (who will be elected president?), and current events (will the Israeli airforce strike Iran next month?). Intrade.com is probably the best known of these prediction markets. Potentially they can provide valuable insurance and information. For example, you can hedge your stock market position by betting that the Dow won't end the year above 14,000, and you might want to cancel a trip to the Mideast when the price of war bets increases. Overall, the prediction markets have proved remarkably accurate, more so than published expert opinion.

Online poker. Online wagers of all sorts are growing rapidly and likely reached $30 billion worldwide by 2011. The convenience to bettors, and the ability to shift easily to low tax jurisdictions, suggests that online sites will become major players in the gaming industry. Delaware became the first state to legalize online gambling in 2012, after Pennsylvania and Maryland began siphoning off its casino customers, and other states will follow. So we now have a causal if twisty path from liar loans to poker bluffs on the laptop.

Poker may be the most dynamic part of this industry. Its roots stretch back to China a thousand years ago, when playing cards first appeared and soon spread across Eurasia. The current 52-card deck took shape in France about 500 years ago, and the ace may beat the king today as a result of the French Revolution. Poker emerged as a distinct game in New Orleans in the early 1800s, with rules published by 1850.

Decks of cards are cheap and easy to carry, and they can entertain dozens of people for months or years. Hence card games spread across the United States in covered wagons, during the Civil War, and in both world wars. Poker is especially appealing to players since it requires skills in detecting and disguising intentions, and in building and exploiting a reputation outside the normal confines of the moral code. Several varieties of poker have evolved, and in casinos Texas hold-em has tended to displace draw and stud.

Until quite recently, poker's commercial appeal seemed limited. Unlike slot machines or roulette, it doesn't funnel much income to casinos. At best, the players buy drinks and the house rakes in part of the pot. However, Hollywood profited from poker, and increased its popularity, with movies like *Big Hand for the Little Lady*, *The Cincinnati Kid*, and *Rounders*. And since 2000 TV coverage has exploded. Tournament viewership now exceeds even NBA basketball, and the big winners are instant celebrities.

Poker became an industry in its own right as the Internet grew. Computer screens capture poker action much better than that of rival sports like darts or billiards, and the Internet reduces players' participation costs. Tens of thousands of players now frequent sites like pokerstars.com every night, and wager tens of millions of dollars. Though the media run occasional horror stories of young lives ruined by an online poker addiction, widespread harm remains hard to see.

In sum, the gaming industry is taking new forms, some socially beneficial and others less so—and the gods of fate are smiling warmly on it.

The Lure of the Bottle

Throughout most of Western civilization, laws and norms have encouraged moderate beer and wine consumption. Distilled spirits with higher alcoholic content, first developed by Persian alchemists, reached Europe in medieval times. Cheap versions ("demon rum") and abuse among the urban lower classes spurred the paternalistic Prohibition movement in the United States by the mid-1800s. Activists pushed through the Eighteenth Amendment to the US Constitution, which outlawed the alcohol industry in 1919.

The result was a classic of morals leading markets awry. Prohibition cut consumption by perhaps 25 to 50 percent but tripled the average price. And enforcement turned out to be far harder than Prohibitionists had predicted—but that really shouldn't surprise anyone who does the math. The estimates imply a doubling, more or less, of industry revenues, and windfall profits for suppliers.

The new profit opportunities degraded morals. Illegal brewing, distilling, importing (bootlegging), and sales (in speakeasies) became widespread and condoned by local norms, encouraging a general disrespect for the law and hypocritical authority. Organized crime got a major boost, and homicides and police corruption increased. Consumption shifted toward drinks with higher alcohol content (easier to smuggle) and greater health risks. Government revenues from alcohol taxes vanished while enforcement expenses increased. Perhaps the best anyone can say for Prohibition is that it reduced liver cirrhosis, by zero to 50 percent (estimates differ). Public support collapsed after 1930, and in 1933 the Twenty-first Amendment ended the "noble experiment."

Current laws support several major subindustries in the United States with quite diverse business plans. Wine makers, brewers, distillers, distributors, and retailers generate annual retail sales of about $100 billion. The industry is a cash cow for government, delivering annual tax receipts of about $20 billion, even though the tax rate now is rather low. At about 25 cents per ounce of alcohol, it is only about one third of its level 50 years ago (after accounting for inflation). Enforcement remains a major enterprise; one federal agency, ATF, has a $1 billion annual budget. (Supposedly most of it goes to firearms control and "antiterror activities," but at least 2 percent of it funds the pursuit of alcohol and cigarette tax evaders.)

Alcohol addiction remains a major problem, and leads to over 100,000 excess deaths annually in the United States. Since 1934 Alcoholics Anonymous has provided peer support to recovering alcoholics. Its decentralized networks currently include millions of members, and it has spawned several other 12-step programs for people such as drug abusers and compulsive overeaters. These are in-groups of mutual aid, and they show the power of morals to overcome chemical dependency itself, for they all work by enmeshing people in the tight, supportive fabric of the tribe. Members sacrifice time and effort for each other; for instance, they take long phone calls from desperate people on the edge of taking a drink. They recognize that each individual needs help, just as they do, and they provide it, often in striking ways. The uncle of one of us (McNeill) was an AA member and McNeill recalls a Christmas dinner at the suburban home of this man who, though highly conservative, invited two unwashed, homeless alcoholics to eat with the family and treated them as equals and partners. It was unforgettable.

The Dead End of Tobacco Road

Tobacco is a vice even more lethal than alcohol. Cigarette smoking accounts for over 400,000 excess deaths each year in the United States and hence is the largest preventable killer. The industry is huge, with worldwide annual revenues currently around $300 billion.

Throughout most of the 20th century, the US industry was a cozy oligopoly, insulated from competition and raking in extraordinary profits from addicted customers. It recruited generation after generation of new customers with sophisticated marketing campaigns featuring rugged cowboys and cool camels.

The industry had just one problem: its product killed people. In December 1953 scientists proved that you could cause cancer in mice by painting cigarette tar on their skin. The finding received global publicity, and panicked industry executives met in New York for damage control. They retained the PR firm of Hill and Knowlton, and John Hill stressed that they had to fund "additional research" and that "scientific doubts must remain." So began the strategy: Counter science with "scienciness." Question rather than prove.

On January 4, 1954, industry leaders printed "A Frank Statement to Cigarette Smokers" in 448 newspapers. It said, "We accept an interest in people's health as a basic responsibility, paramount to every other consideration in our business," and added that "we always have and always will cooperate closely with those whose task it is to safeguard the public's health." Top tobacco executives signed this document. It turned out to be about as honest as if a group of Mafia dons said they'd always cooperated closely with police.

For decades the market has corrupted morals within the tobacco industry. Most notably, it bred institutionalized lying, on a scale and with a sophistication never before seen. Over the decades, the industry funded massive campaign contributions, expensive lawyers and lobbyists, and well-equipped "research" labs. And it pioneered techniques to make people doubt important scientific findings. A key tactic was: Conjure a debate where none really existed and convince the media they had a moral duty to balance two viewpoints. After all, when viewers see newscasters present an argument and counterargument, they naturally assume each side has some weight. If a TV network is in doubt, maybe they should be too. Foes of action on the ozone hole, acid rain, and global warming later used the same strategy. And the moral consequences for people in the tobacco industry went far beyond deceit. The market turned otherwise law-abiding executives into killers—men and women who focused on the bottom line and accepted consumer death as collateral damage.

Meanwhile, researchers went on to show that smoking was the main cause of lung cancer and emphysema and contributed to other fatal ailments. Indeed, since 1954 smoking has ended at least 16 million American lives and saddled millions more with illnesses like heart disease. Scientists also proved that nicotine, a molecule prevalent in tobacco smoke, was highly addictive. Various nongovernmental (and eventually also governmental) organizations publicized the danger. The first breakthrough, in 1969, was the mandatory printed warning from the surgeon general "Smoking may be dangerous to your health," later strengthened to "Smoking causes lung cancer." Antismoking campaigns started to take hold.

In response, the industry began to argue that people knew the risks but decided to smoke anyway. Big Government was taking away their freedom of choice, telling them what to do and what not do. This claim had spectacular flaws. For instance, most beginning smokers are young and ill-informed about the real risks. It doesn't help to give a blindfolded man freedom to choose his course. Moreover, free choice disappears for an addict. His brain punishes him if he doesn't buy a pack at the supermarket. So first you choose and then you don't. And of course tobacco merchants were doing everything they could to hide the real risks from people. Markets realize their potential with complete information and industry falsehoods interfered. So the market initially degraded industry morals, and then low morals worsened the market. Yet the industry always prevailed in the legislature and, as family members of dead smokers began suing, it never lost in court. It seemed a juggernaut.

Life and health are the ultimate currencies, and our institutions eventually responded. The turning point came from evidence about the harm from second-hand smoking. Self-damage radiates, and here nonsmokers were dying. In 1994 trial lawyers allied with state government officials and launched an epic legal battle. Success came suddenly in late 1998. The landmark Master Settlement showered over $250 billion on state governments over 25 years, with tens of billions more going to lawyers and to educational funds.

You might think that the settlement was bad for the industry, but savvy investors saw a bright silver lining. Altria's stock price, for example, rose about 25 percent during the second half of 1998 as investors realized that the settlement locked in a 50 percent market share for the company's Phillip Morris brands, led by Marlboro. State governments now rely on revenue from the tobacco industry and so have become industry stakeholders. The states can't bring further legal action, and the settlement might actually reduce the industry's future tax liability. As a result, it is easier for the cartel to raise prices, extracting even more money from nicotine addicts.

Yet changing norms seem to be reducing the health risk. Smoking has become disreputable in much of the United States, and most of Western Europe seems to be moving in the same direction. Industry growth may be slowing in China too, where Friedman on a recent visit saw far fewer smokers than several years earlier. Teenagers are the key to the future, and their norms began to turn against smoking in the late 1990s. However, the decline in smoking among US high school students apparently ended by 2006, as antismoking campaigns wound down and cash-strapped states diverted more settlement funds into other activities.

The Prodigy and the Penalty Calculus

Where should we draw the legal lines between crime and vice? More broadly, what enforcement policies should the legal system deploy? How much of our scarce resources should we devote to police, courts, and prisons?

Jeremy Bentham (1748–1832) was among the first modern thinkers to tackle these big questions. Exhibited as a child prodigy by his father, a prosperous London solicitor, Bentham emerged at age 16 with an Oxford law degree, a fondness for philosophy, a fear of rough company, and a distaste for actual practice of law. In 1769 he read Joseph Priestley's slogan "the greatest happiness for the greatest number" and found his life's mission: to make this idea the centerpiece of morality. His 1776 "Fragment on Government" caught the attention of leading scholars, who rescued him from his "miserable life" as an unemployed lawyer, and he blossomed as a public intellectual. When his father died and left him a tidy fortune, Bentham bought poet John Milton's former London home and, for the last 40 years of his life, was seldom seen outside its gates.

Bentham lived to write. Every day he rose at 6 a.m., walked around his garden, and then wrote steadily until evening. He wrote to people all over the world and to officials and scholars in London. He wrote notes to himself, and, once in a while, he even wrote for publication. Bentham proposed inventions, such as refrigerators and pneumatic tubes for messages, and most notably, the panopticon. The idea, rather Orwellian, was to build a jail so that a few centrally positioned guards could peer into hundreds of individual jail cells without the prisoners seeing the guards—who could thus take frequent (but randomly timed) coffee breaks. This would be much cheaper, Bentham argued, than maintaining heavily guarded jails or shipping pickpockets and whores to Australia.

Although he didn't actually enjoy human company (he was inordinately attached to his walking stick and cats), Bentham's goal above all was to make more people happier. When he died, he donated his 172 boxes of writings to the new University College of London, where staff is still sorting them out. He wanted his corpse to be useful, too. Following his will meticulously, technicians dissected his body before medical students and reassembled it into a wax-enhanced mummy, the "Auto-Icon," which now sits in a glass case, walking stick in hand, in the lobby outside the university's finest lecture room.

Bentham's lasting legacy is his "hedonistic calculus," a sometimes subtle (and sometimes obtuse) cost-benefit analysis. Here's an example, updated slightly. Suppose a thief steals an heirloom bracelet a family values at $1,000 and sells it for $100, and the family afterwards spends $2,000 changing locks and installing an alarm system. The associated direct cost of the crime is $900, or $1,000 minus $100. (Yes, the thief's gain partly counters the family's loss. A total of $900 has disappeared here.) The $2,000 is an extra private expense of crime prevention. We should also account for public costs of crime prevention and law enforcement, including those for police, courts, and prisons.

The greatest good for the greatest number (or efficiency, in modern jargon) in this context comes down to minimizing the total social cost: the sum of all prevention and enforcement costs balanced against the direct costs of crime. So Bentham asks: Will we get our money's worth? Will an additional expenditure on crime prevention or enforcement reduce the cost of crime by an amount greater than itself? Spending $100,000 on catching jewel thieves, for example, is efficient if it will reduce the costs of theft and other crimes by more than $100,000, and inefficient if it reduces the costs by less than that, say, $90,000.

But how can we know in advance the impact of a policy on crime rates? Bentham assumed (as do his modern followers) that potential criminals try to maximize profit. A rational thief will steal the bracelet if he expects the revenue ($100) to exceed his cost. His cost includes time spent on the crime and disposing of the loot, plus expected jail time (the probability of being caught and convicted times the length of sentence served) and other losses due to conviction.

For example, consider three different ways to raise the cost of theft: (1) increase the probability of catching suspects 10 percent by adding more police patrols, or (2) increase the probability of convicting a suspect 10 percent by boosting the prosecutor budget (or allowing weaker evidence), or (3) increase punishment for convicted thieves 10 percent. Rational thieves would respond equally to any of the three ways, so the more efficient policy would be the cheapest, usually harsher punishment.

Bentham's approach is a useful starting place, but it has its limits. It treats law-breakers as if they were small businesses with ledgers and budgets. Yet criminals are rarely rational profit maximizers. Some are disturbed. Some like the thrill of crime. Jane Austen's wealthy aunt, for instance, was a kleptomaniac. Some law-breakers belong to in-groups that encourage offenses. For example, a small-time hood may commit a spectacular but unprofitable crime in hopes of gaining higher status among his peers. Young criminals seem to worry more about the chance of conviction than the severity of punishment. Also, dollar values can be vexing. What is the direct cost of a rape or murder, for example? What is the cost to the public psyche of a mass murderer on the prowl? What is the cost in lost business to a city with a high crime rate? Bentham's optimum point is a blur and compels a guessing game.

There is a larger issue too: To what extent do we view justice as a business or a service? We have innate moral instincts, and if we have to spend $100,000 to reduce jewel theft by $90,000, it may still make moral sense to do it. We go out of our way to help people. There is a balance between morals and economics here, and people may reasonably disagree about the midpoint. But the baseline seems clear: We have to pay attention to Bentham's cost-benefit approach, yet we can't fully rely on it.

Lawyers and Economics

All developed countries have a court system, but only in the United States does the trial lawyer industry loom so large. Hundreds of billions pass through the system each year, a major increase over the past three decades. The industry's current profit centers (like asbestos, tobacco, and insurance) help fund exploration of potential growth markets (like lead paint, mold, and regulated industries) and new products (like suits against the fast-food industry). The industry's government relations and public relations arms are among the most powerful of business lobbies. They contribute to both political parties, but are a core constituency for the Democrats.

The movie *Erin Brockovich* lays out the business model in product liability: Find sympathetic victims, like young families with major health problems. Find an unpopular, overlord-like defendant who may be responsible, like Pacific Gas & Electric. Appeal to the jury's moral sentiments and ask them to help the injured innocents get even with the bully. (Of course, the defendant's lawyers will counter by portraying the plaintiffs as lazy gold diggers, and will remind the jury that exorbitant fines will hurt the defendant's workers and customers.) Since lawyers can get up to 50 percent of any award and most cases settle before trial, they can sometimes sue profitably even when the chance of winning isn't especially large.

At the same time, the costs of obtaining justice in the US system are so high that many people can't afford them. The simple solutions available in a tribe need a fat wallet today. One of us (McNeill) worked at a top law firm in Los Angeles, and one day he heard an associate attorney make an interesting complaint. A partner had asked her to represent his housekeeper but to keep the bill under $10,000. She shook her head in amazement. It wasn't remotely possible, and hence this attorney would be donating time. And even $10,000 is beyond the reach of many. So when lawyers work on contingency for, say, 40 percent of the settlement, they are often righting wrongs and aiding victims who would otherwise get nothing.

Defendants, like asbestos and pharmaceuticals firms, have found more and more effective ways to fight back. Their political campaign contributions now rival those of trial lawyers. The Bush administration tried, with partial success, to cap the damages juries can award and to make it more difficult to file class action lawsuits. Judges are now more alert for claims "manufactured for money," and one of the most aggressive class action law firms is under indictment for paying people to become plaintiffs. Industry growth has slowed.

Is the trial lawyer industry too large? Consider the benefits and costs. In tort law, lawyers have pushed manufacturers to find safer processes and products. PG&E is much more cautious now with toxic chemicals, for example, and we all benefit from that care. The most obvious cost is higher consumer prices, but others are subtler. For example, the fear of lawsuits has pushed medical doctors to prescribe defensive tests or therapies of dubious value, and the same threat has destroyed the small airplane industry.

Bentham said we're efficient when, on average, the last dollar spent on safety actually reduces harm by more than one dollar. By this standard, the trial lawyer industry is efficient to the extent that the threat of lawsuits pushes everyone toward this goal, and does so more cheaply than other incentives. Yet the formula breaks down when we're dealing with unquantifiable harm, such as death from tobacco and lifelong injury from lead paint. And in the end, even if lawyers have pushed us beyond Bentham's balancing point, without them we would never have gotten near it. We would have paid less in prevention, but far more in harm. A moral system without penalties is just a set of niceties, and without reciprocal pain for, say, dumping toxic chemicals, the practices continue. So morals and markets tug in different directions here too, and we need to keep them in equipoise.

Incarceration Nation

Prisons are as old as civilization, but only in the United States have they become a major industry in their own right. With less than 5 percent of the world's population, we now hold about 25 percent of the world's prisoners. Our incarceration rate is 11 times higher than Japan's and about seven times higher than that in most of Europe. It is difficult to find any country in any era that kept a larger fraction of its population behind bars.

Who are we warehousing? Mainly the nonviolent, especially drug users and sellers. Over 60 percent of our prisoners are nonviolent offenders, and nonviolent *drug* offenders make up some 25 percent of the lockup populace, compared to 10 percent in 1980. The US population grew 33 percent from 1980 to 2008, while the jailhouse population jumped more than 350 percent, to 2.4 million.

The burden to taxpayers is enormous. Overall in 2010 the California prison system cost $7.9 billion, almost as much as the state spent on the 400,000 students at Cal State and the 200,000 at the University of California. Each convict sets California back by more than $47,000 annually, so if it released just one person jailed for marijuana possession three years early, the state could pay a student's full tuition at Stanford Law School. Overall, incarceration is one of the state's larger industries, and its revenues come almost entirely from taxpayers.

So what do we get for our money?

Prisons have always served four distinct purposes. The first is punishment: Make the culprit suffer. It is negative reciprocity, on behalf of the victim and society as a whole. The second is incapacitation: Put the offender on ice for a while so he can't harm anyone else. The third is rehabilitation: Improve the culprit so he'll contribute to society when released and won't commit more crimes. The final purpose is deterrence: Make crime less attractive by highlighting the penalties to potential wrongdoers.

Punishment and incapacitation certainly happen in California. Few offenders enjoy the experience and the state locks up plenty. Officials anticipate 110,000 inmates by June 2013.

What about rehabilitation? In reality, we have the reverse: criminalization. While serving time, California's prisoners learn new lawbreaking techniques from fellow reprobates and expand their criminal networks, but very few have the opportunity to develop the skills, contacts, and attitudes needed to succeed in legitimate society. In 2003 the new boss of the California Department of Correction, Rod Hickman, proudly added "Rehabilitation" to its name. He resigned in frustration after less than three years. The DEA says drug treatment can cut recidivism from over 50 percent to around 20 percent—yet these programs are rare because politicians see upfront costs and not the huge long-term savings. If the DEA is right, it's as if Keats's Cortez let an upfront peak in Darien block his sight of the Pacific.

Deterrence is hard to measure since it's inaction. Crime has been declining throughout the nation in recent years, but the causes are unclear and mixed. Yet available evidence is not encouraging. A recent, statistically sophisticated US study suggests that in the 1980s an additional year behind bars prevented about two violent crimes, but now it prevents less than one half of one violent crime. The authors conclude that we are now jailing less dangerous criminals and thus reducing the incapacitation effect.

In all, California's prison system is a masterpiece of inefficiency. It locks up too many people at exorbitant cost and criminalizes them further. Once released they commit more crimes and keep coming back.

How did the state get into this situation? The answer is actually pretty clear to most policy analysts, though they differ on emphasis and terminology. The cause is government oversensitivity to special interests: the prison industry, its labor union, state and national politicians, and television news. Unable to resist these varied influences, state government has taxed its citizens to pay high salaries to officials it doesn't need and subsistence for prisoners it shouldn't keep.

Let's start with the union, the California Correctional Peace Officers Association (CCPOA). In the early 1980s Don Novey put CCPOA together from fragmented groups of low-paid prison guards. He increased dues and used the money to build public relations and influence in Sacramento. The timing was excellent, and guards' salaries climbed steadily while employment grew. By 2006 members received an average annual base salary of $57,000, the highest in the nation, and with overtime more than a tenth of them earned over $100,000. The union collects about $22 million in dues each year and uses the money to run a sophisticated operation. More than a third of the union's budget goes to political activities. In the aftermath of the 2003–4 state budget crisis and the recall election, the new governor, Arnold Schwarzenegger, tried to reduce prison payrolls by a mere $300,000. The union and its allies forced him to back down, and in the end he offered concessions that made the union stronger and richer than ever.

The union's goals dovetail nicely with those of the construction industry and suppliers of prison services, such as food and medical care. All benefit from more convictions and longer sentences, and from larger annual expenditures per prisoner. The expansion of the state system from 13 prisons in 1985 to 31 in 1995 increased their revenues and political power.

Politicians are key players, since they choose policies and allocate the resources. A politician's business model always involves raising campaign funds and finding messages that resonate with voters. A recipe for success in the late 20th-century United States was to get contributions from the prison industry (especially, in California, from the union) and to talk "tough on crime."

Consider, for example, the 1994 "three-strikes" initiative sponsored by the CCPOA and by "victims' rights committees" funded by the union and its allies. Endorsed by politicians in both parties, the initiative passed with over 70 percent of the vote. It requires life sentences for conviction of a third felony and generally forces the courts to impose longer sentences. The three-strikes law is one reason California's prison population has soared, but it does little or nothing to protect the public. For example, Leonard Scott, a 50-year-old who had stayed out of jail for 20 years following two burglary convictions, was sentenced in January 2000 to 25 years to life for misrepresenting his financial condition on a car lease. The law prevents judges from using their good sense, and makes taxpayers fund an expensive but unpleasant retirement for those who no longer pose much danger to society.

Why do voters support such costly, useless policies? TV local news is part of the explanation. Its business model is to build ratings, and to hold viewers through advertisements. In-depth analyses of sentencing guidelines and their cost effectiveness don't help. They achieve their goals far better with stories and images that appeal to strong emotions, such as fear and our urge to find and punish wrongdoers. Crime rates and actual danger to the public have little to do with what works for TV.

At the same time, tales of inhumane sentences also appealed to viewers. When they saw a man ordered to spend his life in jail for stealing a slice of pizza, their emotions rose. More and more such stories appeared, and in November 2012 the three-strikes law itself struck out. California voters revised it to limit life sentences to those who had committed serious crimes, and it let courts re-sentence third-strike prisoners guilty of innocuous offenses. Morals and markets each improved.

Brain Cells and Jail Cells

The history of the War on Drugs reprises familiar themes. About a hundred years ago, people in some states could purchase heroin and cocaine legally but not tobacco or alcohol. The medical profession initially encouraged those drugs as general and local anesthetics, but early in the 20th century it turned to substitutes like morphine and Novocain that produced fewer side effects. Cocaine remained for a while as a minor ingredient of patent medicines, while consumption of opium products, confined mainly to Chinese immigrants, was declining. Nonetheless, sensational (and often racist) newspaper stories, combined with reformist zeal and foreign policy concerns (mainly, ending opium trade in the Far East) spurred Congress to pass the 1914 Harrison Narcotics Tax Act. It required a doctor's prescription for these and many other drugs. As a result, consumption in the United States dwindled until midcentury, and then began to rise as organized crime discovered the profit potential.

Since then we've been caught in a runaway growth cycle. Advances in the industries that supply illegal drugs provoke growth in the repression industry, which in turn leads to further innovations on the supply side. Harry Anslinger, the entrepreneurial chief of the new Federal Narcotics division in the 1930s, increased his mandate and budget by leading a successful campaign to outlaw marijuana use. The youth culture of the 1950s and 1960s glamorized the use of illegal drugs, especially marijuana and the new psychedelics. Norms can be a bit fuzzy, and the youth culture of the day led to more abuse of the harder illegal drugs.

In 1971 President Nixon escalated the situation by announcing his War on Drugs with a much expanded enforcement budget. Since then, the US government has spent $20 to $25 billion per year on programs like spraying coca fields in South America. The market system responded predictably: prices rose, and so producer and distributor networks expanded. They fought each other for turf, tried to corrupt enforcers in the United States and overseas, diversified their product lines, and sought new customers in the suburbs and small towns. Enforcement, despite all the taxpayer money it commands, has fallen behind since 2000. Indeed, prices for cocaine, heroin, and meth actually dropped about 16 percent from 2001 to 2011. The number of users has fallen slightly, so evidently the suppliers have gotten much more efficient.

The Internet has made deterrence even harder. Dealers have of course used Craigslist, which seems to have sold everything but nuclear warheads. And today anyone can buy illegal drugs on the site Silk Road, where all identities are anonymous and the rip-off opportunities are obvious, and yet customers report a satisfaction rating of 97.5 percent.

The War on Drugs has caused both sides to flourish—the illegal drug industry and the enforcement industry—yet it has brought only misery to taxpayers and ordinary citizens. Illegal drugs now generate about $64 billion in retail sales annually in the United States and account for some 25,000 excess deaths—less than tobacco or alcohol but still depressing figures. The public houses some 600,000 nonviolent drug offenders in prison cells, people who could contribute to the economy if they were free. And authorities have long recognized addiction as a medical problem: It is an incurable brain change and solutions aren't easy. Drug rehabilitation programs have success rates well under 50 percent. Though that doesn't sound impressive, scientific studies still end up with benefit/cost estimates of 3 to 7. Society surely would benefit from further growth of the rehab industry and from the development of more effective prevention programs.

When the "noble experiment" of Prohibition bred ignoble behavior, public opinion terminated it in short order. Why didn't this happen with the War on Drugs? It surely ranks among the worst public policy mistakes, and it has been far more expensive and even less effective than Prohibition and has more malignant side effects. Yet it continues to receive widespread support among elected officials. That support may be waning—funding has declined significantly, and the Obama administration dropped the gung ho name entirely—but the apparatus remains intact. Why has our system failed us so badly?

The War on Drugs has persisted for the same reasons as California's prison-industrial complex. Key players found business models that succeeded for them, and it just so happens that some of the results hurt the general public. Whatever its failings, the War on Drugs has been very profitable for politicians, news media, law enforcement agencies, and prisons.

But this explanation raises a deeper question. If the public is seriously harmed, why don't political and business entrepreneurs come up with a way to solve the problem? Almost by definition, an inefficiency is a profit opportunity: there is surely some less expensive way to meet society's goals, and whoever steers society in that direction should be able to pocket some of the cost savings. Such entrepreneurs ended Prohibition in 1933. Why haven't we stopped the War on Drugs or reformed our prisons?

The difference between the two situations lies in the workings of the moral system. Widely held norms supported moderate alcohol use before Prohibition, and almost everyone knew drinkers. They were part of people's in-groups. And the onset of the Great Depression helped focus people on Prohibition's financial pains: reduced tax revenue and heightened enforcement costs. By contrast, the substances prohibited by US drug laws had not previously enjoyed mainstream acceptance, and addicts more readily fell into an out-group, where they have been easier to punish. At the same time, few citizens are aware of far more effective drug policies in the Netherlands, Switzerland, and elsewhere. As a result, taxpayers and voters misperceive the benefits and don't clearly see the costs.

Perhaps even more important, most people put alcohol and tobacco themselves in different moral categories from heroin and cocaine. For example, former drug czar William Bennett wrote that "drug use degrades human character," and philosopher James Q. Wilson observed:

> Tobacco shortens one's life, cocaine debases it. Nicotine alters one's habits, cocaine alters one's soul. The heavy use of crack, unlike the heavy use of tobacco, corrodes those natural sentiments of sympathy and duty that constitute our human nature and make possible our social life.

This is not really an appeal to sense. It is an appeal to Jonathan Haidt's value of sanctity. These drugs defile our soul, "corrode...our human nature." They tar the semi-divine. With such moral stakes, it is unnatural to give much weight to routine costs and benefits. Our instinct is to absolutely forbid the corrosive influences, whatever the cost.

Such instincts often work well in small cohesive groups, but in the modern world they are manipulated by sensationalist journalism (stories about addiction and violence and parents' heartache sell well), by politicians seeking higher office, and by bureaucrats seeking larger budgets. Competitive political markets and media amplify the appeals to moral outrage and don't help us focus on the actual consequences of current policy. Like Ahab's quest for the whale, these policies hijack our urge to punish and send us on a mad voyage.

9

Underworlds: The Tao of Gangs

I am like any other man. All I do is supply a demand.

—Al Capone

In a year early in this century, you could have seen a small group of men hauling a TV set and a satellite dish up into the beige, bush-speckled mountains around Khost, Afghanistan. Their leader had asked for this equipment for reasons unknown to them, but they trusted him. Yet once in camp, the TV gave nothing but white noise. They aimed the dish at every part of the sky, but all was static. The outside world wasn't reaching them.

Finally someone turned on a radio.

They were just in time. A BBC Arabia announcer stated that a jet had struck a World Trade Center tower in Manhattan.

Osama bin Laden beamed at the men and they erupted in celebration. The attack had ended, they thought, and they had struck a gigantic blow against the United States. But bin Laden shushed them. "Wait, wait," he said.

Soon a jet slammed into the second tower. Bin Laden prayed and wept at this sign of Allah's approval. The al-Qaeda members were astounded, but he turned to them and held up three fingers.

Next came news of a plane dive-bombing into the Pentagon, the nerve center of the US defense establishment.

As his crew gaped, bin Laden held up four fingers, but the last plane, meant for the Capitol dome, wound up in a Pennsylvania field.

Broadcast endlessly, visions of the World Trade Center seared into retinas worldwide. Its stump burned for 100 days.

Bin Laden eluded capture for a decade before Navy SEALs shot him and dumped his body in the Arabian Sea. Most of his fellow murderers are dead or in jail, and since then the United States has shredded the band and stopped most further attacks. Indeed, it almost stopped 9/11.

Gangs are ubiquitous. Over a million people worldwide belong to them, and they transcend borders. So we see Crips in Holland, female Muslim posses in Norway, and Jamaican bands in Kansas, and the Russian *mafiya* all over. About a billion people worldwide live in slums, which are vast incubation fields for gangs, so Maori crews flourish in Auckland and "skollies" in Cape Town. One of us (McNeill) has witnessed child street gangs in Rio de Janeiro, made up of orphans, hard-bitten beyond description.

But al-Qaeda was unusual, for many reasons.

From Informal Code to Governance: Prison Gangs

Where do gangs come from? Prison gangs give us a clue, and insight into how our species may have moved from tribes to governments.

California opened its first prison in 1852, and the system had no gangs for over 100 years. Indeed, the idea that criminal gangs could operate in a prison seemed vaguely outlandish, since guards were everywhere. But gangs began appearing in the 1950s and 1960s and quickly grew to dominate the cellblocks.

According to one study, this change occurred when norms grew inadequate. Since the 19th century, the "convict code" had governed behavior. It had such strictures as: Thou shalt not snitch, thou shalt not help staff, thou shalt not show weakness, and thou shalt not wantonly hurt other inmates. Everyone understood the ethos and men who excelled in it gained prestige. It was informal, like moral codes on the savanna, and it generally kept order.

Then the first prison gang, the Mexican Mafia, formed in 1956 at the Deuel Vocational Institution in Tracy, California. The timing was significant. Over the past year, the inmate population at Deuel had grown by 7 percent, and for the first time the facility exceeded its intended capacity. From 1944 to 1969 the number of prisoners in California would swell from 5,710 to 27,535. Deuel was like an overpacked suitcase. It was starting to strain.

The cramming had unexpected effects. Norms work best when communities are small and homogeneous, and when resources suffice. But as the numbers grew in the jails, goods like space grew scarcer and conflicts sharpened. At the same time, ethnic tensions were heightening, outside the walls and inside. Prisoners needed stronger property rights and greater protection, that is, better governance. The guards had never provided these public goods and the old informal code began creaking. Its penalties were too weak, for one thing. But that wasn't all. The influx of new prisoners alloyed the culture. These novices didn't know the rules so they broke them more often, and showed little respect to older men for living up to them. The informal code had worked through implicit understanding, and that understanding fell away.

So quasi-governments appeared like the Mexican Mafia, the *Emes* (after the Spanish pronunciation of the letter *M*). They were private law and order systems, which have succeeded, if crudely, in places like Gold Rush camps and medieval Japanese monasteries. In the lockup, the *Emes* safeguarded Latinos against brutal whites, punishing anyone who hurt a gang member, and they created and enforced their own rules. The *Emes* also took in members from rival Hispanic street gangs, reducing fights among them. And they very clearly distinguished in-groups from out-groups. You were a member or not—and you knew it.

Once the *Emes* had power, they intimidated and attacked other inmates. Members stole goods—wristwatches, shoes, rings, drugs—from gangless prisoners, who formed new alliances in self-defense. The *Emes* also developed profitable in-prison product lines, such as gambling, narcotics, extortion, and male prostitution. Their Sureño (southerner) network spread outside the prison, and within a few years it dominated Latino barrios (neighborhoods) across Southern California with connections south of the Mexican border.

But the *Emes* didn't assimilate all Latinos. The *Nuestra Familia* or *Enes* formed in the late 1960s to resist *Eme* bullying. It favored the letter *N* and its numerical equivalent 14, in contrast to *Eme*'s 13/*M*. Its Norteños (northerners) network entered the same product lines as the Sureños, but recruited mainly young Latinos born north of the border, or living in Northern California's barrios, or on the north side of large barrios. The gangs are mortal enemies yet feed off each other: if you live in the wrong neighborhood (or in prison), the best protection from one gang is to join the other.

These gangs have distinctive codes of behavior. They advertise their power and territory with eye-catching graffiti featuring 13/*M* or 14/*N*. Personal fashions include tattoos, shaved heads, or slicked back hair and bandannas, baggy pants, and Spanglish speech, an eccentric blend of Spanish and English.

The Enes show one way governance can work at a level up from the tribe. They developed explicit, written rules: the Fourteen Bonds. They kept a log of inmates who deserved punishment, called the Bad News List, and sent List updates to gang leaders throughout the prison system. They appointed certain people as internal police, who monitored members' overall behavior and checked new enrollees against the List. They managed reputation. For instance, when a gangster transferred to a new prison, he often brought a letter confirming his status in the group. It said you could trust him, so it was like credit. It said he had merit, so it was like an employer's letter of recommendation. And it said he belonged, so it was like a club card.

In the Gulag Archipelago, the criminal group *vory-v-zakone* used the moral code in a similar way. It had initiation rites and crisply defined in-groups. It had its own courts and procedures for dispute resolution, and like the *Enes* it could enforce judgments system-wide. When a member transferred, he carried *vory* credentials. And as with many gangsters in the United States, *vory* members bore tattoos that credibly announced their standing in and heroic deeds for the gang.

Latino prison gangs have broader norms. Above all, they value honor or respect among peers. Greater respect brings better access to money and *cholas* (girlfriends), and a gangster earns it by attacking rival gang members and defending his own. A wannabe member can gain acceptance by shooting rivals targeted by senior members; these underage assailants receive lighter sentences and shield the top leadership from the law.

In the mid-1980s, a new product line, crack cocaine, revolutionized the gangs. Their revenues exploded, and so did membership and territory. Conflicts spread. Soon everyone had guns and drive-by shootings became common in larger cities and even in some smaller towns. By 1995, Los Angeles and Fresno, two major battlegrounds of the *M*s and *N*s, had violent crime rates that put them among the four most dangerous US cities.

Gang activity seems to have stabilized since then, but the problem remains acute. As recently as 2004, half of Los Angeles' homicides were considered gang-related, and more than a quarter of the nation's. Gang revenues still come mainly from illegal drugs, with major sidelines in extortion and robbery.

When our ancestors abandoned nomadic bands and began living in villages with fields, they faced pressures somewhat like to those of prisoners in the 1950s and 1960s. Villagers too needed secure rights to property, since they were accumulating it for the first time. The need for protection grew. Use of force increased as farmers repelled marauders and guarded their goods. Norms slowly lost effect. While they can work well in a unified tribe of 80 people, they are less effective in a village of 2,000, and useless by themselves in cities like Uruk. So villagers needed more formal rules, and the Fourteen Bonds is an echo of their lost codes

Yet the similarities only go so far. Unlike early villages, prison gangs exist within a larger system: the prison itself. They serve a special subculture, not everyone, and they have a much darker economy. Their moral codes may not seem very decent to us, but as we've seen, culture can twist morals like a Möbius strip. And this particular strip was unlikely to serve the first human settlements.

From Lemons to Slots: The Mafia

Let's turn to the most famous collection of American criminal gangs: the Mafia. Everyone knows elements of its moral code, if only from movies like *The Godfather* and TV shows like *The Sopranos*. Here too, respect is paramount. A mix of fear and admiration, it holds together a paramilitary organization and weakens opposition in the community. *Omertá*, the code of silence, prohibits telling outsiders about Mafia activities and snitching to police. All this is supposed to support *la famiglia* and somehow protect wives and children.

The Mafia's market plan has changed over the years. The Sicilian Mafia appeared after Italy unified in 1861. Its exact rise remains a mystery as its members didn't chat with reporters. But Sicily had been a virtually feudal realm under the Bourbons, citizens distrusted government, and the new Italian state was weak. Small landowners wanted private protection, and the Mafia likely arose to provide it. In 1949 Don Calo Vizzini, a boss of the Villalba mafia, put it this way: "The fact is that in every society there has to be a category of people who straighten things out when situations get complicated. Usually they are functionaries of the state. Where the state is not present, or where it does not have sufficient force, this is done by private individuals."

But unlike the state, these private individuals can heighten demand for protection. A menacing note here, a burnt barn there—it's an obvious way to gain clientele. So once a few landowners hired the gang, the others paid up or suffered. The Mafia also parasitized commerce. Sicily was the world's leading producer of lemons in the late 19th century, and our first reference to it comes from an 1872 note by a Dr. Galati, condemning a "man of honor" who was threatening violence to force him to sell his grove. Today, Mafia-related GDP equals 12 percent of the GDP of Italy itself. It saps the economy as princes do, by draining wealth and thinning or vaporizing profit margins. Its base, southern Italy, remains the poorest part of the nation.

In the United States, Mafia gangs got started about a hundred years ago, led by young Italian immigrants (with a few Jewish and other ethnic variants helping). Revenues at first came mostly from extorting local Italian shopkeepers, who were easily discouraged from seeking police protection. Some Mafia entrepreneurs developed a second product line, gambling or "numbers rackets." The threat of violence (and codes of respect) helped maintain profitable local monopolies. After 1920, Prohibition created very profitable new product lines, bootlegging and distilling, and the rise of organized labor unions over the next several decades expanded the scope for extortion rackets.

Heroin, an emerging market in the 1950s, created tension between Mafia morals and Mafia markets. *The Godfather* (1972) hinges on the decision by Vito Corleone (played by Marlon Brando) to stay out of narcotics. His advisors favored getting in because "there's a lot of money in that white powder," and, "If we don't get into it, somebody else will…with the money they earn, they can buy more police and political power; then they come after us." But Vito refuses Sollozzo's partnership offer and that touches off a bloody war among the Mafia's families. Eventually Vito brokers a peace agreement, saying, "When did I ever refuse an accommodation, except one time. And why? Because I believe this drug business is gonna destroy us in the years to come" since "even the police departments that've helped us in the past with gambling and other things are gonna refuse to help us when it comes to narcotics."

In part due to the drug trade, federal prosecutors did begin to go after the Mafia in the 1960s, and a few years later legalized gambling began undercutting the numbers rackets. The Mafia responded by spinning off legitimate gambling and entertainment units, which merged with ordinary corporations to run the megacasinos in Las Vegas, Atlantic City, and on Indian reservations. It has also spun off (or ceded to more recent immigrant gangs from Russia and elsewhere) the the high-margin drug and prostitution product lines. Traditional Mafia activities continue but, overall, its style of organized crime seems to be in decline.

All moral codes need effective penalties, and legal codes do too. Profiteering gangs arise when the punishments don't work and they wane, as with the US Mafia, when they do.

From Gang to State: Hamas

We've seen how an informal moral code can morph into gang semigovernment, and how gangs can squeeze an economy. What happens when a gang becomes the state itself?

In 1971 Sheik Ahmed Yassin founded *Mujamah* (Arabic for "Congress") in Gaza to provide local services like medical clinics, schools, sports clubs, and mosques. It gave people public goods—just like a government. And if Mujamah brings a doctor and saves your child's life, you will likely feel grateful toward it. Your moral ties to it will strengthen. Originally, tribes provided the rough equivalent, and gangs can thrive where states don't deliver them and people have poor mainstream alternatives. Initially, Mujamah earned its revenues mostly from families using its services and from wealthy outsiders, though Israel offered tacit support. The moral code involved strict Islamic piety, ethical personal behavior, and political support for an eventual Islamic Palestine state.

Until 1988, the movement was nonviolent, aside from occasional skirmishes with the secular Palestine Liberation Organization (PLO). But as the PLO began to lend support to a violent popular uprising that year, now called the first intifada, the Mujamah leaders worried that their organization would lose out. They founded a secret militia called Hamas. It took a more extreme position than the PLO, calling for immediate jihad to conquer all of Palestine and Israel.

Despite intense repression (sometimes by the PLO as well as Israeli authorities), Hamas grew into one of the most effective terrorist organizations in history. Relying on donations from Iran, Palestinian expatriates, and multimillionaires in Saudi Arabia and elsewhere in the Arab world, Hamas recruited Mujamah clients and other Palestinians, especially young men from Gaza, and instructed them in a strict version of Sunni Islam. It selected a few to participate in deadly attacks, featuring car bombs, roadside mines, and suicide bombings. Hamas took the lead during the second intifada (2000–2005). It was responsible for about half of the roughly 1,100 Israelis killed, some of them soldiers but most of them civilian victims of suicide bombers.

Then Hamas won an upset victory over the PLO in Palestine's January 2006 elections. In June 2007, Hamas ousted the PLO from Gaza, and became the de facto ruler there. Soon after, in December 2008, it learned one difference between being a terrorist group and being a government. After repeatedly firing rockets into Israel, Hamas triggered the Gaza War, a 22-day conflict in which it had nowhere to hide. Israel invaded with little trouble, took over, and imposed a blockade. Violence against a powerhouse can backfire when your group has territory to seize and commerce to kill.

Today Hamas has responsibility for Gaza's 1.4 million residents. It stands in relation to the government as Fatah does to the Palestinian Authority, and the Communist Party to the bureaucracy of China. That is, a gang often remains after it takes over a state. It enfolds the official government rather than replacing it. Now often called a "party," it controls the key policies, and though party and government are formally independent, everyone knows where the power lies.

In Gaza Hamas has been reasonably successful. It improved policing, though the cops ride on horseback. It has created a working if incomplete court system based on secular, not Islamic, law, and citizens actually use it. It has also improved education and stabilized its rule. This ministate still depends on the kindness of others, and most of its revenue comes from backers in places like Saudi Arabia. But the uprisings of Arab Spring never threatened it.

Meanwhile, it confronts its own terrorist band: Jaljalat (Arabic for "thunder"), a network of jihadis disgusted by Hamas's new bureaucratic face and perceived softness toward Israel. It has attacked Internet cafes and, apparently, carried out numerous attacks on Hamas security offices and vehicles. If Jaljalat ever gains control of a state, it may find a new terrorist band lobbing bombs at it.

The Assassins: A Terrorist Cult

The world's first true terrorists, according to historian Bernard Lewis, were a cult of Islamic heretics known as the Assassins. The Assassins were followers of an ascetic warlord and theologian, Hasan-i Sabbah. After joining the Ismailis, a mystical and messianic strain of Shiite Islam, young Hasan visited their Cairo headquarters in 1078. He returned to preach in Persia and in 1090 gained a stronghold at Alamut, commanding a narrow valley in the northern mountains. There he built his band of believers, custodians of circles within circles of sacred mysteries.

Hasan plotted world domination for his brand of the true faith, but he faced very long odds. Most Muslims and their rulers viewed the Ismailis as noxious heretics, and routinely rounded them up and slaughtered them. On the other hand, that part of the world was run by autocrats, who relied on transient personal loyalties of henchmen and notables. Whenever the autocrat died, things fell apart until one of the heirs (or usurpers) gained the upper hand. Hasan and his Assassin successors exploited that weakness by perfecting their eponymous craft.

Their first victim, in 1092, was Nizam al-Mulk, the brains behind the Seljuk dynasty and a fierce antiheretic. A pious volunteer named Bu Tahir Arrani disguised himself as a Sufi, sidled up to Nizam as he was being carried to the tent of his women, and buried a dagger in his heart. The Seljuk dynasty fragmented, and over the years many of the more Ismaili-hostile rulers from Syria to Iran fell victim to Assassin daggers. The executioners often were secret agents who had gained the ruler's trust after years of service, and they showed no remorse or fear once caught.

Often a threat was enough. Sultan Sanjar awoke one morning in 1119 staring at a dagger stuck in the ground beside his bed. A messenger from Hasan delivered a short note: "Did I not wish the Sultan well, that dagger which was stuck into the hard ground would have been planted in his soft breast." For the rest of his reign, Sanjar appeased the sect. He and many other rulers (including several Christians holding territories captured by the Crusaders) sent payments to the Assassins and took it easy on the local Ismailis, and these rulers slept better at night.

Fanatical discipline and loyalty, and inaccessible mountain citadels in northern Persia and Syria, gave the Assassins power far beyond their numbers. Their reputation for systematic terror protected Ismaili enclaves throughout the region and brought revenue to the citadels. A notable exception: in the mid-1200s, the Assassins paid out tribute to the Christian Templars and Hospitallers—partly because of the Christians' skill in assaulting mountain citadels and their often hostile relations with the Assassins' enemies. But, according to the chronicler Joinville, the main reason was that the orders' corporate structure immunized them against Assassin terror. If one master was killed, another just as good would replace him immediately. Hence, the Assassins would lose a top operative for little gain.

Toward the end of the 1200s, the Mongols wiped out the Persian Assassins, and the Syrian branch submitted to Baybars, the Mamluk sultan headquartered in Egypt. Some groups of Ismailis survived, and today most are followers of the Aga Khan, a very modern imam whose family has held high positions in the League of Nations and the United Nations. Fanaticism passed to other branches of the Muslim faith.

TV Terrorism

The Symbionese Liberation Army (SLA) got off to a bad start in November 1973. A ragtag collection of leftist activists, Vietnam vets, and escaped convicts, the SLA wanted to make a splash by killing some authoritarian figure. A careless reading of a news clipping pointed them to Oakland's superintendent of schools, Marcus Foster, and they ambushed and killed him with eight bullets dipped in cyanide. But Foster actually was a beloved progressive, and everyone condemned the action, even other radicals.

The SLA hit pay dirt with their second exploit, the February 1974 kidnap of heiress Patty Hearst. Two months later, Patty shocked the nation by joining her captors in a bank robbery. Six SLA members died in a subsequent shoot-out and fire in Los Angeles, but the remaining three, including Patty, eluded capture for more than a year. Then she was caught, deprogrammed, brought to trial, and convicted. President Carter released Patty in 1979 after two years in jail, and since then she has led a quiet domestic life with her husband and their two daughters, occasionally acting in films directed by John Waters.

Why did Patty join her bumbling kidnappers? Indeed, why would anyone join such a deviant, violent group?

Rational explanations, of the sort Jeremy Bentham would understand, go only so far. To address these questions, we must examine the group's moral code and market plan. The Mafia and the youth gangs have roughly parallel morals and basically similar business market plans. How about the SLA?

Its moral code was a mishmash of leftist rhetoric ("Death to the fascist insect that preys upon the life of the people") and striking, occult symbols (a seven-headed cobra), but it served its purpose. It gave SLA members the feeling that they were part of something noble and important and that they had special ties to each other. Life-and-death shared experiences strengthened their bonds, as they do with commandos. Sexual bonds also contributed, and some journalists are convinced that Patty Hearst fell in love with William Wolfe, a core SLA member who also had a privileged childhood.

The SLA's business plan had a short but memorable run. The gang at first got what it needed by robbing fellow leftists, and then by bank robbery and ransom.

Amateurish luck helped considerably: most kidnap victims would have run at the first opportunity, but Patty's conversion took hold and brought priceless publicity, and inept police work compensated for inept SLA actions.

But what was the ultimate point of it? The SLA had no serious plan to overthrow the "fascist insect," as even the briefest analysis revealed. Rather, its members seem to have been role-playing for media attention, enacting the drama of South American guerrilla bands like the student-founded Tupamaros, but without the context. It was a game of "catch me if you can," played out before a world audience. It was TV terrorism.

Do the SLA and the other gangs really have anything important in common?

Humans evolved in close-knit bands that met members' material and emotional needs, but in a Pleistocene world far different from today's. Overall, the detribalized modern world is much better at providing goods—food, shelter, personal security, medical care, and so forth—but it can fall short in matters of the human spirit.

A sense of community appeals to our evolved psychology. We developed in bands, and our moral DNA presumes a group. We feel satisfied working together and some modern jobs offer a very intense communal experience, in start-up companies, for example, or in the military or in some corporations. The modern world also offers opportunities to join a wide variety of part-time communities, such as regular churches, parent-teacher associations, bowling leagues, and the Elks. Some of us feel that tug more strongly than others, of course, and most of us are reasonably happy with what we can find in the modern world.

Cults and gangs offer a much different proposition. Membership is full time, and it cuts ties to the mainstream. In-group moral bonds become far more intense. Once you join the Mafia (or M or N) family, you are supposed to be in for life, and to forget your old friends and ambitions. You're in a group that cares for you and looks out for you, and you do the same for your fellow members.

Many cults and gangs recruit from a single ethnic group, and their codes appeal to our innate chauvinism. They praise the nobility of their own group, and hammer away at real or imagined oppression or disrespect by the mainstream. In a variation on the theme, the SLA and rival leftist groups claimed to act on behalf of the underprivileged of the world. Some of their members (and leaders) grew up in comfort, but felt guilty about it and tried fervently to identify with oppressed minorities.

The proposition offered by deviant groups obviously has more appeal where the mainstream is unattractive: in countries and neighborhoods where markets and state don't function well, and for low-status individuals with poor mainstream prospects. The SLA and the Latino gangs both began in an ideal center: California's prison system. The Mafia traditionally recruited its foot soldiers from among recent immigrants. So did the *Emes* once their network began to grow. The *Nuestra Familia* also recruited school dropouts in barrios throughout California.

But still, why would a young person join up? It's not just that kids in the barrios and ghettoes see very few examples of mainstream success. Just as important, they see an upside. Top gang leaders seem to lead a glamorous life, with lots of money, girls, and respect. Of course, few make it to the top, and those who do seldom last long. It's a bad bet, but it's just the sort that appeals to low-status young men.

By around 1980, the SLA was long gone and a more competent leftist terrorist group—the Weather Underground—was facing mortality. The FBI had gotten better at infiltration after J. Edgar Hoover's departure in 1972, and recruitment dried up in prisons as gangs became more attractive, as well as among middle-class youth with the end of the draft and the Vietnam War. In Europe the Baader-Meinhof gang lingered on into the 1990s as did the trigger-happy Italian Red Brigades, assassins of politician Aldo Moro. But everywhere, former sympathizers had lost their taste for kidnap, robbery, and murder, and ceased believing that society was ripe for revolution. Donations dwindled, and these terror cells fizzled out.

Just as they were rising elsewhere.

The Faces of al-Qaeda

In 1992 al-Qaeda attempted to bomb a pair of hotels in Aden. Bin Laden was trying to kill US soldiers en route to Somalia to help feed starving people. The explosives went off, but the soldiers were staying elsewhere. In 1996 he tried again, working with others to assassinate President Clinton on a trip to Manila, but the plan failed. The gang leader got luckier in 1998, when al-Qaeda detonated bombs in US embassies in East Africa, killing some 300 people, mostly local civilians. And in 2000 he engineered the suicide bombing of the U.S.S. Cole as it lay at anchor in Yemen. But his group was still little known in the West.

Then on September 11, 2001, al-Qaeda overwhelmed the global media. Since then it has affected our daily lives, so we remove our belts and shoes before boarding airplanes and submit to intense security checks before entering, say, the Department of Justice building in Washington, DC. Bin Laden's ignorant, cave-dwelling gang forced new habits on us.

Yet what exactly was it?

Was it a cult? A cult is a small group whose shared beliefs cut it off from mainstream society. (Of course, most such groups reject the epithet.) Some, like the Amish, coexist peacefully with the mainstream. A few groups, like the Mormons or early Christians, started out as cults, but over time they grew so large and adapted so well that they became part of the mainstream. Cults put their core beliefs above the law, but they seldom exist for the purpose of illegal activity. Nonetheless, al-Qaeda was certainly a cult in many ways, with a charismatic founder whose recruits swore loyalty to him.

Is al-Qaeda a terrorist cult? Terrorists try to achieve political aims by threatening opponents' lives. Powerful countries do the same, but terrorist cults are small groups not usually run by national governments. Al-Qaeda clearly fit this description, since its goal is fear.

Is al-Qaeda a criminal gang? Gangs conduct unlawful core activities. They're cryptogovernments to one degree or another. They bloom when outside law is weak, as in prisons or regions like Somalia or in states undergoing big transitions like South Africa after 1994 (and 1990s Russia, for additional reasons). They prosper in black markets where no court will enforce contracts or reliably protect operators. If someone cheats you in a drug deal, you need your own penalty and threat of penalty. Indeed, criminal gangs can co-opt government officials themselves. The Mexican drug cartels near the US border are spectacular examples. There, drug lords with Rolexes have not only assassinated officials and killed at least 50,000 people since 2006 but have bought off law enforcement and led shoot-outs between branches allied to different gangs. Al-Qaeda was clearly a criminal gang too, since it committed atrocities.

But it was hardly a criminal gang in the sense of the cartels or the *Emes*. It did not traffic in protection. It had no sustaining business model and never penetrated an economy, as the Mafia did. Indeed, years earlier bin Laden had tried to run a business in Sudan, where the admiring son of its dictator summed him up: "There was no hypocrisy in his character. No divergence between what he says and what he does. Unfortunately, his IQ was not that great." It's hard to imagine al-Qaeda running a nation, as Hamas has.

A market plan is essential. Every group (indeed, every living thing) has to acquire resources to sustain itself, and in the modern world the market is the dominant source. Even groups that reject the mainstream somehow must deal with that reality. There are four basic options:

- *Legal selling.* For example, the Amish cling to the old ways and aim for self-sufficiency, but many of their communities compromise by selling food and handicrafts to tourists.
- *Illegal selling.* Smuggling, theft, gambling, and prostitution are gangs' traditional mainstays, but drugs now bring in the big bucks.
- *Extortion.* Protection money, ransom, robbery, and sweetheart contracts are one-sided revenues paid to avoid injury.
- *Voluntary contributions.* Sometimes one-sided revenues are paid to return a favor or just to help out, as with charitable foundations. Of course, the boundary with extortion can get fuzzy, as in *The Godfather* or in ancient royal gift exchange and tribute.

Al-Qaeda survived on largesse,from sympathizers in places like Saudi Arabia who supported its magical thinking.

Despite its varied strains, al-Qaeda was ultimately TV terrorism like the SLA, though much more lethal. Both groups seized world attention with panache. Both jumped aimlessly from one project to another (though al-Qaeda planned attacks years in advance). Neither had the slightest blueprint for overthrowing the United States or taking territory. Al-Qaeda had a bold plot to strike central US institutions, the Pentagon, and the Capitol—but then what?

Today, al-Qaeda is a rump organization. It still stirs fire in certain hearts, but it has become almost a nonentity, a media creature, a name useful for snagging viewer attention. In 2009 this squad was behind far less than 1 percent of the 11,000 or so terrorist attacks in the world. Some 240 other terrorist groups operate on our planet, many far more competent and accomplished than al-Qaeda. But the United States cherishes understandable anger toward this gang and will likely pursue it till it vanishes, as bin Laden himself has.

Fighting Terror

Some cults are harmless or even productive, like the pacificist Hutterites of Canada. But others impose costs on the rest of us. For example, many Israelis believe that the settlers' movement, a cult of extremists who take land from the Palestinians and require protection from the army, is largely responsible for the second intifada, at incalculable cost in lives and treasure. The US Mafia is more or less indifferent to mainstream society, but it still imposes significant costs: protection money, labor racketeering, and the rest are like an inefficient tax. Clearly it is in society's interest to find effective ways to reduce these costs, and to suppress the most harmful gangs and cults.

What methods are most effective? As far back as we can see, the favored tools have been torture, slaughter, and scorched earth. For instance, a sect called the Cathars flourished in 12th and 13th century France, and its Perfecti spurned animal food and condemned war; the papal Albigensian Crusade annihilated them. The SLA ended in a fiery shoot-out in Los Angeles, though a few lucky members survived. Similarly, the United States is intent on wiping out al-Qaeda; as one top official said in 2009, "We have to kill them all, every last one of them."

Regardless of the merits of such cases, slaughter has drawbacks for modern nations. Brutal tactics can undermine our own moral system. The 1993 siege of the Branch Davidian compound in Waco, for instance, provoked a backlash and soul-searching. In most cases our rule of law (especially since the Nuremberg Trials and the Geneva Conventions) keeps us from massacre, yet halfhearted violence can be counterproductive. Persecution of minorities creates martyrs like the Mormons' Joseph Smith, boosts radicals, and makes the mainstream less attractive. Even normal prison terms helped Latino gangsters and jihadis build recruitment networks.

So what other tactics are there?

The United States government has offered large cash rewards for apprehension of top terrorists. Though a $25 million reward might (or might not) have helped US troops capture Saddam, a similar bounty played no role in the killing of bin Laden. Perhaps it's understandable. A tribesman going for the payoff would have to balance mortal danger to himself and family, and a permanent loss of his entire social network, against the prospect of starting a new life of leisure in an alien nation. Apparently, few deemed this a good bargain.

Starve these groups of funding and they'll die. This technique is highly effective, but hard to implement. For instance, the United Arab Emirates have acted energetically to shut down cash pipelines to al-Qaeda and the Taliban, but other Gulf states like Qatar have not, and even Saudi Arabia, a clear foe of these organizations, has resisted. Yet al-Qaeda and other gangs survive on handouts, and it's hard to buy a shoulder-launched surface-to-air missile if you don't have the money for breakfast.

Infiltration is a classic tactic. Economists Eli Berman and David Laitin argue that the key to success in the modern terrorism business is to prevent defection: if the authorities can infiltrate or persuade even one person in the cell to cooperate with them, then the terrorist action will fail. The sacrifices Hamas demanded of its recruits—years at religious schools that teach no marketable skills, five prayer sessions each day, and so forth—drove out those individuals most susceptible to defection. As a result, Hamas was better than the secular PLO at screening out Mossad agents and finding suicide bombers who would follow through. Even so, the CIA under Obama infiltrated both Hamas and Hezbollah, so they are no longer black boxes to us. The tactic is especially powerful against terrorist groups, for two reasons. A single defection can enable authorities to wipe out lots of terrorists, perhaps even top leaders. And the fear of double agents impairs communication and coordination within the terrorist group, and slows recruitment.

Today the main infiltrator is software. In the past, spies might memorize secret dispatches or run classified documents through the copier after hours, but ever since the early 1990s the National Security Agency (NSA) has been scouring emails. This surveillance has reportedly helped prevent terrorist attacks on US soil. In addition, software worms like Stuxnet and Flame have not only opened up some of the most tightly guarded factories in the world, but issued commands through the software they infect. Like the spies of the Assassin cult, they suddenly turned very damaging.

Plenty of information is actually out there in plain sight. Gangsters post information on websites, boast of their deeds, threaten foes, discuss their general operations, and comment on others' posts. The problem lies in sieving the Internet ocean for this data, and two professors at Harvard developed a tool called Mogo that does exactly that. To many people's surprise, they found that most Mexican gangs no longer stake out exclusive territory. For instance, in 2010, 62 percent of gang-ridden towns had more than one, compared to 6 percent ten years ago. The groups are competing more vigorously.

What further tactics might work against modern gang and terrorist networks? More than ever, these organizations need cohesive moral codes and compatible market plans. Antiterror campaigns will be more effective when they tarnish the codes and disrupt the plans.

Decentralized political and religious movements are especially vulnerable to internal division, to splitting into hostile factions. That has always been the downfall of the militant left. Many medieval wars were among Muslim sects, and competing Christian creeds battled almost nonstop in Europe between 1550 and 1650. Modern antiterrorists can stoke internal battles by well-timed covert support of minority factions. It's a tricky business, though, and can backfire. Israel's authorities surely regret their attempt to undermine the PLO by supporting Mujamah.

Religious roots can make a group susceptible to moral suasion. For several years after 2002, Yemen's High Court judge Hamood Al-Hitar organized theological debates with captured militants. He asked them to justify attacks on innocent civilians. They cited various passages in the Quran, but none bore close scrutiny. Then Al-Hitar pointed out numerous passages commanding Muslims not to attack civilians, to respect other religions, and to fight only in self-defense. One of his favorites: "Whoever kills a soul, unless for a soul, or for corruption done in the land—it is as if he had slain all mankind entirely. And, whoever saves one, it is as if he had saved mankind entirely." According to a 2005 report, the judge had released 364 young men who promised to obey the Quran, and none of them had left the country to fight anywhere else. Yemen deported foreign militants, shut down extremist madrassas, and became an "indispensable ally in the war on terror." The judge's approach is important, for the more Muslims believe the Quran mandates nonaggression, the fewer will launch attacks—especially suicide attacks.

Satire can undermine militant morals. A scene in the 2005 film *Paradise Now* shows endless flubbed takes for a would-be suicide bomber's martyr videotape. After seeing it, viewers would be less likely to take this propaganda seriously. Monty Python films skewer leftist pretensions, and self-righteous Muslim fanatics should be even more vulnerable. A caveat: To succeed, ridicule must appeal to the terrorists' potential donors, recruits, and support network. For instance, it might mock militants for failing to understand the Quran and thus riding off to death. Or it might ridicule the notion that copycat al-Qaedas could ever shock the world as the original did. But satire that merely entertains the infidels, like the well-known Danish newspaper cartoons, can backfire.

Similar tactics can help fight youth gangs, and perhaps even the Mafia. Respect is vital for these groups, and ridicule cuts deep. Of course, standup comics might find themselves in personal danger if their riffs get too popular. Perhaps convicted gang leaders should be given the choice between maximum-security isolation, or time off for community service on education campaigns that vividly portray gang life as stupid, ugly, and ridiculous.

Jihadis rely on the Internet to spread their faith and techniques. It could be an equally effective medium for undermining their moral message and market plans. The medium is ideal for circulating jokes and video clips and for misdirecting browsers seeking jihadi propaganda. It should be cheap and easy to flood the Internet with counterfeit websites that carry counterpropaganda.

New York Times columnist Thomas Friedman (no relation) has argued repeatedly that the best way to stop Islamic terrorism it is with a serious carbon tax. He has a point. Funds for Islamic terrorists come mainly from the oil revenues flowing to Saudi Arabia, Iran, and other regional oil producers—that is, from drivers every time they fill up at the pump. Their demand for oil is extremely inelastic in the short run, but in the long run, a tax that put a floor on the price of gas would encourage alternative energy production and conservation. Taxes thus should take money from the Wahhabi and Shiite firebrands and bring it back home. It's another way to starve the gangs.

Likewise, our homegrown gangsters' revenue comes mainly from selling products with extremely inelastic demand. An antidrug policy more like the Dutch—legalize, but discourage by heavy taxes and restrictions—would cut off gangs' air supply.

Details matter, and they're hard to get just right. To take advantage of the modern world's great strengths—science, pragmatism, adaptability—we should systematically try out different forms of oil and drug taxes and restrictions, figure out what works best, and then do more of it.

In the long run, mainstream society's best defense against hostile cults and gangs is the market system. If we give people good prospects for social and material advancement, they'll have something to lose. If they have reasonable jobs, they'll be busy and focused on them. If we tie their societies into others and expand their personal spheres—so, for instance, they view acts like blasphemy less as intrinsic wrongs and more as conventional ones (or even errors)—the fervor will ebb. These changes will happen. In the long run, the solution is the long run itself.

10

Cooling the Earth: The Preservation Markets

Nobody is going to emigrate from this planet, not ever.

—Edward O. Wilson

Just off New England's coast, the cold, mineral-rich Labrador Current mixes with the warm Gulf Stream over a series of underwater plateaus, called banks, and nurtures a startling variety of marine plants, animals, and birds. Some, like pollock, lobster, and scallops, are quite valuable commercially.

But the real prize was cod, "so thick you can scoop them up in a basket." Decades before John Cabot's famous 1497 voyage, some argue, Basque fishermen discovered the banks and kept them secret. By 1550, and for the next 200 years, more than half the fish consumed in Europe were salt cod, most caught in these banks. The proceeds paid for England's first colony in Newfoundland and then the New England colonies, and powered their economies for centuries.

Cod's bounty seemed eternal. The great English biologist Thomas Huxley wrote in 1883 that the cod fishery was inexhaustible. But by 1991, fishermen like Billy Tyne of Gloucester, Massachusetts, had to sail far beyond the banks to fill their boats. Catches were down 80–90 percent from what Billy had seen as a young man, despite (or because of) rapid advances in fishing technology. His search for fish that summer brought him to the middle of the Atlantic Ocean, where his ship, the *Andrea Gail*, sank in the "perfect storm."

Another storm, slower but even more powerful, had already sunk cod fishery. The Grand Banks, off Newfoundland, was closed to commercial fishing in 1992, and then the Georges Bank, off New England, in December 1994. Gloucester plunged into economic depression, joining dozens of other northeast coastal cities and towns. Even now, almost two decades later, many of the young people are gone, and tourism is the region's new economic driver. That man-made storm must rank among New England's worst environmental, social, and economic disasters.

How could an "inexhaustible" resource just disappear? Afterward, of course, everyone involved blamed someone else: out-of-touch scientists, inept government officials, greedy foreign fishermen, local fishermen, or ignorant consumers. Where does the fault really lie?

The environment and the economy can collide, and often the underlying problem is the tragedy of the commons. Our species traditionally averted the tragedy using the moral system, but modern markets and dysfunctional morals aggravate the problem, and threaten our planetary future. But there is a better way. Reformed markets, supported by more sophisticated morals, have brought some local success, and the combination offers hope for lasting global solutions.

Anatomy of a Tragedy

In 1968, ecologist Garrett Hardin published a now renowned article in *Science*. Inspired by game theorists, he identified a variant of the basic social dilemma as the underlying cause of virtually all environmental problems. He entitled the article "The Tragedy of the Commons."

Hardin explains the tragedy by means of a parable. A group of herdsmen has a pasture, the commons, that all can use. Each of them decides how many of his cows to let graze on it. The individual herdsman enjoys the full benefit of an additional cow, but he bears only a fraction of the additional grazing costs: less grass available, more trampling of new growth, and so forth. For example, with 10 equal herds, each herdsman bears only one-tenth the cost of an extra cow. Consequently, each will keep adding cows far past the point that the additional cost equals the additional benefit, and together they'll ruin the pasture by overgrazing.

This sort of social dilemma crops up in all times and places. Both of us grew up in the San Francisco Bay Area and have fond memories of enjoying fresh Dungeness crab in late fall. In recent years, the local haul has been good to excellent for the first two weeks of the season as large crab boats pile in from further north. But the rest of the seven-month season is often meager. The personal benefit is clear if you're the first crab catcher to arrive at a good spot. The cost is that later it is harder to catch crabs there, and most of that cost is borne by the other local crabbers. The result is a minor tragedy: fishermen overinvest in crabbing equipment, unused except for a few weeks each year, and crab consumers have slim pickings most of the time.

Easter Island witnessed a much more acute tragedy. After first arriving about 900 AD, the island's residents enjoyed personally the benefits of cutting another tree (or raising another child) but shared the cost with everyone else. Around 1600 the island's last tree was felled; soil eroded and wildlife vanished. The human population crashed from perhaps as many as 30,000. In 1774 Captain Cook found a few thousand survivors, "small, lean, timid, and miserable." In 1994, one of us (McNeill) saw the island. Chile has preserved it as a national park, and it is still treeless beyond Hanga Roa, the only settlement. Indeed, it is almost all grass and lava, pale green and black, with rocks strewn like wreckage over the meadows. Visitors often meet at a tumbledown bar where they sit on the lanai under a metal awning with a "Coca-Cola" sign and gaze out at dirt road, heaped clouds, and lonely sea. Easter Island has never recovered.

Many anthropologists believe that an opening of the Canadian ice sheet 13,000 years ago allowed several waves of big game hunters to sweep through the Americas and cause the extinction of mammoths, horses, giant sloths, and dozens of other large mammals. Similarly, humans with advanced hunting skills first arrived at the vast commons now called Australia about 45,000 years ago, and drove all sorts of megafauna extinct there over the next few centuries. All future residents share the cost of killing the last breeding stock in an area, but the hunters back then monopolized the benefits.

Moral Management: The Bali Rice Terraces

Other animals, herbivores as well as carnivores, face the same problem. Each animal has an interest in exploiting a depletable resource far past the point that is best for her species.

As Hardin notes, there are ways to cope with the tragedy, or in less poetic language, to more efficiently manage common pool resources. Nature's main device is territoriality. That is, creatures restrict access to the common pool; in a sense, they privatize it. For example, an adult male red-tailed deer will stake out a grazing area and threaten other males who trespass or show interest in the local females. Likewise, prides of lions drive off intruders trying to hunt in their area. Aquarium owners are warned about territorial fish, such as groupers and seahorses, that will attack new arrivals.

The human moral system evolved to cope with social dilemmas of all sorts, including the tragedy of the commons. As our ancestors adopted more sedentary lifestyles, their moral codes began to include territoriality, defending against outsiders. For example, in Akira Kurosawa's *Seven Samurai* (1954), villager Katsushiro recruits warriors to protect his poor hamlet against bandits. Audiences savor watching samurai leader Kambei Shimada rally the townsfolk and outwit and pick off the bandits one by one.

So humans have a traditional way to escape the tragedy. A local group takes control of the common pool resource and evolves a moral code, finely tuned to local circumstances, for excluding outsiders, sharing the resource, and contributing to its maintenance. Cultures that fail to do so fall apart, and cultures that succeed are the ones that last. For example, the descendents of the Clovis hunters eventually evolved cultures that, over the next 10,000 years, efficiently managed the remaining North American grazing animals, such as bison and caribou.

A wonderful example concerns rice farmers on the other side of the planet. Bali's rice terraces rise in stair steps from white sand beaches toward 10,000-foot volcanic peaks. Tourists from around the world visit the equatorial island paradise, lured by the gorgeous landscapes and harmonious culture. Both have the same source—a moral code that has sustained Bali's people for many centuries.

The Balinese call their system Agama Tirtha, the religion of holy water. Rivers rush down the mountainside and hit diversion dams or weirs, and the water then enters a network of tunnels and canals. Each farm family has a small shrine at the top of its terraces, at the gate of the local irrigation canal. The farmers along each canal belong to a *subak*, an organization with its own local temple. Each *subak* has fraternal relationships with the other *subaks* drawing on the same weir, and each pays homage to those upstream. Religious ceremonies focus on the exchange and mixing of waters from upstream and downstream *subaks*, and they promote close ties among people throughout the watershed. As part of their religious duties, the higher priests adjudicate conflicting claims among *subaks* and larger units, for example, whether to develop a new spring or to dig a new water tunnel. The *subaks* and larger units stagger planting cycles to balance water use within the watershed, and they control pests by coordinating fallow times, burning, and flooding.

As part of the "green revolution," the Asian Development Bank launched the Bali Irrigation Project in 1979. Outside experts, who knew nothing about Bali's water temple system and its unique artificial ecology, took over about 10 percent of the island's *subaks* and began continuous rice cultivation. Within five years an "explosion of pests and diseases" and water shortages during the dry season caused major crop failures, and the usual remedies only created dangerous pesticide pollution. By 1988 the Bank acknowledged the problems, and its 1997 final report celebrates working with the water temple system instead of trying to impose a standard structure.

Markets Corrode Morals: Losing Sod and Cod

Moral management worked well in Bali as the Agama Tirtha religion came to embrace entire watersheds and eventually the whole island. At that point, the moral order regulated all the costs and benefits of water management and pest control, and the commons tragedy evaporated.

When farmers produce for distant markets, however, the tragedy can easily recur. The moral control breaks down when individual farmers receive the revenues while their neighbors still share the costs.

A prime example begins with the "sod busters" who first farmed North America's Great Plains in the late 1800s. Most of them had to mortgage the property to purchase machinery and seed and later fertilizers and pesticides. To meet payments, every year they had to sell wheat and other cash crops in the national and international markets. The farmers had little scope for worrying about longer term costs, such as depleted soil and falling water tables; the price signals from global markets drowned out these faint local signals.

In the early 1930s, a drought triggered runaway desertification called the Dust Bowl. Remaining topsoil dried up and blew away, destroying crops hundreds of miles downwind. Bankruptcies spread, and the region has never recovered its population and vitality.

Today things are very different, yet oddly similar. Corporate farms draw down a common pool resource called the Ogallala Aquifer—a vast underground lake stretching from north of Nebraska down through the Texas Panhandle, filled thousands of years ago. Even a huge corporation bears only a tiny fraction of the cost when it depletes the aquifer, and it gains the entire benefit. On present trends the aquifer will run dry in a few decades and decimate the regional economy.

The tragedy strikes at sea as well as on land. Market imperatives undid even the deep commons, the great banks of the northwest Atlantic. When a commercial fisherman finds a new way to sell more fish at lower cost, the other fishermen must copy him or find an even cheaper way or retire. Thus, waves of innovation swept over the banks: Steam-powered fishing fleets and nets instead of hooks. Then came otter trawls, large nets that stayed open as they were dragged across the sea floor. Rock hoppers to cope with rocky floors, and drag chains to flush out the fish. Onboard fish processing and freezing facilities.

By the late 1960s, factory trawlers dragged nets the size of several football fields across the underwater plateaus and turned sea gardens into sea desert. The young cod had nowhere to grow, and sonar (first developed in World War II) tracked down the dwindling schools of adults. Prices rose as cod became scarcer, and higher prices intensified the hunt—all forces that Huxley did not foresee in 1883.

Could territoriality prevent tragedy? Iceland was the first to expand its territorial waters, from 3 miles from shore to 4 in 1950, to 12 miles in 1958, and to 50 miles in 1972. Victory in three "cod wars" enabled Iceland to enforce the new boundaries, and in 1976 most countries, including the United States and Canada, declared a 200-mile limit.

Many observers thought the problem was solved. Surely national control would now internalize the costs, preserve the offshore resources, and halt the tragedy of the commons. Governments could harness science and technology to keep the fishing industry healthy over the long term, to the benefit of all. But it didn't work out that way.

The Great Green Crusade

Let's first look at a larger story unfolding at about the same time, that of toxic pesticides. The benefit to a farmer of spraying poison is obvious: he sees dead bugs and saves his crops for the harvest. The costs are less obvious and are mostly borne by others: 1) the surviving insects evolve greater pesticide resistance, 2) the pesticides kill insect-eating creatures, allowing pests to multiply later, and 3) pesticides accumulate in the crops, soil, rivers, and oceans, imperiling the health of wildlife and ourselves. As usual, the dispersion of costs leads to overuse and inefficient pollution. The kicker is that effects 1) and 2) create an accelerating demand for pesticides, and the chemical industry acquires a vested interest in expanding demand even further for some of its most profitable products.

Rachel Carson's 1962 book *Silent Spring* at first seemed quixotic in so strongly criticizing a very powerful industry, but it gave clear insight into the new science of ecology. Even more important, it evoked a moral obligation to protect the environment for its own sake and for the health of our children. *Silent Spring* was a surprise best seller, and the political response was huge. Environmentalism became a moral crusade, one of the great causes of the 1960s and beyond. Nongovernmental organizations mushroomed, such as the Sierra Club and Greenpeace, and Earth Day gained semiofficial (or even official) status around the world.

Like the original Crusades a thousand years ago, the environmental movement enjoyed initial success. The chemical industry was taken by surprise and overwhelmed. Most industrialized countries passed laws banning the worst toxic chemicals. Other new laws curbed air and water pollution. New agencies such as the US Environmental Protection Agency set standards and monitored compliance.

By 1972 the United States had banned the leading pesticide, DDT, and bird populations soon began to recover. For example, as a student in the early 1970s Friedman seldom saw any pelicans in Santa Cruz, but since returning in the late 1980s he frequently sees dozens, or even hundreds, of brown pelicans dive-bombing the anchovies just beyond the surf line. Likewise, 400 miles south, McNeill sees them patrolling the sky every afternoon off Marina del Rey. Pelicans are back.

Air and water quality improved impressively in the United States and Western Europe during the 1970s and 1980s. Even in Los Angeles the air is far better than in the 1960s. Recycling programs and antilitter campaigns have spread across the industrialized world. Large swaths of land became new wilderness preserves, and many cities grew green belts. The list of environmental improvements is long and varied.

The green crusade took the high moral ground. Its leaders proposed environment-friendly laws, and masses of foot soldiers wrote letters of support and packed public hearings. Supporters donated generously, time as well as money. They all saw themselves as creating a legacy for generations as yet unborn, fighting the good fight against evil corporations. The battle seemed to go their way in the 1970s as they pushed through lots of legislation, and the new laws gave them leverage in the 1980s and beyond, as they filed class-action lawsuits.

Industry Strikes Back

Again like the original Crusaders, the green movement didn't really understand its sworn enemy. In the market system, economic interests have large stakes in the political process. The value to an industry of a favorable law or regulatory decision or legal ruling is often in the hundreds of millions of dollars, and occasionally it is in the tens of billions. Economic logic dictates that firms will spend up to that amount to gain a favorable decision.

As California politico Jesse Unruh famously put it, "Money is the mother's milk of politics." Well-funded industry groups can wear down watchdog agencies by litigation and lobbying. They can use strategic campaign contributions to sponsor friendly politicians and get former employees and consultants appointed as the top regulators.

More imaginatively, industry groups threatened by environmental regulations can learn from Rachel Carson. They too can try to harness moral outrage and scientific research to meet their goals. Consider, for example, the Sagebrush Rebellion of the late 1970s, a populist campaign funded by the mining, oil, timber, and grazing industries in Nevada and nearby states. Under pressure from environmentalists, in the early 1970s the federal Bureau of Land Management (BLM) had begun to raise grazing and logging fees and to restrict access to the more fragile habitats. The foot soldiers in the rebellion, ranchers with property adjoining the vast BLM tracts, demanded a rollback of rules and a transfer of the lands to state or county control or privatization. The rhetoric grew heated and likened the BLM to communist commissars or to King George's minions. The sagebrush rebels formed a core constituency for Ronald Reagan and helped him win the 1980 Republican nomination and then the White House.

Michael Crichton's thriller *State of Fear* is a more recent example of fighting moral fire with fire. The novel's scientist-hero battles evil environmentalists and debunks their fearmongering on climate change.

Scientific research is itself a major front in the battle. For the last hundred years or so, governments in the advanced industrialized countries have funded basic scientific research at universities. The political goal is to catalyze new products and industries that will increase national wealth and prestige. In recent decades, however, government finances have weakened, and a larger share of funding now comes from industry.

Industry has always supported research that translates pure science into commercial products; that is exactly what the biotech and computer industries do in Silicon Valley. But some corporations and foundations also fund research for political purposes. The tobacco industry, as we've seen, sponsored researchers who raised doubts as to whether cigarette smoking really caused cancer; such work delayed consensus for decades. Something very similar is happening on crucial environmental issues such as climate change.

Coda for Cod

Scientific uncertainty and self-interested skepticism helped kill New England's cod industry. In 1976, the United States and Canada established national control over the offshore banks. Scientists assessed the fish populations, while regulatory agencies set total allowable catches (TACs), allocated the rights among fishermen, and monitored compliance. The system was supposed to maximize the economic yield, so that fish and fishermen could live happily ever after. Yet in less than 20 years, the cod fishing industry was dead, and cod almost became extinct.

The fatal dynamics began with uncertainty. Underfunded researchers, relying largely on the industry's reports of cod catches, put wide bands of possible error around their estimates of the live population. For example, in 1977, US scientists estimated that a TAC of 15,000 tons would allow the Georges Bank cod population to sustain itself. Industry advocates argued that the data could justify a TAC of 24,000 tons. The regulators set the TAC at 20,000 tons, and an "emergency amendment" late in the fishing season raised the TAC by about 10 percent. The actual catch probably was considerably higher due to "recreational" fishing as well as underreported catches and misreported species counts. Nevertheless, under industry pressure, the TAC was set even higher the next year. From then on, regulations and quotas were constantly juggled in response to political pressure and overly optimistic interpretations of the data.

Canada's dynamics were even worse. Hoping that the new 200-mile limit would bring prosperity to the impoverished maritime provinces, the Canadian government heavily subsidized factory trawlers and onshore fish processing facilities. The bureaucrats then had a short-term interest in seeing the facilities used, and their pressure (combined with pressure from industry) may have pushed up scientific estimates of the fish population. These pressures certainly biased the TAC and allowed the industry to continue to destroy fish habitat with outsize trawling nets. US and Canadian authorities also squabbled over management of banks that lay partly in each other's territory.

As fish populations waned in the late 1980s, public interest groups and scientists filed lawsuits in the United States and Canada, demanding more realistic measures to protect the fish populations. Industry leaders dug in their heels and delayed decisive action. Perhaps they truly believed the more optimistic reports, or perhaps they suffered from self-serving bias, or were planning early retirement and wanted to leave on a prosperous note. Whatever the reasons, they kept the bureaucracy from lowering the TACs as fast as necessary. Cod populations collapsed in the early 1990s, and so did the fishing industry.

Theories of the Long Haul

The point should now be clear. Environmentalists were naïve to believe that a moral crusade would, by itself, secure a sound and durable policy. Laws may be passed and bureaucracies built, but they will inevitably be eroded when they conflict with market imperatives.

What are the long-term consequences?

An optimistic theory is based on the graph of national environmental quality against average family income. The U-shaped relationship is called the environmental Kuznets curve. It shows that the environment is in pretty good shape in most of the world's poorest and most isolated countries, such as Bhutan, that lack much capacity to pollute. Environmental quality falls sharply as we move to middle-income countries like China, but it begins to rise again in wealthier countries and becomes quite good for the wealthiest. Some economists conclude that greater prosperity automatically spurs demand for a healthy environment, and eventually the whole world will clean up as it becomes richer.

There is also a pessimistic theory, called the "race to the bottom" or the "pollution haven" hypothesis. The key here is international trade. When a country enforces stricter environmental controls, it raises the costs of manufacturing, especially for the industries that generate more pollution. As a result, these industries cannot export as much and face more competition from imports. Free trade then may shift pollution-intensive industries to poorer countries, thus more than offsetting the cleaner world in richer countries. Alternatively, competition for export industries could lead to laxer environmental standards across the board.

Economists have not yet reached consensus on either theory; there are many countervailing trends and the evidence is ambiguous. In our opinion, the long run outcome is not yet determined. Rather, it depends on the policies that governments will adopt during the next decade as they respond to pressures from industry and green interest groups.

The New Grazing Markets: Halibut and Acid Rain

There is another way to look at environmental problems. The tragedy of the commons is the result of missing markets. The herdsman didn't pay the full cost of grazing the extra cow because of a missing market: access to the meadow. If there were a competitive grazing fee that reflected the full cost, then overgrazing would not occur. In the market-oriented modern world, the best way to solve environmental problems is often to build the missing markets and buttress them with moral codes.

Here is an example of success. Halibut, some over 200 pounds, still abound in the waters of southeastern Alaska. Seasonal limits prevented overfishing until the 1960s, when more and more fishing boats began to enter at the beginning of the season. The resulting "derby" got much worse than among Bay Area crabbers. As Alaskan fisherman Arne Fuglvog recounts:

> In the derby days we would set as much gear as possible because we would only have 24 or 48 hours to fish. And a lot of times, you didn't get all of your gear back, especially if the weather was really bad. So there'd be all of this lost gear on the bottom, ghost fishing, and catching and killing millions of pounds of fish. There was an unlimited number of vessels, all trying to race and catch as much fish as possible in this set amount of time. We knew we only had one, maybe two shots at it, to make our entire living.

In the late 1980s, local fishermen, environmentalists, and officials agreed on a market system that solved the problem. Based on estimates of the current halibut population, scientists set an overall limit to the allowable catch that season. Shares of that limit, called ITQs (Individual Transferable Quotas), were awarded to people who had historically fished in those waters. The ITQ holder can catch the fish himself or rent or sell his ITQ to the highest bidder. The usual market magic should put the ITQs into the most efficient hands. Fuglvog explains, "Under the present ITQ system, we have an 8-month season. We can choose when we go out and fish. We can go when the prices are high. We can work it around our crew schedule, our family schedule. We fish totally different now. I do think it's true that ITQs have fostered better stewardship. And one of the main reasons is that we do own part of the resource. We want to keep the resource healthy."

The ITQ market works with the moral system, not against it. Peer monitoring aids enforcement: law-abiding fishermen have an interest in watching for and reporting violators. A fisherman who needs to increase his fish quota to cover fixed costs or who just wants to expand no longer has to hire a lobbyist or a professional expert witness. Instead of trying to bend the political process or the legal system, he can simply go on the open market and purchase the ITQs he wants. Likewise, discouraged fishermen can sell their ITQs and probably end up with more money than they'd get by lobbying for a government subsidy.

ITQ markets are now under development for fishing in the Gulf of Mexico and elsewhere.

Of greater national importance is that in 1990 Congress and the first President Bush introduced the Acid Rain Trading Program for sulfur dioxide (SO_2). The science was pretty clear by then. Coal-fired electricity generating plants produced this air pollutant, which could lead to high concentrations of sulfuric acid in lakes and streams hundreds of miles downwind, killing off fish and other wildlife and endangering human health. The commons here is clean air, and companies graze on it by emitting the chemical. So the Trading Program puts a national limit or "cap" on SO_2 emissions each year—about 10 million tons in 2001, for example—and doles out pieces of the cap, called "allowances," to every generating plant. The EPA measures emissions from each plant, and the owner must have enough allowances to cover the emissions. Extra allowances may be saved for next year or sold to other plants that fall short. Plants that can't come up with enough allowances must pay hefty fines and get fewer allowances the next year.

So far, this cap-and-trade program has been a great success. Overall SO_2 emissions are about 50 percent lower than in 1980, even at the Ohio Valley plants that were the biggest polluters. The lakes and streams seem well on the way to recovery. The economic, bureaucratic, legal, and political costs are quite low: 50–80 percent less than those under traditional "command-and-control" programs, according to EPA estimates. And to the surprise of many, the program yielded its biggest gifts in health. By cutting down on harmful airborne SO_2 particles, it saved an estimated $50 billion by 2010 in health costs—at a total cost of only $0.5 billion.

Greenhouse Gas Markets

Could the market approach also solve the world's biggest and most contentious environmental problem: global climate change? The problem arises from three factors: 1) carbon dioxide, methane, and other greenhouse gasses (GHGs) trap solar energy and warm our planet's surface, 2) the atmospheric concentration of GHGs has risen dramatically since the beginning of the Industrial Revolution and especially in the past 30 years, and 3) current and projected future concentrations of GHGs threaten to warm the globe, make rainfall more erratic, and melt ice packs and raise sea levels, all of which would disrupt the world's environment and economy.

But climate science is notoriously complex and doesn't allow controlled experiments. It leaves a lot of room for uncertainty and self-interested skepticism. A few of the largest industries—oil, cars, and coal—probably would bear a disproportionate share of the costs of reducing GHGs. It should come as no surprise, then, that Exxon and other industry leaders funded think tanks and researchers who argued that the oceans might absorb excess GHGs or that there might be natural causes for observed changes. One important puzzle—that average temperatures recorded in the lower atmosphere didn't seem to be rising in parallel to average surface temperatures—was solved only in summer 2005 when researchers identified incorrect adjustments of the atmosphere data.

Now, however, there is a near-universal consensus that human activity is raising global levels of GHG to such an extent that the global climate will change significantly. But how much? Will the changes be comparable to those seen in recent centuries, or will they be catastrophes of Biblical proportions? Science can't yet say.

For greenhouse gases, the entire planet is a single commons. Since we live in a world of many nations, Garrett Hardin's logic shows that we are in deep trouble. Economist Scott Barrett first worked out the math (and game theory) in a simplified setting with symmetric nations, and came to the dismal conclusion that pursuit of national self-interest will lead to only a tiny fraction of optimal GHG reduction.

Of course, nations differ in their vulnerability to climate change—much of the Netherlands and Bangladesh and some Pacific islands might be wiped off the map, while Russia and Canada might almost break even—and on their costs of reducing GHGs. For example, China and India have lots of primitive coal-fired power plants, and by modernizing they could reduce GHG emissions much more cheaply than countries like Japan or the Netherlands.

It might seem that such asymmetric benefits and costs make bargaining even more difficult. But economist Matt McGinty remembered the old lesson of David Ricardo: Diversity increases gains from trade. What if firms could trade GHG allowances internationally as well as domestically? McGinty worked out the math and reached a much happier conclusion: Self-interested countries with realistic distributions of costs and benefits would have the incentive to form a large coalition, agree on a cap, and trade allowances. This could provide more than half of the potential gains from full cooperation.

If there were a single world government, or if national governments cared more about the good of the planet than their own economies, we'd see an even better solution: a uniform tax on GHG emissions (mainly on carbon) that reflected the costs to the global commons. However, serious new problems would arise from a carbon tax that gradually ratchets up, that differs across countries, or that is not fully enforced in some places. So a global carbon tax seems unrealistic in today's world.

So much for theory. What has actually happened? The first serious attempt to deal with the problem, the 1997 Kyoto Protocol, called for industrialized nations to roll back GHG emissions to about 95 percent of their 1990 levels. The goal is a bit arbitrary and not related to estimated costs or benefits. More important, it doesn't apply to the fastest growing countries such as China and India, and the United States refused to sign. (Australia finally joined following the November 2007 elections.) As a result, climate change is a bigger problem now than it was in 1997.

If nothing else, Kyoto Protocol has been a valuable learning experience. It spurred research, debate, and the first markets for trading carbon allowances in the EU. European nations are bound by their Kyoto limits, and their companies can trade allowances in the European Emissions Trading System (ETS). Prices rose gradually and erratically after the ETS opened in 2004 but crashed in early 2006 when word leaked out that the initial allocations had been far too generous.

ETS trading recovered for later year allowances, and total trading volume reached about €106 billion by the end of 2011.

Overall, reaction from industry seemed remarkably positive. Economist Michael Porter once argued that environmental regulations induce efficiency and innovation and make an industry more competitive. This hypothesis is far too sweeping, but it is true that some companies can profit from cleaning up the environment, and first movers have an advantage. In 2004, the corporate giant GE began seeking profits from products like wind turbines and fuel-efficient jet engines and lobbied for national and international environmental standards. Google announced it was putting up $200 million in venture capital to develop sources of renewable energy cheaper than coal. The banking industry figured out that that GHG allowances could become the world's largest commodities market and monitored developments carefully.

Then political backlash struck. President Obama made the green economy a keystone of his recovery program, and Republican adversaries brought out the knives. Several cap-and-trade bills remain stalled in Congress at this writing. Initiatives are also in limbo to extend cap-and-trade to the other major regional air pollutants, particularly nitrogen oxides and mercury, and to lower the SO_2 caps.

We warmed the earth and it won't cool on its own. Voters respond to immediate feedback far better than to long-term warnings, and the more they sweat in summer heat, the more they'll smile on solutions. Global warming will emerge from the attempts at confusion, as the ozone hole and acid rain did. Some US states and some nations are already taking action. California passed its own GHG regulations in late 2007 and began a cap-and-trade market in November 2012, and several northeastern states have enacted regulatory laws as well. New Zealand launched a cap-and-trade program in 2009, Australia approved one in 2011, and in 2012 South Korea's National Assembly voted 148–0 to start one. The world's leading emitter, China, is now working with the EU to develop a cap-and-trade program for eight of its cities. A carbon tax is probably more efficient, but since cap-and-trade is gaining traction and seems more palatable, it will likely prevail.

There are other inducements. Cap-and-trade markets can merge across nations, and firms in the energy industries know that uniform national (or international) rules are less costly than the patchwork evolving now. In addition, initial allocations of cap-and-trade allowances should be worth something like $40 billion in the United States, and the power companies want to get them for free. If they delay, they might end up having to buy them at auction or face a carbon tax.

However, assigning initial allowances is quite tricky for moral and economic reasons as well as technical. A larger initial allowance is a prize worth billions of dollars to most countries, and therefore, as with the cod TAC in the late 1970s, everyone will look for ways to get more. Bargaining is likely to take the form of dueling approaches to fairness. Countries like China and India will argue that fair means allocations proportional to population, while countries like Russia will argue that it is fairer to set allocations proportional to historical emission levels. To break the bargaining logjam, one should perhaps take a closer look at

McGinty's coalition calculations and then reverse engineer an appealing moral rule that assigns allowances that support the best feasible coalition. Once a sufficiently large coalition stabilizes, it could impose carbon import taxes that give the holdout countries an incentive to join.

Here's the bottom line: Environmental problems now are too pervasive to be dealt with solely by local morals or traditional markets. We need well-engineered replacements for all these missing markets, supported by a pragmatic moral code that insists on a healthy planet for all our grandchildren.

II

The World Ahead

We evolved in terrain of grassland and scattered trees so different from our present-day housing tracts and glass towers that we'd have trouble surviving in it—as our ancestors might in ours. The miracle is that our savanna genome made us so adaptable that we could move from hunting antelopes to trading CDSs and building global webs of finance.

Our success ultimately comes from our adaptable markets and morals. They are both solutions to the basic, universal problem facing every social creature, from forest-loving trees to ants to apes: how to reconcile the good of the individual with the good of the group. That is, how to promote effective cooperation. No other creature has developed either morals or markets, and we will need both to sustain the billions of people on our one small planet.

But they remain in dangerous balance, and always will.

So what's next? In October 2012, in an episode recalling Gilbert and Sullivan, an Italian court sentenced eminent seismologists to jail for failing to predict a deadly earthquake. Wags wondered if this judge would sentence himself to jail for failing to predict the reversal of his decision on appeal. No one has a crystal ball for complex realms. The economy, in particular, is a seemingly infinite, interlocking web of promises, floating almost invisibly all around us and altered by events of every kind. This fact has not stopped economists from predicting its future, but their record isn't heartening.

Even so, we can look forward more broadly, with suggestions on how to keep our morals and markets supporting each other, and thus to maximize wealth creation and minimize gut-wrenching swoons. We can better integrate these two great realms that too often work at cross purposes. We can seek guidelines for a healthy equilibrium.

Evolving Toward Balance

What kind of morals should we want? Philosophers have endlessly addressed this complex question, and we'll refrain from adding another inch to the Himalayan pile. But we can make a few observations about the kind of morals we should and shouldn't want regarding markets.

Fundamentalism

We tend to regard morals as absolute and unchanging, like the formula for the hypotenuse of a triangle. It can make you queasy to think hard about changing your views on what is right and wrong Yet morals evolve. Preagricultural Europeans had different values from the Gauls in Roman times, who had different values from the 21st-century French. Morals have to change to fit the changing world. Today, tribes have vanished, in-groups are much bigger, jets and optic fibers have shrunk the planet, and society has a hyperdimensional intricacy. Without moral evolution we'd still be back in nomad camps.

Yet contemporary morals sometimes seem out of joint, and then it is comforting to think that moral systems of the past worked better. Fundamentalists of all stripes go a step further and demand that we obey an older moral code.

Of course, there has always been a gap between prescribed and actual behavior—that's the way the moral system works. And not even fundamentalist creeds are exact replicas of the past. Christian fundamentalists must reinterpret the Bible, for example, to condemn the sale of morning-after pills. Likewise, suicide bombers targeting civilians stretch, or overstretch, historic Islamic doctrine.

Moreover, fundamentalism undermines cooperation, the very purpose of morals. It does increase cooperation among adherents (as in most in-groups), so it can be deceiving. But it opens chasms between them and others better matched to the current world. Today, cultures are more and more interweaving. Indians run high-tech firms in Silicon Valley, and China is a major trading partner of the United States. The world's top management consulting firm, McKinsey & Co., has branches everywhere and hires partners from every nation on earth. But fundamentalists like the Iranian ayatollahs erect pointless barriers to cooperation and weaken their markets.

The tenets of fundamentalism take morals backward. They typically arose before the Great Transformation and hence are out of kilter with market economies. Tolerance, freedom of speech, the conventionalizing of moral breaches—all help us work with people of varied backgrounds in an information-rich world. Yet fundamentalists follow beliefs which may or may not jibe with an effective market economy.

Saudi Arabia is a good example. To stay in power, the Saudi royals don't need a productive populace with market values; they just need to deflect challenges to control of their vast oil revenues. So it helps to have the backing of the most fanatical religious groups, such as followers of the puritanical and intolerant 18th-century Sunni cleric Ibn Abdul Wahhab, and the royals have long been very generous in financing Wahhabi preachers overseas as well as at home.

Does awareness of a code's evolution weaken its hold? Do we become less moral and more opportunistic? That, we think, is a fear that drives fundamentalism. If a certain act was immoral 300 years ago and is not immoral today, what are we to say? That people erred 300 years ago? That we err now? The real answer is usually that conditions have changed and morals have adapted. They have gotten more effective.

Understanding this fact does not weaken morals. An analogy may help make the point. Biologists and psychologists know more than most of us about the origins and evolution of human sexuality. Such awareness doesn't kill romance or long-term relationships for them or make sex any less pleasurable. Indeed, as a side benefit, awareness may help overcome morbid fetishes.

Overall, knowing that morals have a strong cultural component and that they evolve should make us even prouder of our moral accomplishments and of the bonds of love and friendship that we forge. The success of a moral code comes from its emotional resonance (for internal enforcement), the rewards and sanctions it inspires (for external enforcement), and the productivity it generates (for spreading adherence). It doesn't come from ignorance.

The Perils of Honor

Every society has some idea of honor. It implies respect from others for traits like integrity (and sometimes for more extreme ones, as in the Mafia). But when honor becomes the key mover of a moral code—usually when the legal system has failed, as in 19th-century Corsica—an insult-and-revenge syndrome can arise. A taunt can spur bloodshed.

This kind of honor code makes for a lousy judicial system. The plaintiff becomes judge and jury. He almost always deems his damage worse than impartial onlookers would. The code of the duel, intriguingly, formalizes the revenge and prevents the plaintiff from going too far. But left to his own devices, the punisher typically metes out too great a penalty, an urge for counterrevenge boils up in the original culprit, and violence can volley back and forth. A dishonorable feud can arise.

It all gets worse with groups. Affront one member and you may injure the family or tribe. If it has a Three Musketeers ethic—all for one and one for all—it may retaliate. Honor can also mean prestige from mere exercise of power. My in-group wins honor if men in your group submit to our will. If you won't, we gain by killing your men and taking your women. In short, we win honor by dishonoring your group. So, if we succeed, your group retreats with acid mutterings and plots revenge, and my group has to defend itself. Conflicts escalate rather than shrink. These hostilities divert society's attention (and resources) from more productive activities, and honor-driven rivalries of this sort impoverished much of the ancient and medieval world.

With the rise of market economies and effective legal systems, the old insult-and-vengeance syndrome fell away. For example, in the early 1800s dueling was outlawed and became unfashionable in the modernizing countries, and honor killings declined in Corsica even before 1800. Honor codes softened and changed even in the military. Nowadays, the US Navy and Marine Corps still list honor, courage, and commitment as their core values, but they define honor with modest imperatives like "Deal honestly and truthfully with others," and "Abide by an uncompromising code of integrity, taking responsibility for our actions and keeping our word." Yet the old syndrome remains in areas like rural Pakistan and it is the road to conflict rather than to prosperity.

Bourgeois Values

Hill country shepherds often perceive moral decay in the cosmopolitan city dwellers, who in turn view country folk as ignorant and narrow-minded. One reason is that rural people have always tended to see norm breaches more as intrinsically wrong, while city people may deem them conventionally wrong or not wrong at all. Many of history's great conquerors, including Caliph Umar (AD 581–644) and Genghis Khan (1162–1227), came from herdsmen tribes and launched cleansing missions on behalf of intrinsic wrongs.

Several episodes in the past half-century echo the theme. China's Cultural Revolution (1966–76) was supposed to sweep away bourgeois thinking and purify the Maoist creed, and Cambodia's genocidal Khmer Rouge regime (1975–79) had the same goal. Both were attacks on the market system and its values. The siege of Sarajevo (1992–1996) was on a much smaller scale, with about 10,000 dead rather than millions, but it had a similar source. Serb nationalists in the surrounding mountains wanted to ethnically cleanse a cosmopolitan enclave.

Yet bourgeois values are market values. Truthfulness, tolerance, working hard, and playing by the rules all aid the market system, but their rise has been neither smooth nor universal. For instance, Portugal's vibrant and tolerant new culture of the 1400s was squeezed by Spain in the 1500s. New World plunder gave Spain the luxury of retaining an antimarket honor culture, and of financing religious fanatics at home and halfway around the world.

In recent centuries, bourgeois moral codes spread over the modernizing world, because they breed wealth and lift living standards. Unless we wish to rid the world of billions of people and impoverish most of the survivors, we must rely mainly on moral codes conducive to the market system. They should emphasize bourgeois virtues like tolerance, honesty, prudence, diligence, and obeying the law. Noble traits like courage still have a place, but no longer at the center. The moral codes we should want, then, are perhaps not the most thrilling, but rather those that help support a healthy, wealthy, and populous world.

Marketolatry

Markets are wonderful when they work well. Nothing else known to mankind can scale up so nicely and extract such gleaming gains. But they don't always work so well. Kings can siphon profits. Commissars can breed black markets. Less drastically, intermediate players can break the classic buyer-seller relationship. Professors can assign books, which students have to buy regardless of price. Drug companies can pressure Congress and offer doctors incentives to prescribe, as in the anemia scandal. Moreover, markets don't suit all transactions. They work well spontaneously in some cases, can be engineered cleverly to work well in other cases, but are nonstarters in yet others. Whether specific markets will or can work is a scientific and engineering question, and we need to examine the evidence carefully to understand their limits.

In recent decades, mainly in the United States, a new ideology has taken hold that glorifies markets. As with any other ideology, it is dogmatic and resistant to evidence. This new creed, which some call marketolatry, holds that markets will always deliver the best of all possible outcomes in virtually any circumstance. The main exceptional circumstance is the presence of government. Like kryptonite, government somehow neutralizes markets' superpowers.

Alan Greenspan is a particularly interesting example. As a PhD student in economics at NYU in the early 1950s, he joined the inner circle of Ayn Rand, one of the movement's founders. He dropped out of NYU in 1955 to work full time as a consultant to the financial industry, where he prospered over the next several decades. He returned to NYU in 1977 to submit his dissertation on how household spending increases when home prices rise. Friedman recalls a 30-minute phone conversation with him on this topic soon after in 1978; he seemed enthusiastic and insightful, but cited weak data to back up his claims on the size of this effect.

In 1987, President Reagan appointed Greenspan to succeed the legendary Paul Volcker as chair of the Federal Reserve. Greenspan's deft handling of the brief stock market crash that year gave him instant credibility, and he went on to develop a good working relationship with President Clinton and both Presidents Bush. Yet in the last few years before stepping down in 2006, Greenspan ignored urgent warnings from Federal Reserve Board member Edward Gramlich and others about toxic mortgages and unregulated financial derivatives. By his ideology, private investors would do a better job of managing the risks than government regulators.

Almost alone among marketolators, Greenspan expressed doubt after the 2008 crash. In October 2008, he said, "Those of us who have looked to the self-interest of lending institutions to protect shareholders' equity—myself especially—are in a state of shocked disbelief." Pressed to admit that his ideology was wrong, he replied, "Absolutely, precisely.... That's precisely the reason I was shocked, because I have been going for 40 years or more with very considerable evidence that it was working exceptionally well."

This mea culpa upset Greenspan's fans; they preferred a narrative in which everything would have been fine had the government not let Fannie Mae and Freddie Mac run wild, trying to encourage home ownership by poor people. Greenspan has tried to walk back his apostasy a bit in recent books, but he no longer seems to have good standing among market fundamentalists.

Theory isn't reality. "Forget the antiseptic, well-lighted budget sets and markets of economics textbooks," wrote economist Daniel McFadden in an acute 2006 analysis. "Real-life markets are rough, murky, tumultuous places where commodity attributes shift, supply is uncertain, prices are volatile, and information is imperfect."

Marketolators are like tribesmen who, having first seen the power of an antibiotic, want to use it for everything, even toothpaste. Socialists or unreconstructed leftists are like equally ignorant tribesmen who, having seen unpleasant side effects of the same antibiotic, want to ban it. Both marshal moral outrage to push their points. And unfortunately splitting the difference does not succeed much better. Instead, we need to find the balance. We need to do the hard empirical work, to run experiments and tournaments that expand our understanding and show us how to build productive markets with a sustainable moral basis.

Dark Pools and Nanosecond Trades

Do more bubbles loom in the near future? Bubbles are notoriously had to spot because of poor information. Indeed, deniability is a necessary precondition for them. At the same time, all markets require information—you can't make decisions without it—and the better your knowledge, the shrewder the judgments you can reach. Financial markets in particular need information, and investors are constantly racing to get it.

Asymmetrical information can be very profitable. If you know an important fact that other traders don't, you'll value a stock more accurately than they do, and you can make money. For example, if the owners of a key Apple supplier know that a new device will be late or low-quality, they can profit by selling Apple shares. If other investors learn this fact, or even see who is selling these shares, they will sell too, and the price will drop quickly, limiting the supplier's profit. The owners of the inside information would therefore prefer to hide their trades. The US government made such insider trading illegal in the Securities Exchange Act of 1934.

In the last decade or so, opportunities to hide trades proliferated, as "dark pools" arose. By 2012, some 40 percent of all stock trades were taking place in these murky arenas. Dark pools—some hosted by investment banks like Goldman Sachs (Sigma X) and others independent (such as Instinet and NYFIX Millennium)—hurt the public by slowing the aggregation of information and keeping small investors out. They also could intensify a financial crisis since liquidity dries up faster when traders know less about the range of trading opportunities.

The problem may be more severe when it comes to trading nontraditional assets like CDSs. Investment banks and other financial institutions continue to create and sell them piecemeal. This kind of market reduces competition and transparency and magnifies the counterparty risk to the financial system.

There is a simple technical fix to these problems: Make trades run through a clearinghouse like that used by the Chicago futures exchanges for more than a century. This approach would ensure transparency and eliminate counterparty risk. If used before 2008, it would have mitigated and possibly even prevented the post-Lehman panic and meltdown. There are a few technical details—the customization of CDSs would become an add-on, for instance—but they don't seem especially difficult. Even Timothy Geithner endorsed the idea several years ago. But implementation lags, due to the vested interest of a few large players. The tax approach of A.C. Pigou mentioned below could change their incentives if the road remains blocked.

The Flash Crash of 2010 highlights another fixable problem. At 2:42 p.m. on May 6, 2010, the Dow Jones Industrial Average was down about 300 points on bad news from Greece. But over the next five minutes it plunged more than 600 additional points, representing a 9 percent loss of investors' wealth. Then, over the next 20 minutes, it regained the 600 points, for the wildest one-day roller-coaster ride in the entire history of the US stock market.

Investigations revealed that the Flash Crash was due to an aberrant high frequency trading (HFT) algorithm. Some large hedge funds and other players have spent billions of dollars in software and hardware that can execute orders a few millionths of a second faster than their rivals can. If you know that someone else is about to buy Alcoa, for instance, and you purchase it a sliver of a second faster, you will make money. You know a buyer is coming in at your heels, and that buyer will pay you a slightly higher price. So you've achieved the great dream of speculators: certainty about the direction of a stock, even if just for a moment. And if the deal is for millions of shares and you can execute trades like this all day every day, you can virtually print money. That's why it's called high frequency trading: the payoff on each sale is tiny, but incessant dealing swells it enormously. HFT investments did very well in the early 2000s. Everyone wanted to get in. Soon trading algorithms were battling each other, and an English tech firm claims to have created a chip that completed a trade in 740 nanoseconds. By 2011, according to some estimates, HFT was involved in three-fourths of all trades.

Yet with so many players using HFT, the slivers have grown almost invisibly thin, and it no longer seems very profitable. Some studies have argued that HFT increases liquidity and benefits investors, but we find more plausible recent impartial studies that point to slightly less advantageous prices for ordinary investors and increased systemic risk (exemplified by the Flash Crash, which could have turned out worse). Indeed, some insiders now worry about the moral consequences as well. "What we have today is a complete mess," said HFT pioneer Thomas Peterffy in a 2010 speech to his peers. People don't trust the market, he added, and why should they? "To the public the financial markets may increasingly seem like a casino, except that a casino is more transparent and simpler to understand." To the industry, this was a little like George Washington saying America had become a complete mess.

Regulators have proposed clumsy taxes to discourage rapid in-and-out trading, but there is a very simple solution that could save everyone money (except those who have sunk money into high-speed links to the exchanges). We can just force all trades to take place at discrete intervals, such as every quarter-second, rather than continuously. (More technically, change the market format from continuous double auction, where the first bid received gets priority even if it is only a millionth of a second earlier, to a call market, in which bids are batched and executed simultaneously at a uniform price.) This rule change would end the wasteful arms race to slice microseconds from order execution, and it would help level the playing field and make trading more trustworthy for everyone.

As we see it, the best hope is for the Financial Stability Oversight Council and its research unit to mature as a true guardian of the public interest. Its mandate would not be to forbid new activities, like a questionable new derivative security, but rather to conservatively measure the risk it poses to the financial system and then tax it proportionately Originally developed by British economist A. C. Pigou, this approach has proved to be better than Prohibition in coping with the negative effects of alcohol consumption, and we believe it would improve incentives in the financial market as well. Talented people have devoted much ingenuity in recent decades to evading the regulations rather than to improving financial markets. With a Pigouvian tax on systemic risk, financial firms would have more incentive to earn profits that didn't put markets—and taxpayers—at risk.

Of course, systemic risk is difficult to measure, especially regarding innovations. That's where the research unit comes in. There are actually a fair number of quants, or "rocket scientists" as they are sometimes called, who have the needed expertise and are tired of working on Wall Street. If they compete to be the first to convincingly measure the systemic risk in exotic new financial instruments, the state of the art should move forward rapidly. If members of the Financial Stability Oversight Council seek to advance the public interest rather than curry favor with industry, the next financial calamity may be several decades away rather than only a few years.

Globalization and Them

Henry David Thoreau (1817–1862) spoke of Zanzibar as a place of dreamlike remoteness. But today we can fly there in hours and skype with its citizens for free. In the past 150 years we have witnessed an amazing revolution in communication and transportation. Goods flow across the surface of the earth so quickly and inexpensively that a drought in the Midwest can cause food riots in Bangladesh. Economically, our entire planet is Uruk. We enjoy virtual proximity—Zanzibar *might as well* be nearby—and proximity increases wealth. So today the logical outcome of the market system is a single world market, with goods made and services performed wherever the cost/benefit is best, for consumption by the planet's highest bidders.

Should we encourage such global markets, or try to keep things more local?

Expanding international trade clearly makes the world richer. The global market system especially boosts incomes in the poorer countries that join. China and India are recent examples impossible to ignore, but they follow a path blazed earlier by Japan and many other countries.

Yet resistance to globalization has spread in the past decade or two. It sparked the 1999 Battle of Seattle and several other protests around the world. Critics from the political right (Pat Buchanan and Lou Dobbs, for example) blamed global markets for loss of national sovereignty and excess immigration. Their counterparts on the left (Noam Chomsky and Ralph Nader, say) worried more about threats to economic equality, worker health and safety, and the environment. Critics from both wings claim that global markets destroy local jobs and depress real wages and transfer too much power to international organizations like the World Bank and the World Trade Organization. The economic downturn eclipsed such issues after 2008, but as the world recovers, they will come back to the fore.

Columbia University economist Jagdish Bhagwati has written a very readable refutation of these claims. He summarizes lots of careful studies and concludes that, on balance, opening global markets slightly boosted real wages in the United States and elsewhere. Bhagwati doesn't quite say so, but our us-versus-them moral instincts and self-serving biases may prevent us from seeing clearly the gains that globalization brings to our exporting industries and to our consumers. Likewise, we may blame lost jobs on low-wage foreign competition when the main cause is technological advance.

Bhagwati eloquently points out the cultural benefits from global exchange and the economic and political gains when foreign competition breaks local monopolies and cartels, as it did with the US auto industry. He recommends direct measures to deal with environmental problems that arise when export-oriented businesses expand. For example, when shrimp farming starts to destroy mangrove swamp habitat, the recommended solution is not to ban shrimp exports, but to make sure that shrimp farmers pay the full cost of the damage.

UCLA economist Edward Leamer argues that most jobs in the United States (and elsewhere) are not vulnerable to offshore competition because they can't be commodified. For example, typing can be moved offshore but hairstyling cannot. After discussing the disruptive textile markets in late 1700s England, he concludes, "The lesson is that infrastructure and workforce quality can create deep roots that hold the best jobs firmly in place."

Nevertheless, thoughtful critics of globalization raise three points that deserve analysis. First, joining the global economy brings new vulnerability: distant events are more likely to cause havoc. The crash of 2008 swiftly undermined banks in Iceland, for instance, and sent painful shocks through much of the world. We lean on each other, so we totter when a trading partner falls to its knees.

Harm can reach us in subtler ways. Suppose that my nation becomes specialized in growing Brussels sprouts for export. Normally, our citizens would gain more income—otherwise we would not have specialized—but if a new root fungus kills our crop, we're in much deeper trouble than if we had stayed with mixed agriculture. There are other risks too: New Zealand farmers might suddenly flood the market with lower cost Brussels sprouts, or our sprouts might go out of fashion in key foreign markets.

However, the global economy also brings new opportunities to diversify and share risk. In the premodern era, people could only share risks locally within the extended family or village. And of course they still can. For example, the farmers in my country might rotate sprouts with other crops. But people now can and should partly share risks with others across the globe. For example, imagine a Brussels sprouts futures market or event market. Local farmers could hedge the risk, accommodated by distant investors seeking diversified financial assets. There is also a role for government. "Wage insurance" is a good example: the government could temporarily and partially subsidize workers who take new jobs after losing higher-paying work due to foreign competition. Even Bhagwati approves of this sort of safety net.

The second, related concern is loss of local diversity. Global chain stores replace homegrown operations, eBay and Amazon drive out local antique dealers and bookstores, and outlying shopping malls drain life from Main Street. Everything looks pretty much the same everywhere.

Except that it doesn't, if you look just a little closer. Quirky little businesses spring up that use eBay or their own websites to sell some tiny specialty to the whole world. Three random examples that we experienced in a single week: vintage postcards of Massachusetts' Pioneer Valley, consulting services to biotechnology companies appealing their tax assessments, and a bed-and-breakfast catering to admirers of poet Robinson Jeffers. Long ago, Adam Smith observed that the larger the market, the more specialties it could support. Global markets promote world-class narrow specialties that ambitious people can exploit wherever they have full market access. Diversity doesn't diminish; it just changes shape.

What's Wrong with Inequality?

The League of Shadows has been a check against human corruption for thousands of years. We sacked Rome. Loaded trade ships with plague rats. Burned London to the ground. Every time a civilization reaches the pinnacle of its decadence, we return to restore the balance. . . . Over the ages our weapons have grown more sophisticated. With Gotham we tried a new one. Economics.

—Ducard (Liam Neeson) in *Batman Begins* (2005)

The critics' third point is inequality. Batman fans know of the League of Shadows' dark new weapon: Heighten economic inequality till it rips Gotham's social fabric and leaves the city helpless against the League's final assault. However, in the real world, not everyone fears that weapon. Bhagwati, for example, argues that since globalization boosts incomes for the poor and middle classes, it shouldn't bother anyone that the rich get a bigger slice of the pie than ever.

We're not so sure. This may be one time when Hollywood screenwriters have better insight than an eminent economist. Before jumping to conclusions, though, let's take a closer look at the facts.

We can view inequality in two ways: across and within nations. Globalization and new policies in developing nations have changed both.

Across nations, inequality has dropped. As countries like China and India have gotten wealthier, the gulf between rich and poor nations has narrowed. The world has grown more similar. But the gap remains very wide. Indeed, the biggest factor in determining your lifetime income is your nation of birth. That's why people risk their lives to migrate from Latin America to the United States and from Africa to Europe. Relocation is the most important step they can take toward prosperity.

Within nations, inequality is generally rising. The top and bottom tiers are spreading farther apart. It's happening dramatically in once poor countries like China, but income gaps are also growing in some developed countries. The fraction of income in the United States going to the top 0.01 percent—just 16,000 families—is now almost 5 percent. That's four times the percentage in 1980 and exceeds the percentage in the Gilded Age 100 years ago.

People morally accept a certain amount of inequality, especially if it is some-how proportional to merit. (Ignorance aids acceptance, and few Americans real-ize the current extent of inequality.) Yet the top 0.1 percent in the United States is increasingly populated by investment bankers and less by CEOs. There are now far greater profits in the financial industry than 30 years ago. One reason is the too-big-to-fail subsidy (aka the "Greenspan put" or anticipated bailout effect) and another is the favorable treatment they get in the tax code—the carried interest loophole allows them to pay just 15 percent. Of course, large segments of the pub-lic blame investment bankers for causing the crash of 2008, and the huge bonuses these executives received especially angered people. It's no coincidence that the Occupy movement began on Wall Street.

More broadly, some argue that the wealthy deserve this share of the pie and, in particular, that such inequality improves the economy. Does it?

Inequality can potentially boost economic performance in two ways. First, the rich generally save more than the poor, and their savings can grow capital stock faster when they get a larger fraction of national income. This factor was clearly important in 1800s. However, excessive conspicuous consumption, and keeping up with the Joneses, will attenuate this effect. Second, inequality may increase incentives to work hard to move up the ladder. The University of Chicago school of economics has made this argument, but there is little evidence for it outside the seriously socialist countries that kill incentives for everyone except party members.

Yet inequality can also hurt economic performance in two ways. First, it can limit access or opportunity for a large fraction of the population and thus reduce the supply of available talent. According to a 2012 report from the Organization for Economic Cooperation and Development, or OECD, in countries with more equal incomes like Norway and Finland, a child's future income is less strongly tied to her parents' than in nations with less equal incomes like the United States and Italy. "This suggests," the report notes, "that socioeconomic background plays a strong role in the development of children's skills and abilities in these countries." That is, income inequality slows mobility.

Of course, social mobility is a proud keynote of the American narrative and by letting talents move where they do best, a nation obviously benefits. Gustavo Marrero and Juan Rodriguez compared states in the United States and found that equality of opportunity correlated clearly with growth. Others have reported similar results with nations. Moreover, in virtually all modern societies, we sus-pect, people increase productive efforts when they perceive equal opportunity. Land reform in Japan and Korea (and elsewhere) helped give opportunity to ordi-nary peasants and set these countries on the economic growth path to modernity. Indeed, their Gini coefficients fell as their economies grew. Overall, some scholars find that greater equality is associated with longer and steadier growth; nations with high inequality may have impressive growth spurts, but these are less likely to last. So the Gini increases in recent decades in the United States and China are both quite worrisome, even though their dynamics differ considerably.

Second, inequality can cause a League of Shadows effect, at least to some extent. It can undermine social cohesion, needlessly reducing labor productivity and diverting more resources to crime prevention. When people think hard work won't pay, they slack off or engage in social strife that undermines growth. The Firestone tire/Ford Explorer case highlights the effect, as do labor relations in the United Kingdom over the past 200 years. More subtly, disgruntled employees tend to steal, and by one estimate occupational fraud in the United States amounts to some $650 billion per year or 5 percent of all company revenue.

Modern nations got started when their citizens' sense of in-group expanded from village and region. Indeed, the nationalist movements of the 19th century were partly about establishing this feeling of vast commonality. But people with far different opportunities and lifestyle always seem more like "them" than "us." Inequality thus corrodes the sense of shared national purpose and can harm the moral infrastructure markets need to thrive. And in extreme cases, as in France in the late 1700s or in Russia a century later, their upshot can be as toxic as the disease.

What role does globalization play in the rising inequality? Mainstream economic studies have argued for some time that the main cause is not globalization but rather technological change, which favors the better educated workers, both in the United States and in most other countries. We suspect that the interaction of technology and globalization is the main driver. Just as in early 19th-century England, some people are getting rich much faster than others. In developing nations, people with more education and greater mobility apparently reap most of the gains from globalization, because they can better take advantage of the new opportunities.

However, the fact that countries differ so much in equality but face the same global economy suggests that national policy is of first-order importance.

Government measures to increase opportunity and mobility, if implemented efficiently and not to excess, boost growth. This statement might seem innocuous, but it contradicts the traditional thrust of both US Democrats and Republicans. The classic Democratic approach is to hike tax rates on the rich and transfer benefits to the poor. The traditional Republican approach is to cut spending on public services, including those that increase opportunity and mobility. So we take issue with both of them.

Top marginal income tax rates maxed out at over 90 percent in the 1940–50s. They dropped under Kennedy and hit post-FDR lows under Reagan. Clinton moved them up only slightly, and then George W. Bush dropped them to their current lows. Yet high marginal tax rates are counterproductive at some point. We'd place that phase change at around 50 percent, so we don't see a problem with returning to the rates of the Clinton era. But Belgium and the United Kingdom are skirting the limit at 50 percent, and the recent 75 percent tax on the very rich in France may boomerang.

Other relevant policies include transfers like Social Security, food stamps, and, in the longer run, access to public services like good K-12 schools and health care. In the United States, inequality had risen over the level in the 19th century, but after the Progressive era and especially in the 1930s, the United States reduced it mostly by policy reform—dissolving monopolies, legalizing labor unions, imposing graduated taxation, investing in schools and infrastructure, and creating safety nets like Social Security and unemployment insurance. All mattered, but Harvard economists Claudia Goldin and Larry Katz argue that increasing access to secondary education and college was the prime force in driving the Gini coefficient of the United States down and increasing mobility between 1920 and 1970. A basic safety net is also helpful. For instance, it encourages risk-taking entrepreneurship by folks who are not already wealthy and frees young people to invest in their future instead of taking care of old or sick relatives, or building a large nest egg. Beyond that, however, transfers can be counterproductive. Europe's problems now originate in part from labor market practices and transfers that discourage permanent hiring especially of young people.

In developing countries, sound policy measures include reduction in bribery, effective law enforcement, and sensible regulations to let businesses form easily, compete fairly, and wind up reasonably. For instance, India in the 1990s reduced the fabulous tangle of government red tape called the License Raj and quickly grew more prosperous, and of course we've discussed the adaptations in China. In both cases, opportunity skyrocketed.

Among the most effective policies to reduce inequality and increase mobility are the following:

- *Attacking crony capitalism.* In the United States right now, the most egregious examples are Wall Street privileges, but we'd also include big pharma, telecoms, corporate farmers, and generally industries with a big budget for lobbying and campaign contributions. The *Citizens United* decision will help them elect politicians indebted to them and thus increase crony capitalist favors. This heralds a return to the robber baron era, except that instead of hidden personal payments the plutocrats make campaign contributions and distribute other, less direct favors.
- *Investing in the young.* These programs range from well-baby clinics and Head Start to increasing funds to K-12 programs that work and access to community colleges and universities. We can also benefit by retargeting healthcare funds from medical programs that treat end-of-life conditions expensively without extending life or improving its quality, and funnelling them to younger folks whose lifetime productivity they could boost.
- *Reforming taxes.* The structure should be modestly more progressive and a lot more efficient. More reliance on property tax (especially in California, long deprived of it by Proposition 13) and taxing inheritance at the beneficiary level would help spread the wealth, as would a reduction in sales tax. Many other reforms are long overdue, such as capping deductions, especially on mortgage interest, and removing the tax incentives for employer-provided health care.

Building and Supporting Better Markets

The individuals on US bills, like Benjamin Franklin and Andrew Jackson, lived at a time when US currency wasn't even standardized. No doubt they felt the world shifting as market economies arrived, but markets still played a subordinate role in people's lives. Most US citizens were farmers and largely self-sufficient.

Today, virtually all of us live in a world of money, and a universe of goods exists to satisfy even the rarest tastes. Yet crucial activities still remain outside the market system. Where exactly should we draw the line? Which goods and services should the market provide, and which should come from government or remain unsold?

To approach the question, we'll first perform triage, and sort goods and services into three categories. (We assume good infrastructure: transportation and communication networks and courts that enforce contracts and punish fraud.) The first category includes items the market can reliably provide, such as bread, shoes, computers, and other commodities. The second category consists of things the market could not or should not provide, like slaves or legislation or air.

The third category needs the most attention. It includes services that markets can easily botch, but might provide efficiently with special infrastructure or engineering.

Take California's electric power industry. A partially deregulated power market debuted in 1998 with great fanfare, but it blew up between May 2000 and September 2001. Enron and other power suppliers and traders carved out tens of billions of dollars in windfall profits, while consumers suffered from rolling blackouts, bankrupt local utilities, and inflated bills.

What went wrong? The official report blamed the traders and suppliers who "violated the antigaming provisions," but the real problem was bad design. The politicians and lawyers in charge of deregulation worried mainly about satisfying powerful interest groups. They consulted some economists and engineers, but gave them little latitude in proposing and testing new designs. When the market opened, customers had no real-time information about prices. The market format and special rules were dysfunctional; even worse, the concentrated ownership of generating facilities encouraged suppliers to artificially restrict production and extract monopoly rents. You can't patch those sorts of problems with "antigaming provisions." Of course, it is not straightforward to build a competitive market for electric power—if it were, it probably would have emerged spontaneously. But we have no doubt that economists and engineers could now do so, and despite political scars from the California debacle, there has been cautious progress in the past five years.

For services in the third category, the basic principle is to design the market so that the best profit opportunities come from competitive behavior, from supplying at low cost, and from bidding aggressively. Gaming the system should be self-defeating. The theory of mechanism design, developed largely by the three 2007 Nobel laureates in economics, gives some guidance on how to align participants' incentives with market efficiency.

The basic principle is not enough, however, because there are always crucial details left outside the theory. Laboratory tests, small-scale trials in the field, and tinkering are therefore necessary.

Perhaps even more important are the political obstacles. There are usually special interests growing fat on the inefficiencies, and they will try to strangle the new market. For example, as an assistant professor in the 1980s, Friedman naïvely tried to persuade New York Stock Exchange officials to consider an all-electronic double auction format. They didn't go for it. Eventually the reason dawned on him: The new format would sideline the very specialists who owned the NYSE.

The problem resembles that faced by medieval markets. Western Europe's solution began in the backwaters, in towns beyond the grip of the powerful. Likewise, to spread a new market format, one should seek hungry upstarts at the fringes, build coalitions strong enough to launch, and expand into neighboring niches as they become profitable. In the 1990s, local entrepreneurs brought all-electronic double auctions to new exchanges in Europe, Asia, and Canada, and to US dealers in thinly traded securities. In 2006, the new market formats finally reached the power center, the NYSE, when competition pushed it to merge with Archipelago. Today, the NYSE is all-electronic, as you can tell by looking at its floor during CNBC interviews. It was once a crowded, clamorous marketplace, hard to penetrate; today, you could ride a bike through it.

Selling Health

Health care is a far larger example of the third category. In the United States, it accounts for a huge chunk of the economy, accounting for about 18 percent of GDP in 2011 and expected to hit 20 percent by 2021. But we are a long way from the simple farmers' market here. Indeed, a dysfunctional mix of market and government programs delivers health care. Insurers stand between buyer and ultimate seller, and your policy determines the services and drugs you get, and the additional price you pay. The employer typically stands between end user and seller. The employer buys most coverage (and gets a tax break), but that approach distorts workers' decisions on taking and keeping jobs and artificially raises employers' costs. An increasing part of the coverage comes from government programs, and they create even worse problems for all the usual reasons. To top it off, large numbers of people have no health coverage, and they clog the emergency rooms, where they get extremely expensive but not very effective treatment while putting a burden on everyone else.

Informational problems stymie simple market solutions here. The doctor must have detailed personal knowledge to find the proper treatment, and few patients can judge the quality of the medical services they receive. Insurance is appropriate because occasionally people need costly treatments, and that risk is diversifiable. However, insurance policies are hard for buyers to understand and compare, especially since they come in myriad varieties. On the other hand, adverse selection undermines the market: patients know better than insurers whether they will need lots of expensive care, and the healthiest patients are most likely to opt out, raising premiums for the rest.

Altogether, then, health care reform is one of the great challenges of our time. And several major industries—notably insurance and pharmaceuticals—have large stakes in keeping the current system dysfunctional.

On the savanna, people in tribes cared for others who were injured or ill. Indeed, we can see one relic of this system in the pain expressions on our faces. With mild to moderate pain, we usually show no expression. But when the pain is bad, our faces contort in a manner recognized in every culture, and it prompts people nearby to help. That's why we have it, and this SOS would have worked well in ancient Africa. Moreover, tribal folks had social bonds and trust; they knew each other and indeed needed each other. So they had good reason to aid an ailing in-group member.

But when the in-group becomes a nation, these bonds weaken or disappear. In-groups based on wealth appear. The rich, who can easily pay for their health care, feel everyone else should too; the poor think the state is an ocean of cash and should absorb their medical bills. One upshot: Ideologues of the right and the left cling to obsolete ideas about the role of the government.

Libertarians on the right believe we should phase out Medicare and let individuals negotiate their own deals with insurance companies or health care providers. Most of them haven't taken on board the informational asymmetries in this market and how these lead the invisible hand astray. More economically sophisticated libertarians believe that some sort of entrepreneurs will naturally arise to somehow solve the problem. This is a touching confession of faith, but (as far as we can see) it is unsupported by historical evidence anywhere in the world.

Leftists note that all other industrialized countries use a government-centered model and have achieved better health overall than the United States—and with lower per-capita expenditures. This is true as far as it goes, but different countries involve the government in different ways, and it is unclear which of these ways (if any) would work well for the United States.

In some countries, like the United Kingdom, the government provides health care directly. Doctors and nurses are government employees, and a government agency runs the hospitals. Our Veterans' Administration (VA) works like that, but to scale up the VA to cover all Americans seems prohibitively expensive and politically impossible. One suspects there are much more flexible and efficient approaches than creating a new bureaucracy far more massive than any we currently have.

Other countries, such as Canada, use a single-payer model. The national and provincial governments pay for almost all medical care from general taxes, but doctors and nurses are not government employees, and hospitals are privately owned. The government offers fixed prices for services in contracts with providers. Medicare and Medicaid run like this in the United States. Obama suggested a similar plan for the United States during his 2008 campaign, but it would have cut out the powerful insurance industry, and he abandoned it soon after reaching office.

Dutch taxpayers ensure a basic level of care for everyone, and try to facilitate a competitive market supplying higher quality care to those willing and able to pay for it. That strikes us as the best alternative if we were to start from scratch.

But we can't be entirely sure. The industrialized nations provide many examples of government-centered systems that work better than ours, but the sample of privately run systems is just one: the United States. Perhaps good design might yield a market-driven approach more efficient than the others. We haven't seen it yet but it's possible.

Reality in the United States at this writing is quite strange. Obama decided to make health care his top priority in 2009, but stood back from the political horse-trading for most of that year, hoping for convergence on a bipartisan plan based on proposals originating from Republican think tanks and implemented in Massachusetts in 2006. The Massachusetts law was Governor Mitt Romney's signature accomplishment, and Senator Ted Kennedy and most Democrats supported it. So far, it has worked at least as well as predicted. That plan allows private insurance companies to continue their leading role and indeed increases demand for them by mandating that everyone purchase health insurance. (The logic is like requiring collision insurance for drivers; otherwise, everyone else is on the hook if an uninsured person runs into trouble.)

The Patient Protection and Affordable Care Act, now often called Obamacare, was finally passed and signed in March 2010 over the united opposition of Republicans. They made a moral crusade of opposing Obamacare, calling it a government takeover, socialized medicine, and a violation of freedom of choice. It did indeed violate freedom of choice, but laws often do, and in a surprise decision the Supreme Court, led by hard-line conservative Chief Justice Roberts, upheld it.

As we write, most of the provisions of Obamacare have not gone into effect, and the implementation details remain undetermined. The framework is there for experiments, tournaments, and gradual evolution of more efficient markets for health services. But continued political posturing, inefficiency, and gridlock are also quite possible.

Recess in Education?

Reform of primary and secondary education in the United States is another great challenge, and it too will require an imaginative blend of moral fervor and market design.

Education on the savanna was presumably a matter of imitation, daily experience, and wisdom passed on through instruction and stories. In premodern times it was a simple market good. Some wealthy families hired tutors or sent their children to a private academy, while the other kids became apprentices or learned a trade from their parents. Instruction and experience thus partly bifurcated, with the rich learning Greek and the others hands-on skills. But most jobs remained pretty simple by our standards, and there wasn't much demand for universal education before 1800.

China is an interesting exception. For more than a thousand years, when the empire was working well, a competitive national exam with a pass rate of 1–2 percent selected the country's career civil servants. Participation was hardly universal. From 1500 to 1900, some two to three million people took it every other year—a small fraction of the populace—and sons of farmers and merchants rarely entered at all. In some centuries, however, the government subsidized test-taking schools and encouraged talented students from poor families.

Today, our market economies ride on education. You are much more productive when you and everyone can read and write the same language, and when you know that strangers learned the same things in school that you did. Almost every organization needs a literate and numerate workforce, people who can quickly absorb its training; most companies also require access to professionals in special areas like accounting and engineering. As the economy grows more elaborate, there is more to learn, and the educated become increasingly valuable. The average college graduate earned 38 percent more than the average high school graduate in 1979, for instance, but the difference amounts to 75 percent today.

Without education, a nation limps. In India, for instance, primary schools are almost nonexistent in some rural areas and work poorly in others. The lack of early education handicaps millions of Indian citizens and deprives the nation of their developed skills. The nation owes its rapid growth in technology to its topflight universities. But India is so big that its large number of professionals is deceiving. They remain a fraction of its potential.

Thus, education is a public good, and standard economic theory suggests that it should therefore be subsidized. In the 19th century, the United States led the way in offering universal free public education, at first four years and later eight. In the early 20th century we added kindergarten and high school. The rest of the industrialized world followed our lead. But we fell behind in the last third of the 20th century.

Most other industrialized countries now have better K-12 public education than we do. National taxes finance most of them, and national or province-level authorities run them. The United States retains its basic 19th-century school district boundaries designed for autonomous small towns, with an overlay of state authority and federal programs (which comprise a small part of expenditures on K-12 education).

We also face a moral impasse in K-12 education. Most teachers feel they are sacrificing personal income to do something truly worthwhile, and unions see their mission as preventing exploitation. Such strong moral claims, along with fragmented control, greatly complicate reform. Some call for vouchers or other privatization schemes. The unions resist, and call for smaller classes, higher salaries, and more respect. Taxpayers are skeptical: more money might not be well spent, especially by distant schools. We seem trapped in a bad equilibrium.

There is no easy solution, but three federal efforts have attempted inroads and merit attention here: Head Start, No Child Left Behind, and The Race to the Top.

Head Start is by far the oldest. This school readiness program began under Lyndon Johnson and now every year it serves close to one million kids aged 3–5, at a cost of about $6 billion. Studies of the early cohorts suggest that it was quite effective in raising first graders' test scores, that the test score improvement faded in later grades, but (somewhat mysteriously) adult outcomes were significantly better on scales such as wages, college education, criminal record, and avoidance of teenage pregnancy. The funding was stepped up (partly in response to those findings) in the 1990s, and around 2004 another experiment began that may yield more detailed results. So far, it has revealed an impressive effect on first-grade test scores for those in the lower third of the distribution, but here too this effect washed out after another couple of years. Nobody knows yet whether the adult outcomes will justify this moderately expensive social program.

President Bush's No Child Left Behind program tried to modernize schools, to create national standards and accountability. The goal was worthy, but implementation proved rather clumsy, and results so far have not been impressive.

President Obama's Race to the Top somewhat resembles the tournament that China used to identify effective economic programs. Conducted by the secretary of education, the competition originally offered $4.35 billion in prize money from stimulus funds to states that offered the most convincing plans to develop more effective teachers and principals, to build data systems measuring student success (such as by higher admission rates to college), to turn around faltering schools, and to set world-class student performance standards. Most states entered the contest, and the first winners were announced in December 2010.

China's example shows that tournaments can be very effective under certain conditions. They have to provide substantial rewards (in money and reputation), give contestants plenty of autonomy, and measure results clearly. The stimulus funds provided the rewards, and the fragmentation of public education in the United States has helped their autonomy, but success metrics are tricky and still under construction. Critics on the left have attacked the program for too much reliance on testing, and those on the right have complained about too much federal meddling. Of course, we live in a polarized society where partisans have no trouble turning nonpolitical programs into Thunderdome arenas, and the real question is: Does it work?

By 2012 the amount per year had fallen to $550 million, and educators complained that the grants were too small. But Secretary of Education Arne Duncan claimed the Race to the Top had brought a variety of benefits. It had led to significant academic gains in the turnaround schools, he said, as well as "huge reductions of discipline incidents," a major headache for teachers. Moreover, schools that didn't win copied those that did, so the successful innovations spread. According to Jay Altman, a New Orleans executive who helps rescue failing schools, "Louisiana ended up not winning Race to the Top, but we got close, and the process stimulated Louisiana and other states to think more broadly about educational reform rather than just approach it piecemeal." Despite such assertions, it remains too early to gauge the success of this program.

But we do like the tournament idea itself. It parallels not just China but the market system, where profitable ideas can arise out of nowhere and conquer the earth. It also resembles the scientific enterprise, where even bizarre concepts like those of quantum physics can prevail by proving that they work. This approach greatly improves the discovery, assessment, and spread of useful ideas, and no other is nearly as good at these vital tasks.

So as with our other pressing problems, the answer here is not to launch a new moral crusade to shame corporations (or schools) into social responsibility nor to build big bureaucracies to micromismanage them. Neither is the answer simply to let the global markets rip. There is a better way forward: to experiment, test, and build new structures on solid foundations.

On Balance

We've covered continents worth of territory, so what have we seen? In essence, morals should encourage cooperation but not at the expense of competitive equilibrium (CE), and they should encourage competition, but not at the expense of trust and customer value. Aristotle's golden mean is a good if vague guide for morals and markets: Neither in excess. But we can provide some specific examples.

Some problems arise from too much or misdirected moral emphasis:

1. Antiquated values. Throwback morals, such as fundamentalism and insult-and-revenge syndromes, weaken the values that support markets.
2. Fear of finance. Blaming "finance" for regulatory failings and the sins of some practitioners makes no sense and can harm society.
3. Cronyism. Warm personal favors can destroy economic benefits to the public, as in the Japanese recession.
4. In-group thinking. Big markets work better and global markets may work best of all, but in-group tendencies set up barriers and can shrink markets.
5. Excess "moral" regulation. Markets slow where governments morally oppose them and artificially boost costs, as by requiring high fees and long waits to start a business. Ostensible reasons may be moral, but real-world reasons are often ignoble, such as officials' desire to pocket bribes for cutting red tape.
6. Substitution of moral for market thinking. Surprises often greet the well-meaning. For instance, socially conscious price regulation can create black markets, as people find clever ways to trade at real values. Outlaw competitive equilibrium and you wind up playing whack-a-mole.
7. Attempts at leveling. If everyone must be equal, rewards dwindle and performance lags. People cease caring, so the system loses individual effort and insights, as on the Chinese collective farms. Markets need well-placed incentives.
8. Marketophobia. When governments demonize and try to suppress markets, as under communism, we witness extraordinary, often ghastly events.
9. Marketolatry. When governments themselves demonize government and morally exalt all markets, we risk inefficient oversight and crashes. Markets come in many different kinds, and every one needs a well-tailored moral and legal infrastructure (in some cases with a regulatory component) that facilitates competitive equilibrium.

And some problems arise from too little emphasis on morals:

1. Diversion. The Colorado River no longer reaches the sea, because people divert so much from it. Kings have a similar effect on markets.

2. Expropriation. Why improve your home, neighborhood, or business if a dictator can steal it at any time? Private property needs protection.

3. Monopoly and cartels. It's a rare person who competes with herself. The first word in competitive equilibrium is "competitive," and powerful economic players can kill competitive equilibrium and jack up prices. A classic example is the Southern Pacific railroad in late 19th-century California.

4. Political distortions. Powerful figures can lobby legislators to alter markets by, say, loosening antitrust regulations or perverting patent laws.

5. Slight, poorly enforced, or misdirected regulation. Lax rules breed crashes. One special pitfall is information blackout, as with the CDSs, the Spanish *cajas*, and potentially the dark pools.

6. Cheating. Frauds boost distrust and undercut markets, so everyone may suffer.

7. Stoppers on information flow. Censorship and chilling effects can slow movement of the data essential to smart, quick decisions.

8. Information asymmetry. This is the Grouch Marx Theorem: Why buy from people with superior knowledge? Farmers in India long had no idea where to get the best prices and suffered rip-offs from better-informed middlemen, until mobile devices arrived. Technology wiped out asymmetry here, but in other cases, like the US health care insurance market, the problem is less tractable.

9. Wrist-slap penalties. If traders can get rich through shady practices but don't go to jail, the enforcement system may encourage more rip-offs.

10. Inequality. The harder it is to climb the ladder, the fewer will try. And if the populace becomes less competitive, economic growth may slow or shrink.

These lists are hardly comprehensive, but they highlight some of the themes we have discussed.

Aligning morals and markets so they work together is a premier challenge of our world today, and anyone who doubts it need only reread headlines dating from mid-September 2008. Fortunately, both morals and markets are adaptable and, with vigilance and care, we can keep them from tripping each other up.

Indeed, many aspects of the moral code—especially young peoples' eagerness to fight corruption and willingness to sacrifice for the greater good—are tremendous resources that could be better brought to bear on our problems. For example, a national program could bring college students back to poor high schools near where they grew up to serve as teaching assistants, activity leaders, and researchers. It could be largely financed by student loan forgiveness but animated by idealism.

Markets adapt very quickly. The profit motive is like a hot, ever-flowing stream, and if unattended it can spill out and harm society. But good ground rules can channel it into competition that truly serves the public good. Again, the rules must be readily enforceable by law—or, better, by a nudge from conscience or peers—and ensure that everyone profits most by creating value. The last several chapters of this book have pointed up new possibilities. Global markets for greenhouse gas allowances, heavy taxes on dangerous drugs with the proceeds going to the most effective antidrug campaigns, and antijihadi oil taxes all work in basically the same way. They join morals and markets together to help build a better world.

Morals have already undergone two major transitions, at the dawn of civilization and again at the dawn of the modern era. The changeovers wove new elements into the moral code but did not eliminate the old—for instance, the impulse to liberty remained as we moved into cities like Uruk. To solve our present problems, we don't need a third moral transformation. We have the right equipment.

Yet we do need vigilance over our own ethical and competitive feelings. In both morals and markets, we are prone to placing cardboard crowns on our heads and glorying in them. Everyone is vulnerable. To limit our self-deceit, we need more awareness and discussion of morals and markets, a more conspicuous, ongoing analysis of their relation, and if possible, touchstones for the hazards. Poor understanding of the dangerous balance has sunk us into gigantic troughs, at terrible cost, again and again. Not only can we avoid these disasters, but the cost/benefit ratio is superb. We have met the enemy and he is us, as an old *Pogo* comic trip once said.

But the solution is also us.

Acknowledgments

This book began as a collaborative effort many years ago, with several discussions on the interaction of morals and markets. At the time we felt we were among the few individuals probing the matter. But then came the crash of 2008, and suddenly issues related to this topic were popping up in conversation everywhere, from black-tie galas to grocery lines. Opinions were often intense, conveyed with sarcastic certainty. Yet heads of state and of central banks faced complex choices, and even the brightest minds often failed to grasp the underlying dynamic. Hence this new edition.

We have benefited from the aid of an array of people, so many—and at times so subtly—that the pleasure of naming them all eludes us. But we thank them all.

More specifically:

Friedman: It was my great fortune to learn from a series of generous mentors. Mathematicians Stephen Smale and Ralph Abraham taught me new ways in which to think about dynamic processes. Economists Robert Clower and Jack Hirshleifer (and watching the interbank FX market at Bank of America) helped shape my thinking about the inner workings of markets. My approach to evolutionary games, and especially to social dilemmas, owes much to Ken Binmore and Reinhard Selten. I gained philosophical and historical perspective from Axel Leijonhufvud.

Numerous colleagues helped at crucial junctures. A dinner conversation with Ernst Fehr convinced me to think more systematically about social preferences and their market impact. Repeated contacts with Santa Fe Institute researchers and MacArthur Preference Group members—Sam Bowles, Herb Gintis, Rob Boyd, Pete Richerson, and Stu Kauffman are the first who spring to mind—helped sharpen my thinking about the nature and evolution of morals.

My deepest debt is to my dear wife, Penny Hargrove, who put up with me during countless preoccupied hours and did a complete round of copyediting of the earlier edition.

McNeill: I owe intellectual IOUs to myriad people, such as Laurence Tribe, Duncan Kennedy, and Charles Nesson at Harvard, who refined my thinking about multifaceted moral issues and their relation to society, as well as to novelists Ishmael Reed, Mary Robison, and Monique Raphel High, whose generosity and integrity match their outstanding talent.

I also benefited from my sojourn at the Josephson Institute of Ethics, and I'm grateful to Michael Josephson, Wes Hanson, Andy Acalinovich, Steve Nish, Peter

Chen, and Margaret Bryant for their many insights into the good, the bad, and the ugly. It is a pleasure as well to thank Bart Kosko, Garth Magee, David Leon, Wendy O'Sullivan, Richard Casey, Alexes Razevich, Paul Dillon, Meg X, everyone at the Grant Street conclaves, and the late Mike Elwell and Don Kreuzberger.

And, for so much, the wise and brilliant Rosalind Gold.

We are both grateful to Wade Hastings for helping compile the endnotes and Jenelle Feole for helping develop the bibliography. A shout-out to Jim Spohrer as well.

In addition, we thank our pre-pub readers, who helped us correct errors and clarify our prose and thinking: Art Argiewicz, Nick Despota, Bernie Elbaum, Benjamin Friedman, Paul Goldfinger, Sara Hendrix, Joel Leventhal, Changhua Sun Rich, and an anonymous Palgrave reviewer. And though it seems like a cliché older than Gondwanaland, we must say it: All errors are our responsibility alone.

The bright, big-hearted folks at Palgrave made the transition from manuscript to book a delight. Jaime Marshall introduced this project to the organization, Aaron Javsicas brought it in, and Airie Stuart kept it all alive. We are especially grateful to acquisitions editor Laurie Harting for championing this work and guiding it so astutely and thoughtfully. Editorial assistant Lauren Lo Pinto gave us gentle, much-appreciated prodding, Philip Pascuzzo designed the cover, Ciara Vincent copyedited the prose, Jenelle Feole compiled the index, and the production crew, led by Rosemi Mederos, shepherded it into the form you see before you.

Our heartfelt thanks to all.

Notes

Prologue: A Tale of Two Tilts

The 1991 Gorbachev story draws on Moynahan (1994), especially pp. 249–50.
The Sachs' quote is from Lipton and Sachs (1992).
On the rise of the oligarchs and looting of Russia: see Klebnikov (2000). Leijonhufvud and Craver (2001) is an excellent summary of Russia's economic shocks and policies in the 1990s.
"The European Central Bank had based the euro symbol on the Greek letter epsilon": see European Central Bank (2002).
"'How can you survive on 600 a month, with ever-rising taxes, and continue to pay bills and buy necessary supplies?' he asked": see CBS News, September 26, 2012.
"snapped a bullwhip": see Alderman (2012).
"one college student told the *New York Times* in 2012. 'They keep saying: 'I can't take it'": see Donadio (2012).

1 The Savanna Code: What Good Are Morals?

Adam Smith epigraph: see *The Theory of Moral Sentiments*, p. 393.
"our own species has eight times more biomass than all wild land vertebrates combined": see Hill et al (2009), p. 187.
"In this environment, generalists thrived": see Richerson and Boyd (2013). Their thesis is that extreme climate fluctuations, especially in the last several hundred thousand years, were a primary force behind the evolution of larger brains and human cultural evolution. See also Potts (1996) for a discussion of specialists vs generalists.
Homo erectus: see Bobe and Behrensmeyer (2004). Also see Aiello and Wheeler (1995) who propose an evolutionary tradeoff between robust digestive systems and large brains. On sexual dimorphism and the emergence of male-female pair bonds: see for example, "A Course in Evolution, Taught by Chimps," by Nicholas Wade (*New York Times*, November 25, 2003). Among the wider families of apes, pair bonding is observed in gibbons, but not in species more closely related to humans such as gorillas, orangutans, and chimps.
"By one estimate, our ancestors' brains gained an average of 100,000 neurons and support cells with each generation": see Flinn (2011), p. 13.
"At least twice our ancestors approached extinction": see Turner (2010).

"Australopith males seem to have been significantly larger than females": see McHenry and Coffing (2000), p. 135.

"overall the centers for emotion in our brains are now twice as large as in our ape ancestors": see Turner (2010), p. 134.

"For example, when the Roman orator Cicero was running for consul in 64 BC, his brother gave him the age-old advice: 'Now is the time to call in all favors'": see Cicero, in *Foreign Affairs* (2012), p. 19.

"Man is an animal that makes bargains: no other animal does this": see Smith, *The Wealth of Nations*, chapter 2.

"as one anthropologist noted, "It is my impression that those [Northern Ache] who refuse to share game would probably be expelled from the band": see Hill (2002).

"children actively seek to associate and cooperate with others": see Hare (2011), p. 295.

Kelly (1985) explains the Nuer and Dinka conflict.

"when people internalize [norms] and use them as a way of life, they can react harshly not just to violations, but to novelties that threaten change": see Hill et al. (2009), pp. 188–89.

Oxytocin influences people to "donate more to charity": see Barraza et al. (2011).

Cognitive loads make "no difference in people's performance" when making moral judgments: see Haidt (2012), p. 36.

"moral emotions dye our perceptions, and we view the world in ethical terms": see Moll, Oliveira-Souza, and Eslinger (2003).

"When a friend who lives nearby becomes happy, the chance that you become happy too rises by 25 percent": see Christakis and Fowler (2009), p. 53.

Chimpanzees "not only have elaborate favor systems but possess a sense of justice": see Moll, Oliveira-Souza, and Eslinger (2003).

"Of the 15 animals, 10 prolonged their own hunger rather than inflict the pain": see Masserman, Wechkin, and Terris (1964).

Werner Güth had "1000 marks in my bag for running experiments": see "An Interview with Werner Güth," http://www.econ.mpg.de/english/research /ESI/gueth_ interview.php. The famous published article is Güth et al. (1982). Rejections of unfair offers correlate with brain activity in the anterior insula region associated with disgust, according to Sanfey et al. (2003). Henrich et al. (2001) reports ultimatum games conducted among the Machiguenga and a dozen other small scale societies.

For the celebration of the honor killing of Zahra, see Zoepf (2007).

"Polyandry among brothers…spread among Nyinba farming families": see Durham (1991, Ch. 2).

"Mirror neurons play a key role in maintaining cultures over time": see Losin, Dapretto, and Iacoboni (2009), p. 178.

Children "tend to think that the actions they are imitating are 'right'": see Hill et al. (2009), p. 189.

"on the Pakistan frontier a controversial set of laws imposes liability on a whole tribe," see Leiby (2012).

The six values that people use worldwide to define morals: see Haidt (2012).

"after a man raped a 16-year-old mentally defective girl in rural Pakistan, the tribe's judicial council ruled that she had shamed her tribe and had her executed in front of the group": see Goldstein (2002), p. 31.

"the strict legal code of *sharia* reinforces" honor killings: see Arnold (2001).

"female chimps are reluctant to share food, even with their own offspring": see Hill et al. (2009), p. 187.

"Individuals had reason to join [the hunt] even if just to sharpen their skills, and far more benefited from success": see Gintis (2012).

"After its second year, the brighter the male's plumage, the more females he attracts," see Reudink et al. (2009).

Percentage of India's parliament charged with crimes: see Sanchez (2012).

The experiments with Ngenika and Wolimbka tribesmen are reported in Bernhard et al. (2006).

"when whites and Asians see members of another race pricked by a needle, their brain circuits for empathizing with pain show less activity than when they see members of their own race pricked": see Cikara and Fiske (2011).

"Embarrassment is worse before an in-group than before a low-status out-group": see Eller, Koschate, and Gilson (2011).

"Even among chimpanzees, yawning is more contagious within the in-groups than with members from an out-group": see Campbell and Waal (2011).

In-groups "even appeared swiftly when researchers divided subjects based only on eye color": see Cheng and Douglas (2005), p. 32.

"In-group rivalries have divided paleoanthropologists": see Gibbons (2006).

"Hindu thugs beat their way into the apartment of a Muslim family and attacked the dad with an iron rod": see Mehta (2004), p. 48.

Need to cut hair arose 175,000 to 200,000 years ago: see Wade (2006), pp. 26–27.

2   The Rise of Wealth: How We Became Civilized and Started Shopping

"In June 2011 total global wealth was $231 trillion": Credit Suisse, *Global Wealth Report 2011*.

Dow et al. (2006) presents a technical explanation of why sedentary hunter-gatherers took the first steps in the transition to agriculture. It also mentions the main alternative theories.

"Humans tamed goats around 8000 BC, then sheep, pigs, and cattle in that order": see Watson (2012), p. 126.

Description of the Agora bazaar in Athens: see Dixon (1995).

"Bazaars also existed in almost every small town in the Roman and Aztec empires": see Michael E. Smith (2002), p. 588

Vernon Smith's experiments are nicely described in Smith (1982). The original paper is Smith (1962).

Uruk is called Erech in the Bible. Recent historical accounts include De Mieroop (2006), Bottéro (2001), Nemet-Nejat (1998), and Kramer (1998).

"first cities emerged around the same time as the earliest writing": see Michael E. Smith (2002), p. 6.

"water travel has been far less expensive than land travel": see Glaeser (2011), p. 44.

Trade, "likely played a major role in Uruk's prosperity": see Algaze (2008).

Hammurabi: "I became the beneficent shepherd whose scepter is righteous": see Roux (1992), p. 206.

For more on the community responsibility system and impartial justice, see Greif (2006). The Champagne fairs are mentioned in most standard economic histories; see for example Cameron-Neal (2003) pp. 65. For more on private commercial law, see Bernstein (1998).

"some claim he [Mao Zedong] was responsible for 70 million deaths": see Chang and Holliday (2006).

"30,000 books existed in all of Europe before Gutenberg": see "Gutenberg's Legacy," Harry Hansom Center, The University of Texas at Austin. http://www.hrc.utexas.edu/educator/modules/gutenberg/books/legacy.

"by 1500 there were between 10 and 20 million, and in the next century as many as 150 to 200 million": see Febvre and Martin (1976).

The Spanish gold and silver estimates are from UC Davis professor Richard Cowen's page http://www-geology.ucdavis.edu/~cowen/~GEL115/.

The Florentine banking discussion draws on McLean and Padgett (2011). Malmendier (2011) discusses the Roman "prequel to financial markets."

Dictator "Francisco Macías Nguema of Equatorial Africa, a bloodthirsty near-psychotic who annihilated his own economy": see Meredith (2005), pp. 238–43.

"the world's 600 biggest cities will see their GDP rise by $30 trillion from 2010 to 2025, and they'll need new floor space the size of Austria": see Dobbs et al. (2012).

3   From Melqart to Zombieworld: Adventures in Imbalance

McCredie quote is from *Balance: In Search of the Lost Sense*, p. 265.

Ghalib: "Cities are being lighted without oil lamps. This new law makes all other laws obsolete": see Dalrymple (2008), pp. 122–123.

For more on Basil II's life and times, see Holmes (2005). The millennium edition of the *Wall Street Journal* (January 11, 1999 pp. R6) lists the sources of wealth for Basil and his contemporaries.

"...what economists call 'monopoly rents'." Actually, royal cartels are far less efficient even than a standard textbook monopoly, for three reasons. First, production (or trade) typically involves high cost producers. Second, over time the barriers to entry raise costs. Third, the cartels often include double marginalization. For example, the Afghan silk traders would charge a monopoly markup and then the Byzantine traders would put a monopoly markup on top of that, raising the final price above that of a profit maximizing unified monopolist. Double marginalization is still discussed in some microeconomic texts: see for example Baye (2005), p. 420.

"from 5000 BC to AD 1600, annual worldwide GDP per capita remained almost unchanged, at between \$400 and \$550 (in 1990 dollars)": see Rose (2010), p. xvi.

On the Phoenicians, see Aubet (2001).

"An early example occurred in 1788 BC": see de Mieroop (2005).

"In AD 301, Emperor Diocletian was facing economic decline": see for example Cameron and Neal (2003), pp. 41–42.

"Singapore is a cluster of shining skyscrapers with the highest GDP per capita on earth": see Mahtani (2012).

Moynahan (1994) reports Khrushchev's corn fiasco on pp. 199-201, and gas filching on p. 233.

The pervasive lack of trust, and predictions that the Soviet economy was headed down come from Richard E. Ericson, personal communication, 1977.

Aleksanyan's quote is from Remnick (1994) p. 318. That book also contains lots of very useful background information.

Hirshleifer (1995) is a nice analysis (see also work by Hershel Grossman and Stergios Skaperdas) of competition in the absence of property rights.

"Bathe…" is *from Milton: A Poem*, Book 2, Plate 41, by William Blake, 1810, and the "dark satanic mills" are from his 1804 poem *Jerusalem*. The quoted lines are from Blake (1997, Gnomic Verses viii).

"Seep across the boundaries": see Lasch (1996).

Most history books include a summary of the enclosure movement, e.g., Palmer et al. (2002) p. 430. Dahlman (1980) offers a deeper analysis.

Portsmouth block maker example: see Hicks (1969), p. 149.

On the events of 1848: see Dureau (1984).

Marx (1844) contains the quoted lines on alienated labor.

Ricardo (1817) is still considered an intellectual landmark. Some of Marx's contemporaries (e.g., the economists Gossens, Jevons, Menger and Walras) discovered fatal flaws in Ricardo's labor theory of value, but Marx seemed unaware of their work. Despite heroic efforts of modern economists in the 1970s and 80s (e.g., Roemer, 1986) to find intellectual underpinnings, the labor theory of value is now dead. The consensus view is that typically market values are determined by the intersection of supply and demand, and that labor cost is just one factor affecting supply.

Goldman (1923), Remnick (1994), and Moynahan (1994) contain much of the material on the Soviet system.

Millett (1991, p. 43) discusses Plato's attitudes, and the entire book discusses Athenian financial practices. In modern Greek, *eranos* refers to communal charity, e.g., passing around a collection plate in church (Nikos Nikiforakis, Personal communication, April 2007).

On roscas, see Besley (1995) and Besley et al. (1993).

"Neither a borrower nor a lender be; /for loan oft loses both itself and friend, / and borrowing dulls the edge of husbandry." William Shakespeare, *Hamlet*, Act I, scene 3.

Thurow (1985, p. 284) argues that the US must subsidize key industries to compete with Japan. Page 298 asks the reader to compare US policies like "propping up Harley-Davidson using high tariffs" to the self-evidently better "Japanese policy of subsidizing research on the fifth-generation computer." Punditry is a tough business, and Thurow's example now stands on its head. Harley-Davidson, now a $15 billion company, dominates its industry, with almost a 50% market share in the US, and a rapidly growing share in Europe and even in Japan (now over 25%). Japan's huge subsidy of fifth generation computing seems to have missed the technological boat and her computer industries are far less impressive now than 30 years ago.

Hoshi and Kashyap (2001) describes the *keiretsu* system and includes the Maruzen and Mazda examples in Chapter 5.

The story of the three suicides comes from the article "Death of Three Salesmen – Partners in Suicide," by Mary Jordan and Kevin Sullivan (*Washington Post*, October 7, 1998) http://www.washingtonpost.com/wp-srv/inatl/longterm/brokenlives/broken4a.htm.

The Sogo saga is pieced together from *The Economist* articles "Unforgiven" (June 29, 2000), "Japan's bankruptcy department" (June 13, 2000), "The slow death of Japan, Inc" (October 12, 2000), "New tricks," (October 26, 2000), and "Fiddling while Marunouchi burns" (January 25, 2001), together with the *Asia Times* editorial "Japan: That revealing Sogo saga" (July 14, 2000), the *Mainichi Shimbun* story "Captain of sinking store guilty of hiding assets" (March 29, 2005), and McIntyre (2000).

Wood (1992) is a journalist's account of the bubble years and the beginning of the zombie era.

Hoshi and Kashyap (2004) pp.3-26 describe zombie finance in Japan. For example, pp. 12 cites other studies that conclude that net operating profits for Japanese banking industry have been negative since 1993. Cargill, Hutchison and Ito (1997) discuss liberalization in the 1980s and related topics on pp. 99–108 and discuss jusen on pp. 130–144. Peek and Rosengren (2005) pp. 1144–1166 documents "evergreen lending," government pressure to misclassify bad loans as good. See also Okada and Horioka (2007), who discuss banks' central role in propping up zombies, to the detriment of typical solvent firms. "Dead Firms Walking," (The Economist, September 25, 2004, p. 81–83) discusses remaining zombie sectors.

Immanuel Kant's "the entire final end of the doctrine of right": see Taylor (2010), p. 8.

Percentages of violent deaths among precontact hunter-gatherers: see Hill, Hurtado, and Walker (2007).

"You are struck by the grace of [the Turkana's] carriage and the independence of his demeanor": see Rayne (1919).

"An average Turkana male has a 20 percent chance of dying in warfare": see Mathew and Boyd (2011).

"When Timur the Lame (Tamerlane, c. 1336–1405) conquered Isfahan in Persia, he built a pyramid of some 70,000 skulls": see Black (2004), p. 21.

Montesquieu's "Two nations that trade together become mutually dependent": see Mansfield and Pollins (2003), p. 3.

World Trade Organization: "Sales people are usually reluctant to fight their customers": see Hegre, Oneal, and Russett (2009), p. 1.

"In the 21st century, total deaths from war-related violence have averaged 55,000 a year": see Goldstein (2011).

"By the summer of 1945, the ruins had ceased smoking but people were starving and ailing all over Europe": see Judt (2005).

Goethe's wish that "my luggage may pass unopened through all thirty-six German states": see Keller and Shiue (2008).

Taiwan-China "cross-strait commerce was worth $75 billion" in the first six months of 2012: see Wang (2012).

"market incentives had led doctors everywhere to prescribe them": see Whoriskey (2012) for a full account of the anemia drug story.

In 1994 a drug label stated that it could improve "health, sex life, well-being, psychological affect, life satisfaction, and happiness": see Whoriskey (2012).

Nicholas Sarkozy's "Financial capitalism is a system of irresponsibility and is…amoral": see Schiller (2011).

Lawrence King and other decrying "low levels of official opposition to—or even questioning of—the primacy of markets": see King et al. (2012), p. 2.

4   Madness, Lies, and Crashes: When Prices Run Free

"Timothy Geithner, then chair of the Federal Reserve Bank of New York, could not believe that an insurance company failure might cripple the global economy, but others soon edified him": see Wessel (2009), p. 190.

For a contemporary account of the crisis, see the September 15, 2008 New York Times article "Lehman Files for Bankruptcy; Merrill Is Sold," by Andrew Ross Sorkin.

Useful background sources on the crisis include Gorton and Metrick (2012), and Lo (2012).

Countrywide "launched a program called Hustle (a sort-of acronym for "High-Speed Swim Lane")": see "US Suit Cites 'Brazen' Mortgage Fraud at Countrywide, Even After Bank of America Purchase," Washington Post, Wednesday, October 24, 2012.

Madoff's "There is no innocent explanation": see Henriques (2011), p. 13.

Albanian "[r]ebels stole one million weapons from the government and burned and looted its buildings": see Jarvis (2000).

The Planet Finance section draws on "Beyond Fear and Greed: The Moral Roots of Financial Crises," the 2010 UCSC Faculty Research Lecture by Friedman, and on Friedman and Abraham (2009).

"In the 1550s an early bubble occurred in Lyons around a loan, called *le Grand Parti*, to King Henry II": see Chancellor (1999), p. 8.

"At the peak of Tulip Mania in 1637, for instance, the heirs of deceased tavern keeper Wouter Winkel sold his flower collection for 90,000 guilders": see Dash (1999), p. 154.

5   Blundering Back to Balance: TARP and Tear Gas

Joseph Cassano's "It is hard for us, without being flippant, to even see a scenario…": see Morgenson (2008).

Cost of the $700 billion bailout "will be far less than pundits originally warned": see Isidore (2012).

Grunwald (2012) contains many facts and figures regarding US 2008–09 bailouts and stimulus package.

"Recent research suggests that the reasons were mostly moral": e.g., see Rabanal (2012).

"many of those losses have been processed improperly, in some cases fraudulently, to the banks' advantage": see "Foreclosures (2012 Robosigning and Mortgage Service Settlement)," New York Times, April 2, 2012. http://topics.nytimes.com/top/reference/timestopics/subjects/f/foreclosures/index.html.

"The financial industry spends more money on lobbying": see "Top Interest Group Giving to Members of Congress, 2012 Cycle," Open Secrets, November 2012. http://www.opensecrets.org/industries/mems.php.

Elizabeth Warren's "Some of the largest financial institutions can build a profit model on tricking people": see New Yorker, September 17, 2012.

Neil Barofsky's "Incentives are baked into the system to take advantage of it for short-term profit": see Morgenson (2012).

Neil Barofsky's "The incentives are to cheat, and cheating is profitable because there are no consequences": see Morgenson (2012).

Phil Angelides' "It's perplexing at best": see Boyer and Schweizer (2012).

On Keynes, Bertrand Russell's "the sharpest and clearest [intellect] that I have ever known": see Skidelsky (2009), p. 57.

Papaconstantinou quotes: see Lewis (2011), pp. 47–48.

Finance ministers grew furious at Greece: see Gruyter (2009).

"special interests won immunity for 'almost any unlawful acts they may engage in'": see Bastasin (2012), p. 141.

"This attitude was extended toward Greece's reporting to the European Union": see Bastasin (2012), p. 141.

"while Greeks are very loyal to their families and local areas, they keep the government at arm's length": see Babington and Papadimas, 2011.

Greece's "11 million citizens owe €60 billion in back taxes": see Babington and Papadimas (2011).

"Most [Germans] viewed rescue as a redistribution of funds to distant folks, and they didn't like it": see Bechtel, Hainmueller, and Margalit (2012).

"austerity still hadn't reduced the corruption. It had only reduced the price of bribes": see Tagaris (2012).

"Greeks were also among the bitterest critics of the EU": see Pew Global Attitudes Project (2012).

"In the 1990s austerity had also succeeded, and for similar reasons, in Finland and Sweden. EU officials thought the policy would also work in Greece too, and elsewhere": see Bastasin (2012), p. 151.

"The stink of the fish factory at the end of the quay hovers perpetually over that end of town": see Morris (1986), p. 185.

"one bank flush with cash even considered building a city from scratch, right next to an existing one": see Halpern (2011).

"a British royal commission found the condition of the average Irish home almost beyond description": see Woodham-Smith (1962), p. 24.

"Yet after 2000 the average Dublin home sold for as much as one in Beverly Hills": see Thomas (2009).

"For example, in 2006 Irish companies built over 90,000 new homes, twice as many as the nation needed, and this kind of construction amounted to over 12 percent of the Irish economy": see Capell (2008).

"Many have questioned whether Irish officials acted too quickly or fully understood the extent of the obligation": see McCarthy (2012).

"Ireland would owe a total of €68 billion": see RT, "Ireland Votes for Austerity with EU Gun to its Head," June 1, 2012. http://rt.com/news/ireland-vote-yes-eu-treaty-794.

Peggy Nolan's "The people that bought into a dream inherited a nightmare": see Flynn (2012).

"and in mid-year the Bank of Spain estimated that the total exposure of banks in real estate alone was around €180.8 billion": see Harrington (2011).

Spain "focused too little on its export economy": see Caballo-Cruz (2011).

6   China: Morals and the Rush to Wealth

Quotes from Mao are from Zedong (1966), chapter 3 (originally from a 1945 speech "On Coalition Government") and chapter 4 (originally from a 1957 speech "On the Correct Handling of Contradictions Among the People"). Dikötter (2010) reports the 1959 quote.

General Gu to his daughters: "Don't be threatened by the door-knocking and confiscations during the night": from Branigan (2012).

"The Cultural Revolution shut many of China's ministries, and virtual civil war broke out in many provinces": see MacFarquhar and Schoenhals (2006) for this and other details.

"Now presented as the quintessence of socialism, modernization would restore the party's legitimacy and prevent the developed world from reasserting dominance over China": see Deng (1984).

For the "textbook prescription" see, e.g., Todaro and Smith (2011).

"This novel form of competition and experimentation, some scholars believe, has been the true engine of China's growth": see Xu (2011).

"suave, charming" Bo Xilai: see Dexter Roberts (2004).

"Xilai bulldozed the old neighborhoods": see Li (2001), p. 166.

"Disciplined by regional competition, many TVEs prospered and their CCP patrons got promoted": see Xu (2011).

"a race to the bottom": see Milgrom and Roberts (1990).

"The [Foxconn] workers, many teenaged, complained about their employers' brutal guards, horrible food, and the dorms' filthy shared bathrooms": see Ho and Culpan (2012).

Gini coefficients of various nations: see Benjamin et al (2008).

"income differences are shrinking between regions and growing within villages andcities": Xu (2011), p. 1135ff.

"In Zhu's age group there are about 12 percent more men than women": see Tsai (2012).

"People enjoy a lot more privacy but often no longer know their neighbors": see Zhang (2010).

"Macau is now the world's hub of money laundering": see Osnos (2012).

7   From Hudson's Bay to eBay: Why Some People Like Going to Work

Maslow (1943). Also see Stephens (2000), p. 96.

For the history of the Hudson's Bay Company: see Innis (1999) and Newman (2000).

Organization and management: see also Milgrom and Roberts (1992). Roberts (2004) also mentions Hudson's Bay and covers some of the same ideas as in the present chapter. See page 18 for a very compatible definition of corporate culture. Many business books implicitly assume that coordination and communication are the only problems and ignore social dilemmas and motivation problems: see Malone (2004).

The Caligula University example is based on a conversation in October 2007 with university employees who chose to remain anonymous.

"Economists call this sort of episode a 'holdup,' and it happens all the time in daily life." This problem was analyzed first in Klein, Crawford, and Alchian (1978). Classic empirical work includes Masten (1984) and Monteverde and Teece (1982). Good textbook explanations can be found in Baye (2006) and in Milgrom and Roberts (1992).

On the transition to corporations 100 years ago: see Chandler (1977). The historical account in this section draws on Lamoreaux, Raff, and Temin (2002). On the textile industry: see Scranton (1983).

Economies of scale: see Smith (1776) ch 1. Also, ch. 3 notes the role of mass markets.

Interchangeable parts likely began in prerevolutionary France. Eli Whitney (of cotton gin fame) obtained the first US contract to manufacture guns this way in 1798, and Eli Terry is credited with developing mass production of clocks in 1808.

" ... with general staff, commanders, and geographically dispersed units pledged to execute the orders passed down the ranks." Shades of old Hudson's Bay? Not really. The 19th century companies had the advantage of rapid communication via telegraph, and they offered attractive promotion opportunities.

Hicks (1969) notes contemporary data on the extent of economies of scale.

Leijonhufvud (2007) insightfully discusses how economies of scale and more extensive markets feed on each other.

"When the alternative was subsistence farming or worse..." In many ways corporate blue-collar jobs, although impersonal, were better than most 19th-century jobs in the old family firms. Think of Bob Cratchit's work life under Ebenezer Scrooge in "A Christmas Carol."

"Lowell's successors defeated the Factory Girls' Association strike in 1834, but three years later they went bankrupt in a recession": see Chapter 1 in Sobel (1974) and also Zinn (2005).

The Swiss laboratory experiments are reported in Fehr, Kirchsteiger, and Riedl (1993). Their interpretation is based on Akerlof (1982). The delicate balance is documented in Charness, Kagel and Frechette (2004) and in Falk and Kosfeld (2006) and other studies cited therein.

"A careful study showed that the problem at [Firestone's factory in] Decatur was not technical, but moral": see Krueger and Mas (2004). See also Mas (2008), which analyzes less famous but still large ($400 million) losses in value due to labor problems at Caterpillar.

On the new environment, the particular list is the authors'. Each item on the list has its own extensive bibliography. On deregulation, see for example Kahn (2004). On China and India's entry into the market system, see for example the June 2006 special issue of *CESIfo Economic Studies*.

Cannibalization costs are featured in Christensen (2003). The iPod story is part of the book *Sony vs Sony*, by *Nihon Keizai Shimbun* (a business daily).

Influence costs are featured prominently in Milgrom and Roberts (1992).

"Each trade in each town had a guild with connections to its counterparts in other towns and in other trades": see Dessi and Ogilvie (2003).

"Prato is laced with independent small-to-medium operations": see http://www .prato.turismo.toscana.it/comprare/eng/storia3.htm.

History of Hollywood: see for example Thomson (2006).

"an Italian system administrator detected a dangerous virus attack on his Linux server": see Evans and Wolf (2005).

Google's story is told in numerous books and magazine articles, e.g., Vise and Malseed (2006).

"a 1996 Silicon Valley start-up we'll call Kntek began with a core of Russian engineers.": The real company was founded in 1996 and changed its name in 2005 and again in 2007 following mergers. Its story was recounted to Friedman by MC, an engineer, on May 7, 2007.

"an American Buddhist temple in California supplemented the usual classes in meditation and philosophy with offerings in martial arts and Java programming": Recounted to Friedman by LM, an engineer, in June 2007.

"in 2012 Amazon was growing at three times the rate of e-commerce itself," see Matthews (2012).

EBay data can be found in its annual reports. The figure of 700,000 sellers comes from Tedeschi (2007).

US Army combat networks: see for example Klein (2007), pp. A01. Countering evolved insurgent networks: see Hammes (2006).

"consider the open source movement": see *The Economist*'s special report March 18, 2006, pp.73–75.

"One engineer recently related a life-and-death struggle for control of his company": Related to Friedman by engineer RM in May 2007.

HP's VC Café is discussed in Malone (2004), pp. 93–95. The company had long been noted for its egalitarian moral code, called the HP Way, emphasizing trust and teamwork. Carly Fiorina (the CEO 1999–2005) tried to make the company more aggressive and star-oriented, touching off a culture war: Fiorina (2006) gives her side of the story.

Toyota's emulation of the Linux community is discussed in Evans and Wolfe (2005). Also see *The Economist*'s special report on "The New Organization: A Survey of the Company," (January 21, 2006), which quotes the Toyota Way. Page 17 of that supplement notes that Boeing didn't design the 787 in-house: the development team includes 100 partner companies around the world. Team members constantly videoconference and work from a common real-time data base.

On outsourcing and the holdup problem: "The outsourcing provider and the client company may form alliances and take financial stakes in one another to make sure their interests are aligned," Jon Watts of Booz Allen Hamilton is quoted on pp. 17 of *The Economist* survey just cited.

"The new IBM still sells lots of hardware and software, but most of its revenue now comes from global services": see the corporate website and annual reports. Although panned by Amazon critics as self-serving and shallow, Gerstner (2002) collects the basic facts.

Regarding business consulting services, see Hancock et al (2005). A capsule summary from p. 4: "dividing its business into components, focusing on those that really matter, responding rapidly to market changes, creating a variable [scalable] business model and operating in a resilient manner."

Wal-Mart: see its 2007 annual report. The raft of recent books includes Fishman (2006). See also Lichtenstein (2006), the proceedings of an academic conference.

Sara Horowitz is profiled in the article "Freelancers of the world, unite!" (*The Economist*, November 11, 2006), pp. 76.

8 Markets and Sin: Murder, Megacasinos, and Drug Wars

"Victorian philosophers confidently predicted that crime and vice would fade away as the human species evolved." Here is a quote from a famed Victorian philosopher: "Let us...consider in what particular ways this further evolution...may be expected to show itself....Will it be in strength? Probably not to any considerable degree....Will it be in swiftness or agility? Probably not....Will it be in intelligence? Largely, no doubt....Will it be in morality, that is, in greater degree of self-regulation? Largely also: perhaps most largely. Right conduct is usually come short of more from defect of will than defect of knowledge....A further endowment of those...sentiments responding to the requirements of the social state…must be acquired before the crimes, excesses, [etc.…] that now so greatly diminish the duration of life, can cease.… [Evolution will] work unceasingly towards a state of harmony." Herbert Spencer (1896, chapter 13).

"the State of California used to spend twice as much on universities as jails, but now the two are almost equal": see http://www.sco.ca.gov/state_finances_101 _state_spending.html.

For US annual crime rates by category 1960–2004: see http://www.disastercenter .com/crime/uscrime.htm.

"Hunter-gatherer societies fight crime the old-fashioned way": see Boehm (1999).

"The !Kung, hunter-gatherers in Africa's Kalahari Desert, have been dubbed 'the harmless people'": see Thomas (1958). On /Twi's execution and the quotes: see Lee (1979), pp. 394–395.

"a boy named Napoleon was born to the Buonapartes." Napoleon later changed his last name to Bonaparte, more natural to the French eye.

Wilson (1988) is the main source of material on Corsica. Some specifics: "Towns were relatively unimportant, and only 17 percent of the population lived in them in 1851, after a period of considerable urban growth" p. 5. "Land of the vendetta," attributed to Maupassant, p. 14. Egalitarianism, p. 13. Proverb, p. 182. The Arbellara story is distilled from pp.17–21. On honore, see ch. 4 especially. Male honor demanded ownership of guns pp. 91. Mediation by elders, ch. 9. Zonza, pp. 253. Corsica's recorded homicide rate during most of the 1800s was 20–60 per 100,000 per year, and the actual rate probably was 2–3 times higher, pp. 15–16. The custom of her relatives killing a dishonored woman (especially if she would not divulge the name of her seducer) was fading in Corsica by 1800 pp. 108. Abduction was common, sometimes with the girl's consent, e.g., to overcome her family's objections pp. 102–110.

Bowman (2006) traces Western honor culture back to medieval times and discusses its decline in the 20th century.

"In 2010 Honduras had the highest murder rate in the world": see "Murder Most Foul," *The Economist* (2011).

"What's the harm in vice?": The text distinguishes vice (where the actor is among those harmed) from self-serving crime. In traditional usage, vice is habitual sin. Catholic doctrine defines mortal sin as consisting of three elements: the matter is grave, the sinner has full knowledge, and he sins deliberately or gives full consent. The sin is venial if some of these are absent. The deadly sins are: pride, covetousness, lust, anger, gluttony, envy, and sloth. Those that "cry out to heaven for vengeance" are: murder, sodomizing, oppressing the poor, and defrauding laborers of wages. Thus, the focus is on character flaws, defective moral sentiments, and it includes opportunistic behavior.

"Some teenage girls like to cut their flesh": see Grohol (2009).

"In earlier times, male promiscuity passed on DNA, so this behavior makes sense—genetically, at least": Bridgeman (2003) summarizes the evolutionary psychology approach to vice and other behavior. On adolescent male gamblers, see Rubin and Paul (1979). Paternity is much more concentrated than maternity in most premodern cultures. Technically, the point is that the left skewed wealth-paternity distribution creates a gap between expected wealth and expected biological fitness. Diamond (1992) notes an alternative explanation: risk takers signal their otherwise unobservable talents, because risk taking is more expensive for those less talented.

Revenues and elasticities are a standard topic in economics textbooks, e.g., Baye (2006), ch. 3.

On the history of gambling, see Ezell (1960). Other data comes from US National Research Council (1999), National Opinion Research Center (1999), and Clotfelter et al (1999).

Legal wagers "now over a trillion dollars a year"; revenue (rake) from gambling "expanded from $10 billion in 1982 to over $92 billion by 2006": see Rose (2010).

Grinols (2004) concludes that, after accounting for increased crime and reduced expenditures on other forms of entertainment, etc., the social costs of the megacasinos exceed the benefits in most communities. See also Grinols and Mustard (2006) and the article "As More States Look to Win the Economic Jackpot with Casinos, Evidence Suggests they are Playing a Losing Hand," by Mark Whitehouse (*The Wall Street Journal*, June 11, 2007).

"Macao is the largest casino on the planet": see Osnos (2012).

"Atlantic City's casino revenue": see Cooper (2012).

Prediction markets: see Wolfers and Zitzewitz (2004).

Online wagers "likely reached $30 billion worldwide by 2011": see Stewart (2011).

Much of the material on poker is collected from an unpublished 2004 term paper by Connor Egan. Hundreds of books are now available, e.g., Gordon and Grotenstein (2004), not to mention innumerable websites. Also see "A Big Deal: Poker is Getting Younger, Cleverer, Duller, and much, much Richer," (*The Economist*, December 2007), p. 33–38.

"the media run occasional horror stories of young lives ruined by an online poker addiction": for instance, see "The Gambler: The Hold-'Em Holdup" By Mattathias Schwartz (*New York Times Magazine*, Sunday June 11, 2006).

"The estimates imply a doubling, more or less, of industry revenues and fortunes for beverage makers": The math: $3*(1-.25) = 2.25 > 2.0 > 1.50 = 3*(1-.50)$, so doubling is in the estimated range.

The Centers for Disease Control collect data on binge drinking, e.g., http://www.cdc.gov/alcohol/datatable.htm.

Tobacco statistics appear in MacCoun and Reuter (2001), ch. 8. The terms of the Master Settlement can be found on The National Conference of State Legislatures website, http://www.ncsl.org/statefed/tmsasumm.htm. Altria's share price was $39.38 in June 1998 and rose to $53.50 in December, with most of the increase taking place between September and November. Coller et al (2004) report the tobacco settlement damage award.

Cancer in mice by painting on cigarette tar: see Oreskes and Conway (2010), especially pp. 15–16.

"since 1954 smoking has ended at least 16 million American lives": see Brownell and Warner (2009).

http://www.monitoringthefuture.org/ summarizes what works and what doesn't for tobacco discouragement among teenagers.

Decline in daily smoking by younger teens has ended: University of Michigan's Monitoring the Future press release, December 21, 2006.

The tale of tobacco lawsuits is long and complex. An expert witness for the prosecution reminds us that the tobacco industry settled many cases out of court prior to the Master Settlement, in part to maintain the image of legal invincibility (though also because such settlements are extremely common). He also notes that the industry's "'well funded research labs'…never did any real science, as far as I can tell," their real mission was to muddy the scientific waters (Glenn W. Harrison, personal communication, June 23, 2004).

"When [Bentham] died, he donated his 172 boxes of writings to the new University College of London; where staff is still sorting them out": The Bentham Project website http://www.ucl.ac.uk/Bentham-Project/info/aims.htm notes that 26 volumes of Bentham's collected works have appeared as of mid-2007, but the total might ultimately reach 70 volumes. Keneally (2006) reports Bentham's panopticon proposal and other schemes to profit from Britain's prison system.

Among other intriguing Benthamiana:His panopticon proposal was resurrected and condemned by postmodernist writers, especially Foucault (1995), pp. 195–228.

His early proposal to decriminalize sodomy has made him a hero to many in the gay rights movement.

His second publication, *Defence of Usury,* sought to straighten out Adam Smith on financial markets and advocated dropping interest rate ceilings.

The modern version of Bentham's hedonistic calculus is the core of the academic field known as Law and Economics: see for example Posner (2006) and Wittman (2006).

Prison industry sources include Doyle, "Behind Bars in the US and Europe," (*Scientific American,* September 1999, p. 25); Marc Klaas, "A bad Law, Set in Stone," (*San Jose Mercury News,* November 14,1999, p. P1), on the three-strikes law; "Joe Arpaio, Tyrant of the Desert," (*Economist Magazine,* March 20, 1999, p. 30); "Prisoners: More than Any Other Democracy," (*Economist Magazine,* Feb. 25, 2005, pp. 27–29); "Hotel California," (*Economist Magazine,* Feb. 25, 2005, pp. 27–29); and "California's Prisons: Packing Them in," (*Economist Magazine,* August 12, 2006, p. 23).

"Jailhouse population jumped more than 350 percent to 2.4 million": see Schmitt, Warner, and Gupta (2010).

"Overall in 2010 the California prison system cost $7.9 billion": see http://www.vera.org/files/price-of-prisons-california-fact-sheet.pdf.

If California "released just one person jailed for marijuana possession, the state could pay a student's full three-year tuition at Stanford Law School": see http://studentaffairs.stanford.edu/registrar/students/tuition-fees_11–12.

Aker (2006) is a good overview of California's criminal justice system. See Unger (2007) for a US overview. Some useful background information appears in chapter 3 of Gilmore (2007). See also the articles "High Court Justice Supports

Bar Plan to Ease Sentencing," by Linda Greenhouse (*New York Times*, June 24, 2004) and "US 'Correctional Population' Hits New High," by Fox Butterfield (*New York Times*, July 26, 2004). The $10.1B figure is Corrections and Rehabilitation, from State Government proposed 2007–08 budget; the corresponding figures for UC and CSU are $5.45 and 4.36B.

"Politicians see upfront costs and not the huge long-term savings" see Carmichael (2010).

Johnson and Raphael (2006) is the source of the estimates on deterrence plus incarceration effects. (Unfortunately, the data don't permit a reliable separation of the two different effects.)

Governor Schwarzenegger backs down on prison costs: see "Guard Union in Showdown," by Mark Gladstone (*San Jose Mercury News*, June 22, 2004), p. 1.

Leonard Scott's three strikes are cited in LaDoris H. Cordell's op-ed (*San Jose Mercury News*, July 10, 2006), pp. 16A. Of course, there are dangerous criminals out there, but the three-strikes law only increases the danger. Consider a violent two-time loser who hates jail and is spotted by a burglary victim. Under three strikes, he has little to lose and much to gain by murdering his victim to avoid a third conviction. Likewise, if he sees police approach his car, he is much more likely to endanger bystanders in a high-speed chase.

Drugs and drug wars: see Spillane (2000). Drug use and human character: see Bennett (1989) and Wilson (1990). Bennett himself confessed to compulsive gambling in June 2003. http://www.washingtonmonthly.com/features /2003/0306.green.html. We got a lot of information and useful perspectives from MacCoun and Reuter (2001).

"prices for cocaine, heroin, and meth actually dropped about 16 percent from 2001 to 2011": see Porter (2012).

"today anyone can buy illegal drugs on the site Silk Road": see Greenberg (2012).

"Tobacco shortens one's life, cocaine debases it": Wilson, (1990), p. 26.

9 Underworlds: The Tao of Gangs

On Bin Laden hearing of the destruction of the Twin Towers, see Wright (2007). More on al-Qaeda: Aid (2012), especially pp. 127, 131, and 132–133.

"Gangs began appearing in the 1950s and 1960s": see Skarbek (2012).

Much of the material on Chicano youth gangs comes from 1994 UCSC Economics 106 term papers by Rafael Trevino, Antonio Gomez, Jose Renteria, and Francisco Marquez. They in turn cite Harris (1988), Virgil (1983), Mirande (1985), and Romotsky and Romotsky (1976). See also "Highlights of the 2004 National Youth Gang Survey," Office of Juvenile Justice and Delinquency Prevention, US Department of Justice, April, 2006.

Quote from Don Calo Vizzini and other Mafia material: see Dimico, Isopi, and Olsson (2012).

On Hamas, see Rance (2006), Smith and Myre (2007), and Sayigh (2010). Thomas (2007) is a history of Mossad.

"It gave people public goods—just like a government." Iannocone (1992) focuses on the social dilemma associated with contributing to public good provision and shows that a cult can mitigate the problem by prohibiting mainstream activities and demanding personal sacrifices. Also see Berman and Laitin (2005).

Hamas revenues: see United States Department of State (2006).

On the Assassins: see Lewis (1968) and Joinville (1868). Cairo headquarters: at that time ruled by the great Fatimid Caliph al-Mustansir, the successor of Basil II's contemporary, Al-Hakim. The entire Fatimid dynasty was Ismaili, but the Assassins didn't recognize al-Mustansir's successors as legitimate.

Aga Khan: see The Institute of Ismaili Studies website at http://www.iis.ac.uk/

Marcus Foster: see *Time*, "Murder in California," (November, 19, 1973).

Patty Hearst story: see http://www.crimelibrary.com/terrorists_spies/terrorists /hearst

On the importance of these part-time communities: see Putnam (2000).

"But still, why would a young person join" a violent group exposed to many dangers? See LeBlanc (2003). Levitt and Dubner (2005), ch. 3, offers some fresh evidence on how bad the gamble is: most ordinary gang members make less than the minimum wage and live at home with their moms.

The *American Heritage Dictionary*'s primary definition of a cult is, "A religion or religious sect generally considered to be extremist or false, with its followers often living in an unconventional manner under the guidance of an authoritarian, charismatic leader."

The *American Heritage Dictionary*'s definition of terrorism is, "The unlawful use or threatened use of force or violence by a person or an organized group against people or property with the intention of intimidating or coercing societies or governments, often for ideological or political reasons." We emphasize threats against lives. The dictionary definition above would include groups that target property. For example, the Animal Liberation Front aims to damage laboratories that test dangerous products on mice but does not target human enemies.

"Kill them all"; see Aid (2012), p. 131.

"The problem lies in sieving the Internet ocean for this data, and two professors at Harvard developed a tool called Mogo that does exactly that": see Coscia and Rios (2012).

"skewer leftist pretensions": e.g., the scene "Dennis, the Constitutional Peasant," in *Monty Python and the Holy* Grail (1975). Danish newspaper cartoons controversy of September 2005: see the very detailed Wikipedia entry "Jyllands-Posten Muhammad cartoons controversy," http://en.wikipedia.org/wiki /Jyllands-Posten_Muhammad_cartoons_controversy

Columns of T. Friedman: "The Battle of the Pump," *New York Times* Op Ed page, October 7, 2004, is a typical example.

Saudis fund mosques and madrassas: see for example "Al Qaeda and Saudi Arabia," by Khaled Abou El Fadl, on behalf of the US Commission on International Religious Freedom, op-ed page in *The Wall Street Journal*, November 10, 2003. "Where Boys Grow up to be Jihadis," by Andrea Elliot (*New York Times* Sunday Magazine, November 25, 2007) mentions the role of Saudi-funded mosques and jihadi websites, but emphasizes the young Moroccan recruits' sense of moral outrage and personal ties to their buddies.

"An antidrug policy more like the Dutch—legalize, but discourage by heavy taxes and restrictions—would cut off gangs' air supply": see MacCoun and Reuter (2001), ch. 9.

10   Cooling the Earth: The Preservation Markets

"the real prize was cod, 'so thick you can scoop them up in a basket'": see Kurlansky (1997) for all assertions in the first two paragraphs. The third paragraph relies on Junger (1999).

"Gloucester plunged into economic depression, joining dozens of other Northeast coastal cities and towns": see "Commercial Fishing Industry Needs on Gloucester Harbor, Now and in the Future," a study by the Gloucester Community Panel, released June 6, 2005, which contains background information on the local economy and the role of the fishing industry.

"The personal benefit is clear if you're the first crab catcher to arrive at a good spot": for details of the Dungeness derby, see "Troubled Waters for Local Crabbers," by Marke Krupnick (San Jose Mercury News, November 28, 2003), p. 3C.

Easter Island's environmental catastrophe: see Diamond (2005), ch. 2. Megafauna extinction in America and Australia: see Diamond (1999)

Red tail deer, lions, and other territorial animals: see Hardin (1968) or a standard biology text such as Goldsmith and Zimmerman (2001). Hardin doesn't mention the "open fields" moral system that, as noted in Dahlman (1980), prevented the tragedy in medieval European commons.

"Aquarium owners are warned about territorial fish, such as groupers and seahorses, that will attack new arrivals." For a chart of territorial fish in the home aquarium, check out http://www.liveaquaria.com/general/compatibility _chart.cfm.

Lansing (1991) is the source of the material on Balinese water temples. A more recent book, Lansing (2006), discusses its origins and stability as an "emergent...complex adaptive system." The final Asian Development Bank report is "Reevaluation of the Bali Irrigation Sector Project Loan No. 522-INO in Indonesia," Asian Development Bank RES: INO XXX, December 1997, http://www.adb.org/Documents/PERs/RE-27.pdf.

"the 'sod busters' who first farmed North America's Great Plains in the late 1800s." Sod buster sagas include Rolvaag (1927), and, of course, Little House on the Prairie, by Laura Ingalls Wilder, never out of print since its original publication in 1935. Egan (2005) describes the Dust Bowl.

On the Ogallala Aquifer, see Kromm and White (1992), and the website http://www.waterencyclopedia.com/Oc-Po/Ogallala-Aquifer.html.

On 20th-century cod fisheries and territorial limits, again see Kurlansky (1997).

"Economic logic dictates that firms will spend up to that amount to gain a favorable decision": see Demsetz (1984), for example.

"Money is the mother's milk of politics": Jesse "Big Daddy" Unruh (1922–1987) was the leading power broker in California's legislature for most of the 1960s. Another great Unruh-ism: "Sometimes we must rise above principles."

Cawley (1996) reports on the Sagebrush Rebellion. See also the Colorado University Library's *Sage Brush Rebellion* (Collection No. 32), http://carbon .cudenver.edu/public/library/archives/sagebrsh/sagebrsh.html.

Coda for cod material: see Committee to Review Northeast Fishery Stock Assessments (1998), and Serchuk and Wigley (1992).

Kuznets curve: the original version relates income inequality to economic development as countries progress from agriculture to manufacturing to services. The environmental Kuznets curve incorporates the idea that primitive agriculture and advanced services are less polluting. See for example: Bradford et al. (2005) available at: http://www.bepress.com/bejeap/contributions/vol4 /iss1/art5. A special issue of the same journal, *Advances in Economic Analysis & Policy* 4:2, is devoted to the pollution haven hypothesis and the race to the bottom. See also Copeland and Taylor (2004).

"There is another way to look at environmental problems. The tragedy of the commons is the result of missing markets." Economists recognize that markets go missing mainly for two related reasons—property rights are not well defined, and/or transactions costs are high. The original insight is due to 1991 Nobel laureate Ronald Coase, see for example Coase (1960).

"Shares of that limit, called ITQs (Individual Transferable Quotas) were awarded to people who had historically fished in [Alaskan] waters": see Pautzke and Oliver (1997) and the website http://www.fakr.noaa.gov/npfmc/sci_papers /ifqpaper.htm. Our thanks to Jon Sutinen for pointing out this article. The Fuglvog quotes are from *Viewpoints* in the Alaskan Halibut episode of the PBS series "Empty Oceans, Empty Nets." The website is http://www.pbs.org /emptyoceans/eoen/halibut/viewpoints.html.

The Cap and Trade program for SO2 emissions: see US Environmental Protection Agency (2001). On compliance cost reductions: see table 3–2, p. 25. See also Chan et al. (2012), p. 5.

The consensus on global climate change is summarized and elaborated in "IPCC Fourth Assessment Report: Climate Change 2007," a report in three parts by the Intergovernmental Panel on Climate Change. That panel shared the 2007 Nobel Peace Prize with former US Vice President Al Gore. Their final synthesis report was released on November 17, 2007, and can be found at http://www .ipcc.ch/pdf/assessment-report/ar4/syr/ar4_syr_spm.pdf.

"incorrect adjustments of the atmosphere data": see "Heat and Light," (*The Economist*, Aug. 11, 2005).

"Ally of Bush Is Defeated in Australia," by Tim Johnston (*New York Times*, November 25, 2007) mentions the prime minister's promise to ratify the Kyoto Protocol. "New Zealand launched a cap-and-trade program in 2009": see Han (2012).

ETS trading volume: see Kossoy et al. (2012)

"Special report on business and climate change," (*The Economist* magazine, June 2, 2007) contains recent information on GE and Silicon Valley VCs. See also "Google's Next Frontier: Renewable Energy," by Brad Stone (*New York Times*, November 28, 2007), and "Banks Urging US to Adopt the Trading of Emissions," by James Kanter (*New York Times*, September 26, 2007). The estimate of $40 billion is attributed to Paul Bledsoe of the National Committee on Energy Policy, and is cited on p. 6 of *The Economist*'s Special report.

Self-enforcing international environmental agreements: see Barrett (1994) and McGinty (2007).

The pitfalls of nonuniform carbon taxes: see Sinn (2007). California's climate policy: see Goulder (2007).

Porter hypothesis: see Popp (2005) available at http://www.bepress.com/bejeap /contributions/vol4/iss1/art6.

Paltsev (2007) contains cost estimates for several recent GHG market proposals.

See also "Kyoto's Caps on Emissions Hit Snag in Marketplace: U.N. Mulls How to Fix Pollution-Credit System," by Jeffrey Ball (*Wall Street Journal*, December 3, 2007), pp. A1.

11   The World Ahead

Morals of hill country shepherds versus cosmopolitan city dwellers: the *Gilgamesh* epic contains this theme, as Gilgamesh, a city-dweller, fights but then becomes best friends with the barbarian Enkidu; see, for example, Prichard (1958), pp. 31–40. The Biblical story (1 Samuel 17–31) of how David rose from shepherd to king also echoes some of these themes.

Moral codes evolve: examples include the very different Buddhist practices in Japan vs. India, and the Protestant Reformation as discussed in chapter 3. The Talmud documents a millennium of changes in Jewish religious law.

"But markets don't always work so well": the examples illustrate standard limits of markets mentioned in most economics textbooks—monopoly power, externalities, asymmetric information, and agency problems.

Greenspan mea culpa: see Lanman and Matthews (2008).

"Forget the antiseptic, well-lighted budget sets and markets of economics textbooks": see McFadden (2006), p. 7.

"Dark pools": see Patterson (2012), p. 45.

"A chip that completed a trade in 740 nanoseconds": see Patterson (2012), p. 291.

"HFT was involved in three-fourths of all trades": see Patterson (2012), p. 283.

Thomas Peterffy quote: see Patterson (2012), p. 293.

Globalization critics: see for example, "How Free is the Free Market?" by Noam Chomsky (LiP Magazine, May 15, 1997), http://www.lipmagazine.org/articles/featchomsky_63.htm. One of the more eloquent criticisms is "The Idea of a Local Economy," in Berry (2001). For a classic treatment in a novel, see Callenbach (1982).

Leamer (2007), pp. 110 is the source of his quote.

Wage insurance: see Kletzer (2004).

Adam Smith's observation is encapsulated in the title of chapter 3 of Smith (1776): "That the division of labor is limited by the extent of the market." See also Anderson (2006) for a modern version of the point.

On inequality, see Levy and Temin (2007), Piketty and Saez (2003), and Goldberg and Pavcnik (2007). Alesina and Giavazzi (2006) argue that poorer people are among the major potential beneficiaries of freer international trade. See also "Larry Summers's Evolution," by David Leonhardt (*New York Times* Magazine, June 10, 2007). The 24-page special report on US and world income inequality in the 10/3/12 issue of *The Economist* was particularly useful as a source of facts and figures.

"Yet the top 0.1 percent in the US": see Kaplan and Rauh (2007).

"a child's future income": see OECD (2012).

"impressive growth spurts": see Berg and Ostry (2011).

$650 billion in occupational fraud: see Holton (2009).

Some background on electric power deregulation: The industry was a natural monopoly when it came online a century ago. One company could produce power and deliver it to a town or region at far lower cost per customer than two or more competing companies. To avoid monopoly's ill effects (price far above CE and inefficiently low usage), the government closely regulated the industry, in particular by setting prices. Newer textbooks (e.g., Baye, 2006), chapter 14, point out the ill effects of regulation: overly costly production, sluggish innovation, and costly political struggles over the regulated price—a variant of influence costs discussed in chapter 8. But by mid-20th century, the power grid spanned thousands of generating facilities, so supplying power could be competitive.

Recent popular accounts of deregulated power markets include: "Flaws Seen in Markets for Utilities," by David Cay Johnston (*New York Times*, November 21, 2006), and "Short-Circuited," by Jerry Taylor and Peter Van Doren (*Wall Street Journal*, August 30, 2007), pp. A11. The "antigaming" quotes come from FERC (2003).

The 2007 Nobel Prize in Economics went to three pioneers of mechanism design theory, Leonid Hurwicz, Eric S. Maskin, and Roger B. Myerson.

On early electronic stock exchanges, see Domowitz (1993).

On health care, the 16 percent figure is for 2005, and the 20 percent projection is standard: see for example Borger et al. (2006). Grol (2006) discusses Dutch health care.

Education cites include Tyack and Cuban (1995), Goldin (1999), and Card and Payne (2002). The case for vouchers is made on http://www.schoolchoices.org /index.html. On China's competitive national exam, see *Berkshire Encyclopedia of China* (2009), p. 205. The Jay Altman quote is from (Thomas) Friedman (2012).

Bibliography

Abou El Fadl, Khaled. 2003. "Al Qaeda and Saudi Arabia." *Wall Street Journal*, November 10.

Acemoglu, D., S. Johnson, and J. Robinson. 2005. "The Rise of Europe: Atlantic Trade, Institutional Change, and Economic Growth." *American Economic Review* 95 (3): 546–579.

Aid, Matthew M. 2012. *Intel Wars: The Secret History of the Fight Against Terror.* New York: Bloomsbury Press.

Aiello, L., and P. Wheeler. 1995. "The Expensive-Tissue Hypothesis: The Brain and the Digestive System in Human and Primate Evolution." *Current Anthropology* 36 (2): 199–221.

Aker, E. 2006. "Crime and Punishment." *Policy Today, California Edition* 3 (5): 4–17.

Akerlof, G. 1982. "Labor Contracts as Partial Gift Exchange." *The Quarterly Journal of Economics* 97 (4): 543–569.

Alderman, Liz. 2012. "Greece Warns of Going Broke as Tax Proceeds Dry Up." *New York Times*, June 5. http://www.nytimes.com/2012/06/06/business/global/greece-warns-of -going-broke-as-taxes-dry-up.html?google_editors_picks=true.

Alesina, A., and F. Giavazzi. 2006. *The Future of Europe.* London: MIT Press.

Algaze, G. 2008. *Ancient Mesopotamia at the Dawn of Civilization: The Evolution of an Urban Landscape.* Chicago: University of Chicago Press.

American Heritage Dictionary of the English Language. 2004. Fourth edition. Houghton Mifflin.

Anderson, C. 2006. *The Long Tail: Why the Future of Business is Selling Less of More.* New York: Hyperion.

Aoki, M. 1988. *Information, Incentives, and Bargaining in the Japanese Economy.* New York: Cambridge University Press.

Arblaster, P. 2005. *A History of the Low Countries.* New York: Palgrave Macmillan.

Arnold, Kathryn C. 2001. "Are the Perpetrators of Honor Killings Getting Away With Murder?"*American University International Law Review* 16 (5): 1343–1409.

Associated Press. 2012. "Greeks Turn Violent Amid New Austerity Measures," CBS News, September 26. http://www.cbsnews.com/8301-505123_162-57520452/greeks -turn-violent-amid-new-austerity-measures.

Aubet, M. E. 2001. *The Phoenicians and the West: Politics, Colonies, and Trade.* Translated by M. Turton. New York: Cambridge University Press.

Babcock, L., and G. Loewenstein. 1997. "Explaining Bargaining Impasse: The Role of Self-Serving Biases." *Journal of Economic Perspectives* 11 (1): 109–126.

Babington, Deepa, and Lefteris Papadimas. 2011. "Insight: In Greece, Playing Cat and Mouse with Tax Evaders," Reuters, December 15. http://www.reuters.com /article/2011/12/15/us-greece-evasion-idUSTRE7BE0S020111215.

Bachman, J. G., L. D. Johnston, and P. M. O'Malley. 2011. *Monitoring the Future: Questionnaire Responses from the Nation's High School Seniors, 2010.* Ann Arbor, MI: Institute for Social Research. http://www.monitoringthefuture.org/pubs.html#refvols.

Baldick, R. 1965. *The Duel: A History of Duelling*. London: Chapman & Hall.

Ball, Jeffrey. 2007. "Kyoto's Caps on Emissions Hit Snag in Marketplace: U.N. Mulls How to Fix Pollution-Credit System." *Wall Street Journal*, December 3.

Barraza, Jorge A., et al. 2011. "Oxytocin Infusion Increases Charitable Donations Regardless of Monetary Resources." *Hormones and Behavior* 60: 148–151.

Barrett, S. 1994. "Self-enforcing International Environmental Agreements," *Oxford Economic Papers* 46: 878–894.

Bastasin, Carlo. 2012. *Saving Europe*, Washington, DC: Brookings Institution.

Baumol, W. 2002. *The Free Market Innovation Machine*. Princeton, NJ: Princeton University Press.

Baye, Michael R. 2006. *Managerial Economics and Business Strategy*. 5th edition. New York: McGraw-Hill.

Bechtel, Michael M., Jens Hainmueller, and Yotam Margalit. 2012. "Sharing the Pain: Explaining Public Opinion Towards International Financial Bailouts?" April. http://www.columbia.edu/~ym2297/Sharing%20the%20Pain.pdf

Becker, G. 1974. "A Theory of Social Interactions." *Journal of Political Economy* 82: 1063–1093.

Beecher, J. 1986. *Charles Fourier: The Visionary and His World*. Berkeley CA: University of California Press.

Beecher, J. 2001. *Victor Considerant and the Rise and Fall of French Romantic Socialism*. Berkeley CA: University of California Press.

Beecher, J., and R. Bienvenu (trans. and eds.). 1983. *The Utopian Vision of Charles Fourier: Selected Texts on Work, Love, and Passionate Attraction*. Columbia, MO: University of Missouri Press.

Benjamin, Dwayne, Loren Brandt, John Giles, and Sangui Wang. 2008. "Income Inequality during China's Economic Transition." In *China's Great Economic Transformation*, ed. Loren Brandt and Thomas G. Rawski. Cambridge and New York: Cambridge University Press, 729–775.

Bennett, W. 1989. "Drug Use Degrades Human Character." *National Drug Control Strategy*, Washington DC: Office of National Drug Control Policy.

Ben-Sasson, H. H. 1976. *A History of the Jewish People*. Cambridge MA: Harvard University Press.

Berg, Andrew G., and Jonathan D. Ostry. 2011. "Inequality and Unsustainable Growth: Two Sides of the Same Coin?" International Monetary Fund. http://www.imf.org/external/pubs/ft/sdn/2011/sdn1108.pdf.

Berman, E., and Laitin, D. 2005. "Hard Targets: Theory and Evidence on Suicide Attacks." NBER working paper 11740.

Bernhard, H., E. Fehr, and U. Fischbacher. 2006. "Group Affiliation and Altruistic Norm Enforcement," *American Economic Review* 96 (2): 217–221.

Bernstein, L. 1998. "Private Commercial Law." *New Palgrave Dictionary of Law and Economics*. New York: Palgrave Macmillan.

Berry, W. 2001. *In the Presence of Fear*. Great Barrington, MA: The Orion Society.

Besley, T. 1995. "Nonmarket Institutions for Credit and Risk Sharing in Low-Income Countries." *The Journal of Economic Perspectives* 9 (3): 115–127.

Besley, T., S. Coate, and G. Loury. 1993. "The Economics of Rotating Savings and Credit Associations." *The American Economic Review* 83 (4): 792–810.

Bezemer, D. J. 1999. "Post-Socialist Financial Fragility: The Case of Albania," *Tinbergen Institute Discussion Paper* #99045. http://www.tinbergen.nl/discussionpapers/99045.pdf.

Bhagwati, J. 2004. *In Defense of Globalization*. New York: Oxford University Press.

Black, Jeremy. 2004. "The Western Encounter with Islam." *Orbis* (Winter). http://www.fpri.org/orbis/4801/black.westernencounterislam.html.

Blake, W. 1997. "Gnomic Verses viii." *The Complete Poetry & Prose of William Blake.* Edited by Harold Bloom. New York: Anchor.

Bobe, R., and A. Behrensmeyer. 2004. "The Expansion of Grassland Ecosystems in Africa in Relation to Mammalian Evolution and the Origin of the Genus Homo." *Palaeogeography Palaeoclimatology Palaeoecology* 207 (3–4): 399–420.

Boehm, C. 1999. *Hierarchy in the Forest: The Evolution of Egalitarian Behavior.* Cambridge MA: Harvard University Press.

Boone, J. L. 1992. "Competition, Conflict, and the Development of Social Hierarchies." In *Evolutionary Ecology and Human Behavior,* ed. E. A. Smith and B. Winterhalder. Hawthorne NY: Walter de Gruyter.

Boorstin, D. 1983. *The Discoverers.* New York: Random House.

Borger, C., et al. 2006. "Health Spending Projections Through 2015: Changes on the Horizon." *Health Affairs Web Exclusive* W61.

Bottéro, J. 2001. *Everyday Life in Ancient Mesopotamia.* Translated by A. Nevill. Baltimore MD: Johns Hopkins University Press.

Bowman, J. 2006. *Honor: A History.* New York: Encounter Books.

Boyd, R., and P. Richerson, 1985. *Culture and the Evolutionary Process.* Chicago: University Of Chicago Press.

Boyer, Peter, and Peter J. Schweizer. 2012. "Why Can't Obama Bring Wall Street to Justice?" *Newsweek,* May 6. http://www.thedailybeast.com/newsweek/2012/05/06/why-can-t-obama-bring-wall-street-to-justice.html.

Bradford, D., R. Fender, S. Shore, and M. Wagner. 2005. "The Environmental Kuznets Curve: Exploring a Fresh Specification." *Contributions to Economic Analysis & Policy* 4 (1): 5. http://www.bepress.com/bejeap/contributions/vol4/iss1/art5.

Brandon, J. 2005. "Koranic Duels Ease Terror." *Christian Science Monitor.* February 4.

Branigan, Tania. 2012. "Gu Kailai Profile: Charming Persona Betrayed Inner Turmoil." *Manchester Guardian,* August 20.

Bridgeman, B. 2003. *Psychology and Evolution: The Origins of Mind.* New York: Sage Publications.

Brownell, Kelly, and Kenneth Warner. 2009. "The Perils of Ignoring History." *The Milbank Quarterly,* 87 (1): 259–294.

Butterfield, Fox. 2004. "U.S. 'Correctional Population' Hits New High." *New York Times,* July 26.

Caballo-Cruz, Francisco. 2011. "Causes and Consequences of the Spanish Economic Crisis." *Panoeconomicus* 3.

California State Controller's Office. "State Spending." http://www.sco.ca.gov/state_finances_101_state_spending.html.

"California's Prisons: Packing Them in." 2006. *Economist Magazine,* August 12.

Callenbach, E. 1982. *Ecotopia.* New York: Bantam.

Cameron, R., and L. Neal. 2003. *A Concise Economic History of the World,* 4th edition, New York: Oxford University Press.

Campbell, Matthew W., and Frans de Waal. 2011. "Ingroup-Outgroup Bias in Contagious Yawning by Chimpanzees Supports Link to Empathy." *PLoS ONE* 6 (4). e18283 doi:10.1371/journal.pone.0018283.

Cannon, J. 2005. *Apostle Paul: A Novel of the Man Who Brought Christianity to Western World.* Hanover, NH: Steerforth.

Capell, Kerry. 2008. "Ireland: The End of the Miracle," *Bloomberg BusinessWeek,* March 26. http://www.businessweek.com/stories/2008-03-26/ireland-the-end-of-the-miracle.

Card, D., and Payne, A. 2002. "School Finance Reform, the Distribution of School Spending, and the Distribution of Student Test Scores." *Journal of Public Economics* 83: 49–82.

Cargill, T., M. Hutchison, and T. Ito. 1997. *The Political Economy of Japanese Monetary Policy.* London: MIT Press.

Carlyle, T. 1843. *Past and Present.* London: Chapman and Hall.

Carmichael, Mary. 2010. "The Case for Treating Drug Addicts in Prison." *Newsweek,* June 28. http://www.thedailybeast.com/newsweek/2010/06/29/the-case-for-treating -drug-addicts-in-prison.html.

Carson, R. 1962. *Silent Spring.* Boston: Houghton Mifflin.

Cason, T., and D. Friedman. 1999. "Learning in a Laboratory Market with Random Supply and Demand." *Experimental Economics* 2 (1): 77–98.

Cason, T., D. Friedman, and G. H. Milam. 2003. "Bargaining Versus Posted Price Competition in Customer Markets." *International Journal of Industrial Organization* 21 (2): 223–251.

Cawley, R. M. 1996. *Federal Land, Western Anger: The Sagebrush Rebellion and Environmental Politics.* Lawrence, KS: University Press of Kansas.

Cervellati, M., and U. Sunde. 2005. "Human Capital Formation, Life Expectancy, and the Process of Development." *The American Economic Review* 95 (5): 1655–1672.

Chan, Gabriel, et al. 2012. "The SO2 Allowance Trading System and the Clean Air Act Amendments of 1990," Harvard Kennedy School, January 2012.

Chancellor, Edward. 1999. *Devil Take the Hindmost: A History of Financial Speculation.* New York: Farrar Strauss Giroux.

Chandler, A. D. 1977. *The Visible Hand: The Managerial Revolution in American Business.* Boston: Harvard University Press.

Chang, Jung, and Jon Holliday. 2006. *Mao: The Unknown Story.* New York: Anchor.

Charness, G., J. Kagel, and G. Frechette. 2004. "How Robust is Laboratory Gift Exchange?" *Experimental Economics* 7 (2): 189–205.

Cheng, Antony, and Steven Douglas. 2005. "Getting to 'We,'" *Human Ecology Review* 12 (1): 30–43.

Choi, J., and S. Bowles. 2007. "The Coevolution of Parochial Altruism and War." *Science* 318 (5850).

Chomsky, Noam. 1997. "How Free is the Free Market?" *LiP Magazine,* May 15. http:// www.lipmagazine.org/articles/featchomsky_63.htm.

Christakis, Nicholas A., and Fowler, James H. 2009. *Connected.* New York: Little, Brown.

Christensen, C. 2003. *The Innovator's Dilemma: The Revolutionary Book that Will Change the Way You Do Business.* London: Collins.

Cicero, Quintus T. 2012. *Commentariolum Petitionis* ("Little Handbook on Electioneering"). In "Campaign Tips from Cicero" *Foreign Affairs* 91 (3), May/June, 18–28.

Cikara, Mina, and Susan T. Fiske. 2011. "Bounded Empathy: Neural Responses to Out-group Targets' (Mis)fortunes." *Journal of Cognitive Neuroscience* 23: 3791–3803.

"Civil Service Examinations." 2009. *Berkshire Encyclopedia of China.* Berkshire Publishing Group. http://www.princeton.edu/~elman/documents/Civil%20Service% 20Examinations.pdf.

Clark, G. 2007. *A Farewell to Alms: A Brief Economic History of the World.* Princeton: Princeton University Press.

Clotfelter, Charles T., Philip J. Cook, Julie A. Edell, and Marian Moore. 1999. "State Lotteries at the Turn of the Century.," Washington, DC: National Gambling Impact Study Commission.

Coase, R. 1937. "The Nature of the Firm." *Economica* 4 (16): 386–405.

Coase, R. 1960. "The Problem of Social Cost." *Journal of Law and Economics* 3 (1): 1–44.

Cohen, D., R. Nisbett, B. Bowdle, and N. Schwarz. 1996. "Insult, Aggression, and the Southern Culture of Honor: An 'Experimental Ethnography.'" *Journal of Personality and Social Psychology* 70 (5): 945–960.

Coller, M., G. Harrison, and M. McInnes. 2004. "Evaluating the Tobacco Settlement Damage Awards: Too Much or Not Enough?" *American Journal of Public Health* 92 (6): 984–989.

Committee to Review Northeast Fishery Stock Assessments. 1998. *Review of Northeast Fishery Stock Assessments*. Washington, DC: National Research Council.

"Consider the Open Source Movement." 2006. *The Economist*'s special report, March.

Cooper, C., and M. A. Etnier. 2005. "Mathematical Modeling of Human and Marine Mammal Interaction in the Prehistoric Monterey Bay." Poster presented at 70th Annual Meeting, Society of American Anthropologists, Salt Lake City, UT.

Cooper, Michael. 2012. "States Up the Ante in Bid to Lure Other States' Bettors." *New York Times*, August 2.

Copeland, B., and M. S. Taylor. 2004. "Trade, Growth, and the Environment," *Journal of Economic Literature* 42 (1): 7–71.

Cordell, LaDoris H. 2006. "End Three Strikes." *San Jose Mercury News*, July 10.

Coscia, Michele, and Viridiania Rios. 2012. "How and Where Do Criminals Operate? Using Google to Track Mexican Drug Trafficking Organizations." Unpublished Manuscript, Department of Government, Harvard University, August 14.

Cosmides, L., and J. Tooby. 1992. *The Adapted Mind*. New York: Oxford University Press.

Credit-Suisse. 2011. *Global Wealth Report. 2011*. https://infocus.credit-suisse.com/data/_product_documents/_shop/323525/2011_global_wealth_report.pdf.

Crichton, Michael. 2004. *State of Fear*. New York: HarperCollins.

Dahlman, C. J. 1980. *The Open Field System and Beyond*. New York: Cambridge University Press.

Dalrymple, William. 2008. *The Last Mughal*. New York: Vintage, 2008.

Darwin, C. 1859. *On the Origin of Species by Means of Natural Selection or the Preservation of Favored Races in the Struggle for Life*. London: John Murray.

Dash, Mike. 1999. *TulipoMania*. New York: Crown.

Davies, Paul. 2006. "Class Inaction: Plaintiffs' Lawsuits Against Companies Sharply Decline." *Wall Street Journal*, August 26.

Dawkins, R. 1976. *The Selfish Gene*. New York: Oxford University Press.

De Mieroop, M. V. 2005. "The Invention of Interest." In *The Origins of Value: The Financial Innovations That Created Modern Capital Markets*, edited by W. N. Goetzmann and K. G. Rouwenhorst. New York: Oxford University Press, 17–30.

De Waal, F. 2005. *Our Inner Ape*. New York: Penguin.

Deming, W. E. 2000. *The New Economics for Industry, Government, Education*. 2nd edition. London: MIT Press.

Demsetz, H. 1984. "Purchasing Monopoly." In *Neoclassical Political Economy: The Analysis of Rent-Seeking and DUP Activities*, ed. D. C. Colander. Cambridge MA: Ballinger.

Deng, Xiaoping. 1984. "On the Reform of the System of Party and State Leadership." In *Selected Works of Deng Xiaoping, Volume 2: 1975–1982*. Beijing: Foreign Language Press.

Dessi, R., and S. Ogilvie. 2003. "Social Capital and Collusion: The Case of the Merchant Guilds." CESifo working paper 1037.

Diamond, J. 1992. *The Third Chimpanzee*. New York: HarperCollins

Diamond, J. 1999. *Guns, Germs, and Steel*. New York: Norton.

Diamond, J. 2005. *Collapse: How Societies Choose to Fail or Succeed*. New York: Viking.

Dikötter, F. 2010. "Mao's Great Leap to Famine." *New York Times*, December 15.

Dimico, A., A. Isopi, and O. Olsson. 2012. "Origins of the Sicilian Mafia: The Market for Lemons," University of Gothenburg Working Papers in Economics 532 (May).

Dinwiddy, J. 1989. *Bentham*. New York: Oxford University Press.

Dixon, Donald F. 1995. "Retailing in Classical Athens: Gleanings from Contemporary Literature and Art." *Journal of Macromarketing* 15 (1): 74–85.

Dobbs, Richard, et al. 2012. *Urban World: Cities and the Rise of the Consuming Class.* McKinsey Global Institute.

Domowitz, I. 1993. "Automating the Continuous Double Auction in Practice: Automated Trade Execution Systems in Financial Markets." In *The Double Auction Market: Institutions, Theories, and Evidence,* ed. D. Friedman and J. Rust. Reading MA: Addison Wesley.

Donadio, Rachel. 2012. "Dread and Uncertainty Pervade Life in a Diminished Greece." *New York Times,* June 13. http://www.nytimes.com/2012/06/14/world/europe/greeks -dread-future-as-their-world-deteriorates.html?google_editors_picks=true.

Dow, G. K., N. Olewiler, and C. G. Reed. 2006. "The Transition to Agriculture: Climate Reversals, Population Density, and Technical Change." Economics Department manuscript, Simon Fraser University.

Doyle, Rodger. 1999. "Behind Bars in the US and Europe." *Scientific American,* September.

Dugatkin, L. 1997. *Cooperation Among Animals: An Evolutionary Perspective.* New York: Oxford University Press.

Dunbar, R. 1996. *Grooming, Gossip, and the Evolution of Language.* London: Faber and Faber.

Dureau, G. 1984. *1848.* Cambridge MA: Harvard University Press.

Durham, D. 1991. *Coevolution: Genes, Culture, and Human Diversity.* Palo Alto, CA: Stanford University Press.

Economist. 2005. "Heat and Light." August 11.

Economist. 2005. "Hotel California." February 25.

Economist. 2005. "Prisoners: More Than Any Other Democracy." February 25.

Economist. 2006a. "The New Organization: A Survey of the Company." Special Report, January 21.

Economist. 2006b. "Freelancers of the World, Unite!" November 11.

Economist. 2011. "Murder Most Foul." October 6. http://www.economist.com/blogs /dailychart/2011/10/homicide-rates.

Egan, T. 2005. *The Worst Hard Time: The Untold Story of Those Who Survived The Great American Dust Bowl.* New York: Houghton Mifflin.

Ehrenreich, B. 2001. *Nickel and Dimed: On (Not) Getting by in America.* New York: Holt.

Eller, A., M. Koschate, and K. M. Gilson. 2011. "Embarrassment: The In-group–Out-group Audience Effect in Faux Pas Situations." *European Journal of Social Psychology* 41: 489–500.

Ellickson, R. C. 1991. *Order Without Law: How Neighbors Settle Disputes.* Harvard University Press.

Elliot, Andrea. 2007. "Where Boys Grow Up to Be Jihadis." *New York Times Sunday Magazine,* November 25.

Ernst and Young. 1996. *Compilation of Gaming Data.*

European Central Bank. 2002. "How the Euro Became Our Money." http://www.ecb.int /pub/pdf/other/euro_became_our_moneyen.pdf.

Evans, P., and B. Wolf. 2005. "Collaboration Rules." *Harvard Business Review* 83 (7).

Ezell, J. 1960. *Fortune's Merry Wheel: The Lottery in America.* Cambridge, MA: Harvard University Press.

Fabozzi and Modigliani. 2003. *Capital Markets: Institutions and Instruments,* 3rd edition. Englewood Cliffs, NJ: Prentice-Hall.

Fafchamps, Marcel. 2010. "Spontaneous Markets, Networks, and Social Capital: Lessons from Africa." In *Institutional Microeconomics of Development*, ed. Timothy Besley and Rajshri Jayaraman. CESifo Seminar Series. Cambridge, MA: MIT Press.

Fagan, B. 2003. *Before California*. Lantham, MD: Rowman & Littlefield.

Falk, A., and M. Kosfeld. 2006. "The Hidden Costs of Control." *American Economic Review* 96 (5).

Fama, E. F. 1971. "Risk, Return, and Equilibrium." *The Journal of Political Economy* 79 (1): 30–55.

Febvre, Lucien, and Henri-Jean Martin. 1976. *The Coming of the Book: The Impact of Printing 1450–1800*. London: New Left Books. http://www.hrc.utexas.edu/educator /modules/gutenberg/books/legacy/.

Fehr, E., G. Kirchsteiger, and A. Riedl. 1993. "Does Fairness Prevent Market Clearing? An Experimental Investigation." *The Quarterly Journal of Economics* 108 (2).

FERC. 2003. "Final Report on Price Manipulation in Western Markets." Federal Energy Regulatory Commission.

Fernandez-Armesto, F. 2006. *Pathfinders: A Global History of Exploration*. NY: Norton.

Fiorina, C. 2006. *Tough Choices: A Memoir*. New York: Portfolio Trade.

Fishman, C. 2006. *The Wal-Mart Effect: How the World's Most Powerful Company Really Works—and How It's Transforming the American Economy*. Boston: Penguin.

Flinn, Mark V. 2011. "Evolutionary Anthropology of the Human Family." In *The Oxford Handbook of Evolutionary Family Psychology*, ed. C. A. Salmon and T. K. Shackelford. New York: Oxford University Press.

Flynn, Finbarr. 2012. "Ireland Bulldozes Ghost Estate In Life After Real Estate Bubble." Bloomberg, July 19. http://www.bloomberg.com/news/2012–07–19/ireland-bulldozes -ghost-estate-in-life-after-real-estate-bubble.html.

Foucault, M. 1995. *Discipline & Punish: The Birth of the Prison*. New York: Vintage Books.

Friedman, B. M. 2006. *The Moral Consequences of Economic Growth*. Westminster: Alfred A Knopf.

Friedman, D. 1998. "On Economic Applications of Evolutionary Game Theory." *Journal of Evolutionary Economics* 8 (1): 15–43.

Friedman, D. 2007. "Market Theories Evolve, and So Do Markets." *Journal of Economic Behavior & Organization* 63 (2): 247–255.

Friedman, D. 2008. "Laboratory Financial Markets." In *New Palgrave Dictionary of Economics*. 2nd edition, ed. S. Durlauf and L. Blume. New York: Palgrave Macmillan.

Friedman, D., and R. Abraham. 2009. "Bubbles and Crashes: Gradient Dynamics in Financial Markets." *Journal of Economic Dynamics and Control* 33 (4): 922–937.

Friedman, D. and N. Singh. 2004. "Vengefulness Evolves in Small Groups." In *Advances in Understanding Strategic Behavior*, ed. S. Huck. New York: Palgrave Macmillan.

Friedman, D., and Ostroy, J. 1995. "Competitivity in Auction Markets: An Experimental and Theoretical Investigation." *Economic Journal* 105 (428): 22–53.

Friedman, T. 1998. *From Beirut to Jerusalem*. London: Harper-Collins.

Friedman, T. 2004. "The Battle of the Pump." *New York Times*, October 7.

Friedman, T. 2012. "Obama's Best-Kept Secrets." *New York Times*, October 20. http:// www.nytimes.com/2012/10/21/opinion/sunday/friedman-obamas-best-kept-secrets. html?_r=0.

Garber, P. M. 1989. "Tulipmania." *Journal of Political Economy* 97 (3): 535–60.

Gerstner Jr., L.V. 2002. *Who Says Elephants Can't Dance? Inside IBM's Historic Turnaround*. New York: Collins.

Gibbons, A. 2006. *The First Human: The Race to Discover Our Earliest Ancestors*. New York: Bantam Doubleday.

Gibbons, E. 2003. *The Decline and Fall of the Roman Empire*. New York: Modern Library.

Gies, F., and J. Gies. 1981. *Life in a Medieval City*. New York: Harper.

Gilmore, R. 2007. *Golden Gulag*. Berkeley CA: University of California Press.

Gintis, Herbert. 2012. "Human Evolution: A Behavioral Synthesis." Santa Fe Institute. http://tuvalu.santafe.edu/~bowles/HumanEvolution.pdf.

Gladstone, Mark. 2004. "Guard Union in Showdown." *San Jose Mercury News*, June 22.

Glaeser, Edward. 2011. *Triumph of the City*. New York: Penguin.

Glazer, E. L., B. Sacerdote, and J. A. Scheinkman. 1996. "Crime and Social Interactions." *Quarterly Journal of Economics* 111 (1): 507–548.

Gloucester Community Panel. 2005. "Commercial Fishing Industry Needs on Gloucester Harbor, Now and in the Future."

Gode, D., and S. Sunder. 1993. "Allocative Efficiency of Markets with Zero Intelligence Traders: Market as a Partial Substitute for Individual Rationality." *Journal of Political Economy* 101: 119–137.

Gödel, K. 1931. "Über formal unentscheidbare Sätze der Principia Mathematica und verwandter Systeme, I." *Monatshefte für Mathematik und Physik* 38: 173–98. Translated in J. van Heijenoort. 1967. *From Frege to Gödel: A Source Book on Mathematical Logic*. Cambridge, MA: Harvard University Press: 596–616.

Goetzmann, W. N., and K. G. Rouwenhorst (eds.). 2005. *The Origins of Value: The Financial Innovations That Created Modern Capital Markets*. Oxford: Oxford University Press.

Goldberg, J. 2004. "Among the Settlers: Will They Destroy Israel?" *The New Yorker*, May 31.

Goldberg, P., and N. Pavcnik. 2007. "Distributional Effects of Globalization in Developing Countries." *Journal of Economic Literature* 45 (1): 39–82.

Goldin, C. 1999. "Egalitarianism and the Returns to Education during the Great Transformation of American Education." *Journal of Political Economy* 107: S65-S94.

Goldman, E. 1923. *My Disillusionment in Russia*. Garden City, NY: Doubleday, Page.

Goldsmith, T. H., and W. F. Zimmerman. 2001. *Biology, Evolution, and Human Nature* New York: Wiley.

Goldstein, Joshua S. 2011. "Think Again: War." *Foreign Policy*, Sept/Oct. http://www.foreignpolicy.com/articles/2011/08/15/think_again_war?page=full.

Goldstein, Matthew A. 2002. "The Biological Roots of Heat-of-Passion Crimes and Honor Killings." *Politics and the Life Sciences* 21 (2): 28–37.

Goody, J. 1996. *The East in the West*. New York: Cambridge University Press.

Gordon, P., and J. Grotenstein. 2004. *Poker: The Real Deal*. New York: Simon Spotlight Entertainment.

Gorton, G., and A. Metrick. 2012. "Getting Up to Speed on the Financial Crisis: A One-Weekend-Reader's Guide." *Journal of Economic Literature* 50 (1): 128–150.

Gould, S., and N. Eldridge. 1993. "Punctuated Equilibrium Comes of Age." *Nature* 366: 223–227.

Goulder, A. 1960. "The Norm of Reciprocity: A Preliminary Statement." *Am Soc Rev* 25: 161–178.

Goulder, L. H. 2007. "California's Bold New Climate Policy." *The Economists' Voice* 4 (3): 5.

Grantham, G. 1999. "Contra Ricardo: On the Macroeconomics of Pre-industrial Economies." *European Review of Economic History* 3: 199–232.

Greenberg, Andy. 2012. "Black Market Drug Site 'Silk Road' Booming: $22 Million in Annual Drug Sales." *Forbes*, August 6. http://www.forbes.com/sites/andygreenberg /2012/08/06/black-market-drug-site-silk-road-booming-22-million-in-annual-mostly -illegal-sales.

Greif, A. 1993. "Contract Enforceability and Economic Institutions in Early Trade: The Maghribi Traders' Coalition." *American Economic Review* 83 (3): 525–547.

Greif, A. 2006. "History Lessons: The Birth of Impersonal Exchange: The Community Responsibility System and Impartial Justice." *Journal of Economic Perspectives* 20 (2): 221–236.

Greif, A., P. Milgrom, and B. Weingast. 1994. "Coordination, Commitment, and Enforcement: The Case of the Merchant Guild." *Journal of Political Economy* 102 (4): 745–776.

Grigoriev, L. 1995. "Ownership and Control in Privatization: Consequences for Foreign Investors." In *Foreign Investment in Russia: Salient Features and Trends – Second Report*, ed. A. Z. Astapovich. Moscow: Joint Stock Bank Imperial.

Grinols, E. 2004. *Gambling in America: Costs and Benefits.* New York: Cambridge University Press.

Grinols, E., and D. Mustard. 2006. "Casinos, Crime, and Community Costs." *Review of Economics and Statistics* 88 (1): 28–45.

Grohol, John. 2009. "Cutting and Self-Injury," Psych Central. http://psychcentral.com /blog/archives/2009/01/05/cutting-and-self-injury.

Grol, R. 2006. *Quality Development in Health Care in the Netherlands.* New York: The Commonwealth Fund.

Grunwald, Michael. 2012. *The New New Deal: The Hidden Story of Change in the Obama Era.* New York: Simon & Schuster.

Gruyter, Caroline de. 2009. "Brussels Knew About Staggering Greek Budget Deficit in July." December 20. http://vorige.nrc.nl/article2442172.ece.

Gunderson, L., and C. S. Holling, eds. 2001. *Panarchy: Understanding Transformations in Human and Natural Systems.* Washington, DC: Island Press.

"Gutenberg's Legacy." Harry Hansom Center, The University of Texas at Austin. http:// www.hrc.utexas.edu/educator/modules/gutenberg/books/legacy.

Güth, W. 2002. "An Interview with Werner Güth." http://www.econ.mpg.de/english /research/ESI/gueth_interview.php

Güth, W., R. Schmittberger, and B. Schwarze. 1982. "An Experimental Analysis of Ultimatum Bargaining." *Journal of Economic Behavior and Organization* 3: 367–388.

Haidt, Jonathan. 2012. *The Righteous Mind: Why Good People Are Divided by Politics and Religion.* New York: Pantheon.

Haldane, J. 1955. "Population Genetics." *New Biology* 18:34–51.

Halpern, Jake. 2011. "Iceland's Big Thaw." *New York Times*, May 13. http://www.nytimes. com/2011/05/15/magazine/icelands-big-economic-thaw.html?pagewanted=all.Sailors.

Hamilton, W., 1964. "Genetic Evolution of Social Behavior, I and II." *Journal of Theoretical Biology* 7: 1–16 and 17–52.

Hammerstein, P., ed. 2003. *Genetic and Cultural Evolution of Cooperation.* London: MIT Press.

Hammes, T. X. 2006. "Countering Evolved Insurgent Networks." *Military Review* 18–26.

Han, Sangim. 2012. "South Korean Parliament Approves Carbon Trading System." *Bloomberg BusinessWeek*, May 3. http://www.bloomberg.com/news/2012–05–03/south -korean-parliament-approves-carbon-trading-system.html.

Hancock, R., P. Korsten, and G. Pohle. 2005. *On Demand Business: The New Agenda for Value Creation.* IBM Institute for Business Value.

Hare, Brian. 2011. "From Hominoid to Hominid Mind: What Changed and Why?" *Annual Review of Anthropology* 40: 293–309.

Hardin, G. 1968. "The Tragedy of the Commons." *Science* 162 (3859): 1243–1248.

Harrington, Carrie. 2011. "The Spanish Financial Crisis." April. http//blogs.law.uiowa .edu/ebook/sites/default/files/BP.Spanish%20Financial%20Crisis.

Harris, M. 1988. *Cholas: Latino Girls and Gangs*. London: AMS Press.

Harrison, Glenn W. 2004. Personal communication, June 23.

Hassan, F. A. 1981. *Demographic Archaeology*. New York: Academic Press.

Hauser, M. 2006. *Moral Minds*. New York: Harper-Collins.

Hawkes, K. 1992. "Sharing and Collective Action." In *Evolutionary Ecology and Human Behavior*, ed. E. A. Smith and B. Winterhalder. Hawthorne NY: Walter de Gruyter.

Hawkes, K. 2004. "The Grandmother Effect." *Nature* 428:128–9.

Hayek, F. A. 1945. "The Use of Knowledge in Society." *American Economic Review* 45 (4): 519–30.

Healy, P., and K. Palepu. 2003. "The Fall of Enron." *Journal of Economic Perspectives* 17 (2): 3–26.

Hegre, H., J. Oneal, and B. Russett. 2009. "Trade Does Promote Peace: New Simultaneous Estimates of the Reciprocal Effects of Trade and Conflict." http://www.yale-university .com/leitner/resources/docs/HORJune09.pdf.

Henrich, J., and R. McElreath. 2003. "The Evolution of Cultural Evolution." *Evolutionary Anthropology: Issues, News, and Reviews* 12: 123–135.

Henrich, J., R. Boyd, S. Bowles, C. Camerer, H. Gintis, R. McElreath, and E. Fehr. 2001. "In Search of Homo Economicus: Experiments in 15 Small-Scale Societies." *American Economic Review* 91 (2): 73–79.

Henriques, Diana B. 2011. *The Wizard of Lies*, New York: St. Martin's Griffin.

Hicks, J. R. 1969. *A Theory of Economic History*. London: Oxford University Press.

Hill, K. "Altruistic Cooperation During Foraging by the Ache and the Evolved Human Predisposition to Cooperate." *Human Nature* 13 (1), 105–128.

Hill, K., et al. 2009. "The Emergence of Human Uniqueness: Characters Underlying Behavioral Modernity." *Evolutionary Anthropology* 18: 187–200.

Hill, K., A. M. Hurtado, and R. S. Walker. 2007. "High Adult Mortality Among Hiwi Hunter-Gatherers: Implications for Human Evolution." *Journal of Human Evolution* 52: 443–454.

Hirshleifer, J. 1995. "Anarchy and Its Breakdown." *Journal of Political Economy* 101 (3): 26–52.

Ho, Alexandra, and Tim Culpan. 2012. "Foxconn Workers Labour Under Guard After Riot Shuts Plant." *Sydney Morning Herald*, September 28.

Hofstadter, D. 1979. *Gödel, Escher, Bach: An Eternal Golden Braid*. New York: Vintage Books.

Holmes, C. 2005. *Basil II and the Governance of Empire*. New York: Oxford University Press.

Holton, Carolyn. 2009. "Identifying Disgruntled Employee Systems Fraud Risk Through Text Mining." *Decision Support Systems* 46: 853–864.

Hoshi, T., and A. Kashyap. 2001. *Corporate Financing and Governance in Japan*. London: MIT Press.

Hoshi, T., and A. Kashyap. 2004. "Japan's Financial Crisis and Economic Stagnation." *Journal of Economic Perspectives* 18 (1).

Howitt, P., and R. Clower. 2000. "The Emergence of Economic Organization." *Journal of Economic Behavior and Organization* 41: 55–84.

Hugo, V., and F. Caesar de-Sumichrast. 1896. *Les Miserables*. London: Ginn.

Huxley, A. 1932. *Brave New World*. New York: HarperCollins.

Iacoboni, M., I. Molnar-Szakacs, V. Gallese, G. Buccino, and J. C. Mazziotta. 2005. "Grasping the Intentions of Others with One's Own Mirror Neuron System." *Public Library of Science Biology* 3 (3): e79.

Iannocone, L. 1992. "Sacrifice and Stigma: Reducing Free Riding in Cults, Communes, and Other Collectives." *Journal of Political Economy* 100: 271–291.

Innes, A. 2001. *Czechoslovakia: The Short Goodbye*. New Haven: Yale University Press.

Innis, H. A. 1999. *Fur Trade in Canada: An Introduction to Canadian Economic History*, rev. edition. Toronto: University of Toronto Press.

Institute of Ismaili Studies. 2012. http://www.iis.ac.uk/

"IPCC Fourth Assessment Report: Climate Change 2007." 2007. Intergovernmental Panel on Climate Change. http://www.ipcc.ch/pdf/assessment-report/ar4/syr/ar4_syr_spm .pdf.

Isidore, Chris. 2012. "Taxpayers Still Owed More Than $200 Billion from Bailouts." CNN Money, September 11. http://money.cnn.com/2012/09/11/news/companies /taxpayer-bailouts/index.html.

Jansen, M. B. 2002. *The Making of Modern Japan*. Cambridge, MA: Belknap Press.

Jarvis, C. 2000. "The Rise and Fall of Albania's Pyramid Schemes." *Finance and Development* 37 (1). http://www.imf.org/external/pubs/ft/fandd/2000/03/jarvis.htm.

Johns, C. H. W. 1903. *The Oldest Code of Laws in the World: The Code of Laws Promulgated by Hammurabi, King of Babylon, B.C. 2285–2242*. Edinburgh: T & T Clark.

Johnson, R., and S. Raphael. 2006. "How Much Crime Reduction Does the Marginal Prisoner Buy?" UC Berkeley School of Public Policy manuscript.

Johnston, David Cay. 2006. "Flaws Seen in Markets for Utilities." *New York Times*, November 21.

Joinville, J. de. 1868. *Histoire de Saint Louis*, ed. Natalis de Wailly. Paris. Reprinted, Lille, nd.

Jones, E. 1981. *The European Miracle*. New York: Cambridge University Press.

Jordan, M., and K. Sullivan. 1998. "Death of 3 Salesmen – Partners in Suicide." *Washington Post* October 7, p. A1.

Judt, Tony. 2005. *Postwar: A History of Europe Since 1945*. New York: Penguin.

Junger, S. 1999. *The Perfect Storm: A True Story of Men Against the Sea*. New York: Harper.

Jyllands-Posten. 2005. "Muhammad Cartoons Controversy." http://en.wikipedia.org /wiki/Jyllands-Posten_Muhammad_cartoons_controversy

Kahn, A. 2004. *Lessons from Deregulation: Telecommunications and Airlines After the Crunch*. Washington, DC: Brookings.

Kahn, Alfred. 2004. *Lessons from Deregulation: Telecommunications and Airlines After the Crunch*. Washington, DC: Brookings.

Kaplan, G., and M. Guitierrez. 2006 "How Long Does It Take to Become a Proficient Hunter? Implications on the Evolution of Delayed Growth." *Journal of Human Evolution*.

Kaplan, Steven N., and Joshua Rauh. 2007. "Wall Street and Main Street: What Contributes to the Rise in the Highest Incomes?" NBER Working Paper No. 13270. http://www .nber.org/papers/w13270.

Keller, W., and W. Shiue. 2008. "Institutions, Technology, and Trade." NBER Working Paper No. 13913.

Kelly, R. 1985. *The Nuer Conquest: The Structure and Development of an Expansionist System*. Michigan: University of Michigan Press.

Keneally, T. 2006. *A Commonwealth of Thieves*. London: Vintage.

Keynes, J. M. 1936. *The General Theory of Employment, Interest, and Money*. London: Macmillan.

Kindleberger, C. P. 2000. *Manias, Panics, and Crashes: A History of Financial Crises*. New York: Basic Books.

King, L., et al. 2012. "Making the Same Mistake Again—Or Is This Time Different?" *Cambridge Journal of Economics* 36.

Klaas, Marc. 1999. "A Bad Law, Set in Stone." *San Jose Mercury News*, November 14.

Klebnikov, P. 2000. *Godfather of the Kremlin: Boris Berezovsky and the Looting of Russia.* New York: Harcourt.

Klein, A. 2007."The Army's $200 Billion Makeover March to Modernize Proves Ambitious and Controversial." *Washington Post*, December 7.

Klein, B., R. Crawford, R. Alchian, and A. Alchian. 1978. "Vertical Integration, Appropriable Rents, and the Competitive Contracting Process." *Journal of Law & Economics* 21(2): 297–326.

Klein, R. 1999. *The Human Career: Human Biological and Cultural Origins.* 2nd edition. Chicago: University of Chicago Press.

Kletzer, L. 2004. "Trade-related Job Loss and Wage Insurance: A Synthetic Review." *Review of International Economics* 12 (5): 724–748.

Kossoy, A., et al. 2012. "State and Trends of the Carbon Market 2012." Washington: World Bank.

Kossoy, Alexandre, et al. 2012. "State and Trends of the Carbon Market 2012," World Bank, May.

Kramer, S. 1998. *Sumerian Mythology.* Philadelphia: University of Pennsylvania Press.

Kromm, D. E., and S. White. (eds.) 1992. *Groundwater Exploitation in the High Plains.* Lawrence: University Press of Kansas.

Krueger, A., and A. Mas. 2004. "Strikes, Scabs, and Tread Separations: Labor Strife and the Production of Defective Bridgestone/Firestone Tires." *Journal of Political Economy* 112: 253–289.

Krupnick, M. 2003. "Troubled Waters for Local Crabbers." *San Jose Mercury News,* November 28, p. 3C.

Kugler, T., Z. Neeman, and N. Vulcan. 2006. "Markets Versus Negotiations: An Experimental Investigation." *Games and Economic Behavior* 56 (1): 121–134.

Kurlansky, M. 1997. *Cod: A Biography of the Fish That Changed the World.* New York: Walker.

Lamoreaux, N., D. Raff, and P. Temin. 2002. "Beyond Markets and Hierarchies: Toward a New Synthesis of American Business History." NBER Working Paper 9029: 14.

Landes, D. S. 1998. *The Wealth and Poverty of Nations.* New York: Norton.

Landes, D.S. 2006. "Why Europe and the West? Why Not China?" *Journal of Economic Perspectives* 20(2): 3–22.

Lanman, Scott, and Steve Matthews. 2008. "Greenspan Concedes to 'Flaw' in His Market Ideology." Bloomberg, October 23. http://www.bloomberg.com/apps/news?pid=news archive&sid=ah5qh9Up4rIg.

Lansing, J. S. 1991. *Priests and Programmers: Technologies of Power and the Engineered Landscape of Bali.* Princeton: Princeton University Press.

Lansing, J. S. 2006. *Perfect Order: Recognizing Complexity in Bali.* Princeton: Princeton University Press.

Larsen, M. T. 1976. *The Old Assyrian City-State and Its Colonies.* Volume 4 of *Mesopotamia: Copenhagen Studies in Assyriology.* Copenhagen: Akademisk Forlag.

Lasch, C. 1996. *Revolt of the Elites.* New York: Norton.

Leamer, E. 2007. "A Review of Thomas L Friedman's *The World is Flat,*" *Journal of Economic Literature* 45 (1): 83–126.

LeBlanc, A. 2003. *Random Family: Love, Drugs, Trouble, and Coming of Age in the Bronx.* New York: Scribner.

Lee, R. 1979. *The Kung San: Men, Women, and Work in a Foraging Society.* New York: Cambridge University Press.

Lee, R. 2003. "The Demographic Transition: Three Centuries of Fundamental Change." *Journal of Economic Perspectives* 17 (4): 167–190.

Leiby, Michele L. 2012. "In Pakistan, a Legal System Under Scrutiny." *Washington Post*, May 29. http://www.washingtonpost.com/world/asia_pacific/in-pakistan-a-legal-system-under-scrutiny/2012/05/29/gJQAmJTqyU_story.html.

Leijonhufvud, A. 2007. "The Individual, the Market, and the Division of Labor in Society." *Capitalism and Society* 2 (2): Article 3.

Leijonhufvud, A., and E. Craver. 2001. "Reform and the Fate of Russia." *Documents de Travail de l'OFCE 2001–03, Observatoire Francais des Conjonctures Economiques (OFCE)*.

Lenin, V. I. 1902. *What Is to be Done?* New York: International Publishers.

Levathes, L. 1996. *When China Ruled the Seas*. Oxford University Press.

Levitt, A. 2002. *Take On the Street: What Wall Street and Corporate America Don't Want You to Know*. New York: Random House.

Levitt, S., and S. Dubner. 2005. *Freakonomics*. New York: William Morrow.

Levy, F., and P. Temin. 2007. "Inequality and Institutions in Twentieth-Century America." NBER Working Paper no. W13106.

Lewis, B. 1968. *The Assassins: A Radical Sect in Islam*. New York: Basic Books.

Lewis, Michael. 2011. *Boomerang*. New York: Norton.

Li, Cheng. 2001. *China's Leaders: The New Generation*. Lanham, MD: Rowman & Littlefield.

Lichtenstein, N., ed. 2006. *Wal-Mart: The Face of Twenty-First-Century Capitalism*. New York: New Press.

Ligon, D. 1991. "Cooperation and Reciprocity in Birds and Mammals." In *Kin Recognition*, ed. P. Hepper. New York: Cambridge University Press.

Lipton, D., and J. D. Sachs. 1992. "Prospects for Russia's Economic Reforms." *Brookings Papers on Economic Activity* 2: 213–283.

Lo, Andrew. 2012. "Reading About the Financial Crisis: A Twenty-One-Book Review." *Journal of Economic Literature* 50 (1): 151–178.

Lorenz, K. 1966. *On Aggression*. New York: Methuen.

Losin, Elizabeth A.R., M. Dapretto, and M. Iacoboni. 2009. "Culture in the Mind's Mirror." In *Progress in Brain Research* 178: 175–90.

MacArthur, R., and E. O. Wilson. 1967. *The Theory of Island Biogeography*. Princeton: Princeton University Press.

Maccoby, H. 1986. *The Mythmaker: Paul and the Invention of Christianity*. New York: Harper & Row.

MacCoun, R., and P. Reuter. 2001. *Drug War Heresies*. New York: Cambridge University Press.

MacFarquhar, R., and M. Schoenhals. 2006. *Mao's Last Revolution*. Cambridge, MA: Belknap Press.

Mackay, C. 1941. *Extraordinary Popular Delusions and the Madness of Crowds*. Reprinted in 1996. NY: Wiley Investment Classics.

Maddison, A. 1995. *Monitoring the World Economy, 1820–1992*. Paris: OECD Development Center.

Maddison, A. 2001. *The World Economy: A Millennial Perspective*. Paris: OECD.

Maestripieri, D., ed. 2005. *Primate Psychology*. Cambridge MA: Harvard University Press.

Mahtani, Shibani. 2012. "The World's Richest Country." *Wall Street Journal*, August 15. http://blogs.wsj.com/searealtime/2012/08/15/singapore-home-to-the-worlds-richest-people.

Malkiel, B. 2003. *A Random Walk Down Wall Street*. New York: Norton.

Malmendier, U. 2005. "Roman Shares." *The Origins of Value*, ed. W. Goetzmann and K. Rouwenhorst. New York: Oxford University Press.

Malone, T. W. 2004. *The Future of Work*. New York: Harvard Business School Press.

Mansfield, Edward, and Brian M. Pollins. 2003. "Interdependence and Conflict: An Introduction." http://141.211.86.200/pdf/0472098276-intro.pdf.

"Marine Compatibility Chart." http://www.liveaquaria.com/general/compatibility_chart.cfm.

Marx, K. 1844. "Alienated Labor." *Economic and Philosophic Manuscripts.*

Marx, K., and F. Engels. 2002. *The Communist Manifesto.* London: Penguin.

Mas, A. 2008. "Labour Unrest and the Quality of Production: Evidence from the Construction Equipment Resale Market." *Review of Economic Studies* 75: 229–258.

Maslow, A. 1943. "A Theory of Human Motivation." *Psychological Review* 50: 394–395.

Masserman, J. H., S. Wechkin, and W. Terris. 1964. "'Altruistic Behavior in Rhesus Monkeys." *The American Journal of Psychiatry,* v. 121, n. 6, pp. 584–585.

Masten, S. 1984. "The Organization of Production: Evidence from the Aerospace Industry." *Journal of Law and Economics* 27 (2): 403–417.

Mathew, Sarah, and Robert Boyd. 2011. "Punishment Sustains Large-Scale Cooperation in Prestate Warfare." *Proceedings of the National Academy of Sciences* 108 (28), July 12. www.pnas.org/cgi/doi/10.1073/pnas.1105604108.

Matthews, Christopher. 2012. "Will Amazon Take Over the World?" *Time,* July 16. http://business.time.com/2012/07/16/will-amazon-take-over-the-world.

Maynard Smith, J. 1982. *Evolution and the Theory of Games.* New York: Cambridge University Press.

McAfee, R. P. 2000. "The Real Lesson of Enron's Implosion: Market Makers Are in the Trust Business." *The Economists' Voice* 1 (4): 2.

McBrearty, S., and A. Brooks. 2000. "The Revolution That Wasn't: A New Interpretation of the Origin of Modern Human Behavior." *Journal of Human Evolution* 39: 453–563.

McCredie, S. 2007. *Balance: In Search of the Lost Sense.* New York: Little, Brown.

McFadden, Daniel. 2006. "Free Markets and Fettered Consumers." *American Economic Review* (96)1: 5–29.

McGinty, M. 2007. "International Environmental Agreements Among Asymmetric Nations." *Oxford Economic Papers* 59 (1): 45–62.

McHenry, Henry M., and Katherine Coffing. 2000. "*Australopithecus* to *Homo,*" *Annual Review of Anthropology* 29: 125–46.

McIntyre, D. 2000 "Learning to Let Go." *Time* 156: 4

McLean, B., and P. Elkind. 2004. *The Smartest Guys in the Room: The Amazing Rise and Scandalous Fall of Enron.* New York: Portfolio Press.

McLean, P., and J. Padgett. Forthcoming. "Economic Credit and Elite Transformation in Renaissance Florence." *American Journal of Sociology.*

McLean P., and J. F. Padgett. 2011. "Economic Credit in Renaissance Florence." *Journal of Modern History* 83: 1–47.

McNeill, W. H. 1989. *The Age of Gunpowder Empires, 1450–1800.* New York: American Historical Association.

Mehta, Suketu. *Maximum City.* New York: Vintage, 2004.

Meredith, Martin. 2005. *The Fate of Africa.* New York: Perseus.

Milgrom, P., and J. Roberts. 1990. "The Economics of Modern Manufacturing: Technology, Strategy, and Organization." *American Economic Review* 80: 511–28.

Milgrom, P., and J. Roberts. 1992. *Economics, Organization and Management.* Englewood Cliffs, NJ: Prentice Hall.

Milius, S. 2006. "Naked and Not: Two Species of Mole Rats Run Complex Societies Underground." *Science News* 169 (25): 394.

Mill, J. S. 1848. *The Principles of Political Economy.* London: Longmans, Green.

Millett, P. 1991. *Lending and Borrowing in Ancient Athens*. New York: Cambridge University Press.

Minksy, H. P. 1982. "Can 'IT' Happen Again?" *Essays on Instability and Finance*. New York: M. E. Sharpe.

Mirande, A. 1985. *The Chicano Experience*. Notre Dame: University of Notre Dame Press.

Moll, J., Ricardo de Oliveira-Souza, and Paul J. Eslinger. 2003. "Morals and the Human Brain: A Working Model." *NeuroReport* 14 (3): 299–305.

Monteverde, K., and D. Teece. 1982. "Supplier Switching Costs and Vertical Integration."*Bell Journal of Economics* 13 (1): 206–213.

Morck, R., and M. Nakamura. 2007. "Business Groups and the Big Push: Meiji Japan's Mass Privatization and Subsequent Growth." NBER Working Paper no. W13171.

Morgenson, G. 2008. "Behind Insurer's Crisis, Blind Eye to a Web of Risk." *New York Times,* September 27.

Morgenson, G. 2012. "Into the Bailout Buzz Saw." *New York Times,* July 21. http://www.nytimes.com/2012/07/22/business/neil-barofskys-journey-into-a-bailout-buzz-saw-fair-game.html?pagewanted=all&_r=0.

Morris, D. 1967. *The Naked Ape*. New York: Dell.

Morris, Jan. 1986. *Among the Cities*. New York, Penguin, 1986.

Moynahan, B. 1994. *The Russian Century: A History of the Last Hundred Years*. New York: Random House.

Murphy, R., and Y. Murphy. 1986. "Northern Shoshone." In Warren L. D'Azevedo and William C. Sturtevant, eds., *Handbook of North American Indians,* 11. Washington, DC: Smithsonian Institution.

National Opinion Research Center. 1999. *Gambling Impact and Behavior Study*. Chicago.

Nemet-Nejat, K. 1998. *Daily Life in Ancient Mesopotamia*. London: Greenwood Press.

New York Times. "Foreclosures, Robosigning, and Mortgage Servicing Settlement." April 2. http://topics.nytimes.com/top/reference/timestopics/subjects/f/foreclosures/index.html.

Newman, P. C. 2000. *Empire of the Bay: The Company of Adventurers That Seized a Continent*. New York: Penguin Putnam.

Nisbett, R. E., and D. Cohen. 1996. *Culture of Honor: the Psychology of Violence in the South*. Boulder, CO: Westview Press.

North, D., J. Wallis, and B. Weingast. 2006. "A Conceptual Framework for Interpreting Recorded Human History." George Mason University Mercatus Center Working Paper 75.

OECD. 2012. "How Pronounced Is Income Inequality Around the World?" *Education Indicators in Focus*, April.

"Ogallala Aquifer." 2012. http://www.waterencyclopedia.com/Oc-Po/Ogallala-Aquifer.html.

Ohno, T. 1988. *Toyota Production System: Beyond Large-Scale Production*. Portland: Productivity Press.

Okada, T. 2007. "A Comment on Nishimura, Nakajima, and Kiyota's 'Does the Natural Selection Mechanism Still Work in Severe Recessions?' Examination of the Japanese Economy in the 1990s." NBER Working Paper no. W13298.

Olson, M. 1984. *The Rise and Decline of Nations: Economic Growth, Stagflation, and Social Rigidities*. New Haven: Yale University Press.

Olson, M. 1993. "Dictatorship, Democracy, and Development." *The American Political Science Review* 87 (3): 567–576.

Oreskes, Naomi, and Erik M. Conway. 2010. *Merchants of Doubt*. New York: Bloomsbury Press.

Orwell, G. 1945. *Animal Farm*. London: Secker and Warburg.

Osnos, Evan. 2012. "The God of Gamblers." *The New Yorker*, April 9.

Packer, C., and A. Pusey. 1997. "Divided We Fall: Cooperation Among Lions." *Scientific American* 1: 52–59.

Palmer, R. R., J. Colton, and L. Kramer. 2003. *History of the Modern World*. 9th edition. New York: Knopf.

Paltsev, S., et al. 2007. "Assessment of US Cap-and-Trade Proposals." NBER Working Paper no. W13176.

Parker, I. 2007. "Our Far-Flung Correspondents: Swingers: Bonobos Are Celebrated as Peace-loving, Matriarchal, and Sexually Liberated. Are They?" *The New Yorker*.

Partnoy, F. 2004. *Infectious Greed: How Deceit and Risk Corrupted the Financial Markets*. New York: Holt Paperbacks.

Patterson, N., D. Richeter, S. Gnerre, E. Lander, and D. Reich. 2006. "Genetic Evidence for Complex Speciation of Humans and Chimpanzees." *Nature* 441: 1103–1108.

Patterson, Scott. 2012. *Dark Pools*. New York, Random House.

Pautzke, C. G., and C. W. Oliver. 1997. "Development of the Individual Fishing Quota Program for Sablefish and Halibut Longline Fisheries off Alaska." National Research Council's Committee to Review Individual Fishing Quotas, Anchorage, Alaska. Presented to North Pacific Fishery Management Council, Anchorage, September 4. Document revised October 8, 1997.

Paxton, R. O. 2004. *The Anatomy of Fascism*. New York: Knopf.

Peek, J., and E. Rosengren. 2005. "Unnatural Selection: Perverse Incentives and the Misallocation of Credit in Japan." *American Economic Review*: 1144–1166.

Penso de la Vega, J. 1688. *Confusion e confusions*. Reprinted in 1996. New York: Wiley Investment Classics.

Peters, E. 1992. *St. Peter's Fair: The Fourth Chronicle of Brother Cadfael*. New York: Mysterious Press.

Pettigrew, J. 1975. *Robber Noblemen: A Study of the Political System of the Sikh Jats*. London: Routledge & Kegan Paul.

Pew Global Attitudes Project. 2012. "European Unity on the Rocks," May 29. http://www.pewglobal.org/2012/05/29/european-unity-on-the-rocks.

Piketty, T., and Saez, E. 2003. "Income Inequality in the United States, 1913–1998." *Quarterly Journal of Economics* 118 (1): 1–39.

Plato. 1945. *Republic*. Translated and introduced by F. Cornford. New York: Oxford University Press.

Polanyi, K. 1944. *The Great Transformation*. Boston: Beacon Press.

Polanyi, K., and A. Conrad. 1957. *Trade and Market in the Early Empires: Economies in History and Theory*. Lawrence, KS: The Free Press/The Falcon's Wing Press.

Popp, D. 2005. "Uncertain R&D and the Porter Hypothesis." *Contributions to Economic Analysis & Policy* 4 (1): 6.

Porter, Eduardo. 2012. "Numbers Tell of Failure in Drug War." *New York Times*, July 3. http://www.nytimes.com/2012/07/04/business/in-rethinking-the-war-on-drugs-start-with-the-numbers.html?pagewanted=all&_moc.semityn.www.

Posner, E. 2000. "Law and the Emotions." University of Chicago Law and Economics Working Paper 103.

Posner, R. 2006. "A Review of Steven Shavell's *Foundations of Economic Analysis of Law*." *Journal of Economic Literature* 44 (2): 405–414.

Potts, R. 1996. "Evolution and Climate Variability." *Science* 271: 922.

Prichard, J. B., ed. 1958. *The Ancient Near East: An Anthology of Texts and Pictures*. Princeton, NJ: Princeton University Press.

Provine, W. 1986. *Sewall Wright and Evolutionary Biology.* Chicago: University of Chicago Press.

Pryce-Jones, D. 2002. *The Closed Circle: An Interpretation of the Arabs.* Chicago: Ivan R. Dee.

Putnam, R. 2000. *Bowling Alone: The Collapse and Revival of American Community.* Simon & Schuster.

Pynchon, T. R. 1984. "Is It O.K. to Be a Luddite?" *The New York Times Book Review,* 40–41.

Rabanal, Jean Paul. 2012. "Looking Underwater in the Lab," SIGFIRM Working Paper #9, Department of Economics, University of California Santa Cruz.

Rance, R. 2006. "Hamas Wins Out over PLO Corruption." *Socialist Outlook.*

Rawls, J. 2001. *Justice as Fairness.* Cambridge MA: Harvard University Press.

Rayne, Henry. 1919. "Turkana." *Journal of the Royal African Society* 18 (72), July.

Remnick, D. 1994. *Lenin's Tomb: The Last Days of the Soviet Empire.* New York: Vintage Books.

Reppetto, T. 2006. *Bringing Down the Mob: The War Against the American Mafia.* New York: Henry Holt.

Reudink, Matthew W., et al. 2009. "Plumage Brightness Predicts Non-breeding Season Territory Quality in a Long-Distance Migratory Songbird, the American Redstart *Setophaga ruticilla.*" *Journal of Avian Biology* 40: 34–41.

Ricardo, D. 1817. *On the Principles of Political Economy and Taxation.* London: John Murray.

Richard, K. 1999. *Human Career: Human Biological and Cultural Origins.* 2nd edition. Chicago: University of Chicago Press.

Richardson, E. 1999. "The Struggle for Sobriety: Anti-Alcohol Campaigning Under Gorbachev and Yeltsin." Research Papers in Russian and East European Studies no. REES99/1.

Richerson, P. 2007. *Rethinking Paleoanthropology: A World Queerer Than We Supposed.* Draft manuscript.

Richerson, P., and R. Boyd. 2013. "Rethinking Paleoanthropology: A World Queerer than We Supposed." In Gary Hatfield and Holly Pittman, eds., *Evolution of Mind, Brain and Culture.* University of Pennsylvania Museum Conference Series.

Roberts, Dexter. 2004. "China: A Princeling Who Could Be Premier." *Bloomberg BusinessWeek,* March 15.

Roberts, J. 2004. *The Modern Firm: Organizational Design for Performance and Growth.* New York: Oxford University Press.

Roemer, J. 1986. *Value, Exploitation, and Class.* Washington, DC: Taylor & Francis.

Rolvaag, E. 1927. *Giants in the Earth.* New York: Harper.

Romotsky, G., and S. Romotsky. 1976. *Los Angeles Barrio Calligraphy.* Los Angeles: Dawson's Book Shop.

Rose, Nelson. 2010. "Gambling and the Law: The Third Wave of Legal Gambling." *Villanova Sports & Entertainment Law Journal* 17. http://www.law.villanova.edu/mooradsports lawjournal/wp-content/uploads/2012/08/VXII-2-Gambling-and-the-Law-172.pdf.

Rosen, J. 1997. "The Social Police." *The New Yorker,* 170–181.

Rosen, W. 2007. *Justinian's Flea: Plague, Empire and the Birth of Europe.* New York: Viking.

Rosen, William. 2010. *The Most Powerful Idea in the World.* Chicago: University of Chicago Press, 2010.

Rosenberg, N., and L. E. Birdsell, Jr. 1986. *How the West Grew Rich: The Economic Transformation of the Industrial World.* New York: Basic Books.

Roth, A. E. 2006. "Repugnance as a Constraint on Markets." NBER Working Paper no. W12702.

Roux, Georges. 1992. *Ancient Iraq.* 3rd ed. New York: Penguin.

Rubin, P. H., and C. W. Paul. 1979. "An Evolutionary Model of Tastes for Risk." *Economic Inquiry* 17: 585–596.

Sachs, S. E. 2006. "From St. Ives to Cyberspace: The Modern Distortion of the Medieval 'Law Merchant'." *American University International Law Review* 21 (5): 685–812.

Sahlins, M. 1972. *Stone Age Economics.* Chicago: Aldine.

Sanchez, Andrew. 2012. "India: The Next Superpower? Corruption in India," IDEAS Reports – Special Reports, *London School of Economics and Political Science,* ed. Nicholas Kitchen, 51. http://eprints.lse.ac.uk/43449.

Sanfey, A., et al. 2003. "The Neural Basis of Economic Decision Making in the Ultimatum Game." *Science* 300 (5626): 1755–1758.

Sayigh, Yezid. 2010. "Hamas Rule in Gaza: Three Years On." *Middle East Brief,* n. 41, March. http://www.brandeis.edu/crown/publications/meb/MEB41.pdf.

Schiller, R. 2002. "From Efficient Market Theory to Behavioral Finance." Cowles Discussion Paper, 1385.

Schiller, R. 2011. *Finance and the Good Society.* Princeton, NJ: Princeton University Press.

Schmidt, F. 2000. "Albania's Pharaoh and His Pyramids." RFE/RL Balkan Report 4 (42). http://www.nettime.org/Lists-Archives/nettime-l-0006/msg00030.html.

Schmitt, J., K. Warner, K. Gupta, and S. Gupta. 2010. "The High Budgetary Cost of Incarceration." Washington, DC: Center for Economic and Policy Research, June. http://www.cepr.net/documents/publications/incarceration-2010-06.pdf.

Schumpeter, J. 1942. *Capitalism, Socialism, and Democracy.* New York: Harper.

Schwartz, Mattathias. 2006. "The Gambler: The Hold-'Em Holdup." *New York Times Magazine,* Sunday June 11.

Scranton, P. 1983. *Proprietary Capitalism: The Textile Manufacture at Philadelphia, 1800–1885.* New York: Cambridge University Press.

Segerstrale, U. 2001. *Defenders of the Truth: The Sociobiology Debate.* New York: Oxford University Press.

Serchuk, F. M., and S. E. Wigley. 1992. "Assessment and Management of the Georges Bank Cod Fishery: An Historical Review and Evaluation." *Journal of Northwest Atlantic Fishery Science* 13: 25–52.

Shimer, R. 2007. "Daron Acemoglu, 2005 John Bates Clark Medalist." *Journal of Economic Perspectives* 21 (1): 191–208.

Shiue, C., and W. Keller. 2008. "Markets in China and Europe on the Eve of the Industrial Revolution." *American Economic Review* 97 (4): 1189–1216.

Shkolnikov, V., M. McKee, and D. A. Leon. 2001. "Changes in Life Expectancy in Russia in the Mid-1990s." *Lancet* 357 (9260): 917–21.

Skarbek, David. 2012. "Prison Gangs, Norms, and Organizations." *Journal of Economic Behavior & Organization* 82 (1).

Skidelsky, Robert. 2009. *Keynes: The Return of the Master.* New York: Public Affairs.

Sinn, H. W. 2007. "Public Policies Against Global Warming." NBER Working Paper no. W13454.

Smith, Adam. 1801. *The Theory of Moral Sentiments.* London: A. Strahan.

Smith, Adam. 1776. *The Wealth of Nations.* London: Methuen.

Smith, Craig S., and Greg Myre. 2007. "Hamas May Find It Needs Its Enemy." *New York Times,* June 17.

Smith, Michael E. 2000. "Aztec City-States." In *A Comparative Study of Thirty City-State Cultures,* ed. M. H. Hansen. Copenhagen: Royal Danish Academy of Sciences and Letters.

Smith, Michael E. 2002. "The Earliest Cities." In George Gmelch and Walter P. Zenner, eds., *Urban Life: Readings in the Anthropology of the City*. Prospect Heights, IL: Waveland Press.

Smith, V. L. 1962. "An Experimental Study of Competitive Market Behavior." *The Journal of Political Economy* 70 (2): 111–137.

Smith, V. L. 1982. "Markets as Economizers of Information: Experimental Examination of the 'Hayek Hypothesis'." *Economic Inquiry* 20 (2): 165–179.

Smith, V. L., G. L. Suchanek, and A. W. Williams. 1988. "Bubbles, Crashes, and Endogenous Expectations in Experimental Spot Asset Markets." *Econometrica* 56 (5): 1119–1151.

Sobel, D. 2005. *Longitude: The True Story of a Lone Genius Who Solved the Greatest Scientific Problem of His Time*. New York: Walker.

Sobel, R. 1974. *The Entrepreneurs: Explorations Within the American Business Tradition*. New York: Weybright & Talley.

Soffer, O., J. Adovasio, and D. Hyland. 2000. "The 'Venus' Figurines," *Current Anthropology* 41 (4): 511ff.

Soler, M., J. J. Soler, J. G. Martinez, and A. P. Moller. 1995. "Magpie Host Manipulation by Great Spotted Cuckoos: Evidence for an Avian Mafia?" *Evolution* 49: 770–775.

"Special Report on Business and Climate Change." 2007. *The Economist*, June 2.

Specter, M. 2007. "Letter from Moscow: Kremlin, Inc.: Why Are Vladimir Putin's Opponents Dying?" *The New Yorker*, 50–63.

Spencer, H. 1896. *The Principles of Biology*, vol. 2. New York: Appleton.

Spillane, J. 2000. *Cocaine: From Modern Marvel to Modern Menace in the United States, 1884–1920*. New York: Johns Hopkins University Press.

Stanford University. "Tuition and Fees, 2011–12." http://studentaffairs.stanford.edu /registrar/students/tuition-fees_11–12.

Stephens, Deborah C., ed. 2000. *The Maslow Business Reader*. New York: Wiley.

Stewart, David O. 2011. "Online Gambling Five Years After UIGEA." American Gaming Association. http://www.americangaming.org/files/aga/uploads/docs/final_online _gambling_white_paper_5-18-11.pdf.

Stone, Brad. 2007. "Google's Next Frontier: Renewable Energy." *New York Times*, November 28.

Szathmary, E., and J. Maynard Smith. 1995. "The Major Evolutionary Transitions." *Nature* 374: 227–232.

Tagaris, Karolina. 2012. "Greeks Can No Longer Afford Paying Expensive Bribes." Reuters, July 31. http://www.reuters.com/article/2012/07/31/us-greece-corruption-id USBRE86U1G220120731.

Tawney, R. H. 1926. *Religion and the Rise of Capitalism*. New York: Harcourt, Brace & World.

Taylor, Jerry, and Peter Van Doren. 2007. "Short-Circuited." *Wall Street Journal*, August 30.

Taylor, Robert S. 2010. "Kant's Political Religion: The Transparency of Perpetual Peace and the Highest Good." *The Review of Politics* 72.

Tedeschi, R. 2007. "EBay Moves to Recharge Its Auctions." *New York Times*, January 18.

Temin, P. 2001. "A Market Economy in the Early Roman Empire." *The Journal of Roman Studies* 91: 169–181.

Temin, P., and H. Voth. 2004. "Riding the South Sea Bubble." *American Economic Review* 94 (5): 1654–1668.

Thomas, E. 1958. *The Harmless People*. New York: Random House Vintage.

Thomas, G. 2007. *Gideon's Spies, Third Edition: The Secret History of the Mossad*. New York: St. Martin's Griffin.

Thomas, J. P., and T. Worrall. 2002. "Gift-giving, Quasi-credit, and Reciprocity." CESIfo Working Paper 687.

Thomas, Jr., Landon. 2009. "The Irish Economy's Rise Was Steep, and the Fall Was Fast." *New York Times*, January 3.

Thomson, D. 2006. *The Whole Equation: A History of Hollywood*. London: Vintage.

Thurow, L. 1985. *The Zero-Sum Solution*. New York: Simon & Schuster.

Time. 1962. "Money Is the Mother's Milk of Politics." December 14.

Time. 1973. "Murder in California." November 19.

Todaro, M., and Smith, S. 2011. *Economic Development*. 11th ed. Englewood Cliffs, NJ: Prentice-Hall.

Toobin, Jeffrey. 2012. "The Professor: Elizabeth Warren's Long Journey into Politics." *New Yorker*, September 17.

"Top Interest Group Giving to Members of Congress, 2012 Cycle." 2012. *Open Secrets*, November. http://www.opensecrets.org/industries/mems.php.

Travers, J., and S. Milgram. 1969. "An Experimental Study of the Small World Problem." *Sociometry* 32 (4): 425–443.

Trivers, R. 1971. "The Evolution of Reciprocal Altruism." *Quarterly Review of Biology* 46: 35–57.

Trivers, R. L. 1985. *Social Evolution*. Menlo Park CA: Benjamin/Cummings.

Tsai, Tyjen. 2012. "China Has Too Many Bachelors." *Population Reference Bureau*, January. http://www.prb.org/Articles/2012/china-census-excess-males.aspx.

Turner, Jonathan H. 2010. "Natural Selection and the Evolution of Morality in Human Societies." In *Handbook of the Sociology of Morality*, ed. Steven Hitlin and Stephen Vaisey. New York: Springer.

Tyack, D., and L. Cuban. 1995. *Tinkering Toward Utopia: A Century of Public School Reform*. Cambridge, MA: Harvard University Press.

Unger, H. 2007. "Criminal Justice in America," *Policy Today*, California edition 4 (3): 6–10.

"United States Crime Rates 1960–2011." FBI, Uniform Crime Reports. http://www.sco.ca.gov/state_finances_101_state_spending.html.

United States Department of Justice. 2006. *Highlights of the 2004 National Youth Gang Survey*. Office of Juvenile Justice and Delinquency Prevention.

United States Department of State. 2006. "Country Reports on Terrorism 2005." Office of the Coordinator for Counterterrorism US Dept. of State Publication 11324.

United States Environmental Protection Agency. 2001. "The United States Experience with Economic Incentives for Protecting the Environment," EPA-240-R-01–001 of the Office of Policy, Economics and Innovation.

United States National Research Council. 1999. *Pathological Gambling: A Critical Review.*

Vayda, A. P. 1967. "Pomo Trade Feasts." In *Tribal and Peasant Economies,* ed. G. Dalton. Austin: University of Texas Press.

Vera Institute of Justice. 2012. "The Price of Prisons." http://www.vera.org/files/price-of-prisons-california-fact-sheet.pdf.

Virgil, D. 1983. "Chicano Gangs: One Response to Mexican Urban Adaptation in the Los Angeles Area." *Urban Anthropology*: 45–75.

Vise, D., and M. Malseed. 2006. *The Google Story: Inside the Hottest Business, Media, and Technology Success of Our Time*. New York: Delacorte Press.

Vogel, E. 1979. *Japan as Number One* Boston: Harvard University Press.

Von Glahn, R. 2005. "The Origins of Paper Money in China." In *The Origins of Value: The Financial Innovations That Created Modern Capital Markets*, ed. W. N. Goetzmann and K. G. Rouwenhorst. New York: Oxford University Press.

Wade, N. 2006. *Before the Dawn.* New York: Penguin.

Wang, Andrew. 2012. "Cross-Strait Trade Drops 5% in First Half." *Taiwan Economic News*, July 12. http://news.cens.com/cens/html/en/news/news_inner_40717.html.

Washington Post. 2012 "US Suit Cites 'Brazen' Mortgage Fraud at Countrywide, Even After Bank of America Purchase." October 24. http://www.washingtonpost.com /business/us-sues-bank-of-america-for-1b-for-mortgage-fraud-suit-concerns-countr ywide-loans/2012/10/24/6273f68a-1df7-11e2-8817-41b9a7aaabc7_story.html.

Waters, F. 1963. *The Book of the Hopi.* New York: Viking.

Watson, J. 2007. *Strategy: An Introduction to Game Theory.* 2nd ed. New York: Norton.

Watson, Peter. 2012. *The Great Divide.* New York: HarperCollins.

Watts, D., and S. Strogatz. 1998. "Collective Dynamics of 'Small-World' Networks." *Nature* 393: 440–442.

Weatherford, J. 2004. *Genghis Khan and the Making of the Modern World.* New York: Crown Publishers.

Weber, M. 1930. *The Protestant Ethic and the Spirit of Capitalism.* London: Allen and Unwin.

Wessel, David. 2009. *In Fed We Trust.* New York: Random House.

Weylman, S. T., H. H. Brownell, and H. Gardner, "It's What You Mean, Not What You Say: Pragmatic Language Use in Brain-Damaged Patients." In *Language, Communication, and the Brain,* ed. F. Plum. New York: Raven Press, 229–243.

White, T., and G. Ganley. 1983. "The 'Death of a Princess' Controversy." Research Report P-83-9, Program on Information Resources Policy, Harvard University. http://pirp .harvard.edu/pdf-blurb.asp?id=129.

Whoriskey, Peter. 2012. "Anemia Drug Made Billions But at What Cost?" *Washington Post*, July 19, 2012. http://www.washingtonpost.com/business/economy/anemia-drug -made-billions-but-at-what-cost/2012/07/19/gJQAX5yqwW_story.html?wprss&google _editors_picks=true.

Wilder, L. I. 1935. *Little House on the Prairie.* New York: HarperCollins Children's Books.

Wilkinson, G. 1984. "Reciprocal Food Sharing in the Vampire Bat." *Nature* 308 (8): 181–184.

Williams, G. 1966. *Adaptation and Natural Selection.* Princeton: Princeton University Press.

Williamson, O. E. 1975. *Markets and Hierarchies.* New York: Simon & Schuster.

Wilson, E. O. 1975. *Sociobiology: The New Synthesis.* Cambridge: Harvard University Press.

Wilson, E. O., and B. Hölldobler. 2005. "Eusociality: Origin and Consequences." *Proc. Nat. Acad. Sci. USA* 102: 13367–13371.

Wilson, J. Q. 1990. "Against the Legalization of Drugs." *Commentary* 89: 21–28.

Wilson, S. 1988. *Feuding, Conflict, and Banditry in Nineteenth-Century Corsica.* Cambridge UK: Cambridge University Press.

Wittman, D. 2006. *Economic Foundations of Law and Organization.* Cambridge UK: Cambridge University Press.

Wolfers, J., and E. Zitzewitz, 2004. "Prediction Markets." *Journal of Economic Perspectives* 18 (2): 107–126.

Wood, C. 1992. *The Bubble Economy: Japan's Extraordinary Speculative Boom of the '80s and the Dramatic Bust of the '90s.* Boston: Atlantic Monthly Press.

Wright, Lawrence. 2007. *The Looming Tower.* New York: Alfred A. Knopf.

Xu, Chenggang. 2011. "The Fundamental Institutions of China's Reforms and Development." *Journal of Economic Literature* 49:4.

Yunus, M. 1999. "The Grameen Bank." *Scientific American*: 114–119.

Zedong, Mao. 1966. "On Coalition Government." In *Selected Works*, vol. 3, April 24, 1945, p. 315. www.marxists.org/reference/archive/mao/works/red-book.

Zedong, Mao. 2008. *Quotations from Chairman Mao Tse-Tung (The Little Red Book)*. Peking Foreign Languages Press. Recent English edition from BN Publishing.

Zhang, Li. 2010. *In Search of Paradise: Middle-Class Living in a Chinese Metropolis*. Ithaca: Cornell University Press.

Zinn, H. 2005. *A People's History of the United States, Volume I*. New York: Harper.

Zoepf, Katherine. 2007. "A Dishonorable Affair." *New York Times*, September 23. http://www.nytimes.com/2007/09/23/magazine/23wwln-syria-t.html?pagewanted=all.

Index